T0388972

Reform and Transition in the Mediterranean

Series Editor
Ioannis N. Grigoriadis, Bilkent University, Ankara, Turkey

The series of political and economic crises that befell many countries in the Mediterranean region starting in 2009 has raised emphatically questions of reform and transition. While the sovereign debt crisis of Southern European states and the "Arab Spring" appear prima facie unrelated, some common roots can be identified: low levels of social capital and trust, high incidence of corruption, and poor institutional performance. This series provides a venue for the comparative study of reform and transition in the Mediterranean within and across the political, cultural, and religious boundaries that crisscross the region. Defining the Mediterranean as the region that encompasses the countries of Southern Europe, the Levant, and North Africa, the series contributes to a better understanding of the agents and the structures that have brought reform and transition to the forefront. It invites (but is not limited to) interdisciplinary approaches that draw on political science, history, sociology, economics, anthropology, area studies, and cultural studies. Bringing together case studies of individual countries with broader comparative analyses, the series provides a home for timely and cutting-edge scholarship that addresses the structural requirements of reform and transition; the interrelations between politics, history and culture; and the strategic importance of the Mediterranean for the EU, the USA, Russia, and emerging powers.

More information about this series at
https://link.springer.com/bookseries/14513

Zenonas Tziarras
Editor

The Foreign Policy of the Republic of Cyprus

Local, Regional and International Dimensions

Editor
Zenonas Tziarras
Nicosia, Cyprus

Reform and Transition in the Mediterranean
ISBN 978-3-030-91176-8   ISBN 978-3-030-91177-5 (eBook)
https://doi.org/10.1007/978-3-030-91177-5

© The Editor(s) (if applicable) and The Author(s), under exclusive license to Springer Nature Switzerland AG 2022
This work is subject to copyright. All rights are solely and exclusively licensed by the Publisher, whether the whole or part of the material is concerned, specifically the rights of translation, reprinting, reuse of illustrations, recitation, broadcasting, reproduction on microfilms or in any other physical way, and transmission or information storage and retrieval, electronic adaptation, computer software, or by similar or dissimilar methodology now known or hereafter developed.
The use of general descriptive names, registered names, trademarks, service marks, etc. in this publication does not imply, even in the absence of a specific statement, that such names are exempt from the relevant protective laws and regulations and therefore free for general use.
The publisher, the authors and the editors are safe to assume that the advice and information in this book are believed to be true and accurate at the date of publication. Neither the publisher nor the authors or the editors give a warranty, expressed or implied, with respect to the material contained herein or for any errors or omissions that may have been made. The publisher remains neutral with regard to jurisdictional claims in published maps and institutional affiliations.

Cover illustration: Aleksey Butenkov/Alamy Stock Photo

This Palgrave Macmillan imprint is published by the registered company Springer Nature Switzerland AG
The registered company address is: Gewerbestrasse 11, 6330 Cham, Switzerland

Foreword

Academic interest in Cyprus' foreign policy has predominantly focused on the Cyprus Problem. This is perhaps unsurprising, and a manifestation of the fact that the Turkish invasion of Cyprus in 1974 has had a decisive, transformative effect on Cyprus' foreign policy given its enduring consequences and the scale of the Problem it generated.

In other words, the Turkish invasion arguably carved an inevitable path for our foreign policy, given that an island of less than 10,000 km^2 was violently called to manage a national problem of a disproportionate magnitude to its size. The consequences were devastating and enduring, with over 37% of the country's territory under military occupation, over 200,000 forcibly displaced from their lands and properties, as well as the orchestrated, ongoing policy by Turkey to erode the demographic, cultural and religious character of the occupied areas of the Republic of Cyprus.

As an academic, in my previous professional life, focusing on the history of the Cyprus problem, but also as a practising diplomat for close to 20 years prior to assuming duties as Foreign Minister, I can certainly testify to that. And yet, what cannot be underestimated, or omitted, is that in the sixty years since the establishment of the Republic of Cyprus, its foreign policy has evolved significantly, in a process that can be described as transitioning from introversion to extroversion. Or, as Dr. Tziarras accurately describes, the journey of maturity of Cyprus foreign policy. In this process of evolutionary transformation, academic input is critical.

I am a fervent believer of the benefits yielded by an interdisciplinary approach, of how academics can inform and challenge beliefs of both diplomats and politicians. Dr. Tziarras, along with the rest of the book's authors, are embarking on a path in academic research that very few have tread upon, one that explores this evolutionary process in Cyprus' foreign policy, identifying and assessing its various constituent parts, well beyond the Cyprus Problem. This journey is undertaken in an effort to unravel both from an academic perspective but also from a practical point of view, the various layers in the foreign policy of the Republic of Cyprus and how they are evolving. Moreover, the various threads in Cyprus' foreign policy that have been under construction in recent years are also identified in the book. That while achieving a comprehensive settlement of the Cyprus Problem that reunifies the country in a viable, functional, independent, sovereign European country, fully in line with UN Security Council Resolutions and EU law, and continues to be the foremost priority, at the heart of our foreign policy, in recent years we have embarked on a different strategy.

Our efforts have focused on moving beyond a monothematic foreign policy, projecting into a diverse, poly-thematic one, utilising Cyprus' unique characteristics, amplifying our geostrategic role and promoting a vision for our region that resonates well beyond the boundaries of the Eastern Mediterranean. The rationale is that the benefits accrued would have a beneficial ripple effect in our efforts to reunify Cyprus. This multifaceted foreign policy is anchored on three main pillars, which the authors of the book identify and analyse, in a forward-looking manner.

The first is the enhancement of our relations with countries in our immediate region, the Middle East and the Gulf. Building on the historically excellent relations with our neighbours, we have worked assiduously to deepen our ties and cooperation. Our actions are underpinned by a long-term vision for our region that we believe is relevant not only for the region and its countries but also for Europe. At a time of regional power shifts, we see significant added value in increasing European Union (EU) involvement in the Eastern Mediterranean. A manifestation of this pillar is the trilateral cooperation mechanisms that Cyprus, together with Greece have established with countries of the region, namely Egypt, Israel, Jordan, Lebanon, Palestine and the United Arab Emirates (UAE), that have a strictly positive agenda and are inclusive in nature. While energy developments triggered some of the cooperation mechanisms, once the benefits of these cooperation forums became clear to other countries in the region, they expanded. It undoubtedly constitutes a model of regional cooperation, one firmly anchored on international law, that is open to all countries in the region that respect international law, good neighbourly relations, the sovereignty and the sovereign rights of all their neighbours.

The growing web of regional cooperation has since proliferated in an array of other areas such as security, education, environment, climate change and innovation. The dynamic of the trilateral mechanisms is also evident in the fact that they are constantly evolving and expanding in terms of format and participation. For example, we had the meeting in Cairo at the ministerial level of Cyprus, Greece and Egypt, joined by France and Italy. The United States joined Cyprus, Greece and Israel in a meeting on issues of security. In the midst of the pandemic, a virtual ministerial conference with the participation of Cyprus, Greece, Egypt, France and the UAE, on issues of security took place. In April 2021 the Pafos meeting took place in Cyprus with the participation, for the first time, of Israel, Greece, Cyprus and the UAE at the Ministerial level; such a meeting would have been unimaginable only a year earlier and became possible following the historic normalisation agreements. Further work in this direction is under way, including joint projects in areas such as environment, climate change, education and tourism.

The commitment of countries involved in investing in these regional cooperation forums is proven by the decision taken to institutionalise them, through the establishment of a Permanent Secretariat for the coordination and implementation of decisions taken. At a time when states are turning their backs to multilateralism, opting for insularism, countries in the region are taking a different path, creating a narrative of like-minded countries, with an inclusive agenda coming together to promote a vision of cooperation, peace, stability and prosperity for the Middle East. The message to those countries of the region, which opt for confrontation and gunboat diplomacy of a past era, is to join us and countries of the region on this path of cooperation. Our long-term vision is that the momentum created by the cooperation developed in the region could lead to the creation of a regional Organisation for Security and Cooperation when the political conditions permit. In fact, the Eastern Mediterranean is one of the few regions where such an organisation does not exist. The Organisation would be inclusive, based on a positive agenda, and with the only pre-requisites being respect for international law, and commitment to good neighbourly relations.

The second pillar is the more active involvement of Cyprus within the EU, beyond issues that directly touch upon the Cyprus problem which have been the primary concern for a long time following our accession. The first Cyprus Presidency of the Council of the EU during the second half of 2012 (OXI 2021) was decisive in fully comprehending the remarkable opportunities and tools the EU has to offer. We have systematically worked in recent years to build our voice in Brussels on an array of issues where Cyprus has a strong added value. A prime example is bringing the Eastern Mediterranean's perspective to the EU and acting in practical ways as a bridge between the EU and the region of the wider Middle East and Gulf. The creation of the General Secretariat for the EU, under the Ministry of Foreign Affairs, is an important step towards building a stronger, more effective and more coherent voice in the EU, while enhancing the coordination of competent governmental bodies. A national strategy on EU matters has been formulated for the first time since Cyprus' accession to the EU in 2004 setting short term and long-term goals, including on the headquartering of the EU agency in Cyprus.

The third pillar concerns the strengthening of relations with the five permanent members of the United Nations Security Council, as well as with key players in the international arena. As far as the five permanent members of the Security Council are concerned, we have worked methodically in building our relationship beyond the remit of the discussion of the Cyprus problem at the Security Council, creating an evolving and continuously advancing strategic cooperation in all fields. Through this process, the important role Cyprus can play as a stable, predictable and credible partner in a region of strategic importance is highlighted. There are several examples of the advancement of relations with P5 countries and other key players in recent years. One such example is the establishment of the Cyprus Centre for Land, Open Seas and Port Security, known as CYCLOPS, in partnership with the United States, which bears testimony to the acknowledgement of Cyprus' role in promoting security and stability in the Eastern Mediterranean, as well as of the strategic partnership that has been fostered with the United States. Moreover, in 2018 Cyprus and the United States also co-signed a Statement of Intent to strengthen security cooperation including in combatting terrorism, enhancing maritime security and promoting regional stability.

With Russia, China, the UK and France as well, our cooperation is witnessing a dynamic and steady growth in recent years. With France we concluded a Strategic Agenda, signed in 2016. In particular, cooperation with France has been greatly enhanced in the areas of security and defence—where under a defence agreement the armed forces of the two countries exchange joint naval and air exercises, with the participation of other European countries as well—and an array of other fields of growing cooperation. Additionally, with Japan and India significant, tangible steps are taken in enhancing our cooperation. In 2018 Japan opened its Embassy in Cyprus and the following year Cyprus reciprocated with the opening of its Embassy in Tokyo. In February 2021, amid the pandemic, consultations were held via teleconference with the Indian Foreign Minister, discussing precisely concrete ways to advance, both at the bilateral and the multilateral level, relations between Cyprus and India, two countries that share a historically strong bond of friendship and cooperation.

In this evolutionary journey in Cyprus' foreign policy, there has also been acknowledgement of the fact that beyond traditional foreign policy tools, there is a need to utilise 'soft power' policy tools, particularly for small states such as Cyprus. In this respect, the Foreign Ministry has elaborated in recent years a strategic plan, utilising such 'soft power' foreign policy tools, including economic diplomacy, cultural diplomacy, as well as gender mainstreaming. For example, the Cyprus Investment Promotion Agency has now come under the Ministry of Foreign Affairs, while on gender mainstreaming the Foreign Ministry formulated and announced a strategy. The book touches on the efforts exerted by the Foreign Ministry in this regard.

In this book on the journey of Cyprus' foreign policy to maturity, the editor, Dr. Tziarras, accurately identifies the importance of constantly reflecting and assessing how the component parts of our foreign policy evolve and contribute to our foreign policy goals, as we continue walking this path of a multifaceted foreign policy, firmly anchored on international law.

September 2021

Nikos Christodoulides
Former Foreign Minister of the
Republic of Cyprus (Mar.
2018–Jan. 2022)
Nicosia, Cyprus

Contents

Part I Historical Background, Concepts and Foreign Policy Drivers

1 Introduction: The Foreign Policy of the Republic of Cyprus—The Age of Maturity? ... 3
Zenonas Tziarras

2 The Republic of Cyprus and Its Foreign Policy: A Historical Overview, 1960–2004 ... 19
Andreas Karyos

3 All the President's Decisions: Foreign Policy in the Republic of Cyprus After 2004 ... 45
Anna Koukkides-Procopiou

Part II Between East and West—The International Orientation

4 Stuck in the Middle: Constructing Maturity and Restoring Balance in RoC-EU Relations ... 77
Petros Petrikkos

5 The Republic of Cyprus and the US: A Revamped Relationship with Key Limitations ... 105
Alexandros Zachariades

6   Russia's Place in the Foreign Policy of the Republic
    of Cyprus: Will "Pragmatic Idealism" Survive
    in the 2020s?   137
    Costas Melakopides

Part III   A Newly-Discovered Identity in the Eastern
           Mediterranean?

7   Assessing Maturity in the RoC's Eastern
    Mediterranean Foreign Policy   177
    Ioannis-Sotirios Ioannou

8   The Eastern Mediterranean Disputes in the RoC's
    Foreign Policy: A Socio-Psychological Account   199
    Emine Eminel Sülün

9   Towards a Foreign Policy Actor? Turkish Cypriot
    Perceptions of Cyprus in European Affairs
    and the Eastern Mediterranean   223
    Nur Köprülü

Part IV   Foreign Policymaking, Institutional Capacities &
          Grand Strategic Concerns

10 International Law and the Republic of Cyprus'
    Foreign Policy   245
    Nicholas A. Ioannides

11 Gender Mainstreaming in the Foreign Policy
    of the Republic of Cyprus   267
    Constantinos Adamides and Josie Christodoulou

12 The Republic of Cyprus in International and Regional
    Organizations: Towards a Mature Small State Status
    Seeking Strategy?   287
    Revecca Pedi and Kalliopi Chainoglou

13 Defence Diplomacy by the Republic of Cyprus:
    A Dynamic Policy in the Process of Maturation   311
    Marinos Papaioakeim

14 Foreign Policy Maturity and Grand Strategy: The
   Way Forward for the Republic of Cyprus   343
   Zenonas Tziarras

Index   363

NOTES ON CONTRIBUTORS

Constantinos Adamides is an Associate Professor of International Relations and the Associate Head of the Department of Politics and Governance, at the University of Nicosia (UNic), where he also serves as the Director of the Diplomatic Academy. Beyond his academic activities, Constantinos frequently collaborates on projects and training activities with the Ministries of Foreign Affairs and Defense as well as the National Guard. He also served as a member of the first Geostrategic Council of the Republic of Cyprus (2014–2018). His research focus is on security studies, conflicts and diplomacy. His latest monograph is a book on the Cyprus conflict through the lens of securitisation theory.

Kalliopi Chainoglou holds an LLB (University of Essex), an LLM in Public International Law (UCL), a Ph.D. in International Law (King's College London), and a Postgraduate Certificate in Education and Learning (Bolton University). Dr. Chainoglou is an Assistant Professor of International Law and International Institutions at the University of Macedonia (Greece), a Visiting Professor at the University of Sarajevo (BiH) and a Visiting Research Fellow at the Centre of Human Rights in Conflict at UEL (UK). She has produced a number of monographs and chapters to edited books as well as academic articles in the field of international law and international organisations.

Josie Christodoulou is an independent expert on issues related to women's rights, gender equality, migration, trafficking in human beings and the promotion of gender mainstreaming in policies at national, regional, European and international levels. In February 2019, she was appointed as the Gender Adviser to the Minister of Foreign Affairs of the Republic of Cyprus. She has since contributed to the writing, designing and day to day implementation of the Framework of Action on Gender Mainstreaming in Foreign Policy of the Republic of Cyprus. She continues to work extensively on preventing and combating violence against women including femicides, trafficking in women for the purpose of sexual and labour exploitation, on gender and migration, and on equal representation between women and men, amongst others.

Nicholas A. Ioannides holds a Ph.D. in Public International Law from the University of Bristol. During the academic year 2017–2018, he was a Nippon Fellow at the International Tribunal for the Law of the Sea. He received his LLB from Aristotle University of Thessaloniki in 2010 and earned an LLM in Public International Law from the University of Bristol in 2012. In 2020, he was awarded the 'Daniel Vignes' Prize by the International Association of the Law of the Sea. His monograph entitled *Maritime Claims and Boundary Delimitation: Tensions and Trends in the Eastern Mediterranean Sea* has been published by Routledge.

Ioannis-Sotirios Ioannou has worked as a journalist for Greek, Cypriot and international publications and radio channels. He has been published in academic outlets and served as an expert and associate for MPs in the Hellenic Parliament. He is an expert in the areas of international and regional conflicts, the Middle East, terrorism and security. He holds a B.A. and a M.A. from the University of Piraeus in International and European Studies, a B.A. in Journalism from KAR and a M.A. in International Relations from Carleton University. He currently writes for 'Kathimerini' newspaper is an Analyst at the Diplomatic Academy of University of Nicosia. He is also the co-founder of Geopolitical Cyprus.

Andreas Karyos (B.A. in History & Archaeology, University of Athens; M.A. in Twentieth Century European History, Queen Mary, University of London; Ph.D. in History, School of Advanced Study, University of London) has been teaching faculty in various state and private universities providing education to undergraduate and postgraduate students, but also to Cypriot policemen. His research and publication activities focus on military and political aspects of the Modern History of Cyprus and Greece. Currently, he offers his expertise at the National

Struggle Museum, as well as the Cypriot Commission of Military History (Republic of Cyprus). Moreover, he is member of the board of the Cyprus Society of Historical Studies.

Nur Köprülü has been working on comparative politics of the Middle East region. Köprülü wrote her Ph.D. dissertation on the consolidation of national identity in the Hashemite Kingdom of Jordan at METU, Ankara, Turkey. Her research interests primarily cover the social movements, politics of identity and democratisation processes and foreign policy of Jordan. She published works on the Islamist actors and processes of democratisation in the MENA region as well as consolidated monarchies in the post-Arab uprisings era. She is an Associate Professor and currently works as chair of the Department of Political Science at Near East University, Nicosia, Cyprus.

Anna Koukkides-Procopiou is a Senior Fellow and Member of the Advisory Board of the Center for European and International Affairs, University of Nicosia, and a member of the UN Senior Women Talent Pipeline. She contributes as an independent expert in projects and working groups run by international organisations, such as the OSCE and the World Bank, as well as European institutions. Previously, she held the position of researcher with SeeD-Centre for Sustainable Peace and Democratic Development. A multi-disciplinarian by training, her work focuses on foreign policy, inclusive security, and gender. Anna is an avid public speaker, podcaster and political commentator.

Costas Melakopides studied Law, Philosophy and Political Studies in Athens, Canterbury, and Kingston, ON. After teaching in Canada from 1982 to 1995, he joined the University of Cyprus in 1996. Retired from teaching as Associate Professor, he continues researching and publishing, mainly on Greek-Turkish relations, the Cyprus Problem, Russia-Cyprus relations, and International Ethics. His book, *Russia-Cyprus Relations: A Pragmatic Idealist Perspective*, was published in 1996 by Palgrave.

Marinos Papaioakeim is a Ph.D. Candidate in Diplomacy and International Relations at the Department of Social and Political Sciences of the University of Cyprus. His Ph.D. thesis examines the Small States' Defence Diplomacy in the Protracted Conflict Context: The Evolution of Republic of Cyprus (Roc) Defence Diplomacy (2004–2020). He has a Bachelor degree in History from the Department of History and Archaeology of the University of Cyprus. He also completed an M.A. in Diplomacy and

Foreign Policy at Lancaster University in UK. His main research interests include among others: Defence/Military Diplomacy, Small States, Public Diplomacy, Soft Power and Hybrid Threats.

Revecca Pedi is an Assistant Professor in International Relations at the Department of International and European Studies, University of Macedonia, Thessaloniki, Greece. Her research interests focus on International Relations of Small States, the International Relations of the EU, Small states in the Eastern Mediterranean and Entrepreneurship in International Relations. Her research has been published in international peer-reviewed journals and edited volumes by international publishing houses. She has recently contributed to the *Handbook on the Politics of Small States* and she is co-chairing the *Small States in World Politics Section in the European International Studies Association.*

Petros Petrikkos is a European Security and Defence College–Common Security and Defence Policy (ESDC-CSDP) Doctoral Fellow under the EU's Common Foreign and Security Policy (CFSP) and a Ph.D. candidate in International Relations and European Studies at the University of Nicosia. His Ph.D. focuses on critical security approaches to hybrid threats in Cyprus and Estonia. Petros is also a Project and Research Associate at the Diplomatic Academy—University of Nicosia. He has served in various posts, including Managing and Reviews Editor for *ASEN's Studies in Ethnicity and Nationalism* (SEN) journal.

Emine Eminel Sülün is an Assistant Professor in the Department of International Relations at the Near East University where she has been a faculty member since 2016. She completed her Ph.D. in International Relations at the Middle East Technical University (METU). She holds a B.A. in Sociology from METU and a M.A. in International Politics from the University of Bath. Between 2012 and 2016, Sülün taught at Eastern Mediterranean University (Famagusta) as a part-time member of staff in the Political Science and International Relations Department. Her research interests lie in the areas of geopolitics and security in the Easter Mediterranean.

Zenonas Tziarras is a Researcher at PRIO Cyprus Centre focusing on Eastern Mediterranean geopolitics. He holds a Ph.D. in Politics and International Studies from the University of Warwick (UK) and worked as adjunct lecturer at the University of Cyprus, UCLan Cyprus, the

University of Warwick and Cyprus Police Academy. He completed a Post-Doctoral Fellowship at the University of Cyprus and collaborated with a number of think tanks in Cyprus and abroad on matters pertaining to foreign policy, international security, Turkey, the Middle East and the Eastern Mediterranean. He participates in the editorial board of *New Middle Eastern Studies* and, among other publications, he edited *The New Geopolitics of the Eastern Mediterranean*, and authored *International Politics in the Eastern Mediterranean* (in Greek) and *Turkish Foreign Policy: The Lausanne Syndrome in the Eastern Mediterranean and Middle East*.

Alexandros Zachariades is a Ph.D. Candidate in the Department of International Relations at the London School of Economics. Alexandros' expertise lies in Neoclassical Realism, small states, international relations theories and the Middle East. His research at the LSE is supported by the Alexander S. Onassis Foundation and deals with Greek and Cypriot Foreign Policy in the Middle East since 2004. Alexandros is also the Head of Research for the 89 Initiative.

List of Tables

Table 1.1	Components of a mature foreign policy	7
Table 4.1	RoC Foreign Policy Maturity Levels vis-à-vis the EU	98
Table 11.1	Hiring statistics at the Ministry of Foreign Affairs 1983–2018	275
Table 11.2	Ministers of foreign affairs RoC 1960–2020	276
Table 11.3	Decision-making/Leadership positions-2020	276
Table 12.1	UN resolutions related to the protection of culture and cultural heritage supported or sponsored by the RoC	295
Table 13.1	Bilateral Defence/Military Agreements on Defence Related Issues	336
Table 13.2	Bilateral Memoranda of Understanding (MoUs) on Defence Related Issues	337
Table 13.3	Bilateral Annual / Biannual Military Cooperation Programmes	337
Table 13.4	SOFA Agreements	337
Table 13.5	Trilateral Military Cooperation Programs	337
Table 14.1	Assessing the RoC's foreign policy maturity	353

PART I

Historical Background, Concepts and Foreign Policy Drivers

CHAPTER 1

Introduction: The Foreign Policy of the Republic of Cyprus—The Age of Maturity?

Zenonas Tziarras

INTRODUCTION

Since its foundation in 1960, the history of the Republic of Cyprus (henceforth, RoC) has been one of turmoil. It was not long after independence that ethnic strife dominated Cypriot politics and, by extension, shaped the country's future. The first ethnic clashes took place in 1963. The first United Nations (UN) peacekeeping force (UNFICYP) arrived in Cyprus in 1964 to prevent further fighting between Greek-Cypriots (G/C) and Turkish-Cypriots (T/C). What followed was a decade of tensed bi-communal relations and conflict resolution efforts with various types of involvement by the three guarantor powers of Cyprus's constitutional order (Greece, Turkey, United Kingdom) as well (Anastasiou 2008; Attalides 1979; Dodd 2010; Michael 2009).

Z. Tziarras (✉)
PRIO Cyprus Centre, Nicosia, Cyprus
e-mail: zenonas@prio.org

© The Author(s), under exclusive license to Springer Nature Switzerland AG 2022
Z. Tziarras (ed.), *The Foreign Policy of the Republic of Cyprus*, Reform and Transition in the Mediterranean,
https://doi.org/10.1007/978-3-030-91177-5_1

The 1974 coup d'état by the Greek military junta with the support of the G/C nationalists of EOKA B' against the Cypriot government of Archbishop Makarios III, and the Turkish military invasion that followed as a result, would change Cyprus forever. Since then, Turkey occupies 37% of the island while thousands of Cypriots have been displaced from the north to the south and vice versa. The RoC which since 1963 effectively ceased to be bi-communal and became controlled by the Greek-Cypriots was now faced with a new reality: an internationally recognized Greek-Cypriot dominated republic in the south with amputated sovereignty, and a de facto Turkish-Cypriot state in the north, recognized only by Turkey.

From there on, the Cyprus Problem was meant to become one to consume Cyprus' intra-communal, bi-communal and international politics until today. The RoC in particular, as the only legitimate state in Cyprus with the ability to have foreign relations, tried time and again to internationalize the problem in an effort to pressurize Turkey and bring about a solution that would somehow restore the constitutional order and everything that the republic lost after 1974. The Cyprus Problem is perhaps the most important obstacle in the RoC's foreign policy and its international outlook, with another one being the persisting—if mitigated—economic crisis that broke out in 2013 (Christou and Kyris 2017). Indeed, foreign policy in Cyprus is often seen as merely a means towards the resolution of the Cyprus Problem; international alliances, agreements and even European Union (EU) membership are understood through this prism as well (Ker-lindsay 2007). And this is precisely the problematique that drives this collective volume: the fact that research and scholarly work about the politics and foreign policy of the RoC have been almost entirely seen and analysed through the prism of the Cyprus Problem.

Of course, this reality is not without justification since the Cyprus Problem is indeed central to the social, political and economic life of Cyprus as well as its international position. However, Cyprus is located in a highly neuralgic area of historical and geopolitical importance that is, more often than not, characterized by rapid developments, instability, insecurity as well as opportunities. Therefore, the RoC's politics and foreign policy go well beyond the confines of the Cyprus Problem, or so they should. A "new" and more "mature" foreign policy would be more multidimensional, seeking to strengthen the state's international image and impact, read the newest trends of the international system correctly and adapt accordingly. Some evidence of such change can be found in the RoC's contemporary foreign policy.

The RoC's Contemporary Foreign Policy and the Concept of "Maturity"

Against this background, this book aims to examine the foreign policy of the RoC, particularly since 2004—a landmark year in Cypriot history. On May 1, 2004, Cyprus became a full member-state of the EU. A few days earlier two referenda were held in the two communities of Cyprus; Cypriots were asked whether they approved of Annan Plan V, a UN effort to reunite the island and solve the decades-old political problem. The plan was rejected by 76% of the Greek-Cypriots and approved by 65% of the Turkish-Cypriots. As such, 2004 was a year that simultaneously had an impact on domestic dynamics with respect to the Cyprus Problem as well as on the RoC's foreign relations and international orientation given that with the EU accession Cyprus became, in a sense, officially part of the "West".

On Foreign Policy Maturity

One could also argue that 2004 marked the beginning of a rather long process of maturity in the RoC's foreign policy. Certainly, "maturity" is not a well-established concept in international relations (IR) or foreign policy analysis (FPA); related literature is very limited, and it can thus be seen as an underdeveloped and ambiguous concept. Referring to changes in American foreign policy during the late 1970s, Robert W. Tucker (1979) describes foreign policy maturity as follows:

> Whereas a generation ago the United States was still in its period of youthful exuberance, today it has entered a period of 'maturity.' The former aspiration to preside over and give direction to change in the developing countries has been succeeded by the desire to find a way by which we may get on the side of change we no longer aspire to control, or believe we could control even if we so aspired. And whereas a generation ago the United States enjoyed a marked advantage over the Soviet Union in the means of carrying on the competition in the Third World, today this former advantage has considerably narrowed.

The author goes on to summarize his point by arguing that "catechism on the limits to power" is an expression of "the true spirit and inner wisdom of the foreign policy of 'maturity'" (Tucker 1979). Therefore, for Tucker, foreign policy maturity is reached by striking a balance between aspirations and capabilities (or power limitations); a task that de facto requires well-defined goals.

Similarly, an Op-Ed on Georgia's maturing foreign policy concluded that the country's "foreign affairs in 2010 followed a course of well-defined reasoning and corresponding aspirations" and that the route it "has mapped for the longer term will require sustained maturity, patience and courage". Maturity here is understood as "being more demanding" of a state's "own policy" and learning "to deal more calmly and patiently with the sometimes slow and often elaborate strategic calculations of... foreign partners" (Tabula 2011). Once again, aspirations are central to this conception of foreign policy maturity along with the development of the corresponding capabilities. In addition, a mature foreign policy is here equated with a more demanding and assertive foreign policy, albeit within the well-defined limits of a state's power and capabilities.

A closely related concept in IR and FPA is that of policy optimality/sub-optimality. Barbara Tuchman, for example, mentions "folly" as a kind of "misgovernment"—a suboptimal government, one could argue. Folly, Tuchman argues, is "the pursuit of policy contrary to the self-interest of the constituency or state involved", and self-interest "is whatever conduces to the welfare or advantage of the body being governed; folly is a policy that in these terms is counter-productive" (Tuchman 1984). She then goes on to argue that for a policy to qualify as folly it must meet three criteria: (a) that it was "perceived as counter-productive in its own time, not merely in hindsight"; (b) that there was "a feasible alternative course of action"; and (c) that the folly policy was not the decision of just one individual (e.g. a monarch) but that of a group (Tuchman 1984). Similarly, Randall Schweller demonstrates how underbalancing, underexpansion or underaggression could be suboptimal foreign policy decisions, insofar as they demonstrate "reluctance to use force or build up military power in pursuit of profit or security or both" (Schweller 2008, 104–105).

Defining foreign policy optimality should thus take into account the defined foreign policy objective(s) or discernible national interests, which of course vary across states. In Muhammet Bas's example, "United States sending troops to Afghanistan was a policy intended to enhance US security, but the outcome may be as desired as eliminating the terror threat, but also unwanted, such as leading to further terrorist attacks" (Bas 2012, 801). From this perspective, and in agreement with Tuchman's approach, whereas an optimal policy would maximize security, a suboptimal policy means that other alternatives could serve the objective better, or it could even produce opposite results.

In sum, based on these theoretical and empirical approaches a mature foreign policy could be generally described as that which has clearly defined and set goals/aspirations that match a state's needs, interests and capabilities. Moreover, a mature foreign policy is one with a well weighted strategy; and for that, a state needs the necessary institutions and policymaking mechanisms (see Table 1.1). However, in reality, things are much more complicated. Foreign policymaking and implementation have to deal with various policy sectors and levels of operation. One could assess whether the "whole" of a state's foreign policy is mature only by assessing its "parts". And even then, an overall mature foreign policy does not necessarily mean that it is without mistakes or that suboptimal policies are not followed in certain policy sectors. Therefore, this book leaves it up to the different chapter authors to approach the assessment of foreign policy "maturity" based on their respective policy sectors of enquiry—be it energy security, crisis management, defence diplomacy, etc. Depending on the sector, emphasis might be given to the objectives, the strategy, institutions and so on.

To be in a better position to examine the RoC's foreign policy and assess whether it has matured in its various sectors, it is worth to briefly look at the geopolitical circumstances under which it was ushered into a period of maturation since 2004. The factors listed below are echoed in different degrees by the book's contributing authors. Furthermore, there is a general consensus among the contributors that there has been at least some degree of maturity in the RoC's contemporary foreign policy with the understanding, nonetheless, that there is still a long way to go. The overall maturity and grand strategic prospects of the RoC's foreign policy are further assessed in the concluding chapter of the book.

Table 1.1 Components of a mature foreign policy
Clearly defined objectives and interests
Strategic plan
Functioning institutions and appropriate institutional capacities
Matching material capabilities

The RoC's Road to Foreign Policy Maturity?

As mentioned earlier, it can be argued that since 2004 and even more so since the early 2010s, the foreign policy of the RoC has matured significantly in that it has started, despite some persisting problems and dilemmas, to realize and utilize the island's geostrategic role (see also, Tziarras 2019). To this emerging reality contributed a number of external and domestic factors: (i) the RoC's accession to the EU; (ii) the pressing need to find a solution to the Cyprus Problem; (iii) the maturing of the country's political elites; (iv) the changing world order and the regionalization of the international system; (v) Cyprus' delimitation of its maritime Exclusive Economic Zone (EEZ) with Egypt, Lebanon and Israel and the discovery of hydrocarbons within it; and (vi) Turkey's increasing self-aggrandizement and destabilizing foreign policy (Kontos and Bitsis 2018) which led it to multiple diplomatic and strategic deadends. All these factors and variables are addressed extensively in the chapters of this book.

The RoC's accession to the EU took place at a time when the structure of the international system was undergoing significant changes. This was a result of the post-9/11 international order, the launching of the US's "War on Terror", the 2001 war in Afghanistan and the 2003 invasion of Iraq. To these factors was later added the 2007/2008 global economic crisis that had a great impact on American economy. The 2000s was thus a costly period of overextension for US foreign policy and global power (Zakaria 2011, 190–200). And whether one subscribes to the opinion that American hegemony is in decline or not (for this debate see, e.g., Walt 2005; Friedman 2010; Nasr 2014; Zakaria 2011), it is not hard to see the transition to which Charles Krauthammer was referring right after the end of the Cold War unfolding (Krauthammer 1990):

> The bipolar world in which the real power emanated only from Moscow and Washington is dead. The multipolar world to which we are headed, in which power will emanate from Berlin and Tokyo, Beijing and Brussels, as well as Washington and Moscow, is struggling to be born. The transition between these two worlds is now, and it won't last long. But the instant in which we are living is a moment of unipolarity, where world power resides in one reasonably coherent, serenely dominant, entity: the Western alliance, unchallenged and not yet (though soon to be) fractured by victory.

It has been argued that, as this global transition towards multipolarity has been taking place, middle powers and smaller states have been able to exploit the growing power vacuums in different regions of the world and further their own agendas, independently from the interests of their great power partners or allies (Schweller 2014). In addition, given that the post-Cold War order has been less about global scale rivalries and influences, "region-specific dynamics have been allowed to develop into the primary venues within which most states securitize and de-securitize actors and issues" (Frazier and Stewart-Ingersoll 2010, 734). In other words, international security has been going through a process of decentralization and regionalization that, by extension, creates the need for more regional approaches to managing the geopolitical order, peace, stability and security (Lake and Morgan 1997, 6–7; Tziarras 2018).

Within the context of the increasing importance of the regional level in international relations and the accelerated pace of geopolitical developments particularly in the broader Middle East (Tziarras 2016a), Cyprus has been incentivized by systemic changes and opportunities to acquire a more central role in the Eastern Mediterranean. The RoC's accession to the EU and the delimitation of its EEZ with other states of the Eastern Mediterranean (Israel, Egypt, Lebanon) during the 2000s signified a growing realization of the country's geopolitical position and potential role in the region. Two additional developments created the necessary opportunities for the RoC to further expand its regional outlook and foreign policy activity: (a) the deterioration of Turkish-Israeli relations as of 2008; and (b) the discovery of hydrocarbons in the RoC's EEZ as of 2011 (Proedrou 2012; Kariotis 2011; Moran et al. 2016).

Pushed by the need for security and international support vis-à-vis the Cyprus Problem as well as by the prospects for economic and energy cooperation, the RoC made significant foreign policy openings in the Eastern Mediterranean by being—together with Greece—the main initiator of what has been called "diplomacy of trilateral partnerships" (see, Tziarras 2016b). The two main trilateral partnerships that have been formed so far are the Israel-Cyprus-Greece and Egypt-Cyprus-Greece ones. At least three more are under way: Greece-Cyprus-Jordan, Greece-Cyprus-Lebanon and Cyprus-Greece-Italy. Relations with extra-regional actors such as the United Arab Emirates and France are also improved. To be sure, these foreign policy efforts by the RoC took place in the second half of the 2010s and are thus quite recent. What is more, as any international partnership and alliance, they are not "carved in stone" while their sustainability demands a lot of effort and commitment. Their eventual success will very much depend on both the RoC's handlings, and international developments.

It is also worth mentioning that geopolitical pressures and incentives would perhaps not have the same effect on the RoC's foreign policy had the state's political elites not developed a more regional perspective and gained a better understanding of Cyprus' geopolitical potential since the early 2000s. For example, in 2011 former RoC President, Dimitris Christofias (2008–2013), though coming from a leftist tradition critical of Israel and supportive of the Palestinian cause,[1] became the first Cypriot President to officially visit Israel thus signalling the strengthening of Cypriot-Israeli relations (Tziampiris 2015, 146). Similarly, Nicos Anastasides who was elected to the presidential office since 2013 and re-elected in 2018,[2] though elected with a staunchly pro-Western political programme, he sought to strike a balance between its Western partners (EU and US) and Russia (Cyprus Mail 2018). Both examples demonstrate a more pragmatic and balanced foreign policy approach from the RoC's governing elites, which arguably indicates at least some degree of maturity. This discussion relates to the state's institutional maturity and capacities as well, including the issue of gender equality and gendered foreign policy. The RoC has seen some interesting developments on that front as well though there is still way to go.

Despite the growing importance of the Eastern Mediterranean as a geopolitical space as well as the political and academic interest that it has stirred (see, e.g., Litsas and Tziampiris 2015; Stergiou et al. 2017; Adamides and Christou 2015; Ellinas 2017), the RoC's new foreign policy activism itself has attracted little attention in the literature. Beyond the fixation with the Cyprus Problem, the RoC's foreign policy is usually seen as just another part of the Eastern Mediterranean or in relation to other states particularly in the context of the emerging energy security architecture of the region (e.g. Adamides and Christou 2015; Giannakopoulos 2016; Prontera and Ruszel 2017). There have been of course exceptions which are, however, rather limited and not close to providing a rounded and comprehensive account of the RoC's contemporary foreign

---

[1] Dimitris Christofias used to be the General Secretary of the communist AKEL (the Progressive Party of Working People).

[2] Nicos Anastasiades used to be the president of conservative DISY (Democratic Rally). He was first elected in February 2013 and got re-elected in February 2018.

policy (Melakopides 2016; Tziarras 2019; Kouskouvelis 2015; Pedi and Kouskouvelis 2019; Efthymiopoulos and Tziarras 2013).

Book Aims and Structure

This book aims to at least partly fill this gap in the literature by being the first comprehensive account of the various aspects, drivers and levels that affect the foreign policy of the RoC, especially in the light of important external developments such as regional geopolitical changes, the politico-ideological transformation of Turkey, the discovery of hydrocarbons in the Eastern Mediterranean and the competing international interests in the broader region not least because of the conflicts in Iraq and Syria. Moreover, the book considers both external and domestic dynamics in analysing the RoC's foreign policy while exploring its increasingly important role in the region as well as its traditionally blurry international orientation. It does so by looking at the RoC's relations with key regional and international players (e.g. Israel, Turkey, Greece, Egypt, US, Russia, EU) and different policy sectors (e.g. energy, security, diplomacy, international law).

In this sense the book also covers the role of Cyprus and the wider implications of the RoC's foreign policy for NATO, the EU, Turkey, Russia, etc., thus covering its local, regional and international dimensions. Furthermore, the concept of "maturity", as mentioned earlier, runs through the whole book, and, among other conclusions, each chapter provides an assessment on whether the RoC's foreign policy has matured since the mid-2000s. Apart from the Introduction, Part I consists of two more chapters. In Chapter 2, Andreas Karyos provides the historical background to the book in the form of an original and valuable thematic review of the RoC's foreign policy between the state's establishment in 1960 and its accession to the EU in 2004. Among other things, Karyos's review demonstrates how the Cyprus Problem has been central to the RoC's foreign policy throughout its history. At the same time, Karyos sheds light on other aspects—such as leader perceptions and economic interests—thus showing other issues the RoC's foreign policy has been concerned with, albeit taking second place to the Cyprus Problem. In Chapter 3, Anna Koukkides-Procopiou picks it up where Andreas Karyos left it and looks at the foreign policy drivers of the RoC, particularly since 2004. Koukkides-Procopiou delves into the issue through the examination of what she calls "stages" of foreign policymaking that correspond to different time periods (or milestones) and the most salient foreign policy drivers therein. Koukkides-Procopiou focuses on the forces of Europeanization to a large extent while arguing that during the period in question, there has been "no other more important endogenous driver to policy than the President himself".

Part II focuses on aspects of the RoC's international orientation and its diachronic dilemma between East and West. In Chapter 4, Petros Petrikkos looks at the RoC's relations with the EU and argues that despite the rising status of the country in the international scene since its accession to the EU, its foreign policy is at a cul-de-sac with some of its areas being static and contained. Petrikkos uses an empirical foreign policy analysis approach to understand and explain an unevenly developed foreign policy pursued by the RoC in relation to the EU. His chapter highlights areas of cooperation over security, energy and the economy, as well as the style of diplomacy used to bridge the East and the West through the country's EU membership. However, he points out that despite the progress in some fields, such as the RoC's new strategic approach towards energy and security within the EU, its membership in the Union creates an illusion about the settlement of the Cyprus Problem and prevents the RoC's foreign policy from reaching its full potential.

In Chapter 5, Alexandros Zachariades seeks to account for the relationship of the RoC with the US since Cyprus' 2004 accession to the EU. Zachariades suggests that after the accession, Cyprus-US relations have gradually improved—especially in the late 2010s. Through the analysis, the chapter argues that the current state of US-Cyprus relations is less a product of a "mature" foreign policy strategy on Cyprus' part, and more a result of regional developments in the Eastern Mediterranean and US response to those developments. As such, Zachariades details the systemic—but also unit-level—factors that affected the enhanced American-Cypriot relationship in recent years, as well as its limitations. In Chapter 6, the final chapter of Part II, Costas Melakopides provides a comprehensive account of RoC-Russia relations from the perspective of Nicosia's professed attempts to cultivate a "symmetrical" foreign policy agenda vis-à-vis both Russia and the US. Melakopides's critical argument suggests that Nicosia's stereotypical assurances of a "balance" in its relations with both superpowers appear inauthentic, allowing the current opposition to accuse President Anastasiades of a quasi-opportunistic stance towards Moscow, that amounts to turning towards it primarily when in need.

Part III shifts the attention to the regional level of analysis, particularly the Eastern Mediterranean (and the Middle East) and addresses the RoC's newly discovered regional identity. Ioannis-Sotirios Ioannou in Chapter 7 highlights certain weaknesses in the RoC's foreign policy and missed opportunities to play the role of an "honest broker" in crises starting within the Eastern Mediterranean geopolitical sub-region. Through the examination of regional examples, Ioannou argues that when the RoC fails to play a proactive role in important issues, it also fails to affirm its role as a small but effective EU actor in the broader Eastern Mediterranean region and to capitalize possible rewards both in relation to the Cyprus Problem and in the emerging landscape of regional (energy) cooperation.

In Chapter 8, Emine Eminel Sülün explores the performative link between the foreign policy discourse of RoC policymakers, especially Ministry of Foreign Affairs officials, on the Eastern Mediterranean dimension of Turkish foreign policy since 2002. Sülün argues that this foreign policy discourse has constituted developments—especially regarding hydrocarbons and the RoC's EEZ claims—as important events. At the same time, it has helped the constitution of the Greek-Cypriot self as a homogenous identity who views Turkey as a barrier to the RoC's increasingly important role in the region. Importantly, Sülün also argues that especially the RoC's hydrocarbons and EEZ claims have been instrumental for the RoC to reproduce a self-identity whose sovereignty is continuously threatened by Turkey, but this time goes beyond the confines of the Cyprus Problem.

Nur Köprülü completes Part III with Chapter 9, providing a Turkish-Cypriot view of the RoC's foreign policy. More specifically it aims to highlight the new patterns of behaviour that have accompanied the RoC's foreign policy, which in some circumstances extend far beyond the limits of the Cyprus Problem, and addresses the perceptions and interpretations of Turkish Cypriots regarding the proactive foreign policy choices of the RoC. Detailing the Turkish-Cypriot view, Köprülü argues that despite the RoC's proactive foreign policy since the early 2000s, Nicosia appears unable to fulfil its primary goals and further its proactive policy because of the obstacles that occur from the lack of settlement to the Cyprus Problem.

Part IV is the final part of the book. It consists of five chapters and addresses aspects of foreign policymaking and institutional issues in the RoC as well as the future of the RoC's foreign policy and its ability to have a grand strategy. It begins with Chapter 10 where Nicholas Ioannides examines the role of international law in the RoC's foreign policy. He first scrutinizes the participation of the RoC in the Kosovo Declaration of Independence and the Chagos Archipelago advisory proceedings. Lastly, he analyses the RoC's policy regarding the marine domain and the pertinent regional tensions. According to Ioannides, his study reveals that the RoC is a law-abiding state observing its international law obligations. The author ultimately argues that the RoC has demonstrated maturity in the international law domain given that it does not merely deem this branch of law a foreign policy "tool". Rather, the author suggests, the RoC has been prudent in invoking international law and "has been inclined to play a part in the evolution of the legal framework governing international relations".

In Chapter 11, Constantinos Adamides and Josie Christodoulou present the first review and study on the RoC's strategy of gender mainstreaming in foreign policy. They specifically examine whether the RoC's foreign policy aspiration is in line with the state's needs and interest in women's rights and gender equality through the strategy of mainstreaming gender. To this end they look at the past and current gender representation gap in the RoC's foreign affairs institutional structures and the efforts undertaken to rectify the problem. Moreover, they explain how a more focused gender strategy can contribute to a state's foreign policy goals broadly speaking and, lastly, they explore ways in which there can be foreign policy actions that can contribute to the advancement of women's rights. Adamides and Christodoulou find that despite "some very positive steps", the RoC has "still a long path ahead" as regards mainstreaming gender in foreign policy.

In Chapter 12, Revecca Pedi and Kalliopi Chainoglou focus on the RoC's underexplored foreign policy in International and Regional Organizations. The authors combine literature on status seeking with studies on small states in International Organizations (IOs) and examine the role(s) the RoC assumes within IOs, its means and ends, priorities and areas of activity as well as the values and norms the small island state supports and sponsors. Their empirical analysis looks at the case studies of the UN, the Council of Europe (CoE) and the EU focusing on the issue of the protection of culture and cultural heritage. Pedi and Chainoglou argue that the RoC's foreign policy activity in the cases in question has been successful in advancing its position in multilateral settings even though it is directly related to the Cyprus Problem.

In Chapter 13, Marinos Papaioakeim offers a highly interesting and original review of the RoC's defence diplomacy since the country's accession to the EU based on primary research and never-before-accessed documents. Papaioakeim argues that the current foreign defence relations of the RoC are unprecedented as it is the first time since the republic's establishment in 1960 that its external defence relations have develop to such an extent. He suggests, however, that although the RoC has shown a great degree of dynamism and evolution in defence diplomacy its way to maturity is still long and he identifies specific areas that either hinder the further evolution of the RoC's defence diplomacy or need to develop more.

In the final and concluding chapter of the book (Chapter 14), Zenonas Tziarras analyses the challenges and obstacles to grand strategic planning by the RoC. The chapter draws conclusions regarding the overall "maturity" of the RoC's foreign policy and ties together the arguments and findings of the book's chapters thus juxtaposing the RoC's levels of foreign policy maturity with its capacity to develop a grand strategy. The argument is that the Cyprus Problem has been inevitably and negatively affecting grand strategic formulation in the RoC even as it often complicates and hinders the country's day-to-day foreign policy and diplomatic practice. From this perspective, the argument sometimes found in Cypriot or Greek literature that the RoC either has or can have long-term foreign policies or a grand strategy without the resolution of the Cyprus Problem is put to the test. Lastly, it is argued that the RoC should not stop engaging in capacity building and a proactive foreign policy while setting the resolution of the Cyprus Problem as a strategic objective, among others, that will allow the country to reach its full potential in the region and the world.

Epilogue

Although the book provides a detailed account of the RoC's contemporary foreign policy, it also touches upon many regional and international dimensions. This renders it relevant for anyone who wants to better understand not just Cyprus but also the broader region and its importance for regional and international actors. It could particularly interest those concerned with the security, stability, and the economic and energy development of the Eastern Mediterranean and the Middle East vis-à-vis the EU, given that Cyprus is an EU member-state that is trying to acquire an important role in the future plans of Europe's energy security and relations with the Middle East. It is also relevant for those who want to better grasp the Eastern Mediterranean dimension of Turkish foreign policy as seen from Cyprus' perspective and that of other actors in the Eastern Mediterranean that have improved their relations with the RoC in recent years. As the significance of the region grows, the book's relevance will grow as well.

References

Adamides, Constantinos, and Odysseas Christou. 2015. "Energy Security and the Transformation of Regional Securitization Relations in the Eastern Mediterranean." In *Societies in Transition: The Social Implications of Economic, Political and Security Transformations*, edited by Savvas Katsikides and Pavlos Koktsidis, 189–206. New York: Springer.

Anastasiou, Harry. 2008. *The Broken Olive Branch: Nationalism, Ethnic Conflict, and the Quest for Peace in Cyprus. Volume I: The Impasse of Ethnonationalism*. Syracuse, NY: Syracuse University Press.

Attalides, Michalis A. 1979. *Cyprus: Nationalism and International Politics*. Edinburgh: Q Press.

Bas, Muhammet A. 2012. "Democratic Inefficiency? Regime Type and Suboptimal Choices in International Politics." *The Journal of Conflict Resolution* 56 (5): 799–824.

Christou, George, and George Kyris. 2017. "The Impact of the Eurozone Crisis on National Foreign Policy: Enhancing Europeanization in the Case of Cyprus." *Journal of Common Market Studies* 55 (6): 1290–1305.

Cyprus Mail. 2018. "Cyprus Has Looked More to the East than West During Anastasiades' Term." http://cyprus-mail.com/2018/01/04/view-cyprus-looked-east-west-anastasiades-term/.

Dodd, Clement. 2010. *The History and Politics of the Cyprus Conflict*. New York: Palgrave Macmillan.

Efthymiopoulos, Marios P., and Zenonas Tziarras, eds. 2013. Κυπριακή Δημοκρατία: Διαστάσεις Εξωτερικής Πολιτικής [Republic of Cyprus: Dimensions of Foreign Policy]. Thessaloniki: University Studio Press.

Ellinas, Charles. 2017. "The Eastern Mediterranean: An Energy Region in the Making." In *The Political and Economic Challenges of Energy in the Middle East and North Africa*, edited by David Ramin Jalilvand and Kirsten Westphal. London: Routledge.

Frazier, Derrick, and Rober Stewart-Ingersoll. 2010. "Regional Powers and Security: A Framework for Understanding Order Within Regional Security Complexes." *European Journal of International Relations* 16 (4): 731–753.

Friedman, George. 2010. *The Next 100 Years: A Forecast for the 21st Century*. New York: Anchor Books.
Giannakopoulos, Angelos, ed. 2016. "Energy Cooperation and Security in the Eastern Mediterranean:A Seismic Shift Towards Peace or Conflict." Research Paper 8. Tel Aviv: The S. Daniel Abraham Center for International and Regional Studies.
Kariotis, Theodore C. 2011. "Hydrocarbons and the Law of the Sea in the Eastern Mediterranean: Implications for Cyprus, Greece, and Turkey." *Mediterranean Quarterly* 22 (2): 45–56.
Ker-lindsay, James. 2007. "The Policies of Greece and Cyprus towards Turkey's EU Accession." *Turkish Studies* 8 (1): 71–83.
Kontos, Michalis, and George Bitsis. 2018. "Power Games in the Exclusive Economic Zone of the Republic of Cyprus: The Trouble with Turkey's Coercive Diplomacy." *The Cyprus Review* 30 (1): 51–70.
Kouskouvelis, Ilias I. 2015. ""Smart" Leadership in a Small State: The Case of Cyprus." In *The Eastern Mediterranean in Transition: Multipolarity, Politics and Power*, edited by Spyridon N. Litsas and Aristotle Tziampiris. New York: Routledge.
Krauthammer, Charles. 1990. "The Unipolar Moment." *The Washington Post*. Accessed 10/04/2018. https://www.washingtonpost.com/archive/opinions/1990/07/20/the-unipolar-moment/62867add-2fe9-493f-a0c9-4bfba1ec23bd/?utm_term=.7bf798880cf5.
Lake, David A., and Patrick M. Morgan. 1997. "The New Regionalism in Security Affairs." In *Regional Orders: Building Security in a New World*, edited by David A. Lake and Patrick M. Morgan. University Park, PA: The Pennsylvania State University Press.
Litsas, Spyridon N., and Aristotle Tziampiris, eds. 2015. *The Eastern Mediterranean in Transition: Multipolarity, Politics and Power*. New York: Routledge.
Melakopides, Costas. 2016. *Russia-Cyprus Relations: A Pragmatic Idealist Perspective*. New York: Palgrave Macmillan.
Michael, Michalis Stavrou. 2009. *Resolving the Cyprus Conflict: Negotiating History*. New York: Palgrave Macmillan.
Moran, Ayla Gürel, Harry Tzimitras, and Hubert Faustmann, eds. 2016. "Global Energy and the Eastern Mediterranean." PCC Report 1/2016. Oslo, Nicosia, and New York: PRIO Cyprus Center.
Nasr, Vali. 2014. *The Dispensable Nation: American Foreign Policy in Retreat*. New York: Anchor Books.
Pedi, Revecca, and Ilias Kouskouvelis. 2019. "Cyprus in the Eastern Mediterranean: A Small State Seeking for Status." In *The New Eastern Mediterranean: Theory, Politics and State in a Volatile Era*, edited by Spyridon N. Litsas and Aristotle Tziampiris, 151–167. Cham: Springer.

Proedrou, Filippos. 2012. "Re-conceptualising the Energy and Security Complex in the Eastern Mediterranean." *The Cyprus Review* 24 (2): 15–28.

Prontera, Andrea, and Mariusz Ruszel. 2017. "Energy Security in the Eastern Mediterranean." *Middle East Policy* 24 (3): 145–162.

Schweller, Randall L. 2008. *Unanswered Threats: Political Constraints on the Balance of Power.* Princeton and Oxford: Princeton University Press.

Schweller, Randall L. 2014. *Maxwell's Demon and the Golder Apple: Global Discord in the New Millenium.* Baltimore: Johns Hopkins University Press.

Stergiou, Andreas, Kivanç Ulusoy, and Menahem Blondheim, eds. 2017. *Conflict & Prosperity: Geopolitics and Energy in the Eastern Mediterranean.* New York: Israel Academic Press.

Tabula. 2011. "Foreign Policy in 2010: Increased Maturity, Courage and Patience." http://www.tabula.ge/en/story/70029-foreign-policy-in-21-increased-maturity-courage-and-patience.

Tuchman, Barbara. 1984. *The March of Folly: From Troy to Vietnam.* New York: Ballantine Books.

Tucker, Robert W. 1979. "America in Decline: The Foreign Policy of 'Maturity'." *Foreign Affairs* 58 (3): 449–484.

Tziampiris, Aristotle. 2015. *The Emergence of Israeli-Greek Cooperation.* London: Springer.

Tziarras, Zenonas. 2016a. "The Changing World Order and the 'Acceleration of History': The Middle East Example." In *Acceleration of History: War, Conflict, and Politics*, edited by Alexios Alecou, 17–35. London: Lexington Books.

Tziarras, Zenonas. 2016b. "Israel-Cyprus-Greece: A 'Comfortable' Quasi-Alliance." *Mediterranean Politics* 21 (3): 407–427.

Tziarras, Zenonas. 2018. "The Eastern Mediterranean: Between Power Struggles and Regionlist Aspirations." Re-Imagining the Eastern Mediterranean: PCC Report, 2. Nicosia: PRIO Cyprus Centre.

Tziarras, Zenonas. 2019. "Cyprus's Foreign Policy in the Eastern Mediterranean and the Trilateral Partnerships: A Neoclassical Realist Approach." In *The New Geopolitics of the Eastern Mediterranean: Trilateral Partnerships and Regional Security*, edited by Zenonas Tziarras, 53–72. Nicosia: PRIO Cyprus Centre.

Walt, Stephen M. 2005. *Taming American Power: The Global Response to U.S. Primacy.* New York and London: W. W. Norton.

Zakaria, Fareed. 2011. *The Post-American World and the Rise of the Rest.* 2nd ed. London and New York: Penguin Books.

CHAPTER 2

The Republic of Cyprus and Its Foreign Policy: A Historical Overview, 1960–2004

Andreas Karyos

INTRODUCTION

The foreign policy of the Republic of Cyprus (henceforth, RoC) has been investigated to a very limited degree so far. The few works that contain a foreign policy perspective (for instance Tzermias 2001; Mallinson 2005; Tsardanidis 2006) focus on the various initiatives of the RoC in response to the development of the Cyprus Problem or on Nicosia's efforts to deal with its dilemmas in the field of Strategic Planning for National Security (Kontos 2014). Another study (Ker-Lindsay 2010) briefly describes the choice of the RoC to become member of the Non-Alignment Movement instead of the North Atlantic Treaty Organisation (NATO), and later on, the European Union (EU) leaving outside from the research

A. Karyos (✉)
University of Nicosia, Nicosia, Cyprus
e-mail: karyos.a@unic.ac.cy

Open University of Cyprus, Nicosia, Cyprus

© The Author(s), under exclusive license to Springer Nature Switzerland AG 2022
Z. Tziarras (ed.), *The Foreign Policy of the Republic of Cyprus*, Reform and Transition in the Mediterranean,
https://doi.org/10.1007/978-3-030-91177-5_2

agenda Nicosia's other strategic choice—the Commonwealth. Consequently, the limited literature has resulted in an indefinite understanding of the landscape of the foreign policy of the RoC.

This chapter's task is twofold. First, to provide a historical background to the present book. Second, to contribute to the international literature about the RoC by exploring the important drivers (global or regional actors, views of political personalities or quarters of the society, ideology of political parties, etc.) behind the RoC's foreign policy, from 1960 until 2004. These drivers encompass not only the unfolding of the Cyprus Problem and important international developments but also the concepts of national survival and prosperity. The present overview is done through the prism of the RoC's relations with international organisations. This approach accommodates the better understanding of the country's international orientation at various periods of its Modern History.

The chapter adopts a thematic structure to tie together the drivers behind the RoC's alignment (or not) with key international organisations. Therefore, apart from the Introduction and Conclusion, the chapter is divided into five sections, each one accounting for the following organisations, respectively: the United Nations (UN), the Non-Alignment Movement, the Commonwealth, NATO and the EU. The period under examination expands from 1960, when the RoC was established and became part of the international community—the UN—to its accession to the EU, in 2004.

THE RoC AND THE UN

In February 1959 the governments of Greece, Turkey and Britain, as well as Archbishop Makarios III on behalf of the Greek-Cypriots (G/C) and Dr. Fazil Küçük, leader of the Turkish-Cypriots (T/C), reached a compromising agreement on the international status of the British Colony of Cyprus (Richter 2011, 939–963). The settlement took the shape of the Zurich and London Agreements and did not fulfil the desire of London for continuation of the British colonial rule, or that of Greece and the G/C for union of Cyprus with Greece, or that of Turkey and the T/C for partition of the island (Crouzet 2011, 1131–1134).

The resolution of the Cyprus Question in February 1959 was followed by an eighteen-month period that proved to be crucial for the transition of Cyprus from a colony to an independent republic. During this period, intense negotiations were carried out for the regulation of two important issues: the drafting of the Cypriot constitution (April 1960) and the determination of the size of the British Sovereign Bases (July 1960). The arrangement of these two important matters paved the way for the constitutional foundation of the RoC on 16 August 1960 (ibid., 1134–1136; Lambrou 2008, 75–76; Crawshaw 1978, 351, 356–361).

One of the strategic priorities of the newly founded RoC was to consolidate its presence within the international community as an independent and sovereign state (Tsardanidis 2006, 2). It therefore applied for accession to the UN soon after its independence was officially declared. In late August 1960 the UN Security Council (UNSC) considered the Cypriot candidacy and gave its approval. Eventually, the RoC's membership was actualised on 20 September 1960 (Kranidiotis 1981, 453–455). Since its incorporation into the UN, the RoC has remained committed to its values and principles, acknowledging the Organisation as "the guardian of international legal order" (Ministry of Foreign Affairs 2021). Hence, the RoC's membership has been moving along "in respect of human rights, the implementation of International Law provisions, and the peaceful settlement of disputes" (ibid.)

The RoC—through its UN membership—tried to promote its vision for peace, security, respect of human rights and the rule of law at the international level. The RoC used the UN also as diplomatic leverage to attain its own political aims. Such a conduct should not take someone by surprise. As Joseph S. Joseph (2011, 245) acutely points out "states are using and abusing it [the UN] in many ways and for a variety of purposes, such as a platform for political debate, a means for the mobilization of world public opinion and concern, an arena for diplomatic maneuvering, and an instrument of collective legitimization and support".

The RoC, indeed, tried to make the UN become involved for purposes beyond the latter's mission to promote peacekeeping and conflict resolution (ibid.). More specifically, Nicosia's short-termed objective was to make explicit to the international community that the constitutional order established by the Zurich and London Agreements created serious dysfunctions to the newly born state. In the long term, the key preoccupation of the RoC's foreign policy was the partial amendment of the constitution, thereby abolishing the provisions that allowed Greece, Britain and Turkey to interfere in Cypriot domestic affairs. In this way, the RoC would eventually achieve complete self-determination (Tsardanidis 2006, 2).

The eruption of ethnic strife between the G/C and the T/C in 1963, and the strenuous diplomatic negotiations it ignited, provided the RoC with an opportunity to fulfil some of its foreign policy objectives. Nicosia tried to settle the Cyprus Question through an appeal to the UN. Thus, internationalisation became the dominant tactic of the foreign policy of the RoC for many decades. An examination of the first recourse to the UN is therefore necessary.

In late November 1963, Archbishop Makarios III, the President of the RoC, proposed to the T/C side a thirteen-point constitutional reform to revamp the dysfunctional nature of the constitution (Mallinson 2005, 35; Stylianou 2010, 87; Tzermias 2001, 475–484). This initiative was perceived by T/C as a threat against their constitutional privileges (Kazamias 2013, 273). A few weeks later, an incident between G/C policemen and T/C passengers was the pretext to an intercommunal violent crisis, during which the T/C withdrew from their posts in the RoC government and state institutions and moved to fortified enclaves/cantons (Kazamias 2013, 274; Papademetris 2010, 106–108; Tzermias 2001, 521–540). Due to the alarming deterioration of the situation and in view of Turkey's declared threat to take forceful action against the RoC, Nicosia appealed to the UNSC asking for support to safeguard the RoC's territorial integrity and political independence. The RoC's request for a UN intervention invoked articles 1 (1),[1] 2 (4)[2] and 24 (1)[3] of the UN Charter (Joseph 2011, 246). After a short session of the UNSC, Nicosia decided to participate in the Five-partite Conference held in London (15 January–10 February 1964), a British initiative to resolve the (re-emerging) Cyprus Question. After all, article 33 of the UN Charter stated that it was desirable to seek all possible alternative solutions before seeking a settlement through the UN institutions. However, the London Conference reached a deadlock and Nicosia made recourse to the UN again (Christodoulides 2010a, 148; Kazamias 2013, 277–278; Tzermias 2001, 553–555; Bitsios 1975, 130–132, 138).

---

[1] This article states that the primary aim of the UN is the preservation of international peace and security.

[2] According to this article, all states must refrain from the threat or use of force against the territorial integrity or political independence of any other state.

[3] This article accepts the UNSC as the primary organ responsible to keep the international order and security.

What drove the RoC to choose the internationalisation of the Cyprus Question instead of relying solely on the G/C superiority in numbers and resources to turn the ethno-political balance of power to its benefit? After all, the T/C reaction led the state institutions and economy of the RoC to come under the absolute G/C control (Syrigos 2015, 159; Kyriakides 1968, 113–115). Basically, the RoC government appealed to the UN to strengthen its position both domestically and internationally, aiming ultimately at a revision of those constitutional provisions that seriously restricted the newly established state's political independence. Through its appeal, Nicosia pursued the following objectives: first, it tried to exploit the UN to strengthen the legality of the RoC government, which was directly disputed by Ankara and the T/C. The latter had abandoned their public posts but also started establishing separate administration mechanisms in the enclaves/cantons (Tzermias 2001, 527–540; Kyriakides 1968, 116–119). A UN resolution would mean a direct or indirect recognition of Makarios' government as the sole legitimate authority in the RoC (Joseph 2011, 248).

Second, by taking the issue to the UN, Nicosia tried to obstruct the efforts of Britain and the United States (US) to settle the Cyprus Question within the framework of NATO (Tsardanidis 2006, 30, 33–34). The RoC believed that the Anglo-American stance was favourable to Turkey (Syrigos 2015, 159, 161). In quest of international leverage at the UN forum, it decided to present foreign intervention (by other actors than the UN) as a case of "neo-colonialism" to secure support from the African and Asian countries—especially the recent post-colonial states—as well as the communist states of the Eastern bloc. These two groups of UN members believed that the RoC should follow an international orientation away from NATO or the West. In addition to increasing its diplomatic leverage, a possible UN debate on the RoC's troubles would provide an opportunity to the USSR for another round of competition with the Western powers (Joseph 2011, 249; Tsardanidis 2006, 34).

Third, the RoC government considered that the recourse to the UN would facilitate its effort to amend various provisions of the Cypriot constitution and abrogate the Treaty of Guarantee (Tsardanidis 2006, 30, 33). Nicosia hoped for a UN declaration endorsing the view that the Zurich and London Agreements provided for an imperfect independence. Such a declaration would "greatly strengthen Makarios' position and free his hand to reshape the internal political structure and external relations of Cyprus as he wished" (Joseph 2011, 249).

Finally, it was crucial for the RoC to secure—through the appeal to the UN—peacekeeping force under the international organisation's mandate. The dispatch of a UN force would satisfy the G/C, who were greatly suspicious of British peacekeeping operations; they considered them as an instrument that originated in Britain's guarantor capacity that promoted, however, Turkey's plans against the RoC (Joseph 2011, 248). Moreover, a force under UN mandate would enable Nicosia to continue resisting the pressures of London and Washington for the establishment of a peacekeeping force comprising NATO contingents (indeed this is what the so-called Ball Plan proposed).[4] More importantly, though, a UN force in Cyprus would improve the RoC's capability to counter the Turkish threat of an invasion. The latter was Ankara's most serious bargaining chip in its contest with Nicosia (Joseph 2011, 248–250; Syrigos 2015, 161, 178; Tsardanidis 2006, 33).

Eventually, the reactivation of the RoC's appeal and the UNSC debate that followed produced a resolution on 4 March 1964 in which most of Nicosia's goals were attained. With references to the "sovereign Republic of Cyprus", the resolution urged all sides to respect its territorial integrity and political independence. For this reason, any foreign intervention or interference should be avoided. Moreover, a peacekeeping force (UNFICYP—United Nations Force in Cyprus) was to be deployed in the RoC to collaborate with the RoC government (the Makarios government; not the T/C administration) in the preservation of peace and order. Finally, a UN mediator[5] was commissioned to the RoC to consult with all parties and promote a peaceful arrangement of the Cyprus Question that would be in line with the UN Charter (Mallinson 2005, 41–42; Christodoulides 2010a, 148; Tzermias 2001, 558–562).

---

[4] See more on the so-called Ball Plan in Kazamias (2013, 278) and Christodoulides (2010a, 148).

[5] The UN mediator was Gallo Plaza (from Ecuador). Plaza, after consultations with all the interested parties submitted a report in March 1965 in which he pointed out the weaknesses of the Zurich and London Agreements that produced the dysfunction of the Cypriot constitution, suggested the commencement of intercommunal talks (between the G/C and the T/C) under UN auspices and proposed the establishment of a genuinely independent Republic of Cyprus with majority rule and guaranteed minority rights for the T/C. However, his report on the solution of the Cyprus Question met fierce reaction by Turkey (Christodoulides 2009, 175–176; Tenekidis 2009, 225–230; Tzermias 2000, 475).

Britain and the USA tried to counter the UN and USSR involvement in the RoC (Christodoulides 2010a, 149; Joseph 2011, 257). They took the initiative to call a conference in Geneva, in August 1964, to regulate the Cyprus Question (in consultation with the governments of Athens and Ankara) based on the Acheson Plan.[6] The RoC reacted by exploiting the momentum and pursuing further involvement of the UN in the Cyprus Question. More specifically, with its recourse to the UN General Assembly Nicosia intended to attract a substantial sum of votes—African and Asian votes. Many of those member-states were former colonies who had recently gained their independence. As such, they opposed any exogenous intervention that would compromise the unity or the survival of the RoC (Tzermias 2001, 613; Tsardanidis 2006, 33). The latter presented its case before the UN General Assembly, through the lens of continuing colonialism, supporting that self-determination—in its genuine form—was never applied in Cyprus. Also, the RoC government argued that Turkey abused its capacity of a guarantor power (imposed by the Zurich and London Agreements of 1959) to threaten the newly founded state's sovereignty and independence. In addition, it called the UN member-states to declare their respect for the sovereignty, unity, independence, territorial integrity and non-alignment of the RoC (Joseph 2011, 257–258). Eventually, in late December 1965 the General Assembly adopted a resolution that called all countries to respect the RoC's unity, sovereignty, independence and territorial integrity (Tzermias 2000, 475; Tsardanidis 2006, 53). Joseph S. Joseph's (2011, 259) analysis of how the RoC's membership (and activism) in the UN served as an instrument of policy is again illuminating:

> A closer look at the vote clearly shows that the General Assembly functioned as a political forum, and the votes of the individual states were determined by political consideration and sympathies... The forty-seven votes cast in favor of the resolution came mainly from the Afro-Asian countries which approached the issue in the context of self-determination and anti-colonialism... There is no doubt that the resolution represented another major diplomatic victory for Makarios who successfully used

[6] See more on the Acheson Plan in Kranidiotis (1984, 129–145), Kranidiotis (2000, 211–223), Rizas (2000, 123–164), Syrigos (2015, 173–176), Tzermias (2001, 587–603) and Christodoulides (2009, 138–174).

the General Assembly as a means for the articulation, channeling, and publicization of international support for his position.

Tzermias (2001, 613–614) in his assessment of the results of the UN General Assembly resolution makes a similar argument.

After 1964 and especially after the Turkish invasion of 1974, Nicosia enforced a strategy involving, among others, successive appeals to the UN (Tsardanidis and Nicolaou 1999, 175). These efforts produced successive UN resolutions with respect to the independence of the RoC. To properly assess the motive behind the RoC's foreign policy to resort to activism within the UN, we note that the UN resolutions did not constitute a legally binding force to sanctions that would reverse Turkey's strategic planning for the partition of Cyprus. On the other hand, these UN resolutions were proven to be more than mere paper victories. Ankara has since then been disputing the legitimacy of the RoC through the formation of dependencies in the Turkey occupied part of Cyprus, such as the "Turkish Federated State of Cyprus" of 1975 and the "Turkish Republic of Northern Cyprus" of 1983. Such unilateral initiatives were not accepted by the international community. UN resolutions have been, indeed, one of the methods that the RoC used to deal with the Turkish attempts to legitimise *faits accompli* created by force. From this perspective, membership and activism in the UN has been to the benefit of the RoC's pursuit to solidify its statehood and position in the international arena (Coufoudakis 2006, 210; Joseph 2011, 260–261; Syrigos 2015, 360–361). It should be clarified, however, that such a success was partial: the most important aim, namely the resolution of the Cyprus Problem was not achieved (Tsardanidis and Nicolaou 1999, 177).

THE RoC AND THE NON-ALIGNMENT MOVEMENT

During the Cold War, a period marked by the strong and multidimensional antagonism between the East and the West, the RoC chose an alternative path: non-alignment. A driver behind this orientation was Makarios' personal beliefs of Cyprus' position within the international system (Sakkas 2015, 69). Makarios envisaged at least since the late 1940s that, after union with Greece, Cyprus could be a bridge between Greece, Asia, Africa and the Middle East region, playing the role of a regional and international stabiliser (Kranidiotis 1981, 30). In the famous speech

"Nenikikamen" ("We have triumphed"),[7] delivered on 1 March 1959, he reaffirmed his views on Cyprus' key international role (especially in the region of the Eastern Mediterranean), although as an independent country (*Eleftheria* 1959d; *Phileleftheros* 1959; *Times of Cyprus* 1959).

Another motivation behind Makarios' turn to the post-colonial states of Africa and Asia was his view of the decolonisation process of the 1950s and the early 1960s; a momentum that he wanted to capitalise for the benefit of Cyprus. As the G/C movement for termination of the British colonial rule and union with Greece took a more dynamic turn in the 1950s, Makarios intensified his efforts to attract international support for Cyprus. He therefore succeeded in developing close relations with leaders of other anti-colonial movements or newly independent states. Stavros Panteli (1984, 243) notes that Makarios' "political thinking, still in the formative stage, must have been influenced by his visits to the middle east and later the far east". Makarios even attended the Bandung Conference in 1955, which aimed at Afro-Asian collaboration to contain colonialism in all its manifestations (Christodoulou 1987, 113–114).

In the early post-independence years, the RoC deepened its relations with the countries of the Third World. After all, joining NATO or the Warsaw Pact were not favourable orientations. In 1961, the RoC was one of the twenty-five states that participated in the summit of leaders of the Non-Aligned Movement, in Belgrade, thereby becoming one of the founding members (Christodoulou 1987, 319; Ker-Lindsay 2010, 69). As explained by a prominent G/C politician of that time, Glafkos Clerides, the RoC's sense of cohesion with the member-states of the Non-Aligned Movement should not take someone by surprise. Most of the former colonial possessions felt more comfortable within the Movement rather than in a coalition where the dominant members were their former rulers. Also, these countries would have fewer conflicting interests, thereby acting in a spirit of goodwill, seeking solutions to the common problems and challenges they faced. In addition, the RoC expected that Non-Aligned member-states would be able to exercise significant influence had they acted collectively rather than individually (Clerides 1988, 134).

James Ker-Lindsay (2010, 68) points out that the RoC's shift towards non-alignment shaped the "island's ties with the rest of the world for

---

[7] For the historical context and the rhetorical tactics of the speech see Serafim and Karyos (2020).

the next three decades". Indeed, in the years that followed, the RoC attained significant diplomatic gains due to its close relationship with the Non-Aligned Movement. We have already mentioned that in 1965 Nicosia tried to improve its diplomatic leverage through support received by UN partners in the Non-Aligned Movement (Tzermias 2000, 475; Tsardanidis 2006, 53). One year earlier, Nicosia had participated in the Second Conference of the Heads of State or Government of Non-Aligned Countries in Cairo and succeeded in getting a resolution supporting the RoC's independence (Republic of Cyprus 1997, 3; Sakkas 2015, 69). Similarly, membership in the Non-Aligned Movement became an important part of the RoC's strategy to obstruct the efforts of Turkey to achieve legitimisation for the self-proclaimed, in 1983, "Turkish Republic of Northern Cyprus" on an international level (Ker-Lindsay 2010, 69; Republic of Cyprus 1997, 26). In addition, the RoC concentrated its efforts exerting pressure over Turkey to adopt a less negative stance for the settlement of the Cyprus Problem; this task was sought to be accomplished through Non-Aligned members states support within the UN General Assembly (Tsardanidis and Nicolaou 1999, 175; Republic of Cyprus 1997, 20–52). However, such a tactic did not lead to the resolution of the Cyprus Problem.

THE RoC AND THE COMMONWEALTH

The UN and the Non-Alignment Movement were not the only international organisations to which the RoC pursued membership. The question of the RoC-Commonwealth ties came to the fore by the British as soon as the initial settlement of the Cyprus Question was reached in February 1959 (*Ethnos* 1959b).

A debate was ignited during which various quarters of the G/C society weighed the pros and cons of a RoC-Commonwealth relationship focusing on the economic dimension and not the ideals the Commonwealth claimed to represent.[8] This was true among the G/C that were in favour of accession to the Commonwealth: they were motivated by financial incentives instead of any sense of loyalty to the specific international organisation (Karyos and Papaioakeim 2021). As for Lieutenant-General George Grivas, the military commander of the EOKA

---

[8] For the arguments made in favour or against membership to the Commonwealth see *Eleftheria* (1959a, b, c), *Ethnos* (1959a), and *Charavgi* (1959c).

anti-colonial movement in the late 1950s, he opposed the membership to the Commonwealth and publicly criticised Makarios' efforts to secure the RoC's accession to the international organisation (TNA. KV 2/3883 1959; TNA. KV 2/3883 1959; *Charavgi* 1960b). Membership in the Commonwealth was also opposed by the G/C Left. The communist party of AKEL preferred the RoC to be linked to the USSR and satellite states so that the island would receive substantial financial aid by communist countries. Additionally, AKEL argued that the RoC's membership in the Commonwealth would certainly result in the involvement of NATO in Cyprus: in the event of war, such an intervention would put the new republic at risk (TNA. FCO 141/4523, Public opinion 1959).

Eventually, the question of Commonwealth membership was considered by the RoC Parliament on 16 February 1961: 41 G/C and T/C MPs voted in favour and nine G/C MPs voted against (*Eleftheria* 1961). The Patriotic Front (whose representatives originated from EOKA's ranks), the dominant G/C political party in the parliament, held a negative stance. However, an intervention by Makarios led to the alignment of most Patriotic Front MPs with the view in favour of accession to the Commonwealth (Karyos and Papaioakeim 2021). Regarding the Communist Left, AKEL also reversed its negative stance and voted for membership in the Commonwealth for five years. AKEL MP and General Secretary, Ezekias Papaioannou, explained his party's position. He said that it would be preferable for the RoC to withdraw from the Commonwealth, but AKEL acknowledged the economic dependencies emanating from the 80-year colonial rule over Cyprus; thus, it considered that a five-year interim period would be adequate to actualise a smooth detachment from the Commonwealth (*Eleftheria* 1961).

Makarios' personality and political strength undoubtedly drove the majority the MPs of the Patriotic Front to vote for the parliamentary resolution in favour of stronger RoC-Commonwealth ties. The President of the RoC probably envisaged his country's membership in the Commonwealth from the beginning. Initially, he was very cautious in his public statements and consistently pointed out that this responsibility must be undertaken by the people and the Cypriot House of Representatives. Progressively, he revealed his personal views through the Press, stating that the RoC should join the international organisation (*Charavgi* 1960a). What were the reasons behind Makarios' positive stance? The President of the RoC was aware of the particularly active Cypriot communities in various Commonwealth countries envisaging to capitalise such links for the benefit of the RoC on economic grounds or to promote the country's soft power.[9] More importantly, he endeavoured to add more substance to the Cypriot sovereignty (compared to the limited independence the RoC had achieved in the constitutional framework of the Zurich and London Agreements), as well as attain a genuine majority rule (an innate demand in any anti-colonial struggle).

Therefore, Makarios tried to give the RoC a more international stature, beyond the (tight) Greek-Turkish framework that the Agreements of February 1959 created. The path to achieve so was distancing the RoC from both Greece[10] and Turkey and pursuing accession to various international organisations (particularly the political groups where Turkey did not belong) such as the Commonwealth and the Non-Alignment Movement. In addition, participation in the Commonwealth served Makarios' famous policy to bridge East and West. Strong RoC-Commonwealth relations created a sense of "Westerness", thereby preventing the destruction of bridges with those (international or domestic) groups who did not feel comfortable with the RoC's membership in the Non-Alignment Movement (Markides 2021).

The RoC and NATO

The question of the RoC's accession to NATO was discussed by the Greek government and Makarios, even before the Zurich Agreement. More precisely, in a meeting held on 29 January 1959, the G/C leader was informed by the Greek Prime Minister, Konstantinos Karamanlis, on the development of Greek-Turkish consultations for the settlement of the Cyprus Question. Among other things, Karamanlis referred to the Turkish proposal for the establishment of (Greek-Turkish-Cypriot) Tripartite Headquarters in the future RoC. He pointed out that if the new-born state joined NATO, the ethnic composition of the units in the military bases of the alliance would be immaterial. Makarios agreed, replying that "it would be to the absolute benefit of the Cypriots if the independent

---

[9] For instance, Makarios promoted Cyprus in Kenya through religious diplomacy (Constantinou and Tselepou 2017, 179–193).

[10] Cyprus' membership in the Commonwealth and the Non-Alignment Movement, two international organisations in which Greece did not participate, also conveyed the message that Nicosia was not under the influence of Athens and remained loyal to the implementation of the Zurich and London Agreements (Diana Markides 2021).

Cyprus participated in the defence alliance of NATO" (Papageorgiou 2000, 45–46).

Karamanlis' views for the future of the RoC originated from the same pro-Western strategic principles along which he had moved to strengthen the national security of his homeland. According to Karamanlis, the ultimate strategic aim of the RoC must be the complete alignment with the West. This would fulfil the RoC's primary goal to maximise its own national security. Therefore, the new state had to attain the following two objectives: accession to NATO and undeviating application of the Zurich and London Agreements. The latter would indicate to the Western states that the RoC had initiated a route of domestic stability and development, thereby facilitating Nicosia's strategic aim of strengthening the RoC's ties with the West.

Aside from gains on the grounds of national security, Karamanlis' pro-Western perspective for the RoC envisaged benefits in the fields of regional and domestic relations. For instance, tensions in the Middle East usually triggered Great Power politics that benefited Turkey and had implications for the RoC. If the RoC actualised a partnership with the West, the impact of such exogenous factors on the RoC would be significantly reduced. Similarly, Nicosia's alliance with the West (again from Karamanlis' point of view) and the consequent minimisation of Ankara's influence would result in gains for the G/C community domestically. Up to that point, any advantage that the G/C could gain due to their population majority, or their economic status was outweighed by Turkey. Karamanlis believed that the RoC's close ties with the West would confine Ankara's interventions, thereby allowing the restoration of the G/C leading position in Cypriot society (Hatzivassiliou 2020, 110).

The question of whether the RoC should join NATO or not came again to the fore during the Zurich Conference (5–11 February 1959) held by Greece and Turkey. One of the articles in the "Gentlemen's Agreement" concluded by Konstantinos Karamanlis and Adnan Menderes, the Prime Ministers of Greece and Turkey, respectively, stated that the two countries would support the accession of the RoC to NATO (Mallinson 2005, 49). In addition, the Gentlemen's Agreement provided for the establishment of NATO military bases as well as the approval of both Athens and Ankara on the ethnic composition of the units that would comprise the NATO forces in the island. Later, because of British hesitations, one of the topics on which the Foreign Ministers of Greece, Turkey and Britain agreed in the London Conference (17–19 February

1959) was that any discussion about a Cypriot accession to the Western alliance would be premature before the declaration of the Cypriot independence. On the other hand, the three countries agreed that the RoC would be allowed a right to decide whether it would remain or not in the British sterling area (Hatzivassiliou 1998, 122, 125–126).

Despite that Makarios had agreed in January 1959 with Karamanlis' view to opt for the RoC' accession to NATO, he changed his mind and did not follow through. The Archbishop was probably driven to this decision because of AKEL's strong criticism. The G/C powerful communist party had publicly stated in February 1959 its disagreement with aspects of the formula for the settlement of the Cyprus Question such as the military bases and the stationing of Greek and Turkish contingents in the future RoC (*Charavgi* 1959a, b). Another factor to be considered was the bitter experience of the political and militant struggle of Cyprus against the British colonial rule, and the prevalent ideals of the G/C population against colonialism. The G/C had to fight to bring British colonial occupation to an end and gain their freedom. The fact that a power with colonial possessions, Britain, was one of the pillars of NATO might make it difficult for various quarters of the G/C public to accept the idea of joining the Western alliance; on the contrary, a path of non-alignment seemed more attractive (Hatzivassiliou 2020, 114).

It is worth mentioning that the debate about NATO membership was revived in 1963. The RoC government commenced discussions with Greece and Britain aiming at their support to propose amendments on the Cypriot constitution. Athens gave a negative response (Averoff-Tossizza 1982, 324–329). However, when the RoC Minister of Foreign Affairs, Spyros Kyprianou, met the British High Commissioner to Cyprus, Sir Arthur Clark, the British diplomat proposed joining NATO as the path towards stabilisation of the Cypriot domestic front (where fierce disagreements and tensions between the two main ethnic groups were progressively rising). More specifically, the RoC's accession to NATO would make the Treaties of Guarantee and Alliance unnecessary while anticipating the T/C reactions.

Nicosia was immediately attracted by the prospect of exploiting NATO to overcome some of the negative consequences of the Zurich and London Agreements. Nonetheless, the British Foreign Office, for various reasons,[11] opposed such an idea. Thus, the British government decided to abstain from promoting the RoC's membership to NATO. The British High Commission to Nicosia informed the Cypriot government on the gloomy prospect of a possible path towards NATO: Turkey would decline any effort to revise the Treaty of Guarantee. Moreover, NATO would possibly ask for permission for the installation of a military base to the Cypriot landmass. These two arguments undoubtedly discouraged the RoC government to pursue incorporation into NATO as the way towards a partial revision of the Agreements of February 1959 (Hatzivassiliou 2020, 118, 120). To these factors could be added the belief of Makarios that if the RoC became a NATO member, the geostrategic significance of Turkey would still outweigh that of the RoC. As a result, Nicosia would not be able to draw on the support of its partners in its effort to amend certain provisions of the Zurich and London Agreements. Therefore, from Makarios' standpoint, deepening the RoC-NATO relationship would be inconsequential (Clerides 1988, 134).

The RoC and the EU

The European prospect of the RoC was considered by Nicosia in the early post-independence years, for reasons that were not connected with any sense of "Europeannes" (European consciousness). The RoC pursued closer ties with the European Economic Community (EEC) in 1962, one year after Britain declared its interest to join the international organisation. Nicosia feared that the British initiative would undermine the protectionist status that the Cypriot agricultural goods enjoyed within the Commonwealth. However, France's veto against British candidacy made a milder interest on behalf of the RoC. The latter's European prospect was revived in 1970 when links between Britain and the EEC became considerably stronger and the negotiations for British membership advanced to a point that accession to the Community would become soon a *fait accompli* (Joseph 2000, 488).

The signing of the Association Agreement, in 1972, marked the establishment of official relations between the RoC and the EEC. The economic criterion was the main driver for the RoC to seek closer ties with the Community. First, with this agreement the RoC gained access to new

---

[11] For the reasons behind the opposition of the Foreign Office to a Cypriot candidacy for accession to NATO see Hatzivassiliou (2020, 119).

markets. Also, the damaging effects on Cypriot exports that the British membership to the EEC would cause were thus avoided. Moreover, through the Agreement the RoC planned to safeguard the competitiveness of its goods in the face of the framework for trade transactions that was recently shaped between the Community and other Mediterranean states (Joseph 2000, 488; Tsardanidis 2006, 63). Another prospective advantage would be ease of access to financial aid and new technologies to help finance Cypriot projects for rural economic advancement, industrialisation and development of infrastructure (Joseph 2000, 488).

The Association Agreement[12] provided for a deepening of the economic and trade relations of the two parties in two phases. The second phase of the Agreement should have started in 1978 to progressively lead to the creation of a Customs Union by 1983 (Vassiliou 2004, 25). However, the Turkish invasion of the RoC, in 1974, significantly hindered the completion of the Agreement within the agreed time limit; the first phase, after successive extensions lasted fifteen years (Kranidiotis 2001, 36; Tsardanidis and Nicolaou 1999, 184). The Customs Union was substantially promoted only after the accession of Greece to the EEC in 1981 (Vassiliou 2004, 25). Indeed, Greece's activation in the European organisation gave a new boost to the RoC-EEC relationship that entered a new phase with the signing of an additional protocol, in 1987. The latter provided for the materialisation of the Customs Union by 2002 (Joseph 2000, 488; Kranidiotis 2001, 37).

In 1988, two leading officials of the Greek Ministry of Foreign Affairs suggested to the President of the RoC, George Vassiliou, to aim at membership in the EEC. This proposal coincided with the Turkish application for accession to the same political group. According to the Greek strategy, if the RoC applied for membership in the European Community, its application would be unavoidably linked to that of Turkey. Consequently, the EEC would exert pressures for progress on the efforts to resolve the Cyprus Problem, thereby overcoming the Turkish intransigence (Christodoulides 2010b, 75). Vassiliou decided not to adopt the Greek proposal. He prioritised the effort to deal with the Cyprus Problem via intercommunal talks. In addition, the leading member-states of the EEC were not favourably inclined towards a Cypriot application. It should be also considered that the communist-led party of AKEL,

[12] For a sophisticated analysis on the EEC-Cyprus Association Agreement see Tsardanidis (1988).

the most powerful associate to Vassiliou's elevation to power, opposed to the strengthening of ties between the RoC and the EEC due to its anti-Western ideology (Christodoulides 2010b, 76–77).

Eventually, after nearly two-year efforts by the UN, negotiations over the Cyprus Problem formally broke down and another impasse emerged. The firm stance of the T/C leadership that did not facilitate progress of the intercommunal talks and growing pressure from the Cypriot political scene (the House of Representatives had resolved twice in favour of the RoC joining the EEC) prompted the RoC government to reconsider the European prospect of the country and apply for accession to the European Community in 1990 (Christodoulides 2010b, 78). The Cypriot initiative was a clear sign that it was ready to align with the West, thereby opening the way for new avenues of diplomatic cooperation. Aside from political advantages regarding the resolution of the Cyprus Problem, other gains would be obtained too. Through membership in the EEC, the RoC would consolidate its independence and national survival, thereby upgrading its international position even further (Kranidiotis 2001, 45; Hatzivassiliou 2010, 73; Ker-Lindsay 2010, 70–72; Tsardanidis and Nicolaou 1999, 185).

Thereafter, the RoC mobilised its state mechanism to promote all necessary reforms on a political, legislative and institutional level in order to comply with the *acquis communautaire* and attain positive results for its European prospect (Vassiliou 2004, 45–46). The application of the RoC was considered by the European Commission in 1993. The Commission's Opinion concluded that beyond all doubt the RoC had a "European identity and character and… [a] vocation to belong to the Community" (Christodoulides 2010b, 78–79). The Corfu European Council of 1994 acknowledged the significant progress made in the preparation process for accession to the EU[13] and noted that the next phase of enlargement would include the RoC. At the 1994 European Council in Essen, it was confirmed that the next phase of the Union's enlargement would include the RoC (Kranidiotis 2001, 53; Tsardanidis and Nicolaou 1999, 186). The suitability of the RoC for incorporation in the EU was reaffirmed by the EU General Affairs Council in 1995. The Council, also, stipulated that the accession negotiations between the EU and the RoC would start six months after the conclusion of

---

[13] With the Maastricht Treaty (the foundation treaty of the EU) the EEC evolved to the EU.

the Inter-Governmental Conference of 1996 taking into consideration its results.

In 1997, the Luxembourg European Council decided the commencement of a new enlargement process with ten applicant countries, including the RoC. Another important outcome was the explicit decision to launch accession negotiations with the RoC as well as with Hungary, Poland, the Czech Republic, Estonia and Slovenia. The negotiation process was initiated in March 1998 (Joseph 2000, 489–490). At that time, the President of the RoC, Glafkos Clerides, invited the T/C to appoint representatives as full members of the Cypriot negotiating team for the accession of the RoC to the EU. Although the invitation was welcomed by the EU, the T/C leadership held a negative stance and rejected it (Kraniidiotis 2001, 59; Christodoulides 2010b, 80; Heraclides 2006, 281). At Helsinki, in December 1999, the European Council concluded that the political settlement of the Cyprus Problem would help the accession of the RoC to the EU. However, if no settlement was achieved by the completion of accession negotiations, the Council noted that decision on accession would be made without the above being a precondition. It was therefore made very clear that failure to resolve the Cyprus Problem could not obstruct the European prospect of the RoC (Christodoulides 2013, 356; Heraclides 2006, 282).

The long process of the accession negotiations was concluded at the Copenhagen European Council, in December 2002. The Council took a landmark decision which materialised EU's largest expansion: the RoC and nine other candidate states were to join the Union. Full member-state status was granted in May 2004.[14] On 16 April 2003, the President of the RoC, Tassos Papadopoulos, signed in Athens the Treaty of Accession of the RoC to the EU. On 1 May 2004, Cyprus became a full EU member-state (Christodoulides 2013, 370, 376; Rizas and Stefanides 2004, 59). By attaining this prime foreign policy objective, the RoC ceased to be member in the Non-Alignment Movement. In fact, this was one of the requirements it had to fulfil for its incorporation into the EU (Ker-Lindsay 2010, 70).

---

[14] It is worth specifying that the Copenhagen European Council decided that, in the absence of a settlement for the Cyprus Problem, the application of the *acquis communautaire* in the areas not under effective control of the government of the RoC would be suspended until the restoration of the political unity of Cyprus (Rizas and Stefanides 2004, 59; Christodoulides 2013, 370).

Conclusion

The chapter had set out to investigate the determining motives behind the strategic orientations of the RoC's foreign policy within the international system during the first fifty years after its constitutional foundation. It has been shown that, on a macrohistorical level, a recurring driver that shaped the foreign policy of the RoC was its quest for national survival and the arrangement of the Cyprus Question/Problem. This was the most influential factor in the decision-making process for the accession or non-participation to an international group of states. Prosperity—or economic development—had a motivating dynamic only in the cases of closer relations with the Commonwealth and the EEC/EU. Domestic factors such as state institutions, political parties, professional associations or quarters of the public played a role in the alignment of the RoC with the Commonwealth and the rejection of a NATO prospect. The international-universal values and norms have been a catalytic driving force, according to the RoC Ministry of Foreign Affairs (2021), solely in the case of membership in the UN. Finally, leader ideas or national visions (e.g. the prospect of the RoC functioning as a bridge between the East and West) were important and one of the driving forces that prompted the RoC to pursuit stronger ties with the Non-Alignment Movement and the Commonwealth.

In terms of the incentives behind the foreign policy of the RoC between 1960 and 2004, three main points should be made. First, despite the various restrictions that the Zurich and London Agreements imposed, the RoC was able to build a substantial level of autonomy as far as its relations with the various forms of cooperation of the international community (Ker-Lindsay 2010, 73). This realisation is connected to the second point: Did the foreign policy of the RoC go through a process of maturation? The answer to this question is complex and cannot be given in a manichaeistic fashion. For instance, the excessive reliance on UN resolutions for the settlement of the Cyprus Problem cannot be described as mature foreign policy given that it did not pave the way to the settlement of the conflict. In addition, the aspirations of the RoC to play the role of a bridge between the East and West were, at that point, not realistic and thus not mature given that a small and newly formed state did not possess the capabilities to pursue such a role. On the other hand, deepening ties with the Commonwealth and the EEC/EU were vital choices in the quest for prosperity. The RoC experienced economic development and in the long term it was able to overcome the negative consequences of the intercommunal strife of the 1960s and the Turkish invasion of 1974. Lastly, it should be noted that alignment with the various organisations should neither be taken for granted nor is it a panacea. The domestic political scene of the RoC, as well as the regional and international environments do not remain static. They constantly produce new debates, challenges and opportunities regarding the RoC's foreign policy orientations. The international system and its evolving dynamics constantly provide the RoC with new opportunities to demonstrate whether its foreign policy is evolving and maturing.

References

TNA, FCO 141/4523, "Public Opinion-Cyprus and the Commonwealth." March 17, 1959.

TNA, KV 2/3883, "Political: Grivas' Views on Outstanding Problems Connected with the Cyprus Settlement." December 30, 1959.

TNA, KV 2/3883, "Meeting Between General Grivas and Emissaries from Archbishop Makarios." December 30, 1959.

Charavgi. 1959a. "Προκαταρκτικά" [Preliminarily]. 12 February.

Charavgi. 1959b. "Την Τελευταία Λέξη" [The Last Word]. 7 February.

Charavgi. 1959c. "Τα Προβλήματα της Εθνικής μας Οικονομίας και οι Βασικές Αρχές για την Ανάπτυξή της" [The Problems of our National Economy and the Basic Principles for Its Development]. 13 March.

Charavgi. 1960a. "Οι Χθεσινές Δηλώσεις του Μακαρίου" [Yesterday's Statements of Makarios]. 18 August.

Charavgi. 1960b. "Θερμός Χαιρετισμός της ΕΔΑ προς την Κύπρο με την Ευκαιρία της Ανακήρυξης της Δημοκρατίας" [Warm Greeting from EDA to Cyprus on the Occasion of the Declaration of the Republic]. 16 August.

Eleftheria. 1959a. "Αι Οικονομικαί Σχέσεις της Κύπρου μετά της Κοινοπολιτείας και της Περιοχής της Στερλίνας" [The Economic Relations of Cyprus with the Commonwealth and the Sterling Area]. 29 March.

Eleftheria. 1959b. "Αι Οικονομικαί Σχέσεις της Κύπρου μετά της Κοινοπολιτείας και της Περιοχής της Στερλίνας" [The Economic Relations of Cyprus with the Commonwealth and the Sterling Area]. 1 April.

Eleftheria. 1959c. "Αι Οικονομικαί Σχέσεις της Κύπρου μετά της Κοινοπολιτείας και της Περιοχής της Στερλίνας" [The Economic Relations of Cyprus with the Commonwealth and the Sterling Area]. 3 April.

Eleftheria. 1959d. "Η Βαρυσήμαντος Ομιλία του Εθνάρχου κ. Μακαρίου" [The Momentous Speech of Ethnarch Makarios]. 3 March.

Eleftheria. 1961. "Δια Ψήφων 41 Εναντίον Εννέα η Βουλή Ενέκρινε Ψήφισμα υπέρ της Εντάξεως της Κύπρου εις την Κοινοπολιτείαν δια Περίοδον Πέντε Ετών" [With 41 Votes in Favour and Nine Against the Parliament Resolved in Favour of the Accession of Cyprus in the Commonwealth for a Period of Five Years]. 17 February.
Ethnos. 1959a. "Η Σημασία της Ανεξαρτησίας από Οικονομικής Πλευράς" [The Importance of Independence from an Economic View]. 10 March.
Ethnos. 1959b. "Προς την Κοινοπολιτείαν;" [Towards the Commonwealth?]. 20 March.
Phileleftheros. 1959. "Ο Ιστορικός και Μνημειώδης Λόγος του Εθνάρχου Μακαρίου" [The Historical and Momentous Speech of Ethnarch Makarios]. 3 March.
Times of Cyprus. 1959. "We Have Triumphed." 2 March.
Averoff-Tossizza, E. 1982. Ιστορία Χαμένων Ευκαιριών: Κυπριακό, 1950–63 [Lost Opportunities: The Cyprus Question, 1950–63]. Vol. 2. 2nd ed. Athens: Estia.
Bitsios, Dimitri S. 1975. Cyprus: The Vulnerable Republic. Thessaloniki: Institute for Balkan Studies.
Christodoulides, Nikos. 2009. Τα Σχέδια Λύσης του Κυπριακού (1948–1978) [The Plans to the Solution of the Cyprus Question (1948–1978)]. Athens: Kastanioti.
Christodoulides, Nikos. 2010a. "Διπλωματική ιστορία του Κυπριακού, 1964–1969" [Diplomatic History of the Cyprus Question, 1964–1969]. In Ιστορία της Κυπριακής Δημοκρατίας [History of the Republic of Cyprus], edited by Petros Papapolyviou, vol. 1, 147–157. Nicosia: Phileleftheros.
Christodoulides, Nikos. 2010b. "Η Αίτηση Ένταξης στην ΕΟΚ και η Ευρωπαϊκή Πορεία της Κυπριακής Δημοκρατίας τη δεκαετία του 1990" [The Application for Membership to the EEC and the European Course of the Republic of Cyprus in the 1990s]. In Ιστορία της Κυπριακής Δημοκρατίας [History of the Republic of Cyprus], edited by Petros Papapolyviou, vol. 4. 75–81. Nicosia: Phileleftheros.
Christodoulides, Nikos. 2013. "The Annan Plan and the April 2004 Plebiscite. Cyprus Entry to the EU, 1999–2004." In Introduction to the History of Cyprus, edited by George Kazamias, Antonis K. Petrides, and Emmanouel Koumas, 268–287. Nicosia: The Open University of Cyprus.
Christodoulou, Miltiadis. 1987. Η Πορεία μιας Εποχής: η Ελλάδα, η Κυπριακή Ηγεσία και το Κυπριακό Πρόβλημα [The Course of an Era: Greece, the Cypriot Leadership and the Cyprus Problem]. Athens: I. Floros.
Clerides, Glafkos. 1988. Η Κατάθεσή μου [My Deposition]. Vol. 1. Nicosia: Alithia.
Constantinou, Costas, and Tselepou, Maria. 2017. Branding Orthodoxy: Religious Diplomacy and the Makarios Legacy in Sub-Saharan Africa. Place

Branding and Public Diplomacy 13 (3): 179–193. https://doi.org/10.1057/s41254-016-0034-6.

Coufoudakis, Vangelis. 2006. Κύπρος: Ένα Σύγχρονο Πρόβλημα σε Ιστορική Προοπτική [Cyprus: A Contemporary Problem in Historical Perspective]. Translated by George Demertzidis. Athens: Pataki.

Crawshaw, Nancy. 1978. *The Cyprus Revolt: An Account of the Struggle for Union with Greece*. London: Allen and Unwin.

Crouzet, François. 2011. Η Κυπριακή Διένεξη 1946–1959 [The Cyprus Conflict 1946–1959]. Translated by A. Phrydas. Vol. 2. Athens: MIET.

Hatzivassiliou, Evanthis. 1998. Το Κυπριακό Ζήτημα, 1878–1960: η Συνταγματική Πτυχή [The Cyprus Question, 1878–1960: The Constitutional Aspect]. 2nd ed. Athens: Hellinika Grammata.

Hatzivassiliou, Evanthis. 2010. "Το Κυπριακό Ζήτημα" [The Cyprus Question]. In Η Ελληνική Εξωτερική και Ευρωπαϊκή Πολιτική 1990–2010 [The Greek Foreign and European Policy 1990–2010], edited by Giannis Valinakis. 71–87. Athens: Sideris.

Hatzivassiliou, Evanthis. 2020. "Bon pour l' Orient: το Ζήτημα της Ένταξης της Κύπρου στο NATO, 1959–1963" [Bon pour l' Orient: The Question of Cyprus' Accession to NATO, 1959–1963]. Η Δέλτος [The Tablet] 7 (2): 101–124.

Heraclides, Alexis. 2006. Κυπριακό Πρόβλημα 1947–2004: Από την Ένωση στη Διχοτόμηση [Cyprus Problem 1947–2004: From Enosis to Partition]. Athens: Sideris.

Joseph, Joseph. 2000. "Εσωτερικές Πολιτικές Εξελίξεις και η Ευρωπαϊκή πορεία της Κύπρου 1974–1998" [Domestic Political Developments and the European Course of Cyprus 1974–1998]. In Ιστορία του Ελληνικού Έθνους [History of the Greek Nation], vol. 16, 484–490. Athens: Ekdotiki Athenon.

Joseph, Joseph. 2011. "The UN as an Instrument of National Policy: The Case of Cyprus." In *Independent Cyprus 1960–2010: Selected Readings*, edited by Hubert Faustmann and Emilios Solomou. 245–263. Nicosia: University of Nicosia Press.

Karyos, Andreas, and Papaioakeim, Marinos. 2021. "Cyprus in the Commonwealth: Pre-membership Perceptions by the Greek Cypriot Elites, 1959–1961." Paper presented at the conference *Cyprus and the Commonwealth 1961–2021*. Accessed 26 July 2021. https://www.youtube.com/watch?v=rYgHu79bMOk&t=23s.

Kazamias, George. 2013. "Cyprus, 1960–1974: Internal Developments." In *Introduction to the History of Cyprus*, edited by George Kazamias, Antonis K. Petrides, and Emmanouel Koumas, 268–287. Nicosia: The Open University of Cyprus.

Ker-Lindsay, James. 2010. "Shifting Alignments: The External Orientations of Cyprus since Independence." *Cyprus Review* 22 (2): 67–74.
Kontos, Michalis. 2014. "Στρατηγικός Σχεδιασμός Ασφάλειας και Επιβίωσης της Κυπριακής Δημοκρατίας: Οι Επιλογές του Παρελθόντος και οι Προοπτικές του Μέλλοντος" [Strategic Planning for the Security and the Survival of the Republic of Cyprus: Past Choices and Future Prospects]. In *Η Κύπρος σε Νέα Εποχή: Γεωστρατηγικές Παράμετροι, Οικονομία, Εξωτερική Πολιτική* [Cyprus in a New Era: Geostrategic Parameters, Economy, Foreign Policy], edited by Christina Ioannou, Demetris P. Soteropoulos, and Achilles K. Emilianides, 81–98. Nicosia and Athens: Foreign Affairs: The Hellenic Edition, Hippasus Publishing.
Kranidiotis, Giannos. 1984. *Το Κυπριακό Πρόβλημα: Η Ανάμειξη του ΟΗΕ και οι Ξένες Επεμβάσεις στην Κύπρο, 1960–1974* [The Cyprus Problem: The Involvement of the UN and the Foreign Interventions in Cyprus, 1960–1974]. Athens: Themelio.
Kranidiotis, Nikolas G. 2001. *Η Κύπρος στην Ευρώπη* [Cyprus in Europe]. Athens: Estia.
Kranidiotis, Nikos. 1981. *Δύσκολα Χρόνια: Κύπρος 1950–1960* [Difficult Years: Cyprus 1950–1960]. Athens: Estia.
Kranidiotis, Nikos. 2000. *Ανοχύρωτη Πολιτεία: Κύπρος 1960–1974* [Unfortified State: Cyprus 1960–1974]. 2nd ed. Vol. 1. Athens: Estia.
Kyriakides, Stanley. 1968. *Cyprus: Constitutionalism and Crisis Government*. Philadelphia: University of Pennsylvania Press.
Lambrou, Giannis K. 2008. *Ιστορία του Κυπριακού: τα Χρόνια μετά την Ανεξαρτησία, 1960–2008* [History of the Cyprus Question: The Years After Independence, 1960–2008]. 2nd ed. Athens: Parga.
Mallinson, William. 2005. *Cyprus: A Modern History*. London: I. B. Tauris.
Markides, Diana. 2021. "Diplomatic Ambiguity: Cyprus, the Commonwealth, the Non-aligned Movement, and the Greek-Turkish Framework, 1961–1963." Paper presented at the conference *Cyprus and the Commonwealth 1961–2021*. Accessed 26 July 2021. https://www.youtube.com/watch?v=rYgHu79bMOk&t=23s.
Ministry of Foreign Affairs. 2021. "International Organisations." Accessed 26 July 2021. https://mfa.gov.cy/themes/.
Panteli, Stavros. 1984. *A New History of Cyprus: From the Earliest Times to the Present Day*. London: East-West Publications.
Papademetris, Panayiotis. 2010. "Η Ρήξη με τους Τουρκοκύπριους" [The Rupture with the Turkish Cypriots]. In *Ιστορία της Κυπριακής Δημοκρατίας* [History of the Republic of Cyprus], edited by Petros Papapolyviou, vol. 1, 103–113. Nicosia: Phileleftheros.

Papageorgiou, Spyros. 2000. *Τα Κρίσιμα Ντοκουμέντα του Κυπριακού (1957-1967)* [The Crucial Documents of the Cyprus Question (1957-1967)]. vol. 1. Nicosia: Epiphaniou.
Republic of Cyprus. 1997. *Non-aligned Declarations on Cyprus 1964-1997*. Nicosia: Press and Information Office.
Richter, Heinz. 2011. *Ιστορία της Κύπρου 1950-1959* [History of Cyprus 1950-1959]. Translated by Ch. Papachristou. Athens: Estia.
Rizas, Soreris. 2000. *Ένωση Διχοτόμηση Ανεξαρτησία* [Enosis Partition Independence]. Athens: Bibliorama.
Rizas, Soreris, and Stefanides, Ioannis. 2004. "Το Κυπριακό 1974-2004: Οι Ατελέσφορες Μεσολαβητικές Προσπάθειες" [The Cyprus Problem 1974-2004: The Ineffectual Mediatory Efforts]. In *Ιστορία του Νέου Ελληνισμού* [History of Modern Hellenism], vol. 10, 51-62. Athens: Hellenica Grammata.
Sakkas, Giannis D. 2015. *Η Ελλάδα στην Μεσόγειο, 1950-2004: Εξωτερική Πολιτική και Περιφερειακές Διενέξεις* [Greece in the Mediterranean, 1950-2004: Foreign Policy and Regional Conflicts]. Athens.
Serafim, Andreas, and Karyos, Andreas. 2020. "The Politics of Language: Linguistics, Rhetorics and Political History in Makarios' *Nenikikamen* ('We Have Triumphed')." *Journal of Mediterranean Studies* 29 (2): 177-196.
Stylianou, Philippos. 2010. "Τα 13 Σημεία" [The 13 Points]. In *Ιστορία της Κυπριακής Δημοκρατίας* [History of the Republic of Cyprus], edited by Petros Papapolyviou, vol. 1, 87-101. Nicosia: Phileleftheros.
Syrigos, Angelos. 2015. *Ελληνοτουρκικές Σχέσεις* [Greek-Turkish Relations]. Athens: Paraki.
Tenekidis, George K. 2009. "Διεθνοποίηση και Αποδιεθνοποίηση του Κυπριακού πριν και μετά την Τουρκική Εισβολή" [Internationalisation and De-internationalisation of the Cyprus Question Before and After the Turkish Invasion]. In *Κύπρος: Ιστορία, Προβλήματα και Αγώνες του Λαού της* [Cyprus: History, Problems and Struggles of Its People], edited by George K. Tenekidis and Giannos. Kranidiotis. 3rd ed, 195-323. Athens: Estia.
Tsardanidis, Charalambos. 1988. *The Politics of the EEC-Cyprus Association Agreement: 1972-1982*. Nicosia: Social Research Centre.
Tsardanidis, Charalambos. 2006. *Η Κυπριακή Εξωτερική Πολιτική: 1960-1974* [The Cypriot Foreign Affairs Policy: 1960-1974]. Athens: Institute of International Economic Relations.
Tsardanidis, Charalambos, and Nicolaou, Yannis. 1999. "Cyprus Foreign and Security Policy: Options and Challenges." In *The Foreign Policies of the European Union's Mediterranean States and Applicant Countries in the 1990s*, edited by Stelios Stavridis, Theodore Couloumbis, Thanos Veremis, and

Neville Waites, 171–194. London: University of Reading European and International Studies, University of Reading, Palgrave Macmillan. https://doi.org/10.1007/978-1-349-27161-0_8.

Tzermias, Pavlos N. 2000. "Από τις Συμφωνίες της Ζυρίχης και του Λονδίνου ως και την Τουρκική Εισβολή (1959-1974)" [From the Zurich and London Agreements to the Turkish Invasion (1959-1974)]. In *Ιστορία του Ελληνικού Έθνους* [History of the Greek Nation], vol. 16, 464–483. Athens: Ekdotiki Athenon.

Tzermias, Pavlos N. 2001. *Ιστορία της Κυπριακής Δημοκρατίας* [History of the Republic of Cyprus]. Athens: Libro.

Vassiliou, George. 2004. *Κύπρος-Ευρωπαϊκή Ένωση: Από τα πρώτα βήματα στην ένταξη* [Cyprus-European Union: From the First Steps Until the Accession]. Athens: Kastanioti.

CHAPTER 3

All the President's Decisions: Foreign Policy in the Republic of Cyprus After 2004

Anna Koukkides-Procopiou

INTRODUCTION

Any present analysis of the drivers of Cyprus' foreign policy will be found lacking, unless it is placed in the context of history and within the constraints of geography. On the one hand, history shapes experience; experience shapes perception; perception shapes policy. On the other, geography determines one's bedfellows. Once geography and history meet, Cyprus' main foreign policy predicament can be easily defined as that of escaping the strangling embrace of Turkey, which has been occupying one-third of the island's territory since its 1974 invasion. It is no surprise, then, that Cyprus' past and present foreign policy-making can be reflected in the struggle to secure a number of United Nations Security Council (UNSC) Resolutions, with regard to the Cyprus Problem. Moreover, Cyprus' foreign policy is primarily driven by the

A. Koukkides-Procopiou (✉)
Cyprus Center for European and International Affairs, University of Nicosia, Nicosia, Cyprus
e-mail: koukkides@cytanet.com.cy

© The Author(s), under exclusive license to Springer Nature Switzerland AG 2022
Z. Tziarras (ed.), *The Foreign Policy of the Republic of Cyprus*, Reform and Transition in the Mediterranean,
https://doi.org/10.1007/978-3-030-91177-5_3

seeking of potential security providers, whether in the form of common defence arrangements with Greece,[1] European Union (EU) membership per se and corresponding bilateral defence arrangements with European nations thereafter[2] or more recently, trilateral regional cooperation alignments,[3] enabled and further enhanced by the blessings of Washington.[4] In the same security light, there have also been pre-election promises by the current president, Nicos Anastasiades, of applying for membership in Partnership for Peace (PfP), but so far, they have remained exactly that—promises.[5]

Within the above context, the framework of currently readjusting geopolitical realities in the region, as well as within the quicksand that the international system has become, this chapter will examine exogenous and endogenous foreign policy drivers during a rather fascinating period in the island's foreign policymaking. A period which counts

---

[1] The so-called Common Defence Doctrine (Ενιαίο Αμυντικό Δόγμα) between Cyprus and Greece was short-lived and lasted only between 1993 and 1999, coming to an end, more or less, with the S300 missiles fiasco. Recently, there have been suggestions to re-enact this doctrine, as an underlying theme to the already existing trilateral cooperation with other regional players, but mostly on the basis of renewed Turkish aggression, directly aimed against Greece and Cyprus, in the Aegean and the Eastern Mediterranean. Many security analysts would point out the obvious: common threats require common action.

[2] See, for example, the Defence Cooperation Agreement between the Republic of Cyprus and the French Republic, which was signed on 4 April 2017 and came into force on 1 August 2020 and the recent declarations of enhanced Cypriot-German defence cooperation, also focussing on deepening PESCO ties.

[3] The nature of such regional alignments has been aptly described as one of "quasi alliances" by analysts such as Tziarras (2016).

[4] During the Trump administration, Secretary Pompeo led the path of the "three-plus-one" formula, especially as regional cooperation between Greece, Cyprus and Israel was concerned. The more recent establishment and inauguration of CYCLOPS (The Cyprus Centre for Land, Open-Seas and Port Security) in January 2021 was preceded by the appointment of the first military attaché of Cyprus in the United States, back in 2019.

[5] It is noteworthy that despite Anastasiades' pre-electoral promises, in 2013, to proceed with PfP and even NATO membership upon election, this never materialized. One could argue that the leftist AKEL's vehement protests could have possibly marked the President's change of heart. Nonetheless, there is great probability that the opposition's protests did not matter so much, as did Moscow's arm-twisting to an economy substantially living off Russian money. However, the fact that such promises were made, to lure more voters into the fold, proves the importance of Cyprus' security predicament, as a critical issue affecting domestic decision-making on the island.

three presidents (Tassos Papadopoulos, Dimitris Christofias, Nicos Anastasiades) and six foreign ministers (George Iacovou, Yiorgos Lillikas, Erato Kozakou-Marcoullis, Markos Kyprianou, Ioannis Kasoulides, Nikos Christodoulides), while spanning sixteen years, from 2004 to 2020. It is marked by important milestones: the rejection of Annan Plan V for a settlement of the Cyprus Problem by 76% of the Greek Cypriot community and the almost concurrent Cyprus' accession to the EU in 2004, despite vehement Turkish protests[6]; Cyprus' joining of the Eurozone in 2008; a foreign policy debacle involving Syria, Iran and the United States (US), which culminated into the Mari tragedy in 2011, with the tragic loss of 13 lives, the destruction of Cyprus' main power station and grave consequences for the island's already dithering economy (Orphanides 2016). Last but not least, in 2013, came the final blow in a perfect storm—the unprecedented, although perhaps not unexpected, haircut of Cyprus bank deposits, which wiped out a chunk of Cypriot savings and Russian oligarch money, but, most importantly, wiped out the thin veil of credibility that the island's banking sector had fought to keep intact. When the banking bastion fell, so did the economy.[7] Rarely, if ever, has a small European state in modern times suffered such setbacks of such magnitude in such a confined space in time.

Yet, there, for a moment, seemed to be hope amidst calamity, with the discovery of hydrocarbons in the Eastern Mediterranean considered a game-changer for regional politics and for Cyprus itself. The reshuffling of energy cards in the region indeed brought in the international players, with local players all jostling for attention, ensuring their piece of the pie remained intact. This, initially, seemed to endow the RoC with a comparative advantage in the region, since it served as the common

---

[6] Kaymak and Vural (2006) provide an account of the Turkish Cypriot view of ensuing isolation vis-à-vis EU accession of what they refer to as the "Greek-Cypriot led Republic of Cyprus".

[7] "Urgent work is now underway to repair the damage, much of it under the terms of the Memorandum of Understanding (MoU) reached by Cyprus with the Troika of the EU, the European Central Bank (ECB) and the International Monetary Fund (IMF) as a condition for a €10bn loan in March 2013. The country's two largest banks have been merged and re-capitalised, the co-operative sector has been restructured with an emergency capital injection of €1.5bn, and important improvements are being made to the country's supervisory system. But the country is in recession, confidence in the banks has been severely damaged, and capital controls are holding back recovery, meaning that uncertainty about the outlook remains considerable" (Independent Commission on the Future of the Cyprus Banking Sector, Final Report and Recommendations, 2013).

denominator for the trilateral cooperation agreements and later on, the Eastern Mediterranean Gas Forum (EMGF), established mainly through energy considerations and involving Cyprus, Greece, Israel, Egypt, occasionally Jordan, Lebanon and Palestine, while also ensuring that the US, France and Italy[8] kept a close eye on regional activity. Nonetheless, the recent global economic crisis, stimulated by the COVID-19 pandemic, has increased uncertainty in the recovery of the energy market, creating ambivalence for many regional aspirations to this end.[9] Commercial considerations, regarding deep sea drilling costs and monetization, as well as climate change considerations, seem to create the same ambivalence for the feasibility of the ambitious East Med pipeline project, which could place Cyprus on the European energy map (Knews 2021).

All in all, in 2021, even with the Cyprus Problem still unresolved, the RoC finds itself the perennial strategically located hub, where energy, security and diplomacy overlap. The Cyprus Problem, albeit with an added twist of renewed Turkish threats at the level of energy geopolitics at sea and a recent encroaching over the ghost town of Varosha, in direct violation with previous UNSC resolutions, still dominates foreign and domestic policy narratives alike, constituting the platform by which presidents, policymakers and political parties distinguish themselves. The RoC's security dilemma is, as always, seen through the prism of opposition to Turkish scheming and remains unchanged as the main driver on the foreign policy agenda.

An all-powerful president still calls most foreign policy shots, in the conspicuous absence of a National Security Council[10] or a National

---

[8] It is important to note that glimpses of Italy and France still reflected on the troubled waters of the Eastern Mediterranean have more to do with their own individual power and energy pursuits, rather than any European Union ambitions. The EU is yet to have a common foreign policy and still practically remains a non-entity as far as security is concerned. No concrete actions, apart from verbal declarations and a semblance of sanctions (against individuals), have ever been taken by Brussels, whilst Turkey has been continuously violating Republic of Cyprus sovereign rights and overriding French and Italian commercial interests, by the commencement of illegal drilling activity in the very same area off the coast of Cyprus allocated to the Total-ENI energy consortium.

[9] At the point of writing this paper, the Energy Minister of the RoC, Natasa Pilides, publicly confirmed that Exxon Mobil has already announced the reverse of its decision of postponement of drilling in Cypriot waters during the initial pandemic shock. There are strong indications that ENI-Total will probably take steps to that same direction.

[10] In December 2020, the Council of Ministers of the RoC approved the establishment of a Foreign Policy, Defence and Security Council, under the joint auspices of the RoC

Security Strategy Document (Adamides 2018) and with little qualitative contribution from political parties,[11] think tanks or experts. The National Council of parliamentary party leaders and former statesmen usually meets to be informed rather than to advise the President.[12] Women are conspicuously absent from the process (Koukkides-Procopiou 2017). Additionally, available room for manoeuvre for the Ministry of Foreign Affairs (MFA) itself is partially taken up by the functions of the Presidential Diplomatic Office (established by President Papadopoulos in 2003 and tellingly enough housed at the Presidential Palace) and the Office of the Chief Negotiator for the Cyprus Problem (a position so far held by prominent, knowledgeable and well-connected senior diplomats such as Ambassador Tasos Tzionis and Ambassador Andreas Mavroyiannis, accountable only to the President himself). Thus, foreign ministers can be influential, but there are limits as to what they can independently do, especially as far as the more important item on their agenda is concerned—relations between Turkey and Cyprus. One cannot stress enough that in Cyprus, due to historical reasons which will be examined in the main body of this paper, presidential leadership matters in the making of foreign policy because the president matters. Therefore, foreign policymaking will be analysed hereafter as the direct product of the President's making.

MFA, the Ministry of Defence, and the Central Intelligence Service. Up to the point of writing this paper, no further announcements or actions have been taken to this effect.

[11] Despite repeated twisting and turning between parties and president, the buck stops with the President, when decisions are made. An example illustrating the President's absolute authority on policy are DIKO's protests in 2014 against President Anastasiades' signing of a joint declaration with Derviş Eroğlu, the leader of the Turkish Cypriot community, prior to Cyprus Problem negotiations. These protests fell on deaf ears and DIKO was forced to leave the coalition government. Much earlier, in 2004, Papadopoulos had also ignored the pleas of AKEL, his government coalition partners, not to take a position on the Annan Plan referendum. Instead, he very openly and publicly urged the Greek Cypriot community to reject the plan and indirectly forced AKEL leadership to reconsider its YES position and turn it into a NO, succumbing to grassroots pressure, probably stirred up by the President's firm position. Consequently, AKEL did not support Papadopoulos' second election bid. It is noteworthy that even in one of the most disastrous cases of foreign policymaking by the Republic, the Mari debacle of 2011, President Christofias seems to have taken significant decisions on his own, without consulting or informing any of the political parties of the island, but also keeping his own cabinet of ministers in the dark.

[12] An excellent account of the (non) workings of the National Council is provided by Ker-Lindsay (2009).

The Four Stages of the RoC's Foreign Policymaking

In the short period since its inception in the summer of 1960, the RoC endeavoured to define and position itself as a newly arrived player in the international system. Being a post-colonial small state, stuck at a geographical and political crossroads between East and West, situated in Turkey's soft southern underbelly and chaperoned by three guarantor powers, it spent the first years of its existence on a fact-finding foreign policy mission:

> The challenges have been numerous, daunting and far-reaching. From the fragility and vulnerabilities inherent to all newly emerged states, to the lofty fight for political development and the building of structures that guarantee democracy and the rule of law without prior experience in self-administration, the never-ending task of economic and social development, and the fulfilment of the responsibilities emanating from sovereignty and international relations, in the cold war era no less. (Mavroyiannis 2020)

This was a stage in policymaking which commenced in turmoil in the 1960s and ended in catastrophe in the mid-1970s, marking the end of the Cypriot age of innocence.

Consequently, there followed a "long-term" ("makrohronios" according to Archbishop Makarios) and rather intense struggle for survival of state and people, characterized by attempts to reverse a de facto situation, imposed on the island by Turkey, using various *de jure* means. This second stage of foreign policymaking, beginning with the 1974 cataclysm and ending with glimpses of European hope, in the early 90s, can be identified as the years of idealization, followed by a third stage of approximately twenty years of Europeanization thereafter and a final, more mature, fourth stage of multilevel, multifaceted and polythematic foreign policy under the current government, in power since 2013.

Signs of such maturity can be mainly seen in the means, if not the end of foreign policymaking, which remains as steadfast as ever—a solution to the Cyprus Problem. As in most democratic states, foreign policy is usually conducted within the space confined by the parameters of public opinion. Thus, recent proclamations of new-found multilateralism have started to be formalized and made known to the public in Cyprus, often crediting the government with open-mindedness and a forward-looking vision. Digital diplomacy and digital communication have started to make their presence felt, in the workings of the foreign ministry. At the same time, there has been a revision not only in means but also in the perspectives of foreign policy. A rather monolithic rhetoric has been replaced by a multidimensional and multilevel agenda. The opening up of space in the Eastern Mediterranean and the Middle East, with aspirations for collaboration stretching as far as the United Arab Emirates (UAE), Saudi Arabia and India, has replaced a previously held primarily Eurocentric approach, which had been a necessity during the RoC's Europeanization process. In this more mature state of affairs, Cyprus' geostrategic location in the Middle East is flaunted as an ace rather as an embarrassment, whereas Nicosia's expectations of Athens have become more practical and less aspirational, allowing for more obvious give-and-take manner.

Furthermore, Burke's centuries-old adage that a state is its revenue has become a harsh realization, especially so after the economic crises of 2013 and 2020, when international politics and international political economy began to overlap paths rather precariously, amidst the face of recurrent financial shocks. The importance of economic diplomacy has come to the forefront, and the MFA has aptly adjusted. It has also started focusing on the caveats of energy diplomacy, cultural diplomacy and the women, peace and security agenda, supported globally through the implementation of UNSCR 1325 and subsequent complementary resolutions. At the same time, Cyprus' MFA did not hesitate to dabble its fingers into vaccine diplomacy during the current pandemic.

At the same time, interconnectedness between the Cyprus MFA and other government ministries, courtesy of full-fledged Europeanization of the RoC, which is now both a member of the EU and of the Eurozone, translates into another new reality. Among others, the Ministry of Finance, and the Ministry of the Interior (handling migration/asylum seeker issues) are constantly navigating their way through troubled European waters. Another example stems from the thrust of trilateral regional cooperation, which means that the Ministry of Energy and the Ministry of Defence are, too, joining forces into a (semi-alignment) of their policies with the MFA, especially with the recent establishment in the RoC of a Permanent Secretariat for the Trilateral Mechanisms, between Cyprus, Greece and Israel. Local ministries are, thus, forced to work closer with the MFA than ever before, the dots connected in a more effective and efficient way than in the past. While the interdependency between foreign and domestic policy has become more pronounced, so has the blurring of lines between the two begun to fade away.

So, where does that leave us? As the third decade of the twenty-first century is dawning, Cyprus remains a "hostage to history", despite multiple attempts to break free from it.[13] Turkey still[14] covets what Turkey sees and Cyprus' foreign policymakers have not yet managed to escape the Turkey conundrum to the Cyprus Problem, i.e. the eternal dilemma, ever since the Republic was established in 1960, of whether and how to keep Turkish fingers in or out the Cypriot honeypot. *Plus ça change*, but the stakes are now much higher, in a much more unstable regional and global context.

War Is a Stern Teacher—A Historical Security Conundrum

No country ever exists in a vacuum. Nor can it easily escape from itself. The RoC is a case in point. Enter history and the obvious becomes inescapable: the predicament of Cyprus has always been much more of a political affair and much less of a local ethnic struggle between two communities, as it has become fashionable nowadays to present it. It cannot be understood unless the meddling of the so-called guarantor powers (Britain, Turkey and Greece) and other foreign players is seen as part and parcel of power politics in the region.

Going back to Cyprus' anti-colonial struggle against the British Crown, in the first half of the twentieth century, sensing the danger of colonial instability, the British proceeded to divide and rule Cyprus, as they pretty much did elsewhere; first enlisting the local "Muhammadans", as they called them, to poise themselves against the Greek community on the island and then, as a last resort, inviting Turkey to take its pick—despite Ottoman claims on Cyprus having officially being waived by modern-day Turkey through the Treaty of Lausanne in 1923. Thus, the British added a regional game-changer to an otherwise ordinary, for its time, colonial struggle between peoples and empire, a struggle hitherto chaperoned on national grounds only by Greece. The scene

---

[13] As per Christopher Hitchens' eponymous book.

[14] Throughout past decades, the unchanging geostrategic importance of Cyprus for Turkey can be seen through a range of indicative documents affecting/portraying Turkish policy. See, for example, Professor Nihat Erim's report on Cyprus for Prime Minister Adnan Menderes in 1956 (see e.g., Erim 1978), as to what Turkey's official position on the island should have been (see, Davutoğlu 2010; Kasapoğlu 2017).

was set for what was to follow once Turkey decided to take up the "Muhammadan" cause and turn it into a national cause for the Turkish state.[15] Enter Turkey, exit Enosis. The struggle for union with Greece, the much-anticipated outcome of the EOKA struggle, during 1955–1959, culminated instead into the birth of a supposedly independent state— an affront to most Greek Cypriots, a coup de grace for most Turkish Cypriots.

This first, post-colonial stage (1960–1974) in foreign policymaking by the young state of Cyprus was characterized by the weighing in of the three guarantor powers, whose presence and say made independent policy of any sort close to impossible. The decision of the Turkish Cypriots to withdraw from government and barricade themselves in a number of separate enclaves all over the island in 1963, on a number of constitutional disputes, was followed in less than a year by the bombing of Tylliria with napalm bombs by Turkey. In the meantime, bi-communal strife had been wreaking havoc to the newly found state's resilience. By 1964, the clock of division seemed impossible to turn back.

No further proof is needed than the island's forceful separation since 1974, which marks the traumatic commencement of a second stage in the island's foreign policymaking. That is the stage of idealization, i.e. the deification of international law and institutions, accompanied by a perception of the United Nations as *deus ex machina*, in restoring a "return to normal conditions" (UNSCR 186, 1964), with the underlying belief that, in any case, there could never be peace in Cyprus in the absence of justice. This is a rather common occurrence among small states,[16] which often succumb to the Thucydidean dictum of "the weak suffer what they must" and yet choose to clutch on moral dictums and international law, while making their dying case. The most prominent anomaly in this sequence would, of course, be the state of Israel. Cyprus was no Israel. Nonetheless, naivete should not be presumed. As Foreign Minister at the time, the late Nicos Rolandis, admitted, Cypriot recourses to the UNSC and appeals to the UN General Assembly were never deemed panacea, but "a reminder to the world community that this problem existed" (Rolandis 2020).

---

[15] For further analysis of the history of the Cyprus Problem in a regional power politics context, see Koukkides-Procopiou (2018).

[16] Tziarras (2013) takes up this case, drawing upon East's (1973) model of analysis of small state behaviour.

Today, even in the absence of an official, long-term, well-defined and comprehensive National Security Strategy document, nothing drives Cyprus foreign policy harder than the traditional concept of national interest, deriving from the island's history. Based on the 1974 wartime experience and what ensued thereafter, the Cypriot *raison d'etat* cannot be translated in any other terms than in raw terms of security and survival vis-à-vis the historic Turkish threat. This has become "part of the country's security culture, mentality and practices" (Adamides 2018). Undoubtedly, any sign of success of Turkish policy in promoting its strategic goals on the island is, as would be expected, seen as inversely proportional to Cyprus' security (Kontos 2014), the result of a zero-sum geopolitical game.

It is no exaggeration by any means to conclude that the response to the imminent Turkish threat has monopolized most foreign policy decisions taken since the inception of the Republic. It was exactly in the light of this modus operandi that the decision to apply for membership in the EU was taken, as it was considered at the time perhaps a potential security provider,[17] even if in a broader sense of the word. The only other option, Greece, seemed too bewildered within her own problems to offer any kind of real consolation vis-à-vis Turkey. The Non-Alignment Movement, to which Cyprus had belonged, was by now more or less obsolete. The Commonwealth was irrelevant. The Communist Bloc had already crashed and burned its way out of existence.

Openly enough, the decision to apply for membership was mainly political rather than economic and aimed at one thing and one thing alone—to deal with Turkey, but in a different context and from an empowered standpoint. To say that "our foreign policy, our EU policy is always made in reference to Turkey and the Turkish stance vis-à-vis the Republic of Cyprus…[,] you cannot make foreign policy while overlooking the Cyprus Problem and definitely not while overlooking Turkey" can be no exaggeration, when uttered by a man in the know, who handled both the process to accession, as well as foreign policy at a later, more mature, stage of Europeanization (Kasoulides 2019).

---

[17] Following a number of other incidents, the boisterous 2018 ENI blockade by the Turkish navy within Cyprus' EEZ plus a number of ensuing illegal drilling actions by Turkey in the area, have so far failed to mobilise the European Union into action. Thus, the chimera of EU as security provider of any kind has by now been duly dispelled.

Indeed, the RoC's decision to join the EU was a big thing, similar to jumping second-rate ranks in order to play first division. EU accession did mark an important turning point in Cypriot history. Even if EU membership did not turn out to be the smoothest of rides, the application for EU membership was initially greeted in euphoria by most Cypriots. As Andreas Theophanous put it (2014),

> The country had a very pro-EU record: during the accession negotiations, polls had revealed a record level of pro-EU sentiment in Cyprus. This was related to high expectations from the EU; that accession to the EU would contribute to a solution for the Cyprus problem and that it would also help modernise social, economic and political structures.

To conclude, when discussing this third stage in Cyprus foreign policymaking, i.e. the one of Europeanization,[18] commencing in the early 1990s and running as an underlying policy theme up until 2013, one cannot escape security as the driver of foreign policymaking. First and foremost, the starting premise for security considerations would be concerns for the physical existence of the state's *citizens,* in the face of 40,000 Turkish troops stationed in the northern, occupied part of the island since 1974 and the continuous threats still hurled by Turkish officials, with Turkish President Recep Tayyip Erdoğan himself being no exception (Andreou 2018; Turner 2018; Babolias 2019).

However, there is also an additional underlying existential predicament, in the RoC's foreign policymaking—that is, serious concerns about the survival of the *state* itself. Minister Kasoulides' past exclamation that the EU "is the greatest guarantee to our existence" (Arsalidou 2017) exactly epitomizes past and present attempts by the Cypriot government to address such a concern. The primary importance placed on the recognition of the RoC—although this is only really disputed for obvious reasons by Turkey—is proven by its positioning as a central and overarching theme in both President Anastasiades' and former Foreign Minister Christodoulides' public statements, following denunciations by the Turkish government (see, e.g., e-Kathimerini 2014). In one instance, Christodoulides stated: "Cyprus wants Turkey to be involved in the development of energy in the region, but the prerequisites are that it must

---

[18] A thorough account of Cyprus' Europeanisation and, according to the authors, Re-Europeanisation paths, can be found in Christou and Kyris (2015).

recognise the Republic of Cyprus and the resolution of the Cyprus problem" (see, Ellinas 2018). Christodoulides has publicly reiterated this same statement at regular occurrences.

Owing to the turning of current political tides, a similar carrot-and-stick rhetoric has been deployed by the EU, regarding the fulfilment of Turkey's obligations towards the RoC prior to Turkish accession, even prior to visa-free entry into EU territory (see, for example, publicly announced terms on visa-free entry to Schengen areas for Turkish citizens; Schengen Visa Info 2018). However, it should be noted that even the most fervent advocates of such policy in the past nowadays pose serious doubts, as to whether this can actually work to safeguard Cypriot security concerns, in the face of Turkish obnoxiousness and the different path which Ankara has chosen, straying away from democratic values, Europeanization and westernization (Kasoulides 2019).

To this concoction of security threats as drivers of foreign policy, one should also add the serious preoccupation, not only with those threats posed to the existence of the Cypriot state in present times, but, also, with those possibly posed by a future solution of the Cyprus Problem. With 37% of its territory still under occupation by the army of a state which considers the RoC already "defunct", its possible political and legal deconstruction and delegitimization still echoes[19] as a publicly expressed policy concern among high-ranking, seasoned Cyprus diplomats (Tzionis 2017). In an international system where the State is still king, this seems to be a very legitimate concern.

Over and above the concerns of policymakers, one should not forget public opinion, whose perceptions of Turkey have been shaped by the wartime experience of 1974. Public opinion may not formulate policy, but it certainly sets the parameters within which policy can be made. This is very much the case in Cyprus, as the core of its foreign policy doctrine, that is the endeavour to engineer a bearable solution to the Cyprus Problem, while keeping Turkey at bay, is not just another foreign policy issue, for which the public would rarely care, as it happens in most societies. Where you stand as a policymaker on the Cyprus Problem, defines

---

[19] Back in 2004, the late President of the Republic, Tassos Papadopoulos, had urged the Greek Cypriots to reject Annan Plan V, on the premises of that same fear of losing the state: "I received an internationally recognised state, and I cannot deliver a community" (Greek News 2004). The plan was overwhelmingly rejected by the Greek Cypriots, while a Turkish Cypriot majority voted in favour.

where and if you sit in your political future. It is an issue affecting the everyday lives of hundreds of thousands of citizens and an issue where the lines between foreign and domestic policy are seriously blurred. Current Turkish threats and provocations aside, security fears and concerns for a post-solution state, albeit sometimes expressed in more inclusive, human security terms, are, also, regularly reflected in qualitative and quantitative research findings conducted among the Cypriot population (see, e.g., Cyprus SCORE Index/SeeD, 2009–2018).

War is a stern history teacher and Greek Cypriots have already had their fingers badly burnt by Turkey, several times. Following the coup orchestrated by the Greek Junta on the island to depose then-President Archbishop Makarios III, Turkey carried out two invasions in the summer of 1974—the second one planned and executed while supposedly the two sides were still in ceasefire and embroiled in negotiations. The canning untrustworthiness of Turkey is something Greek Cypriots cannot easily forget. To add insult to injury, casualties between the two sides since 1974 have been mostly of Greek Cypriot ethnic origin; namely a number of Greek Cypriot soldiers shot in cold blood in the buffer zone in the 1980s and early 1990s, culminating in the Tasos Isaak-Solomos Solomou civilian killings during a bikers' demonstration in the buffer zone. The effect of these two brutal murders (one by mob lynching, the other a cold-blood shooting) was magnified, as they took place while the UN stood by and watched and were witnessed by a shell-shocked television audience. The fact that Solomou's assassin, while on Interpol's wanted list, has been dragged along to international negotiation venues by the Turkish-Cypriot leadership, as a member of their delegation, adds to negative perceptions of lawlessness, under Turkish patronage, in the occupied areas of the Republic.

Based on such historical experiences, it is not surprising that Greek Cypriots simply refuse to trust and agree on Turkey's future presence on the island. It must, of course, be noted that on the other hand, to this persistent fear, the Turkish Cypriots juxtapose their own, stemming from the 1963 bi-communal troubles, which for them make Turkish military presence on the island a necessity (Cyprus SCORE Index/SeeD, 2009–2018). In turn, such notions of public opinion are what galvanizes Cypriot and Greek leaders enough to manoeuvre Cyprus Problem negotiations and by extension, foreign policy, along these same lines, when need be. Tassos Papadopoulos found himself amid an international furore, as the President who instigated the rejection of Annan V by the Greek

Cypriots, in 2004. However, his obituary in the Times (Theodoulou 2008) was quite telling of his capacity to withstand foreign pressure:

> Opprobrium abroad left Papadopoulos unruffled. He had support where it counted-at home. He was admired as a steadfast champion of Greek Cypriot rights, who had the gutsy strength of character to resist Anglo-American pressure to accept an unworkable and unfair peace deal...- Papadopoulos, his supporters believed, had saved Cyprus from Turkish dominance.

In this same light, one can explain the former Greek Foreign Minister, Nikos Kotzias' stance on Cyprus. Kotzias insisted on what he called the making of "a normal state" out of a post-solution Cyprus, before negotiations crashed at Crans Montana, in June 2017. In his book *Cyprus, 2015–2018. A three-year period which changed the Cyprus issue*, he makes the point that although his views on the negation of security guarantees and the removal of Turkish occupation troops from Cyprus made him very unpopular abroad and a victim of vitriolic attacks, he could still afford to ignore all these, as his views reflected majority opinion both among Greeks and Greek Cypriots (Kotzias 2018, 7–8).

Such argument can also be substantiated by more recent claims against the current President of the RoC, Nicos Anastasiades. Anastasiades had been a fervent supporter of the Annan Plan V, who lost face when the Plan was defeated by majority referendum vote back in 2004, with most of his party voters declining the party line and voting NO, too. He had been considered unelectable for a long time, his party bitterly divided, when salvation arrived in the form of a communist president, who so clumsily handled the economy and the Mari disaster that Anastasiades imminently came to be regarded as the lesser of two evils. In 2013, he came to the presidency with the mandate of a pro-solution leader. Despite negotiations gaining ground during his first term, things came to a standstill by 2017 at Crans Montana. According to Anastasiades, Turkish insolence over armies and guarantees brought a halt to the process.

The stance of some of his disappointed former close associates, who bitterly accused him of not acquiescing to signing a deal as "his sights were set on his re-election" (Drousiotis 2020), exactly proves the case in point—that is, the significance of public opinion when making core foreign policy decisions. Any Greek Cypriot politician taking home a deal, which did not secure removal of Turkish guarantees and Turkish troops from the equation, would be designing an electoral falling on one's own sword, as, in all probability, such deal would never make it through a referendum, as fear of Turkey still runs high. Anastasiades, knowing his politics "ABC" only too well, seemed to have refused to take that final leap of faith, which would have gone against Greek Cypriot (and probably his own) survival reflexes. It is quite astounding that amidst the ad hominem and political accusations hurled against Anastasiades, what his critics myopically disregarded was that his decision reflected the wishes of most Greek Cypriots voters on their own future, which Anastasiades' recent policy "redesign" was supposed to please (if such sources as Drousiotis are as they claim right). Contrary to his former associates, Anastasiades was too much of a politician to ignore public opinion and make the same mistake twice. His instincts proved him right. He was thereafter easily re-elected for a second term.

Anastasiades' political instincts on sensing domestic issues were coupled with the ability to understand rising disappointment vis-à-vis Brussels' treatment of Cypriots and growing disillusionment with EU foreign policy and security capabilities. When the opportunity presented itself, he gave the go ahead to proceeding with a revised multifaceted approach, as far as foreign policy was concerned. Both Anastasiades' terms in power and the making of foreign policy during his presidency can be characterized as the initiation to a more mature stage of foreign policy for Cyprus.

HISTORY IN THE MAKING: PRESIDENTIAL AUTHORITY AND FOREIGN POLICY

Ever since the 1963 political stalemate on the island and the withdrawal of Turkish Cypriots from government,[20] Cyprus is stuck with a president in almost absolute control of the executive for a period of five years, with no checks and balances in place, mainly due to the absence of the Turkish

---

[20] Because of Turkish Cypriot withdrawal from Cypriot government in 1963, the foreign ministry of the RoC has only ever been headed by Greek Cypriots, despite the constitutional stipulation that 3 ministries out of 10, with one of them being the Ministry of Foreign Affairs, Ministry of Defence or Ministry of Finance are to be held by a Turkish Cypriot, as per the 1960 Constitution. Events usually move faster than constitutions and regularly beat them to the ground. This is one such case.

Cypriot Vice President as counterweight. As James Ker-Linsay (2006) puts it:

> Under the 1960 constitution, the president is both the head of state and the head of government and in this dual capacity wields considerable power. The position is also strengthened by the fact that the post of the vice-president, the main check on presidential power, is currently in abeyance. At the same time, the president is also regarded by Greek Cypriots as the national leader, both in an historic, cultural sense and in terms of handling the peace negotiations. This means that the office, which is vested with significant powers under the constitution, has also developed considerable political and moral authority. In overall terms, it is argued that the president of Cyprus exerts greater control over domestic political affairs than any other EU leader.

Over and above the personal touch of any minister, the overall vision of what the RoC foreign policy should be all about, for reasons already discussed, seems to make its way to the Foreign Ministry via the Presidential Palace and not vice versa; although some foreign ministers have admittedly been more proactive, imaginative and productive than others. The President's values, style of leadership, furniture of mind, as well as his credibility at home and abroad, lay the foundations of foreign policy thinking and shaping on the island. In the period examined in this chapter, there can really be no other more important endogenous driver to policy than the President himself.[21]

TASSOS PAPADOPOULOS (2003–2008)

Europeanization—A Tricky Start

Despite initial celebrations regarding EU membership, things turned sour, when immediately upon accession in 2004, Cyprus had to face an array of negative comments and reactions, as the other European states tutted unapologetically at the Greek Cypriot decision to reject Annan Plan V, while eulogizing the Turkish Cypriots. As Gorvett writes (2004),

> The result was greeted with statements of official disappointment, along with anger at the Greek Cypriots, by the U.N., the EU and the U.S. EU

---

[21] There has never been a female president in Cyprus.

Commissioner for Enlargement Gunter Verheugen even went so far as to accuse the Greek Cypriots of lying to him when they earlier had given their commitment to reunification. Indeed, the EU's strong backing of the U.N. plan led Greek Cypriot "no" campaigners to ban Verheugen from making an address on the subject on Greek Cypriot TV during the run up to the vote. The Greek Cypriot government also accused the EU of trying to interfere in its domestic affairs, an allegation that an aghast Verheugen then claimed had "never been made before in EU history." Following the vote, EU ministers and parliamentarians agreed to open an office in the Turkish Cypriot north of the island, along with providing $260 million in aid.

as compensation for Turkish Cypriots being left behind. For most Greek Cypriots, it was beyond comprehension how a club of democratic states, such as the EU professed to be, could frown upon the result of a democratic referendum, which had clearly signified citizens' wishes regarding their own future.[22] Brussels choosing to play Mother Superior did not go down very well in Nicosia, but Papadopoulos' government decided to stand its ground, with the President himself spearheading the campaign.[23] In any case, in the eyes of the international community, Papadopoulos personified what had been an incomprehensible act of defiance, as he had urged the Greek Cypriot community to reject the plan. His election had been bad news right from the start: "the right man at

---

[22] The suspicions that many Greek Cypriots still project, when pondering about the involvement of the international community, in efforts to resolve the Cyprus Problem, were obviously magnified by such reactions. The disappointment felt for being vilified by the EU topped long-term Greek Cypriot disappointment at UN failure to exert any kind of pressure on Turkey, despite its obvious violations of international law and human rights. "The weak suffer what they must" approach may reflect harsh realities, but it can still be resented by those who bear its brunt. Let's not forget that Cyprus' foreign policy had for years anchored itself on the near deification of international law and international institutions. Thorough accounts on how foreign actors are perceived by Cypriots are provided by Adamides (2014) and Adamides and Kontos (2018).

[23] Papadopoulos may not have been an outward-going communicator, but he was gifted with an astute legal mind, made sharper by the practical approach of the seasoned politician. In the period immediately after the referendum, he produced a number of speeches and articles, at an international level, personally defending the Republic's decision, in a very capable way, but they still fell on deaf ears. See for example his statements at the UN General Assembly (Papadopoulos 2004b, 2005b), his article in *The National Interest* (Papadopoulos 2004a) and the *European Voice* (Papadopoulos 2005b). In the years that followed, Lillikas, as his Foreign Minister, followed the same line of defence, albeit in a more bombastic and dramatic tone.

the wrong time", "a talented and respected political veteran", but at the same time "a hardline nationalist" (Politico 2003).

Despite such initial acrimony and tense relations, the not-much-liked Papadopoulos and his team proceeded in a "business as usual" mode. During his presidency, in 2008, Cyprus joined the Eurozone. This was yet another political decision, according to Orphanides, who had served as Central Bank governor during the Papadopoulos administration, when this took place. "As with so many other decisions…the reasons Cyprus sought to join, were not economic but primarily political in nature… the decisions to join the European Union in 2004 as well as the euro area in 2008 were made to strengthen the political standing of the nation and to promote greater stability" (Orphanides 2016).

DEMETRIS CHRISTOFIAS (2008–2013)
Europeanization—Tricky Gets Trickier

As political tides often turn, a change in Cyprus government, in 2008, reversed the gradual normalization of relations between the RoC and the EU, when the first (and possibly last) communist president of Cyprus, Demetris Christofias, came to power. Christofias had no inhibitions in showing that his loyalties (and by extension the loyalties of the RoC) lied elsewhere. He began flirting with Syria and Iran and paid lip service to Chavez and Castro, even inaugurating RoC's first ever embassy in Cuba by 2009, during a presidential official visit.

In the gravest incident of mismanagement marking his presidency, the 2011 Mari explosion, 13 people were killed, hundreds injured, and the country's main power station came to lay in waste, causing island-wide power cuts and industrial disruption in costs, production and services. An official investigation into the explosion of this dangerous cargo of arms, intercepted while heading from Iran to Syria (an interception that the RoC had only reluctantly acted to carry out, upon American demands on embargo violation) showed that Christofias, despite repeated warnings by a number of experts and chief officials, had refused to comply with safety precautions and allow the shipment to be destroyed, hoping to return it to Assad in due time (Polyviou 2011). This was in defiance and at odds not only with common sense, but, also, with the official EU policy of sanctions against Syria (BBC 2011). Despite a damning investigation and the public outcry that ensued, Christofias continued undeterred, even while, at some point, forced to hold Council of Ministers meetings in his private home, as the Presidential Palace was surrounded by seething protesters.

Christofias had made no secret of his despise of capitalism and the free market, in contrast to his admiration and adherence to communism, even when Cyprus found itself at the helm of the European Presidency in 2012. At a crucial point in time, when Cyprus could have used its EU presidency to capitalize on the status presented by the occasion and negotiate an assistance programme on better financial terms, while it found itself on the brink of financial catastrophe, Christofias, instead, chose to close the presidency by giving a speech at the European Parliament, where he made full use of his communist pride.

He only succeeded in antagonizing and alienating his peers, many of whom had suffered under communism or fought against it, as a Cypriot academic pertinently observed (Ioannou 2012). In any case, Christofias had repeatedly chosen to ignore their heeds regarding the RoC's reckless spending spree, refused to engage in constructive dialogue with any of them or pay attention to ECB warnings. (Orphanides 2016). On the one hand, he was forced to invite over the Troika team for negotiations, as the economy was junked, but at the same time refused to fully cooperate with them, when on the ground, his wife and children protesting outside the Parliament, in condemnation of Troika's presence on the island.

To add insult to injury, while Christofias kept chastising his EU partners, he sang the Russian praise. Christina Ioannou (2012) commented thus:

> Demetris Christofias has ruffled diplomatic feathers one too many times in the EU, with statements upholding Russian 'generosity' over the terms of their loans, as opposed to the EU stringent conditions and measures. While Christofias has declared Russia a "strategic partner" of Cyprus, he has openly charged the EU and the IMF with behaving as "colonial forces". Both Christofias' rhetoric and ideology, as well as his Soviet veteran profile which he projects through statements such as "I won't create a revolution, don't worry", have stung diplomatic and other circles in Europe. The President's determination to seek additional loans from Russia, while also flirting with Beijing, at a time when debates over the IMF rescue package are ongoing, has also been negatively criticized in Cyprus and in Europe. Such behavior raises the question of whether this is the best of times to create doubts in Brussels over the country's allegiance.

In the same way that Papadopoulos had personified the anti-Annan wrath in previous years, this time, Christofias seemed to personally embody the hitherto unprecedented despise he had against Europe and its ideals. Despite dignified attempts by his highly educated, world-travelled Foreign Ministers (Erato Kozakou-Marcoullis and Marcos Kyprianou) to save the day, by projecting a more open-minded image and working on a global agenda, what stuck with the international audience watching was the parochialism of a rather anachronistic President, out of touch with modern realities.

Nicos Anastasiades (2013 to Present)
Moving Beyond Europeanization Towards Maturity

It was not long before Christofias left the presidency in 2013 that the Cypriots experienced a Eurogroup-imposed haircut on their bank deposits, as a remedy to the island's failing banking sector. This was the second time that Brussels appeared vindictive, in what was seen as disproportionate punishment for the doings of a small nation, treated as guinea pig. Debate whether the European card had been an ace or anathema began anew. In Theophanous' (2014) words,

> Nevertheless, when Cyprus found itself in deep crisis, due both to endogenous and exogenous factors, its treatment was unexpected and extremely harsh. By 2012 Cyprus was facing a huge banking crisis, serious fiscal imbalances and a real estate bubble. Admittedly Cypriot policy-makers and other stakeholders had engaged in imprudent practices with devastating results. But exogenous factors had also contributed: the global financial crisis, the Eurozone crisis and above all the haircut of the Greek debt in October 2011 during which Cypriot banks lost €4.5 billion – about 25% of Cyprus' GDP...The decisions of the Eurogroup were influenced by other considerations as well: these included the timing of the upcoming German elections, the objective to contain Russian presence in Cyprus, to use Cyprus as an experiment for future crises and to send particular messages to other, bigger, more troublesome countries. Cyprus did not deserve this treatment.

These words echoed the sentiments of many Greek Cypriots.

The 2013 financial crisis was an eye opener and a coming of age for Cyprus. Whether the correct lessons have been learned is another story

(Stockwatch 2019). Having by accident or design demolished the RoC's economic model, which had been based on its banking sector, the EU offered no remedy other than austerity to kick start the economy back into growth. But the RoC realized that the EU card (and passport) could be played when partnerships were struck with others, exactly based on the value added ascribed to Cyprus by its EU membership, in the eyes (and pockets) of third parties (Charalambous 2019). It was not long before such tactics recreated the already existing acrimony between Brussels and Nicosia (Reuters 2019), though in the meantime, the RoC had already begun setting its sights elsewhere. Once more, it was the President himself who bore the brunt or credit for foreign policy choices.

Going back to previous years, despite occasional verbal proclamations to the opposite by Papadopoulos and Christofias' roaming eye to the East, the pursuit of the RoC's foreign policy had hitherto been mostly monothematic, exclusively, and directly linked to efforts to secure state and people against Turkish aggression and to resolve the Cyprus Problem, Europe or no Europe. Today, although dealings with Turkey and the reunification of the island undoubtedly remain the primary focus of the current government, its foreign policy agenda has become multi-layered, "a multidimensional realpolitik" (Karides 2015). As such, it comprises a range of issues: primarily, the addressing of regional concerns through energy cooperation and security, as well as climate change and gender, while also paying attention to soft power pursuits, through economic and cultural diplomacy.

Although this is by no means a new approach in the Cyprus Foreign Ministry,[24] the shift in using new means to achieve an old end has especially picked up momentum under the Minister, Nikos Christodoulides. Christodoulides has made an intense effort to promote a more transparent, inclusive, and participatory process for foreign affairs (Cyprus News Agency 2018), as well as to open up foreign policy public discourse to a range of additional topics. Nonetheless, such a diverse approach would have hardly worked in the absence of the newly introduced multifaceted foreign policy doctrine that had already started to unfold, in previous years, under the auspices of Minister Kasoulides (2013–2018).

---

[24] For example, Minister Erato Kozakou-Marcoullis, especially in her second term, between 2011 and 2013, pioneered important multi-dimensional issues; several her public speeches and statements focused on strategizing on women's rights, food security, cultural diplomacy, etc.

The origins of what Nicos Anastasiades, in the beginning of his own first term in office, described as "my new foreign policy dogma" (Cyprus Profile 2013), can most likely be traced back to the experienced foreign policy veteran that Kasoulides is.

Anastasiades elaborates on this new dogma, as "the conscious reorientation of the foreign policy of Cyprus, based on a comprehensive and extrovert approach", with five specific aims: (a) the solution to the Cyprus Problem as a means of domestic and regional stability (b) the exploitation of natural resources, benefitting country and region, (c) the enhancement of participation in EU pillars and mechanisms, mainly security, (d) the promotion of bilateral relations with neighbouring countries, and (e) the creation of a grid of alliances with China, Russia, Israel, the US, the United Kingdom (UK) and the Arab World (Anastasiades 2014).

This "dogma" has now been further developed into a concise and coherent three pillar policy of which both Minister Christodoulides and President Anastasiades make good use at every given opportunity. In Christodoulides' (2019) own words (with these foreign policy tenets closely reflected in most of the President's speeches):

> The first pillar is the enhancement and expansion of our relations with countries in our immediate region: the Middle East and the Gulf… The second pillar of Cyprus foreign policy is a more active involvement of Cyprus within the European Union beyond issues that directly touch upon the Cyprus problem or Turkey, which for a long time following our accession to the European Union in 2004 was the case. We have worked methodically to build our voice in Brussels on an array of issues where Cyprus has a strong added value. Take, for example, issues relating to our region…The third pillar of our foreign policy relates to the strengthening of relations with the five permanent members of the United Nations Security Council as well as with key players in the international arena, such as Japan and India. So far as the five permanent members of the Security Council are concerned, we have worked in building our relationship beyond the remit of the discussion of the Cyprus problem at the Security Council…

The important point made in the second pillar of Anastasiades' foreign policy is, in turn, made possible by Christodoulides' gregariousness. This projects on the role of Cyprus as bridge and communication pathway between the EU and the RoC's other partners in the Eastern Mediterranean. Such suggestion has been much welcomed by Jordan, Egypt,

Lebanon and Israel, who often see in Cyprus another friendly broker mediating for promotion of their interests in Europe (see, e.g., Gold News 2015). In addition to this, the reinforced venture of seeking additional fortunes elsewhere (the third pillar of current foreign policy) "allows" for the further building of bridges with China and Russia, in the name of good UNSC member relations, without brushing the Americans off. Focus on the Gulf area, in what used to be hostile ground for Cyprus, comes as no surprise. The cultivation of a special relationship between the RoC and the US is also in process, whereas bilateral relations between with the UK remain more than friendly and ties are expected to become closer now that Brexit is final.

In essence, as per the above, there has been a revised policy of conveniently playing the European card rather than passively being rebuked and played by it. This being a sign of maturity is one thing, a sign of necessity another. All in all, it has translated into focusing less energy on the collective (yet bureaucratic) EU identity and instead strengthening bilateral defence cooperation and energy relations with the big guns (Germany, France and Italy). The oil drilling by French TOTAL and Italian ENI in Cyprus' waters was hoped to create the necessary synergies for cooperation spilling into energy security arrangements (as has happened with Exxon Mobil creating somehow tighter US-RoC ties), while German troops have already been provided the use of military facilities in Cyprus. Bilateral and trilateral diplomacy seems to be working (KNews 2018), although a note of warning is necessary: when analysing the existing situation, one should not confuse intentions with results, especially under current market conditions which have made/will make drilling happen later rather than sooner. Relations stipulated on possible energy successes now need to be rethought and restarted.

The COVID-19 pandemic and the ongoing uncertainty has only added insult to injury, by highlighting how lacking the EU is in dealing with crisis management, not only as far as traditional security structures are concerned, but, above all, in terms of being a collective entity which can act at least as a human security provider. In the recent past, Cypriot (high) expectations were not really met, especially in the face of Turkish threats and outright violations of Cyprus' (and by extension EU's) EEZ, wreaking havoc on ENI's drilling plans (Paraskova 2018). Currently, it has been duly noted that Cyprus initially received aid from China and the UAE, while close to nothing from its EU counterparts. Under these circumstances, insisting that the EU can act as a catalyst to the Cyprus peace process seems quite unlikely, to say the least. Even with a solution to the Cyprus Problem having future ramifications for Europe, close to two decades past accession, the EU remains nothing but an observer in the process, although admittedly its role has been more active now than it has ever been in the past.[25]

Conclusion

All in all, the recently revised informal doctrine of the RoC's foreign policy, under Anastasiades, can be summed up as: the development and deepening of multilevel, multilateral, bilateral and trilateral diplomacy; the principle of reciprocity defining relations with other states rather than allowing the Cyprus Problem to monopolize discussions; the RoC acting as the bridge between Europe and the Eastern Mediterranean, capitalizing on its stability (the Cyprus issue is a frozen conflict after all), its strategic location and its EU membership; and, the RoC moving away from a passive/reactive stance to a more energetic, innovative and proactive one (see also, Tziarras 2019). Energy and defence policy are attempting to follow suit. There has also been emphasis on the tools and means of public diplomacy, digital diplomacy, economic diplomacy and cultural diplomacy, as well as the women, peace and security agenda.

Thus, under the guise of a newly found confidence, but, also, permitted by the breaking down of the traditional regional order and power structure (as well as current antipathy towards Turkey) trilateral cooperations and a move away from Europeanization were both made possible. It can be perhaps said that the RoC found an entry point and attempted a long overdue disentanglement from the conditionality hitherto placed on its standing in the world order through the prism of the Cyprus Problem. Whether ambitions are surpassing capabilities remains to be seen, especially as the global balance of power could one day soon enough turn into a seismic shifting of tectonic plates, which could either make it extremely difficult for Cyprus to continue to rock many boats at once or extremely lucky not to have placed all its eggs in the European basket. The primordial question though remains—has the RoC's

---

[25] For extensive references regarding the EU's complementary role in Cyprus peace process, especially in Crans Montana, see the Report of the Secretary-General on his mission of good offices in Cyprus (UNSC 2017).

current foreign policy attempts managed to disentangle it from its very own existential problem vis-à-vis Turkey? The answer is no.

References

1960 Constitution of Cyprus, http://www.cypnet.co.uk/ncyprus/history/cyproblem/1960.html.
Adamides, Constantinos. 2014. "Negative Perceptions of Foreign Actors". In *Great Power Politics in Cyprus: Foreign Interventions and Domestic Perceptions*, edited by M. Kontos, N. Panayiotides, H. Alexandrou, and S. C. Theodoulou, 197–222. Newcastle: Cambridge Scholars Publishing.
Adamides, Constantinos. 2018. "The Challenges of Formulating National Security Strategies (NSS) in the Presence of Overarching Existential Threats." *The Cyprus Review* 30: 1.
Adamides, Constantinos, and Michalis Kontos. 2018. "Greek Cypriots Perceptions of the UN". In *Cyprus Roadmap for Peace: A Critical Interrogation of the Conflict*, edited by Michael Michael and Vural Yucel. Northampton, MA: Edward Elgar Publishing.
Anastasiades, Nicos. 2013. "Η κρίση θέλει ηγέτη" [Crisis Needs a Leader]. Election Programme, Presidential Elections 2013.
Anastasiades, Nicos. 2014. "The True Story About the Geopolitical Role of Cyprus: David or Goliath?" *LSE Hellenic Observatory Public Lecture*, January 16. http://www.lse.ac.uk/europeanInstitute/research/hellenicObservatory/CMS%20pdf/Events/2013-14_Events/Public-Lectures/LSE-SPEECH-ROLE-OF-CYPRUS-FINAL-ONE.pdf.
Andreou, Evie. 2018. "Erdogan Threatens to Increase Number of Soldiers in the North." *Cyprus Mail*, September 17. https://cyprus-mail.com/2018/09/17/erdogan-threatens-to-increase-number-of-soldiers-in-north/.
Arsalidou, Athena. 2017. "EU Participation the Greatest Guarantee for Our Own Existence." *Cyprus News Agency*, May 9. http://www.cna.org.cy/WebNews-en.aspx?a=ed7bbaa5f24946258625cbc2b79fb426.
Baboulias, Yiannis. 2019. "Turkey Is Hungry for War with Cyprus." *Foreign Policy*, May 21. https://foreignpolicy.com/2019/05/21/turkey-is-hungry-for-war-with-cyprus-erdogan/.
BBC. 2011. "EU Imposes Sanctions on President Assad," 23 May, https://www.bbc.com/news/world-middle-east-13500395.
BBC HardTalk. 2017. "President Erdogan Tells the BBC Most Turkish People," 12 July. https://www.bbc.com/news/av/world-europe-40577220/president-erdogan-tells-the-bbc-most-turkish-people-don-t-want-the-eu-anymore.
Charalambous, Annie. 2019. "Commission Warns Cyprus over Golden Passports." *In-Cyprus*, January 22. https://in-cyprus.com/commission-warns-cyprus-over-golden-passports/.

Christodoulides, Nicos. 2019. "Cyprus and the Future of Eastern Mediterranean Security and Co-Operation." *Speech Given at ERPIC- European Rim Policy and Investment Council*, January 23. https://erpic.org/portfolio-post/mediterranean-security-operation/.

Christou, George, and George Kyris. 2015. "The Financial Crisis and Cypriot Foreign Policy: Re-Europeanisation?" *Hellenic Studies* 23 (1).

Cyprus Mail. 2020. "Cyprus Protests Turkish Violations of Its Air and Sea," February 22. https://cyprus-mail.com/2020/02/22/cyprus-protests-turkish-violations-of-its-air-and-sea/.

Cyprus News Agency. 2018. "Δημόσια Διαβούλευση ΥΠΕΞ για Στρατηγικό Πλάνο Δράσης" [Public Deliberation of Foreign Ministry on Strategic Action Plan], July 11, http://www.cna.org.cy/WebNews.aspx?a=1d7e51ff49734b0ea069852132170ae4.

Cyprus Profile. 2013. "Interview with Nicos Anastasiades," 12 July. https://www.cyprusprofile.com/en/articles/interview-president-of-cyprus-nicos-anastasiades/.

Cyprus SCORE Index, USAID/SeeD-Centre for Sustainable Peace and Democratic Development, 2009–2018 Publications of Research Findings, available at https://www.scoreforpeace.org/.

Davutoğlu, Ahmet. 2010. *Στρατηγικό Βάθος: Η Διεθνής Θέση της Τουρκίας* [Strategic Depth: Turkey's International Position]. Athens: Politia.

Droussiotis, Makarios. 2020. "Anastasiades Got His Way at Crans Montana." *Cyprus Mail*, February 22, https://cyprus-mail.com/2020/02/09/anastasiades-got-his-way-in-crans-montana/.

E-Kathimerini. 2014. "Turkey Calls Cyprus a Defunct State," June 25, http://www.ekathimerini.com/161010/article/ekathimerini/news/turkey-calls-cyprus-a-defunct-state-reports-say.

East, Maurice A. 1973. "Size and Foreign Policy Behaviour: A Test of Two Models". *World Politics* 25 (4).

Ellinas, Charles. 2018. "Cyprus Wants Turkey to Be Involved in Regional Energy Plans." *Cyprus Mail*, November 4. https://cyprus-mail.com/2018/11/04/cyprus-wants-turkey-to-be-involved-in-regional-energy-plans/.

Erim, Nihat. 1978. "Reminiscences on Cyprus. " *Foreign Policy Quarterly* 4 (2–3). http://foreignpolicy.org.tr/reminiscenses-on-cyprus-nihat-erim/.

Greek News. 2004. "Greek Cypriots applaud Papadopoulos' Rejection," April 12. http://www.greeknewsonline.com/greek-cypriots-applaud-papadopoulos-rejection/.

Gold News. 2015. "Cyprus Proposes EU Migrant Crisis Assistance to Jordan-Lebanon," November 13. http://www.goldnews.com.cy/en/energy/cyprus-proposes-eu-migrant-crisis-assistance-to-jordan-lebanon.

Gorvett, Jon. "Vote on Annan Plan Results in Reversal of Fortune for Turkish, Greek Cypriots." *Washington Report on Middle East Affairs*, June 2004,

40–41, https://www.wrmea.org/004-june/vote-on-annan-plan-results-in-rev ersal-of-fortune-for-turkish-greek-cypriots.html.
Hazou, Elias. 2021. "Gas Drilling to Resume Later This Year Says Pilides." *Cyprus Mail*, June 29. https://cyprus-mail.com/2021/06/29/gas-drilling-to-resume-later-this-year-says-pilides/.
Independent Commission on the Future of the Cyprus Banking Sector, Final Report and Recommendations, October 31, 2013, available at https://www.centralbank.cy/images/media/pdf/LSE_ICFCBS_Final_Report_10_13.pdf.
Ioannou, Christina. 2012. "Cyprus' 'Bailout Presidency.'" *In Depth* 9 (4). http://cceia.unic.ac.cy/wp-content/uploads/article04-C.Ioannou-9-4.pdf.
Karides, Nicholas. 2015. "Cyprus' Foreign Policy Ambitions." *Cyprus Mail*, July 5. https://cyprus-mail.com/2015/07/05/cyprus-foreign-policy-ambitions/.
Kasapoğlu, Can. 2017. "Turkey's Forward-Basing Posture." *EDAM Foreign Policy and Security Paper Series 2017/4*. https://edam.org.tr/en/turkeys-forward-basing-posture/.
Kasoulides, Ioannis. 2019. *30 χρόνια παρών: Ιδέες και σκέψεις για την Κύπρο μας* [30 Years Present: Ideas and Thoughts on Our Cyprus]. Nicosia: Kathimerini.
Kaymak, Erol, and Yucel Vural. 2006. Intra-Communal Dynamics: EU Discourses Among Turkish Cypriot Political Actors Since the Failed Referenda. *European Consortium of Political Science*. https://ecpr.eu/Filestore/PaperProposal/64475397-2150-4c38-8e06-116f7042ea8b.pdf.
Ker-Lindsay, James. 2006. "Presidential Power and Authority in the Republic of Cyprus." *Mediterranean Politics* 11 (1): 21–37.
Ker-Lindsay, James. 2009. "The National Council." In *The Government and Politics of Cyprus*, edited by James Ker-Lindsay and Faustman Hubert. Oxford: Peter Lang.
Knews. 2018. "President: US, France interested in Greece, Cyprus, Israel Cooperation," 4 December, https://knews.kathimerini.com.cy/en/news/president-us-france-interested-in-greece-cyprus-israel-cooperation.
Knews. 2021. "EastMed Pipeline Viability Under Scrutiny," https://www.ekathimerini.com/news/1157014/eastmed-pipeline-viability-under-scrutiny/.
Kontos, Michalis. 2014. "The Strategic Security and Survival Planning of the Republic of Cyprus: Past Choices and Future Prospects [In Greek]." In *Cyprus in a New Era: Geostrategic Parameters, Economy, Foreign Policy*, edited by Christina Ioannou, Dimitris P. Sotiropoulos, and Achilles K. Emilianides, 81–98. Nicosia: Hippasus.
Kotzias, Nikos. 2018. "Cyprus, 2015–2018. A Three-Year Period Which Changed the Cyprus Issue," Hellenic Republic, Ministry of Foreign Affairs. Athens: Livanis.
Koukkides-Procopiou, Anna. 2018. "Cyprus History: Ignore at Your Own Peril." *Eurasia Review*, June 1. https://www.eurasiareview.com/01062018-cyprus-history-ignore-at-your-own-peril-oped/.

Koukkides-Procopiou, Anna. 2017. "The Cyprus Problem: When We All Think Alike, no One Thinks Very Much." *In Depth* 12 (4).

Lillikas, Yiorgos. 2007. "Interview with Cypriot Foreign Minister Yiorgos Lillikas: Why Should We Adopt the Turkish Culture?" *Der Spiegel*, May 4. https://www.spiegel.de/international/europe/interview-with-cypriot-foreign-minister-yiorgos-lillikas-why-should-we-adopt-the-turkish-culture-a-481079.html.

Mavroyiannis, Andreas. 2020. "Cyprus Foreign Policy: Always Investing in Effective Multilateralism." *In Depth* 17 (6).

Ministry of Foreign Affairs of the Republic of Cyprus. All Speeches and Statements of Previous and Current Ministers Mentioned in the Paper Can Be Accessed Through www.mfa.gov.cy.

Oprhanides, Athanasios. 2016. "What Happened in Cyprus? The Economic Consequences of the Last Communist Government in Europe." *The Cyprus Bail-Policy Lessons from the Cyprus Economic Crisis*, edited by Alexandros Michaelides and Athanasios Orphanides. London: Imperial College Press.

Papadopoulos, Tassos. 2004a. "A People's Decision." *The National Interest*, April 28. https://nationalinterest.org/article/a-peoples-decision-2636.

Papadopoulos, Tassos. 2004b. Statement by H.E. Mr. Tassos Papadopoulos, President of the Republic of Cyprus, at the 59th session of the UN General Assembly, September 23. https://www.un.org/webcast/ga/59/statements/cypeng040923.pdf.

Papadopoulos, Tassos. 2005a. Statement by H.E. Mr. Tassos Papadopoulos, President of the Republic of Cyprus, at the 60th Session of the UN General Assembly, September 18. http://www.cyprusun.org/?p=1443.

Papadopoulos, Tassos. 2005b. "Why Greek Cypriots Wisely Said 'No' to Solomon's Justice." *European Voice*, March 17–23.

Paraskova, Tsvetana. 2018. "Turkey's Navy Threatens to Sink Eni Drilling Ship Offshore Cyprus." *OilPrice.com*, February 23. https://oilprice.com/Latest-Energy-News/World-News/Turkeys-Navy-Threatens-To-Sink-Eni-Drilling-Ship-Offshore-Cyprus.html.

Polyviou, Polys. 2011. Report of Investigation Committee Regarding the Explosion of 11 July 2011 in the Naval Base of Evangelos Florakis at Mari [in Greek].

Reuters. 2019. "EU Warns of Crime Risks from Governments' Passports and Visa Sales," January 23. https://www.reuters.com/article/us-eu-passports/eu-warns-of-crime-risks-from-governments-passports-visa-sales-idUSKCN1PH13M.

Rolandis, Nicos. 2020. "Foreign Policy Perspectives." *In Depth* 17 (6).

Schengen Visa Info. 2018. "Turkey Must Recognize Cyprus to Gain Visa-Free EU Travel: EU Report," July 6. https://www.schengenvisainfo.com/news/turkey-must-recognize-cyprus-to-gain-visa-free-eu-travel-eu-report/.

SeeD-Centre for Sustainable Peace and Democratic Development, Cyprus Project Research Data on Cyprus Accessible at https://www.seedsofpeace.eu/ and https://www.scoreforpeace.org/.

Stockwatch. 2019. "The European Commission Identifies Excessive imbalances in Cyprus," February 27. https://www.stockwatch.com.cy/en/article/eyropi/european-commission-identifies-excessive-imbalances-cyprus.

Theodoulou, Michael. 2008. "Tassos Papadopoulos: Greek Cypriot President." *The Times*. https://www.thetimes.co.uk/article/tassos-papadopoulos-greek-cypriot-president-wqfchsbvv2l.

Theophanous, Andreas. 2014. "Troika Fixes Fail: How to Fix the Troika." *Friends of Europe*, December 4. https://www.friendsofeurope.org/future-europe/troika-fixes-fail-fix-troika.

Tziarras, Zenonas. 2013. "Κύπρος και Εξωτερική Πολιτική: Κεφαλαιοποιώντας την Περιφερειοποίηση του Διεθνούς Συστήματος" [Cyprus and Foreign Policy: Capitalizing on the Regionalization of the International System]. In *Κυπριακή Δημοκρατία: Διαστάσεις Εξωτερικής Πολιτικής* [Republic of Cyprus: Dimensions of Foreign Policy], edited by Marios Efthymiopoulos and Zenonas Tziarras, 75–95. Thessaloniki: University Studio Press.

Tziarras, Zenonas. 2016. "Israel-Cyprus-Greece: A 'Comfortable' Quasi-Alliance." *Mediterranean Politics* 21 (3): 407–427.

Tziarras, Zenonas. 2019. "Cyprus's Foreign Policy in the Eastern Mediterranean and the Trilateral Partnerships: A Neoclassical Realist Approach." In *The new Geopolitics of the Eastern Mediterranean: Trilateral Partnerships and Regional Security*, edited by Zenonas Tziarras, 53–72. Nicosia: PRIO Cyprus Centre.

Tzionis, Tasos. 2017. "The 'Defunct Republic of Cyprus' (according to Turkey) in the Present Phase of the Cyprus Problem." *Eastern Mediterranean Policy Note*, no. 13, January 10, https://cceia.unic.ac.cy/wp-content/uploads/EMPN_13.pdf.

Turner, Katie. 2018. "Erdogan Makes New Threats Against Cyprus." *Cyprus Mail*, December 2. https://cyprus-mail.com/2018/12/02/erdogan-makes-new-threats-against-cyprus/.

UNSC Resolution 186. 1964. Resolution of March 4, 1964. (S/5575) http://unscr.com/en/resolutions/186

UNSC Presidential Statement. 2021. (S/PRST/2021/13). https://www.un.org/press/en/2021/sc14586.doc.htm.

UNSC. 2017. Report of the Secretary-General on His Mission of Good Offices in Cyprus, September 28. http://www.uncyprustalks.org/wp-content/uploads/2017/10/2017-09-28-SG-GO-Report-S-2017-814.pdf.

Winneker, Craig. 2003. "Right Man, Wrong Time." *Politico*, February 26. https://www.politico.eu/article/right-man-wrong-time-tassos-papadopoulos/.

PART II

Between East and West—The International Orientation

CHAPTER 4

Stuck in the Middle: Constructing Maturity and Restoring Balance in RoC-EU Relations

Petros Petrikkos

INTRODUCTION: HOW CYPRUS "FITS" IN THE EU

Small states can be vulnerable in an international system that is largely characterised by alliance-building. This does not necessarily mean that small states find themselves without support, nor does it imply that such a system is unstructured. Rather, it is constructed by way of framing and redefining one's image within a greater agenda, by projecting interests, common objectives, as well as adapting to a fixed routine that secures such interests (Adamides 2020, 77–78). This means that small states address the constrained material capabilities by placing emphasis on agency, in their quest for emancipation (Steele 2008, 14, 69). Effective leadership, alliance-building, and addressing ideology, identity, and existential security concerns are key foreign policy issues for small states (Steele 2008, 14, 69; Wendt 1992, 401; Schweller 2009, 227; Frazier and Stewart-Ingersoll 2010, 732). To paraphrase Mitzen, raising awareness over the

P. Petrikkos (✉)
University of Nicosia, Nicosia, Cyprus
e-mail: petrikkos.p@unic.ac.cy

© The Author(s), under exclusive license to Springer Nature Switzerland AG 2022
Z. Tziarras (ed.), *The Foreign Policy of the Republic of Cyprus*, Reform and Transition in the Mediterranean,
https://doi.org/10.1007/978-3-030-91177-5_4

problem triggers boosted anxiety, thus states choose more comfortable routines they have grown accustomed to (Mitzen 2006, 350). The way the Republic of Cyprus (RoC) has formulated its foreign policy in recent years since 2004 has been sporadic and uncertain. In its ambition to re-adapt and to overcome the challenges posed by the Cyprus problem, the RoC has been forced to adjust its image, priorities, and to shift alliances in order to retain, justify, and secure its ontological security. As a matter of fact, because of its frozen conflict, Cyprus has been characterised as "the graveyard of diplomacy" (Gramer and Surana 2017). To be more precise, the conditions revolving around RoC diplomacy have effectively sustained the conflict, often failing to go beyond this fixation (Adamides and Constantinou 2012, 244; Constantinou 2015, 30).

This brings forth the question of *maturity* in foreign policy. For the purposes of this chapter, foreign policy maturity refers to simultaneously balancing and framing RoC foreign policy against that of the European Union (EU). This means that the expectations and power of the state in terms of foreign policy can meet realistic targets and objectives (Tucker 1979, 470), on the one hand, while projecting and maintaining a narrative that situates the state within the bloc as a whole, on the other hand (Bailes and Thorhallsson 2013, 100, 102, 109). Maturity, therefore, is the ability to match means to ends. This can either mean to set goals that correspond to means or develop the necessary means to achieve desired goals. For instance, states having sufficient economic or military power, energy capabilities, and other capacity and material-focused factors are the means that may help a state fulfil its foreign policy objectives successfully. On the contrary, if the state mismatches its objectives due to a lack of resources or a realistic agenda, then it risks poor decision-making, and as a result, an immature foreign policy (Economides 2005, 475; Schweller 2008, 105–106). In states like the RoC, foreign policy may even be disrupted due to "mismanagement, corruption, bureaucratic inefficiency, and deep ethnic, religious, and regional cleavages" (Schweller 2008, 105–106). As such, a key problem that has contained and inhibited foreign policy maturity in the RoC is the Cyprus problem.

Through its accession to the EU, the RoC's foreign policy has also been guided strategically through EU institutions. Cyprus has been an EU member-state since 2004. The country entered negotiations for its accession as a full member on 4 July 1990. Seeing that the collapse of the Soviet Union created a vacuum, Cyprus had to pick a side for security reasons, thus it turned to institutions. It was only 16 years after the island was *de facto* divided, following years of intercommunal violence, a military coup, and a subsequent Turkish invasion and occupation. Prior to this, the guerrilla-style war of 1955–1959 against the British rule was the basis for the breakout of intercommunal violence. The ambitions of *enosis* on the one side and *taksim* on the other[1] eventually drove the two communities apart.

A mistake that happens far too often in the studies of the RoC foreign policy is the overemphasis on the conflict itself. Past literature and other accounts profiling the RoC foreign policy have often concentrated on the Cyprus problem (Attalides 1979; Coufoudakis 2006; Hannay 2005; Ker-Lindsay 2005). These accounts often put the problem in question in the spotlight, implying that policy is formulated or at least based solely on how the RoC approaches and utilises the conflict in the international scene. Other more recent accounts have also suggested that all foreign policy actions are solely based on the notion that "Cyprus seeks to better its position and harness the gains from that improvement, especially with regard to the settlement of the 'Cyprus question' and the exploitation of the Republic's natural resources" (Pedi and Kouskouvelis 2019, 151).

Indeed, the conflict was also an integral part of the Cypriot membership to the EU. Throughout the negotiation process, the EU constantly stressed the importance of the entire island joining the bloc (Skoutaris 2011, 13). It was a key request set by other European leaders, for a number of reasons: (a) the liberal ideology and principles of the bloc as a whole; (b) the possibility of opening further accession and enlargement with Turkish membership to the EU; (c) bridging the East and the West; and (d) ending the long dispute that has kept the island *de facto* divided.

The excess focus on the conflict itself, however, has shifted attention away from other foreign policy areas. These include social welfare, defence and security, unemployment, crime, and agriculture (Zachariades and Petrikkos 2020, 108; Petrikkos 2019; Dağlı 2017). Despite ongoing improvements, the RoC's foreign policy is contained due to the persistence of the Cyprus problem. The *de facto* division, the current energy dispute, and ongoing developments with Turkey in the Eastern Mediterranean, as well as blocking Turkish membership to the EU are only some of the spill-overs that result from the continuation of the *status quo*.

---

[1] "Enosis" (in Greek: union) refers to the idea of uniting Cyprus with Greece, whereas "taksim" (in Turkish: division) refers to the idea of partitioning the island between Turkish and Greek portions.

Because of these issues, we must begin answering questions pertaining to the actual relations of Cyprus and the EU. Therefore, instead of focusing solely on the conflict itself, there is a growing need to assess how Cyprus *fits* in the EU. This includes answering serious questions pertaining to what the country's place and future within the Union is, and what other priorities it seeks to address in this partnership. Although it has encouraged a solution to the issue, the EU bloc does not hold a "RoC-centric" view on international affairs, nor does it wish to engage in a partnership that is one-sided as such.

There is a gap in the studies of RoC foreign policy that has created this overreliance on the Cyprus problem. Consequently, we must begin looking beyond the conflict's confines. This chapter specifically focuses on understanding RoC-EU relations and foreign policymaking across various sectors. It addresses the gap in the literature by using both structural and behavioural theory methods to explain how (a) the RoC's foreign policy is redefined by regional and international developments, and (b) the Cyprus problem impedes certain aspects within the RoC's foreign policy. Utilising in-depth interviews collected between 2017 and 2019, as well as participant observation data obtained in 2015, this chapter incorporates qualitative research methods to address the relations of Cyprus and the EU at the foreign policy level. Concurrently, it considers the question of whether the Republic has become more strategic (or *mature*) in its foreign policy and strategic objectives, in line with the overarching theme of this book.

The first part makes a foreign policy analysis broken down into three levels: (a) a systemic-level analysis of the RoC-EU relations and the background behind joining the Union; (b) a unit-level analysis, looking at the domestic and executive levels that shape policymaking; and (c) questions pertaining to policies, cooperation, and governance. The second part of this chapter looks at the areas in which the RoC's foreign policy has matured and the areas in which it has not yet matured in. The third part covers the RoC's role as a mediator or a bridge between the EU and the Eastern Mediterranean. The fourth part looks at some of the internal problems, with a table summarising all relevant findings pertaining to foreign policy maturity. Lastly, the conclusion offers a reflection of the overall argument of this paper: that the RoC's foreign policy has not fully matured because of the impediments posed by the country's long-lasting conflict.

Foreign Policy Analysis: Balancing and Constructing a Cypriot Agenda

Systemic-Level Analysis: RoC-EU

With the collapse of the Soviet Union, the RoC decisively entered negotiations with the European Economic Community (EEC). Prior to the accession and during the negotiations, the RoC retained its status as a member of the Non-Aligned Movement. The bloc originally set out to act as a balancing and mediating force between the Soviet Union and the United States (US), with its members never siding to either superpower. The power vacuum generated at the collapse of the USSR meant the US or the EU itself could jump in to dominate the international scene as a hegemon, as some accounts have suggested (Waltz 1979; Costalli 2009: 332). The Consul-General of the Republic of Cyprus to the Court of St James's, Theodoros Gotsis[2] also confirmed that the breakdown of the Soviet Union created new opportunities for Cyprus: "It is not by coincidence that we submitted our application for EU accession in 1990" (Gotsis 2019). Nevertheless, this had merely formed a multidimensional arena up for contestation, with countries experiencing multipolarity in international affairs, and with new opportunities up for grabs (Schweller 2014). The RoC's foreign policy was undergoing drastic changes in order to meet the requirements for EU membership.

Following the 2003 opening of checkpoints between the two communities and the subsequent referenda for reunification in 2004, the RoC eventually joined alongside the Czech Republic, Estonia, Hungary, Latvia, Lithuania, Malta, Poland, Slovakia, and Slovenia (Bindi 2010, 37). With new opportunities on the rise and its accession to the Union, RoC Non-Aligned membership formally came to an end in May 2004. Despite the failure of the 2004 Annan Plan, the RoC was able to proceed with its EU accession. Strictly speaking and based on EU governing treaties and international law, the entire island is considered a member-state. The RoC was, in effect, guaranteed EU membership prior the referenda (Loizides 2014, 241–242). That was because the regime in the north remains unrecognised by the rest of the international community to this day. Despite this acknowledgement from the EU, however, the RoC is

---

[2] Interview with the author (2019).

unable to assert its control over the rest of its designated territory in the northern part.

In establishing a Common Foreign and Security Policy (CFSP) following the Maastricht Treaty, the EU's foreign policy has largely focused on promoting international peace and security, stability, interdependence and economic prosperity for its members, consolidating liberal democracy, and upholding basic liberal rights and freedoms (Bindi 2010, 28–29). The CFSP was kept after the introduction of the Lisbon Treaty, but its scope expanded further. Foreign and security priorities also began focusing on international development, including sending neutral observers to monitor elections, and eventually created a European Security Strategy (ESS) and the European Defence Agency (EDA) by 2003 and 2004, respectively (Bindi 2010, 34, 37). Through the EU Near Abroad and the 2004 European Neighbourhood Policies, the Union has also focused on enlargement and getting involved in regional politics, including the Eastern Mediterranean and the Middle East (Kreutz 2015, 204, 208). This led to the European Commission employing the CFSP as a tool to justify intervention via civilian and military means in the delivery of humanitarian aid (Orbie et al. 2014, 161).

At the same time, these policies have led to a stronger political union throughout the years. This is an important transformation that has embraced a stronger integration than the EU's predecessor—the EEC. Even so, national sovereignty is by no means diminished. Member-states still have an equal say in EU bodies such as the Council of Ministers, and they can effectively veto decisions, due to the Council being a body whose authority is derived by consensus (Smeets 2016, 24). Based on this premise, the RoC joined a supranational bloc that has a liberal worldview on matters such as regional stability and security, among others. The way the RoC behaves within the EU, however, is an entirely different matter.

Unit-Level Analysis: Inside RoC Policymaking

The chief executioner and decision-maker over matters of foreign policy is the President of the Republic. At the moment of writing, this office is occupied by Nicos Anastasiades, who currently serves in his second term since 2018. The second-in-command is the foreign minister, up to January 2022 Dr Nikos Christodoulides. During different presidencies, the approach to foreign policy and diplomacy had been a dependent variable. This means that foreign policy would shift depending, to some extent, on the approach taken by its key practitioners.

Under the leadership of Demetris Christofias, AKEL (Progressive Party for the Working People) and the executive branch of government often dependent on previous tactics as set by the predecessor,[3] when dealing with the EU. This is because Christofia's AKEL was in a coalition government with DIKO (Democratic Party). Upon winning the 2008 presidential elections, however, Christofias had an unclear policy towards the EU. This was equally reflected in AKEL's party documents, which made little to no reference to anything else beyond the Cyprus problem (Katsourides 2014, 649). On the other hand, DISY[4] (Democratic Rally) has had a better structured policy towards the EU, particularly because it was the party that negotiated the accession deal between 1993 and 2003 (Katsourides 2014, 650–651). This should not be taken out of context, however. Despite the internal dynamics of party politics, the systemic conditions are the real prerequisites that transform state behaviour. When it comes to policy application, for instance, the current minister of foreign affairs has emphasised Cyprus's geopolitical role in the Eastern Mediterranean. During a scheduled interview[5] at the Ministry of Foreign Affairs in June 2018, Christodoulides explained the need to look for a more modernised structure. He explained that recent changes have only taken place in the last five years.

Policies as such had not been developed nor implemented in the past. With each successive government and with each geopolitical change, the way actors respond to their surroundings changes. As a result, RoC foreign policy has been undergoing changes. These changes usually depend on the unravelling events that shape the RoC's state behaviour, both domestically, as well as externally. The very fact that the RoC has had an inconsistent and unclear policy in previous years was revealed after its accession to the EU. In this case, the behaviour of the executive

---

[3] This refers to the Tassos Papadopoulos government. This government was responsible for finalising EU accession negotiations.

[4] The party supporting the current President and its former leader, Mr Nicos Anastasiades.

[5] Colleague Alexandros Zachariades was the primary researcher and interviewer during our visit to the Ministry. The file of the recorded interview belongs to Zachariades, who has kindly permitted the use of the material for the purpose of this paper.

branch of government would be inconsistent with that of their predecessors. However, this is not due to ideological reasons. Rather, this is down to the limitations the Cypriot state is exposed to.

Even so, an important question that has not been addressed properly is how we assess the RoC's foreign policy. Whilst internal dynamics may be relevant to policymaking, it is important to understand the RoC's foreign policy at a systemic level, not least due to existing systemic structures, but also the ontological dynamics that generate anxiety and trigger a policy response to such anxiety (Taliaferro et al. 2009, 35; Schweller 2009, 249; Rumelili 2020, 258). This is because leaders respond to events taking place at the international level. This, as a result, prompts them to act upon these challenges and engage in policymaking, by distinguishing between both the material and normative factors that shape foreign policy (Rumelili 2015; Lobell 2009, 42–43). Specifically, when looking at the EU and Cyprus, what are the main factors that contribute to an appropriate foreign policy analysis? This is one of the main questions we must begin addressing to understand how and why the state itself behaves in certain ways.

Even when actors compete for office, each winning entity has to abide by a set of international norms, treaties, and other agreements. For instance, the RoC follows several security-related treaties, in line with official EU policy. Such treaties include the Charter of Fundamental Rights of the European Union (EUR-Lex 2019). Nonetheless, treaties alone do not define a state's foreign policy. To analyse the RoC foreign policy better, we must turn to current affairs, the existing application of said treaties, and even theory.

Policy, Cooperation, and Governance

The RoC policymaking agenda is balanced in order to preserve RoC interests against external threats. For example, some EU Council decisions are only reached with a consensus, rather than simple majority or any other ruling. As previously mentioned, all member-states, including Cyprus, have *de facto veto* powers in key political decisions. Whilst EU primary law dictates that EU legislation is superior to domestic law, member-states still preserve their autonomy and sovereignty within the bloc (Avbelj 2011, 753). In fact, cooperation within the EU is voluntary. Both in theory and in practice, states can take decisions against the bloc, and sometimes, they face repercussions (Avbelj 2011, 746). At the same time, however, cooperation has benefits that can help boost a member-state's image and "soft" power on the international scene. For example, the RoC, alongside other member-states, has often exercised its veto to delay or block further talks for Turkish accession to the bloc (Suvarierol 2003, 57; Kerr-Lindsay 2007, 75). This is a good illustration of how the RoC can promote its own self-interest against Turkey through the use of institutions (Steele 2008, 4, 26; Mearsheimer 1995, 7).

Regarding the lead up to RoC accession to the EU, the pursued discourse and language employed by both Cypriot communities were framed following a niche security narrative, thus securitised, in order to project each other as an existential threat (Adamides 2020; Buzan et al. 1998, 5, 23–24). The reaction of both the Greek-Cypriot and Turkish-Cypriot communities to the negotiation process up until 2004, as well as the social relations that emerged as a result had contributed to the state itself behaving in certain ways (Jackson and Sorensen 2007, 162). Certain "myths" and incorrect claims regarding the EU *acquis communautaire* reduced the scope for settling the conflict, for instance. At the same time, each leadership (both in the RoC as well as in the self-proclaimed "Turkish Republic of Northern Cyprus – TRNC") misinformed the wider public on the existing practices and policies in the EU (Tocci 2004, 162). Tocci describes this rather well:

> Between 1993 and 2001, the presentation of costs and benefits of EU membership in Cyprus was frequently based on misinformation about the EU or about existing practices within the Union. The gains to the Greek Cypriots were presented as political and security losses to the Turkish Cypriots, and as such reduced the incentives of both leaderships to reach an agreement before membership.

The misinformation constructed conflicting identities, disincentivising each respective community from further engaging in the peace process. By bringing forth these questions, each community effectively framed the other as a security concern (Huysmans 2007, 376–377; Neumann 1996; Gecas 1982). However, in recent years, EU policies are much more accessible and widely available in the public domain. There is better information as to what the EU stands for. Similarly, the state is more vested in following EU policy.

In this regard, the RoC has placed emphasis on constructing its foreign policy via EU institutions, especially in the fields of economic and political security. Institutional identity in this sense is particularly strong. Former RoC foreign minister, Nikos Christodoulides, for example, tried to incorporate new institutional approaches as such. Christodoulides explained that the real drivers behind any developments on the Cyprus problem always have to do with international and regional politics, thus the RoC should turn towards addressing these developments by abandoning a "monothematic" foreign policy (Christodoulides 2018).

In utilising an appropriate framework to explain the development of the RoC foreign policy, we need to consider different approaches. The key lies somewhere between turning from what is known as an *institutional understanding of a constructed identity*, down to breaking it up by changing the *physical and materialistic nature* of RoC foreign policy. As such, the RoC foreign policy is receptive of the international systemic changes. Simultaneously, however, identity-related questions matter. The combination of both themes might be a useful addition when assessing the RoC's foreign relations with the EU and its member-states post the 2004 accession.

Addressing New Priorities Against (Im)maturity

Relations Within the EU

Since 2004, the RoC has been on the path of revolutionising its foreign policy. Progress has been made in key areas, including technology, trade, and as of lately, security cooperation and energy. For instance, its participation in the Permanent Structured Cooperation (PeSCo) project is a "national priority" in the context of the RoC's commitment towards the CFSP (Efstathiou 2019b, 3). In addition, the RoC ranks low on the Statelessness Index compared to other EU members, making it among the only four members of the bloc that have an underdeveloped policy on asylum seekers. As the Index reads, "Cyprus is not state party to any of the four core statelessness conventions, being one of only four European Union member states yet to accede to the 1954 Convention on the Status of Stateless Persons" (UNHCR Cyprus 2019). These policies reflect an obsolete and incompatible set of mechanisms that does not fall in line with EU priorities. On the contrary, these policies reflect the priorities that sit on the RoC foreign policy agenda. The crude reality is that sometimes, these priorities are incompatible with the EU's agenda, reflecting that the RoC's agenda may focus on safeguarding its own interests first above those of the Union. Even so, the fact that the RoC sets the agenda to focus on matters revolving around security and energy cooperation is equally beneficial to the EU (Adamides and Christou 2015, 184).

Relations Outside the EU

Prior to the collapse of the USSR and joining the EU bloc, its Non-Aligned status designated uncertainty over its foreign relations. The RoC is now seen as an economic hub, bridging the East and West. Russia is a notable investor contributing to Foreign Direct Investment (FDI), recently followed by others such as the US, Asia, and Eastern Mediterranean and Gulf countries. Between 2004 and 2017, the RoC had a net flow of FDI of US$ 1,118.84 million (World Bank 2019), ranking 27th on CIA World Factbook figures[6] (CIA World Factbook 2019).

It is generally assumed that the EU as a bloc largely abides by pro-Western liberal democratic ideals and policies (Smith 2011, 144, 153). Liberalism and theories on liberal democratic concepts such as Michael Doyle's Democratic Peace Theory assume that liberal states do not wage war on other liberal states, but they will move aggressively against illiberal entities in order to export their liberal values to them (Doyle 1983, 324–326).

The RoC does not quite abide by that. Even after the dissolution of the USSR and post-EU accession, the country maintains good financial relations with Russia. Relations have been so good, that Nicosia has refused to turn against Russia diplomatically, when in fact other EU leaders condemned Russia for its interventionist actions. These are issues of "contestation and geopolitical interests" that pre-existed the collapse of the USSR, with the RoC still striking a balance between the East and the West (Gotsis 2019). For example, following the 2018 Salisbury nerve gas poisoning of former Russian agent in the UK Sergei Skripal and his daughter Yulia, the RoC was one of the very few EU member-states that did not condemn the attack. Where over 20 western states expelled Russian diplomats from their countries in protest, the RoC was among the eight EU member-states that refused to proceed with such a measure (Borger et al. 2018).

---

[6] The CIA database differs, showing that the 31st December estimate for the year 2018 was at $179,800,000,000.

Furthermore, the RoC foreign policy on migration and visa also makes it attractive for investors who wish to buy off a European passport. Until recently and before the corruption and passport scandal of August and October 2020, RoC legislation dictated that foreign nationals making a sizeable contribution or investment in real estate can acquire RoC citizenship, which posed a sizeable problem not only for foreign and bloc relations, but also for domestic politics, leading to the resignation of former Speaker of the House and MP Demetris Syllouris (Al Jazeera Investigative Unit 2020). Despite generating some public revenue, the RoC's approach towards passport policy was criticised by the European Union, in multiple occasions preceding and during the unravelling of the scandal, as blindly handing out rights and European citizenship to foreign oligarchs. The same policy is similarly followed by countries like Malta, that has also faced criticism regarding this (Psyllides 2019). Such policies are not consistent with current EU policies on citizenship.

The Conflict

The *de facto* division was still in place. This has consumed much of the RoC's foreign policy. Despite promises that the RoC would make sure the island would resolve its decades-long dispute, this latter requirement was never met. The failure of the Annan Plan[7] reflects this rather well. The country still joined the EU, with the bloc guaranteeing that it would begin lifting certain sanctions against the illegitimate, self-proclaimed "TRNC"—a regime that is only recognised by Turkey (Skoutaris 2011, 3). Among the objections on the RoC's side were security-related concerns and the issue of resettlement of displaced persons and property (Tocci 2004, 156). These prevented a sound settlement on the dispute. On the other hand, EU membership under Article 6.1 automatically provides security guarantees, securing basic liberties, human rights, and the rule of law (Tocci 2004, 156).

Does the RoC Match Its Foreign Policy Objectives?

The answer to such a question is far from simple. Despite the state being able to assert power via the EU, the RoC is still struggling to overcome its

---

[7] Named after the UN Secretary General Kofi Annan

ethnic conflict. It has also not been able to meet some of its EU partners' objectives in terms of transnational issues such as migration. However, the country is still exercising an agenda that is beneficial to the EU as a whole. This helps the RoC match other objectives, particularly in the energy-defence-security nexus. So, what makes the RoC a reliable partner? The answer might be in its status as a mediator between the EU and the Eastern Mediterranean.

Stuck in the Middle: The RoC as a Mediator Between Its Neighbours and the EU

The RoC's geostrategic location gives it an edge over matters that concern the regional relations between the EU and the Eastern Mediterranean. The RoC has constantly addressed the importance of its role as a mediator, by projecting such ideas on the rest of the EU bloc. As such, it has been able to help coordinate high level summits between the EU and the Arab world, with the example of the February 2019 League of the Arab States (LAS)-EU Leaders Summit at Sharm El-Sheikh in Egypt (Cyprus Presidency 2019). One of the main objectives of the Summit, as part of the CFSP, has been to focus on tackling regional instability through economic, foreign, and regional defence cooperation (European Union External Action 2019).

Before the LAS-EU summit, another key event took place in the same month. The 5th Summit of the Southern European Countries (known as South EU Summit) took place in Nicosia, with a focus on migration, energy, and the future of the EU (Alsaafin 2019). These regional collaborations between the RoC and its neighbours are important for key foreign policy objectives in the region. According to Gotsis, the way the RoC foreign policy has recently evolved is important in emphasising RoC participation in these summits. His pivotal role as the RoC's negotiator and representative in Brussels helped bring forth a stronger image for the RoC. "We have to show them that we really mean business", said the diplomat during his interview, in reference to how the RoC can use its access to EU to tackle "Turkish intransigence" (Gotsis 2019).

What is more, Minister Christodoulides has differentiated between the "low politics" and "high politics" the Republic pursues. "Lower" policy refers to issues such as healthcare, the environment, and cultural heritage that are of general interest to all neighbouring states. This is one of the strategies the RoC employs in order to attract the interest of its neighbours. On the other hand, "higher" politics are focused on defence, national security, negotiations, and the Cyprus problem. In order for "higher" politics to be taken seriously, governments need to "build bridges with the people", according to Christodoulides. The minister also broke down the regional foreign policy the RoC pursues between the EU and its neighbours:

> We are focusing on three pillars within our foreign policy. The first one is our immediate neighbourhood, where we believe we have an added value to contribute, particularly when we consider how the neighbouring states approach us, and the role we can play inside the European Union. This is a theoretical approach. It is the product of specific discussions and policies we have followed. The second pillar in our foreign policy is – and this is directly related to the first one – the European Union. We acceded to the European Union, as it is known in Cyprus, to resolve the Cyprus problem [...]

These two pillars are particularly important. They reflect an old foreign policy that had exceedingly prioritised the conflict. What the minister subsequently shared, however, is rather significant:

> For many years, however, it had not occurred to us that we could play a significant role within the European Union, at least to the degree we can actually be a major player [...] Considering our first foreign policy pillar and especially in the last five years, we have gradually reached the point where when major discussions concern the region [EU and Eastern Mediterranean relations], they turn to us for our own input [...] Unfortunately, for many years, our foreign policy has been rather monothematic. As I have been a diplomat for this Ministry as well, I could see we were under the false impression that the entire world revolved around the Cyprus problem [...] This has certainly changed in the last five years. Of course, the Cyprus problem is still our number one priority. However, if we want to accomplish our end goals and to resolve the problem, we also focus on other key issues that also interest everyone else [...].

This indeed reflects the overarching argument presented throughout this chapter. The fact that the minister himself, a former academic and career diplomat, is well-aware of this issue is noteworthy. He then proceeded to talk about the last foreign policy pillar:

The third pillar is the five Permanent Members of the United Nations Security Council [...] With the five Permanent Members we would discuss the Cyprus problem about 90% of the time. At some point when I was a diplomat, I happened to meet with foreign ministers representing the Permanent Members, and our sole conversation topic would revolve around the Cyprus problem. This is not the case anymore. We nowadays talk about the Middle East, energy-related issues, we talk about the European Union – this is a rather pleasant feeling to embrace and witness, because through these discussions, we also highlight our own significance and expertise, and when the Cyprus problem becomes part of the conversation, they will pay closer attention to what you have to say.

It becomes apparent, then, that agency has been instrumental in guiding RoC foreign policy in the Eastern Mediterranean. Agency, however, is responsive to structures. States behave in certain ways in order to address the changing structures they find themselves in (Rose 1998, 144, 146; Steele 2008, 15, 18). For this, the most important "higher" politics within foreign policy is examined in more detail below.

The Geopolitics of Energy

The discovery of hydrocarbons in the region has created new dynamics that are beneficial to both the RoC, as well as to other EU memberstates. With the RoC declaring its Exclusive Economic Zone (EEZ) as early as 2004 (CNA News Service 2019), natural gas discoveries within its EEZ were made by giants such as US-owned Noble Energy in the bloc 12 in 2011 (Aphrodite field), Italian ENI's findings in bloc 6 in 2018 (Calypso field), and Exxon Mobil's discovery in bloc 10 (Glafkos field) earlier in 2019 (Petrikkos 2019). Georgios Lakkotrypis, former Minister of Energy, Commerce, Industry and Tourism has also commented in an interview at the 2018 South EU Summit on how the findings are so important that can help transform EU and regional Mediterranean security, peace, and stability. He specifically explained that "geopolitics is an important element" of what the RoC is concerned with when it comes to the extraction of hydrocarbons and the trilateral meetings (South EU Summit 2018). This is also in line with the overall policy the administration holds regarding energy since 2013 (AJC Transatlantic Institute 2018).

Scholarship and research in this field have also increased, evident in the particular interest the RoC has posed to researchers and policy makers (Adamides and Christou 2013, 2015; Pedi and Kouskouvelis 2019; Tziarras 2018, 2019). The Political Affairs Counsellor at the High Commission of the RoC to the Court of St James's, Andreas Eliades,[8] commented on the uniqueness of the opportunity the discovery provides for the RoC:

> The Turkish system is obsolete. Indeed, Cyprus is geographically close to Turkey, but it would take billions to modernise Turkey itself for such a system to be installed. Besides, Turkey is a non-EU member, the security implications are risky, and thus Turkey is unreliable for the EU [...] On the other hand, the Aphrodite field within Cyprus's EEZ is much more appealing to companies and there are serious considerations for investment due to the presence of hydrocarbons. Expansion as such in the sea has led to further developments on the land: investment in other companies, ports, and the economy overall.

In terms of the economy more specifically, Consul-General Gotsis also commented on current regional affairs. The discovery of hydrocarbons and crises like "the Arab Spring turning winter" were an opportunity for the RoC to utilise "high politics", bringing forth a regional balance:

> The previous and current 5-year term of the Presidency of Nicos Anastasiades also focuses on Arab-Gulf relations. Within the first year of Nicos Christodoulides' term as foreign minister, for example, he visited most countries in the Gulf [...] Last year, in 2018, the minister was the first Republic of Cyprus minister visiting Riyadh.

These symbolisms and steps the RoC has taken are part of a greater foreign policy plan that contributes to *regional integration*, combating instability and regional disintegration (Diez 2019; Gotsis 2019; Tziarras 2018). Such agreements and deals, however, depend on the initiative of the elite—the governments themselves, as the Consul-General explained. This is equally reflected in the current trilateral partnerships with fellow EU member-state Greece and other countries in the Eastern Mediterranean. These partnerships have been an important steppingstone in securing further cooperation and balancing against potential threats (Tziarras 2016, 418). The minister also acknowledged that "the issue of energy five years ago was a catalyst for engaging in conversation at

---

[8] Interview with the author (2017).

a regional level – the same way we began participating in trilateral partnerships with the neighbouring countries".[9] As more research and more interest are developed on the geopolitical implications in the region, current developments might grow even more beneficial to RoC-EU relations.

Defence and Its Problems

On the other hand, new energy prospects bring forth new security challenges. In recent years, the RoC has become more committed to critical infrastructure protection, and so are all EU members (Commission of the European Communities 2006). In 2014, the RoC hosted the 9th International Conference on Critical Information Infrastructures Security (Panayiotou et al. 2016) with President Anastasiades investing in partnerships between the state-funded University of Cyprus and universities like Imperial College London. The aim of these partnerships has been to work on further improving the security and defence infrastructure (Scheuber 2017).

Moreover, the prospects within PeSCo have allowed a stronger Cypriot presence and actions in Common Security and Defence Policy (CSDP) practices. The RoC has taken part in missions abroad, together with EU partners through the EU Battlegroups, the EDA, and others (Ministry of Foreign Affairs, Republic of Cyprus 2010). Even though the RoC is not a NATO member, PeSCo has provided a framework in which Nicosia can elevate its status by participating in defence and security-related tasks that otherwise would have not been within reach (Wolfstädter and Kreilinger 2017, 7; Ertürk 2018, 7).

During his interview, Political Affairs Counsellor Eliades explained that "the last 2-3 years, because of current affairs (ISIS, our collaboration with our neighbours, the presence of other countries near our territory), the paradigm for Cyprus has shifted to this field of security". This shows that defence and security as part of the RoC's foreign policy is dependent on external factors that prompt the leadership to take precautionary measures. In line with this, the Consul-General also commented on the Turkish challenges posed by the state-owned seismographic exploration

---

[9] This specifically refers to Egypt, Lebanon, and Israel.

vessel RV Barbaros Hayreddin Paşa violating Cypriot EEZ: "We are determined not to follow Turkey down a path of gunboat diplomacy" (Gotsis 2019).

A more technical and insightful analysis has paved the way for understanding the RoC foreign and defence policies within the EU better. According to Yvonni-Stefania Efstathiou,[10] Defence and Military Analyst at the International Institute for Strategic Studies (IISS) DMAP division, the RoC and fellow European member-states like France have upgraded their bilateral relations over defence. Although the RoC is not a superpower, stronger ties have led to an upgraded infrastructure over naval and airspace partnerships (Efstathiou 2019a). France also wishes to develop vessels facilities on the island, whilst also focusing on enhancing its cybersecurity practices with Greece (IISS 2019, 96). This is evident in how the RoC has been conducting joint military exercises with other EU member-states as part of the PesCo project. For example, in 2019, it completed a naval exercise known as "CYP/FRA-01/2019" (National Guard General Staff of Cyprus 2019). These exercises with France have been taking place since 2016. A memorandum between the two countries was signed in July 2018, but its contents have not been made public yet (Efstathiou 2019a).

At the same time, Nicosia-Berlin relations have also improved, evident in direct one-to-one meetings at the ministerial level, between the respective ministers of defence. Discussions over PeSCo and the EU's CFSP have allowed the RoC to proactively voice its demands and concerns over defence (Efstathiou 2019b). Specifically, Efstathiou explained:

> We have seen that most discussion have been around PeSCo rather than bilateral relations. Germany has been congratulating Cyprus for being very active within the framework [...] [Cyprus] ranks 7th in terms of how many projects it has signed up [for], and we also see that Cyprus starts feeling a bit more comfortable in its bilateral relations to ask for things in the defence field. So, we know that the [Cypriot] Minister had a conversation with the German Defence Minister on the Leopards to Turkey. They want Germany to have a role, maybe restrict the use of the Leopard tank, at least within Cypriot soil [...] We don't know what will come out of it, but it's the first time Cyprus seems to be voicing some demands in the area of defence.

---

[10] Interview with the author (2019).

It seems that the RoC has gained a better understanding of its geopolitical situation and its place within the EU and the Middle East. The fact that the state is able to push for containing its security concerns through the EU and diplomacy is significant. As the RoC cultivates strong foreign and defence relations, it also fulfils its requirements towards the CSDP. The national GDP has been growing, from 19.2bn USD in 2017 to 20.2bn USD in 2018. Similarly, defence expenditure rose from 352 m EUR in 2018 to 357 m EUR in 2019 (IISS 2019, 96). Although these figures are short compared to other EU members, the RoC has prioritised boosting its defence capabilities in order to be taken more seriously in foreign policy circles. At first glance, this seems to be working. Even so, we need to look elsewhere to determine the extent to which RoC-EU relations have truly matured.

EU COOPERATION AND THE CYPRUS PROBLEM: INTERNAL PROBLEMS

Considering how the RoC has contributed to EU relations in recent years, it would be unjust to vaguely declare that RoC foreign policy is immature and lacks strategy. In terms of security-related questions within the EU, Nicosia has significantly improved in multiple key areas. It has complied with joint military exercises in the region, contributing significantly to EU defence strategy. According to the PesCo project, the RoC is among the top 10 member-states that has followed the Lisbon Treaty closely (Efstathiou 2019a).

Despite the ongoing improvements within the foreign policy nexus, the RoC foreign policy is seriously hindered by the continuation of the status quo. Some technical issues pertaining to problems within the administration lie in infrastructural developments within the civil service, and specifically the Ministry of Foreign Affairs.

The Bureaucratic Graveyard: Observations in Executing RoC Diplomacy

Despite the rise of new security dynamics since 2004, the RoC has only begun addressing its security and policy infrastructures very recently. Unfortunately, it seems there are gaps that deter further maturity at a diplomatic level. This is particularly dangerous, as it concerns the current apparatus of the Ministry of Foreign Affairs. Although it is systemic reasons that primarily shape and guide the RoC foreign policy, the bureaucratic concerns must be also addressed. Neglecting this aspect may impact the way the RoC is portrayed to its EU and regional partners.

During an interview with a RoC diplomatic source who wished to remain anonymous, concerns that go beyond the traditional security challenges presented by the Cyprus problem were mentioned. The interviewee specifically commented on foreign and security policy trends within the EU bloc that the RoC should abide by:

> Leaving the Turkish threat aside, our infrastructure has not adapted to new threats. Look at the current state of our financial and cyber intelligence. None of that is being addressed. We had taken additional measures against terrorism, we had focused on the financial crisis which severely affected our banking institutions and supporting mechanisms, yet there is a lack of attention to security. The current mentality is to withhold discussion and to dismiss security altogether.

On the other hand, during an interview with Andreas Eliades, the RoC diplomat explained that "Cyprus has obligations towards its airspace and territorial blocks. It is part of its integrity to guarantee the security and the supply of energy, which makes up most of its critical infrastructure security" (Eliades 2017). An outdated infrastructure, however, may seriously inhibit the implementation of these policies. As an intern for the Ministry in 2015 I saw, for example, how it was impossible to send file attachments exceeding the size of 10 MB via email. Diplomats have confirmed that this has been recently resolved, yet it shows the need to take such issues more seriously.

In a public lecture organised in 2016, the High Commissioner of the RoC to the Court of Saint James's Euripides L. Evriviades delivered a speech on RoC-EU relations (Facebook 2016). The lecture focused on the pivotal role the RoC has been playing in bridging the EU and the Mediterranean, including the possibility of new partnerships and closer economic cooperation. As I was the main organiser and host of the event, my responsibility laid with promoting, structuring the event, as well as providing all the relevant logistics to ensure the delivery of the lecture. As an independent observer, I was able to see how RoC diplomats take their role seriously in promoting RoC-EU relations to the wider academic audience abroad. Working directly with the High Commissioner's office revealed the importance of communications and public relations in diplomacy.

Indeed, communications and public relations policies have been improving, something that has been taken seriously in RoC foreign policy circles. Thanks to initiatives put forward by diplomats such as Consul-General Gotsis and the Minister of Foreign Affairs, the electronic infrastructure of the civil service and elsewhere are undergoing changes. "We are currently setting up our new website and updating our social media accounts", the minister said (Christodoulides 2018). Gotsis has specifically referred to the need to modernise both the Ministry, but also its embassies around the world. By developing and improving electronic databases. In terms of diplomatic personnel and representatives both in the RoC and across the world, the Ministry is understaffed. Responding to a question on whether the current infrastructure and personnel numbers in the civil service are sufficient, Mr Gotsis emphasised the following:

> [With the accession to the EU] at a technocratic level, the Republic had to immediately fill up new positions, and to hire people for areas that we previously had no access to. Consequently, even by simply being present to different meetings, the shape and the face of the state itself changes. It engages [with policy] in greater depth, it has greater input [...] As per our work within the EU, it is known that we have general problems pertaining to understaffing in the civil service, because of the financial crisis and the periods we went through without hiring new people. Even so, states like Cyprus do not necessarily rely solely on numbers. It is about the state's ability of putting this low human capital into good use. This is dependent on the capacity of the state for effective organisation, and of course developing an electronic database and infrastructure.

In summary, the RoC exercises a hybrid foreign policy, in terms of maturity. Some policy objectives are balanced effectively against their targets. This reflects the reality of the situation. On the other hand, some elements have not been addressed at all. Table 4.1 demonstrates the RoC foreign policy maturity levels in relation to the EU. It looks at three key areas where the RoC foreign policy has: (a) matured, thus meeting its objectives; (b) begun addressing its objectives, thus in the process of maturation; (c) not matured, thus there is a need for stronger commitment and better policy development.

Table 4.1 RoC Foreign Policy Maturity Levels vis-à-vis the EU

Achieved maturity	On the road to maturity	Not matured
Energy and economic cooperation	Communications Online presence	Migration policies Cybersecurity and cyber intelligence
Security (external threats, e.g., Turkey)	Defence (CSDP, PeSCo, EU treaties)	Bureaucracy and e-databases
	Healthcare, environment, cultural heritage	Civil service

Conclusion: Restoring Balance

The RoC has shown great determination in restoring balance and maintaining good relations with the EU. It has effectively boosted its foreign policy by utilising all relevant EU frameworks, as well as acting as an important mediator and partner in the Eastern Mediterranean. With new prospects for defence, energy, and the economy, the RoC foreign policy will continue being responsive to the unravelling geopolitical conditions that the state is part of. This constructs an image that is beneficial for the RoC decision-makers in their day-to-day business with the EU.

Despite its accomplishments, RoC-EU relations suffer from adaptability and infrastructural issues. It seems that the focus should be on improving several protocols, in order to make the RoC foreign policy compatible with that of other EU member-states. The gradual standardisation of diplomatic training and reforming of the Ministry of Foreign Affairs, as seen through the interviews, are two important pillars. Simultaneously, developing a better electronic and security infrastructure would enhance the RoC's status and adaptability within its regional security domain. These issues are well-known to RoC state officials, and this is in itself very positive. These approaches, once addressed appropriately, would help incorporate a better and more effective way of developing a stronger foreign policy. However, a serious impediment is the ongoing status quo in the island. As already mentioned, this impacts both domestic and external politics. The Republic is aware that the long-lasting dispute has exhausted its foreign policy agenda, which is the main reason for branching out to other fields. The endgame is for the RoC to be seen as a serious, reliable partner. Despite the growth of the RoC policy, the conflict still haunts and inhibits maturity in foreign policy. If this issue is left unanswered, the RoC will be stuck between appearing as a reliable regional partner and remaining an internally problematic EU member-state.

References

Interviews

Christodoulides, Nicos. 2018. "Minister of Foreign Affairs of the Republic of Cyprus." Nicosia, June 17. Primary interviewer was Alexandros Zachariades. Interview was kindly shared with the author.

Eliades, Andreas. 2017. "Political Affairs Counsellor to the High Commission of the Republic of Cyprus to the Court of St James's of the United Kingdom of Great Britain and Northern Ireland." London, March 1. Interview in the possession of the author.

Efstathiou, Yvonni-Stefania. 2019a. "Defence and Military Analyst (DMAP), International Institute for Strategic Studies." London, March 18. Interview in the possession of the author.

Gotsis, Theodoros. 2019. "Consul-General to the High Commission of the Republic of Cyprus to the Court of St James's of the United Kingdom of Great Britain and Northern Ireland." London, February 27. Interview in the possession of the author.

Bibliography

Adamides, Constantinos. 2020. *Securitization and Desecuritization Processes in Protracted Conflicts: The Case of Cyprus*. Cham: Palgrave Macmillan.

Adamides, Constantinos, and Costas M. Constantinou. 2012. "Comfortable Conflict and (Il)liberal Peace in Cyprus." In *Hybrid Forms of Peace: From Everyday Agency to Post-Liberalism*, edited by Oliver P. Richmond and Audra Mitchell. Basingstoke: Palgrave Macmillan.

Adamides, Constantinos, and Odysseas Christou. 2013. "Energy Securitization and Desecuritization in the New Middle East." *Security Dialogue* 44 (5–6): 507–522.

Adamides, Constantinos, and Odysseas Christou. 2015. "Energy Security and the Transformation of Regional Securitization Relations in the Eastern Mediterranean." In *Societies in Transition: The Social Implications of Economic, Political and Security Transformations*, edited by Savvas Katsikides and Pavlos Koktsidis, 189–206. New York: Springer.

AJC Transatlantic Institute. 2018. "The Geopolitical Role of Cyprus in the Eastern Mediterranean: Regional Stability, Energy Security and Counterterrorism." https://transatlanticinstitute.org/event/geopolitical-role-cyprus-eastern-mediterraneanregional-stability-energy-security-and-0. Accessed 27 March 2019.

Al Jazeera Investigative Unit. 2020. Cypriot Parliament Speaker Quits After Passport Scheme Scandal. https://www.aljazeera.com/news/2020/10/15/cyprus-house-speaker-resigns-following-al-jazeera-investigation. Accessed 20 March 2021.

Alsaafin, Linah. 2019. "What to Expect from the 2019 South EU Summit." *Al Jazeera*, January 29.

Attalides, Michalis. 1979. *Cyprus, Nationalism and International Politics*. New York: St Martin's Press.

Avbelj, Matej. 2011. "Supremacy or Primacy of the EU Law—(Why) Does it Matter?" *European Law Journal* 17 (6): 744–763.

Bailes, Alyson JK, and Baldur Thorhallsson. 2013. Instrumentalizing the European Union in Small State Strategies. *Journal of European Integration* 35 (2): 99–115. https://doi.org/10.1080/07036337.2012.689828.

Bindi, Federica. 2010. "European Union Foreign Policy: A Historical Overview." In *The Foreign Policy of the European Union: Assessing Europe's Role in the World*, edited by Federica Bindi, 13–40. Washington, DC: Brookings Institution Press.

Borger, Julian, Patrick Wintour, and Heather Stewart. 2018. "Western Allies Expel Scores of Russian Diplomats over Skripal Attack." *The Guardian*, March 27.

Buzan, Barry, Ole Waever, and Jaap de Wilde. 1998. *Security: A New Framework for Analysis*. Boulder, CO: Lynne Rienner Publishers, Inc.

CIA World Factbook. 2019. Country Comparison – Stock of Foreign Direct Investment – Abroad. https://www.cia.gov/library/publications/the-world-factbook/rankorder/2199rank.html. Accessed 19 February 2019.

CNA News Service. 2019. "Cyprus Protests Turkish Provocations in EEZ to UNSG." *Cyprus Mail*, January 3.

Commission of the European Communities. 2006. "COM(2006) 786 – Communication from the Commission on a European Programme for Critical Infrastructure Protection." http://eur-lex.europa.eu/legal-content/EN/TXT/PDF/?uri=CELEX:52006DC0786&from=EN. Accessed 14 March 2019.

Constantinou, Costas M. 2015. "In Pursuit of Crisis Diplomacy." *The Hague Journal of Diplomacy* 10 (1): 29–34.

Costalli, Stefano. 2009. "Power over to the Sea: The Relevance of Neoclassical Realism to Euro-Mediterranean Relations." *Mediterranean Politics* 14 (3): 323–342.

Coufoudakis, Van. 2006. *Cyprus: A Contemporary Problem in Historical Perspective*. Minneapolis, MN: Minnesota Mediterranean and East European Monographs, University of Minnesota.

Cyprus Presidency. 2019. "Statement by the President of the Republic at the 1st EU-Arab League Summit." Greek edition: Κυπριακή Δημοκρατία – Πρόεδρος της Δημοκρατίας. 2019. Παρέμβαση του Προέδρου της Δημοκρατίας στην 1η Σύνοδο Κορυφής ΕΕ–Αραβικού Συνδέσμου. https://presidency.gov.cy/international-presence/2019/02/25/παρέμβαση-του-προέδρου-της-δημοκρατίας-στην-1η-σύνοδο-κορυφής-εε-αραβικού-συνδέσμου/. Accessed 26 February 2019.

Dağlı, İlke. 2017. "The Cyprus Problem: Why Solve a Comfortable Conflict?" https://www.oxfordresearchgroup.org.uk/blog/the-cyprus-problem-why-solve-a-comfortable-conflict. Accessed 19 February 2019.

Diez, Thomas. 2019. "Transforming Identity in International Society: The Potential and Failure of European Integration." *Comparative European Politics.* https://doi.org/10.1057/s41295-019-00170-9.

Doyle, Michael W. 1983. "Kant, Liberal Legacies, and Foreign Affairs Part 2." *Philosophy and Public Affairs* 12 (4): 323–353.

Economides, Spyros. 2005. The Europeanisation of Greek Foreign Policy. *West European Politics* 28 (2): 471–491. https://doi.org/10.1080/01402380500060528.

Efstathiou, Yvonni-Stefania. 2019b. *PeSCo: The Cyprus Perspective* – Policy Paper. Paris: Armament Industry European Research Group.

Ertürk, Ahmet C. 2018. *EU's PeSCo: A New Foreign Policy Instrument or the Same Old Story?* – Policy Paper Vol. 51. Istanbul: Global Political Trends Centre and Istanbul Kültür University.

EUR-Lex. 2019. "Treaties Currently in Force." https://eur-lex.europa.eu/collection/eu-law/treaties/treaties-force.html. Accessed 26 March 2019.

European Union External Action. 2019. "EU – Arab League Summit: End Conflicts in the Region Through Cooperation, Not Shortcuts." https://eeas.europa.eu/topics/common-foreign-security-policy-cfsp/58673/eu---arab-league-summit-end-conflicts-region-through-cooperation-not-shortcuts_en. Accessed 26 February 2019.

Facebook. 2016. "Event – No Island Is an Island: Cyprus, the EU and Eastern Mediterranean." https://www.facebook.com/events/591243447693404/. Accessed 17 February 2019.

Frazier, Derrick, and Robert Stewart-Ingersoll. 2010. "Regional Powers and Security: A Framework for Understanding Order Within Regional Security Complexes." *European Journal of International Relations* 16 (4): 731–753.

Gecas, Viktor. 1982. "The Self Concept." *Annual Review of Sociology* 8 (1): 1–33.

Gramer, Robbie, and Kavitha Surana. 2017. "Cracking the Cyprus Code." *Foreign Policy*, March 14.

Hannay, David. 2005. *Cyprus: The Search for a Solution.* London: I.B. Tauris.

Huysmans, Jef. 2007. "James Der Derian: The Unbearable Lightness of Theory." In *The Future of International Relations: Masters in the Making?*, edited by Iver B. Neumann and Ole Waever. London: Routledge.

IISS. 2019. "Chapter Four: Europe." In *The Military Balance 2019*, 66–165. London: International Institute for Strategic Studies.

Jackson, Robert, and Georg Sorensen. 2007. *Introduction to International Relations Theories and Approaches*. Oxford: Oxford University Press.

Katsourides, Yiannos. 2014. "Partisan Responses to the European Union in Cyprus." *Journal of European Integration* 36 (7): 641–658.

Kerr-Lindsay, James. 2005. *EU Accession and UN Peacemaking in Cyprus*. Basingstoke: Palgrave Macmillan.

Kerr-Lindsay, James. 2007. "The Policies of Greece and Cyprus Towards Turkey's EU Accession." *Turkish Studies* 8 (1): 71–83.

Kreutz, Joakim. 2015. "Human Rights, Geostrategy, and EU Foreign Policy, 1989-2008." *International Organisation* 69 (1): 195–217.

Lobell, Steven E. 2009. "Threat Assessment, the State, and Foreign Policy: A Neoclassical Realist Model." In *Neoclassical Realism, the State, and Foreign Policy*, edited by Steven E. Lobell, Norrin M. Ripsman, and Jeffrey W. Taliaferro, 42–74. Cambridge: Cambridge University Press.

Loizides, Neophytos. 2014. "Negotiated Settlements and Peace Referendums." *European Journal of Political Research* 53: 234–249. https://doi.org/10.1111/1475-6765.12043.

Mearsheimer, John J. 1995. "The False Promise of International Institutions." *International Security* 19 (3): 5–49.

Ministry of Foreign Affairs, Republic of Cyprus. 2010. "Common Foreign and Security Policy / Common Security and Defence Policy (CFSP / CSDP)." http://www.mfa.gov.cy/mfa/mfa2016.nsf/mfa25_en/mfa25_en. Accessed 19 February 2019.

Mitzen, Jennifer. 2006. Ontological Security in World Politics: State Identity and the Security Dilemma. *European Journal of International Relations* 12 (3): 341–370. https://doi.org/10.1177/1354066106067346.

National Guard General Staff of Cyprus. 2019. "Joint Passing Exercise (PASSEX) titled "CYP/FRA-01/2019" Between Cyprus Naval Forces and the French, La Fayette class, Frigate ACONIT F-713." http://www.army.gov.cy/en/announcements/details/event-712. Accessed 19 February 2019.

Neumann, Iver B. 1996. "Self and Other in International Relations." *European Journal of International Relations* 2 (2): 139–174.

Orbie, Jan, Peter Van Elsuwege, and Fabienne Bossuyt. 2014. "Humanitarian Aid as an Integral Part of the European Union's External Action: The Challenge of Reconciling Coherence and Independence." *Journal of Contingencies and Crisis Management* 22 (3): 158–165.

Panayiotou, Christos G., Giorgos Ellinas, Elias Kyriakides, and Marios M. Polycarpou. 2016. *Critical Information Infrastructures Security: 9th International Conference, CRITIS 2014 Limassol, Cyprus, October 13–15, 2014 Revised Selected Papers*. Basel: Springer International Publishing.

Pedi, Revecca, and Ilias Kouskouvelis. 2019. "Cyprus in the Eastern Mediterranean: A Small State Seeking for Status." In *The New Eastern Mediterranean: Theory, Politics and States in a Volatile Era*, edited by Spyridon N. Litsas, and Aristotle Tziampiris, 151-167. Cham: Springer.

Petrikkos, Petros. 2019. "Energy and Security in the Eastern Mediterranean." *Global Risk Insights*, March 26.

Psyllides, George. 2019. "EU Sees Crime Risks from Malta, Cyprus Schemes to Sell Passports." *Cyprus Mail*, January 21.

Rose, Gideon. 1998. "Neoclassical Realism and Theories of Foreign Policy." *World Politics* 51 (1): 144–172.

Rumelili, Bahar. 2015. Identity and Desecuritisation: The Pitfalls of Conflating Ontological and Physical Security. *Journal of International Relations and Development* 18 (1): 52–74. https://doi.org/10.1057/jird.2013.22.

Rumelili, Bahar. 2020. Integrating Anxiety into International Relations Theory: Hobbes Existentialism and Ontological Security. *International Theory* 12 (2): 257–272. https://doi.org/10.1017/S1752971920000093.

Scheuber, Andrew. 2017. "President of Cyprus Launches Critical Infrastructure Partnership." http://www3.imperial.ac.uk/newsandeventspggrp/imperialcollege/newssummary/news_17-3-2017-10-25-48. Accessed 17 March 2019.

Schweller, Randall L. 2008. *Unanswered Threats: Political Constraints on the Balance of Power*. Princeton and Oxford: Princeton University Press.

Schweller, Randall L. 2009. "Neoclassical Realism and State Mobilisation: Expansionist Ideology in the Age of Mass Politics." In *Neoclassical Realism, the State, and Foreign Policy*, edited by Steven E. Lobell, Norrin M. Ripsman, and Jeffrey W. Taliaferro, 227–250. Cambridge: Cambridge University Press.

Schweller, Randall L. 2014. *Maxwell's Demon and the Golder Apple: Global Discord in the New Millenium*. Baltimore: Johns Hopkins University Press.

Skoutaris, Nikos. 2011. *The Cyprus Issue: The Four Freedoms in a Member State Under Siege*. Oxford and Portland, OR: Hart Publishing.

Smeets, Sandrino. 2016. "Consensus and Isolation in the EU Council of Ministers." *Journal of European Integration* 38 (1): 23–39.

Smith, Michael E. 2011. "A Liberal Grand Strategy in a Realist World? Power, Purpose and the EU's Changing Global Role." *Journal of European Public Policy* 18 (2): 144–163.

South EU Summit. 2018. "Cyprus is Europe's Answer to Energy Security." https://www.southeusummit.com/europe/cyprus/cyprus-is-europes-answer-to-energy-security/. Accessed 20 April 2019.

Steele, Brent J. 2008. *Ontological Security in International Relations: Self-Identity and the IR State*. Abingdon: Routledge

Suvarierol, Semin. 2003. "The Cyprus Obstacle on Turkey's Role to Membership in the European Union." *Turkish Studies* 4 (1): 55–58.

Taliaferro, Jeffrey W., Steven E. Lobell, and Norrin M. Ripsman. 2009. "Introduction: Neoclassical Realism, the State, and Foreign Policy." In *Neoclassical Realism, the State, and Foreign Policy*, edited by Steven E. Lobell, Norrin M. Ripsman, and Jeffrey W. Taliaferro, 1–41. Cambridge: Cambridge University Press.

Tocci, Nathalie. 2004. *EU Accession Dynamics and Conflict Resolution: Catalysing Peace or Consolidating Partition in Cyprus?* Hampshire: Ashgate Publishing Limited.

Tziarras, Zenonas. 2016. "Israel-Cyprus-Greece: A 'Comfortable' Quasi-Alliance." *Mediterranean Politics* 21 (3): 407–427.

Tziarras, Zenonas. 2018. "The Eastern Mediterranean: Between Power Struggles and Regionalist Aspirations." *Re-imagining the Eastern Mediterranean Series: PCC Report*, 2. Nicosia: PRIO Cyprus Centre.

Tziarras, Zenonas. 2019. "Cyprus's Foreign Policy in the Eastern Mediterranean and the Trilateral Partnerships: A Neoclassical Realist Approach." In *The New Geopolitics of the Eastern Mediterranean: Trilateral Partnerships and Regional Security*, edited by Zenonas Tziarras, 53–72. Re-Imagining the Eastern Mediterranean Series. Nicosia: PRIO Cyprus Centre.

Tucker, Robert W. 1979. "America in Decline: The Foreign Policy of 'Maturity'." *Foreign Affairs* 58 (3): 449–484.

UNHCR Cyprus. 2019. "The Statelessness Index Now with Data on Cyprus." https://www.unhcr.org/cy/2019/02/12/the-statelessness-index-now-with-data-on-cyprus/. Accessed 15 February 2019.

Wendt, Alexander. 1992. "Anarchy is what States Make of It: The Social Construction of Power Politics." *International Organisation* 46 (2): 391–425.

Waltz, Kenneth N. 1979. *Theory of International Politics*. Long Grove, IL: Waveland Press, Inc.

Wolfstädter, Laura M., and Valentin Kreilinger. 2017. *European Integration Via Flexibility Tools: The Cases of EPPO and PESCO* – Policy Paper. Berlin: Jacques Delors Institute.

World Bank. 2019. "Foreign Direct Investment, Net Inflows (BoP, Current US$)." https://data.worldbank.org/indicator/BX.KLT.DINV.CD.WD?end=2017&start=2004. Accessed 19 February 2019.

Zachariades, Alexandros, and Petrikkos, Petros. 2020. "Balancing for Profit: The Republic of Cyprus' Grand Strategy in the Eastern Mediterranean Sea." *Cyprus Review* 32 (1): 89–136.

CHAPTER 5

The Republic of Cyprus and the US: A Revamped Relationship with Key Limitations

Alexandros Zachariades

INTRODUCTION

This chapter seeks to account for the relationship of the Republic of Cyprus (RoC) and the United States (US) since the former's accession to the European Union (EU) in 2004. In the pre-2004 period, the relationship between the RoC and the US was in many cases turbulent due to the island state's close links with the USSR and Russia and the view of many Cypriots that the US played a role in the events of July 1974 that led to the current division of the island. After the accession of the RoC to the EU relations gradually improved and in more recent years we have witnessed a revamped relationship. In view of this change, three crucial questions arise:

A. Zachariades (✉)
International Relations Department, London School of Economics and Political Science, London, UK
e-mail: a.zachariades@lse.ac.uk

i. What caused this rejuvenated relationship?
ii. What are the limits of this relationship?
iii. Is this the result of a mature foreign policy from the RoC's part?

The argument put forth in this chapter is that the current state of US-RoC relations is less of a product of a mature foreign policy strategy on the RoC's part. Instead, it is a result of regional developments in the Eastern Mediterranean and the US's response to those developments. Firstly, the region has witnessed important hydrocarbon discoveries. Secondly, Turkish revisionism has placed Turkey at odds with the US, Egypt and Israel. Thirdly, this in turn has allowed the RoC along with Greece to form two trilateral partnerships with Israel and Egypt, two vital US allies in the region. The US response, I will argue, is employing a soft balancing strategy against Turkey and part of that strategy is a closer relationship with the RoC that approximates that of a strategic partnership.

Nonetheless, essential issues remain that limit the further development of this relationship. The centrality of the Republic's President in the foreign policy decision-making process means that his perception and images are vital for the progression and conduct of foreign policy. Notably, on the matter of US-RoC relations, not all political forces on the island view the US as a crucial ally. The case of AKEL and Demetris Christofias is a case in point. Apart from the possibility of an anti-US administration in Nicosia, US-RoC relations will unlikely progress substantially unless the RoC shifts away from its alignment with Russia and its importance for the RoC's economy and military. Moreover, the centrality of Turkey in the Eastern Mediterranean region makes it a far more critical partner for the US than the RoC. After all, as elaborated below, the primary aim of the US's soft balancing strategy in the region is to lure Turkey back into its fold. Turkey is still a NATO member and a potential change in its government could lead to a pro-Western administration that could realign Turkey with the US to the detriment of US-RoC relations. Finally, the capacity of Eastern Mediterranean gas to diversify European markets away from Russian supplies is highly questionable, thus, making it less significant for US policymakers in the long term.

This chapter begins with a short historical background on US-RoC relations prior to 2004 before moving on to the theoretical framework. It then focuses on the Eastern Mediterranean as a regional space, Turkey's revisionism and the trilaterals that have enabled the current state of US-RoC relations which will be analysed in the next section. Finally, the limitations mentioned above will be explored before assessing the maturity of the RoC Foreign Policy in relations to the US in the chapter's conclusion.

A History of US-Cypriot Relations: From Independence to the EU Accession

Although this chapter deals with the contemporary state of US-RoC affairs, these relations have a turbulent history, linked both with the invasion of 1974 and the development of the Cold War in the Eastern Mediterranean. For the US, Cyprus was of paramount importance because the Greco-Turkish antagonism on the island could bring two US and NATO allies on the brink of war amid the Cold War (Coufoudakis 1976). A war between Greece and Turkey over Cyprus would dissolve NATO's south-eastern flank allowing Moscow to lure either Greece or Turkey on its side. The existence of AKEL, a strong Communist Party, fully obedient to Moscow, that supported Cypriot President Archbishop Makarios III made nothing to alleviate the fears of US policymakers (Ball and Freedman 1982; Güney 2004). At the same time, for many Greek Cypriots, the US is not an "honest broker" in the region (Güney 2004). In fact, the US and NATO are viewed by many Greek Cypriots as a perpetrator of the events that led to the island's split in two (Güney 2004, 34). I should note at this point that it is not my goal here to assess the historical validity of these beliefs. My goal is to report them to facilitate the reader's understanding of the development of US-Cypriot relations.

The independence of Cyprus in 1960 along with the Zurich-London constitution which was imposed by the three guarantor powers—Greece, Turkey and the United Kingdom (UK) —on the Cypriot people sowed the seeds of division between the two sides. The 1963–1964 fights between the two communities over constitutional reform led to the withdrawal of Turkish Cypriots from the government. More importantly, from a US perspective, the crisis led to the active involvement of the USSR in the Cyprus Problem (Norton 1992, 102–105). In February 1964, Soviet Premier Khrushchev warned that the interference of Atlantic partners in the internal politics of Cyprus could endanger "the general peace" (*New York Times* 1964). The USSR then moved forward and supplied the RoC with Soviet arms to bolster its defence (Aslim 2016, 253). The

US response was formulated in a letter by President Lyndon Johnson to the Turkish Prime Minister Ismet Inonu warning him against a Turkish invasion of Cyprus (Johnson and Ismet 1966).

That invasion eventually came ten years later in July 1974. On the 15th of July the Greek military junta along with far-right Greek nationalist paramilitaries mounted a coup d'etat that deposed President Makarios and installed Nikos Sampson as the new head of state. Sampson's reign was short since the Turkish army invaded the island on the 20th of July and by the end of August, controlled approximately 37% of its territory. The US failed to successfully mediate this crisis, unlike the previous one in 1964, and Turkey's grip on the island was solidified in the coming years (Güney 2004). The post-invasion status quo remains to this day with diplomacy repeatedly failing to provide a solution to the Cyprus Problem. In 1983 the Turkish Cypriot leadership with the support of Turkey declared the occupied territories as an independent state under the name "Turkish Republic of Northern Cyprus" (TRNC). Although the TRNC remains unrecognised by the international community, except for Turkey, it has added another facet to an already protracted diplomatic issue.

Analysts have long argued that the US knew about the coup and did nothing to prevent it pointing to the close ties between the Greek junta and the Nixon administration as well as the role of US Secretary of State Henry Kissinger (Mirbagheri 1998; Hitchens 1984; Güney 2004; Joseph 1997). The US stance infuriated the Greek Cypriots as well as Greeks elsewhere. Soon after the invasion, massive demonstrations in Athens and Nicosia condemned not only the Turkish invasion but what was viewed as US support for the military junta in Athens, the Greek coup d'etat and the Turkish invasion. In the years following the invasion, the US placed an arms embargo on both the RoC and the TRNC in 1987, intending to reinforce reunification efforts by the two actors. This move pushed the RoC to increase its dependency on Russian arms for its defence, thus, pushing the two sides further apart.

Theoretical Framework

In line with the central theme of this volume, this chapter employs the concept of foreign policy maturity. For the purposes of this chapter, this refers to whether the RoC's foreign policy has a well-defined and reasoned strategy in its relations with the US.[1] To examine this, I rely on two theoretical strands. The first deals with the study of regions within international affairs that will aid in making the case for an Eastern Mediterranean region that serves as the backdrop to the analysis of US-RoC relations. The second is based on the balance-of-power theory and, more specifically, the concept of soft balancing. The argument is that the relationship between the US and the RoC can be seen as soft balancing vis-à-vis Turkey.

It is vital to adopt a regional approach looking at the effects of international anarchy within a distinct geographical locus—the Eastern Mediterranean. In the post-Cold War era, International Relations (IR) theorists of various strands have argued for the importance of regions and regional perspectives to world politics and international relations (Buzan et al. 1998; Paul 2012; Hurrell 2007; Buzan and Wæver 2003). Although the structural characteristics of the global system like the system's polarity pertain to international relations globally, in many cases it is useful to zero in on specific geographical spaces and view the nature and effects of international anarchy at a regional level. Buzan et al. have described regions as "miniature anarchies" which are constituted by the common and interlinked securitisation and desecuritisation processes among the units of the region giving rise to Regional Security Complexes (RSC). As a consequence, the resolution or analysis of any security problems of any of the units within the RSC cannot be conceivably achieved without taking into consideration the other units within this territory (Buzan et al. 1998, 201). Although I do not share the view that regions are primarily constructed in discursive ways through securitisation processes as Buzan and Weaver argue, I agree that geography and geographic adjacency are key to comprehend the effects of international anarchy for a state (Buzan and Wæver 2003).

Moving on to the second part of my theoretical framework, I focus on the idea of soft balancing. Soft balancing is a relatively new concept in international relations theory which developed out of the necessity to describe, analyse and explain the attempts to restrain the US during its unipolar moment in the post-Cold War international environment. Analysts like Robert Pape (2005) and T.V. Paul (2005, 2018) have argued that due to the vast disparity in hard power capabilities between

---

[1] For a definition of the term "maturity" see the volume's Introduction by Tziarras.

the US and the rest, states were unable to resort to hard balancing measures like formal alliances and internal military build-ups. Instead of attempting to match the US in military terms, a futile task at the time, actors like Japan, Germany, France and Russia, took non-military measures to "delay, frustrate and undermine aggressive unilateral U.S. military policies" (Pape 2005, 10). These measures include economic statecraft, sanctions, diplomatic means like the construction of "strategic partnerships", and international institutions. The ultimate goal as Paul (2018, 20) notes is to make the actions of the target state seem "less legitimate in the eyes of the world and hence its strategic goals more difficult to obtain". Another key prerequisite for the employment of soft balancing is that threat balancing is not seen as critical. In such a case one would expect that the options would be either to resort to a hard balancing strategy or if the power differential is so great then bandwagoning would become a viable option (Schweller 1994).

A prime example of soft balancing is the opposition of France and Russia against the US invasion of Iraq in 2003 where they used their positions as permanent members of the UN Security Council (UNSC) to prevent the US from gaining a UNSC resolution sanctioning the invasion of Iraq—something that would have legitimised its actions. Although both France and Russia along with Germany vehemently opposed the Iraq invasion, they knew that they could do very little to prevent the US from moving forward with its plan. At the same time, despite their opposition, the invasion of Iraq was not an existential threat to them. Hence, soft balancing was the strategy of choice.

A term that requires clarifying and is vital to the aim of this article is that of "strategic partnership" (Paul 2018, 26). A strategic partnership is not a formal alliance since it does not include alliance agreements, common military command structures and extensive military cooperation. A strategic partnership, nonetheless, is not a simple trade relationship since it has a security element. This element takes the form of periodic meetings, joint exercises and some equipment transfer that is not at the scale of a fully fledged alliance.

The literature on soft balancing has to my knowledge exclusively focused on how lesser powers use soft balancing measures to restrain Great Powers or how it is employed as an approach in the relationship between powers of the same status (Pape 2005; Paul 2005, 2018; He and Feng 2008; Saltzman 2012; Tziampiris 2014). Diversifying from the original soft balancing argument, He and Feng (2008) argued that in the existence of extensive economic interdependence between two parties soft balancing can become a viable strategy if hard balancing becomes too costly in economic terms. In this case I seek to illustrate that soft balancing can become the strategy of choice for a Great Power vis-à-vis a weaker state if that state is a key ally that attempts to follow an independent foreign policy path. By employing a soft balancing strategy in the form of sanctions or the formation of a strategic partnership with a regional adversary the Great Power has a two-pronged aim: (i) through soft balancing the Great Power seeks to incur costs to the target state and thus bring it back in its fold and if that fails and (ii) the Great Power is creating alternative partnerships in the region that if need be they can elevate to that of a formal alliance.

THE EASTERN MEDITERRANEAN REGION: CONFLICT, GAS AND SHIFTING ALIGNMENTS

The starting point of our analysis is the Eastern Mediterranean region, the international backdrop to US-RoC relations. Although historically the region has been split between Southeastern Europe and the Middle East, in recent years analysts have argued for the need to reconceptualise this geographical space as a new and distinct region within IR. Novel conceptualisations of the region have varied with different states appearing to be part of it (Adamides and Christou 2016; Tziampiris 2019; Tziarras 2018; Stivachtis 2019). Nonetheless, Cyprus, Greece, Israel, Turkey, the Palestinian Authority, Syria, Lebanon and Egypt are identified as the core states of the region by most analysts with Libya and Jordan often included.

Basing their account on a case study in the relations between Greece, Turkey and Cyprus, Adamides and Christou (2016) have argued that the region can be described as an RSC with energy securitisation playing a pivotal role in the construction of the Complex. In another account, Tziampiris views the Eastern Mediterranean Sea as a regional subsystem in which both Great and regional powers are utilising it as a "laboratory for balance of power policies" (Tziampiris 2019, 25). Importantly, for him and other analysts, the region is seen as one of the West's ultimate frontiers in which "Western" polities and "attitudes" to politics meet non-Western challenges (Tziampiris 2019, 25–26; Inbar and Sandler 2001; Alterman et al. 2018). Similarly, Alterman et al. (2018, 1) have labelled it as a "geostrategic fault line" between the East and West, which should play an essential role in the mindset of American strategists.

Another important necessity in defining a new region acknowledged by many analysts is the internal and external recognition of the new region as well as the creation of organisations and institutions facilitating the relations of regional states (Tziarras 2018). In the case of the Eastern Mediterranean internally, most states of the region acknowledge the existence of the Eastern Mediterranean as a conceptual and analytical space in their foreign policies. The trilateral partnerships that involve Greece and Cyprus along with other regional states like Israel, Egypt, Jordan and Lebanon pay lip service to "Eastern Mediterranean politics". Additionally, in July 2019 we saw the first step in the creation of a region-wide institutional platform—the Eastern Mediterranean Gas Forum (EMGF). Egypt, Cyprus, Greece, Israel, Italy, the Palestine and Jordan convened in Cairo with the aim of lowering infrastructure costs and secure competitive gas prices. The forum's inaugural conference was attended by a representative of the US Energy Department while France has asked to become part of the group. Although the EMGF is by no means an equivalent of other regional bodies like the GCC or the ASEAN, its creation indicates that the Eastern Mediterranean has been gaining both external and internal recognition as a distinct region.

The debacle and turmoil that embroiled the region since the dawn of the twenty-first century also seem to provide evidence for the need of this conceptualisation. The 9/11 attacks and the launch of the War on Terror by the Bush administration brought Iraq and the Middle East to the forefront. The subsequent withdrawal of US troops under President Barack Obama from the region and the scaling down of US involvement in the early 2010s led to the creation of a power vacuum (Harrison 2019; Walt 2015). In conjunction, with forces unleashed by the 2011 Arab Uprisings, the consequences were catastrophic (Gerges 2016). Syria and Iraq were embroiled in a civil war while Egypt saw its long-time ruler Hosni Mubarak overthrown and then replaced by the democratically elected leader of the Muslim Brotherhood only for him to be deposed by the military soon after. Terrorism also resurged in the region in an unprecedented manner through the Islamic State of Iraq and the Levant (ISIS), which, laid claim to large swathes of land of modern-day Syria and Iraq (Gerges 2016). At the same time, persistent conflicts like the Cyprus Problem and the Israeli-Palestinian conflict remain unsolved.

Apart from strife and conflict, the Eastern Mediterranean has witnessed a series of hydrocarbon discoveries off the coasts of the RoC, Egypt and Israel. These discoveries illustrate the Eastern Mediterranean's potential to become an energy hub. According to a 2010 US Geological Survey, the Eastern Mediterranean may hold 355 trillion cubic feet of recoverable natural gas.[2] These estimations have been backed up by a string of discoveries in the Egyptian, Israeli and Cypriot EEZs (Ward 2018; Ratner 2016). On the backbone of these discoveries and the sustained political turmoil, the region's international relations have been in a state of flux with old alliances shaken and new partnerships emerging (Karagiannis 2016). A crucial factor in this reshaping of the region's international relations is Turkey's revisionist foreign policy.

Turkey's Bid for Regional Hegemony and the US Response

Under the leadership of Recep Tayyip Erdogan and the Justice and Development Party (AKP), Turkey is making a bid for regional hegemony that simultaneously challenges the country's pro-Western trajectory since its creation. In 1952 Turkey became a NATO member and a vital ally of the US. As Nikolaos Zahariadis (2015, 85–86) argues, US policy in the Eastern Mediterranean was based on two crucial alliances: US-Israel-Turkey and US-Israel-Egypt. Nonetheless, the rise of the Islamist AKP in Turkey and the party's politics since the early 2010s have threatened Turkey's relationship with the US and have raised questions regarding the country's position within NATO.

In terms of foreign policy, the AKP has been critical of Turkey's fixation on the West and NATO arguing for a more active role within the Muslim world and other geographical spaces. The AKP's foreign policy vision was expressed by the former Turkish Prime Minister Ahmet Davutoğlu in his "strategic depth" doctrine. Davutoğlu maintained that Turkey's international position is determined by its strategic depth which in turn is based on its country's historical past and geography. Turkey's "historical depth", as Davutoglu calls it, is defined by Turkey's position as a "modern nation-state which was established as the heir to the Ottoman Empire" (Davutoglu 2010b, 33). Turkey's Ottoman past determines its geographical depth. In Davutoğlu's words, Turkey "is in a unique position in geopolitical terms, in the midst of Afro-Eurasia' that makes it 'a

---

[2] In 2010 the US Geological Survey estimated that the Levant Basin holds a mean 122 trillion cubic feet of recoverable gas while the Nile Delta Basin holds a mean of 223 trillion cubic feet of recoverable gas (Schenk and Robertson 2010; Kirschbaum and Robertson 2010).

European, Mediterranean, Balkan, Caucasian and Middle Eastern country all at the same time" (Davutoglu 2010b, 33). Turkey's unique geographic position and historical past as the heir of the Ottoman Empire provide it with the potential to become not only a regional but also a power of global stature that could unify and lead the Muslim world (Mufti 2014; Davutoglu 2010a, 2010b; Walker 2011). Hence, despite its initial pro-Western stance, by the late 2000s Turkish foreign policy shifted towards the Middle East, eventually leading to collapsing relations with regional allies.

The first point of rupture was the breakdown in relations with Israel. The Turkish bid to lead the Muslim world is underpinned by a proactive pro-Palestinian stance which led to the Mavi Marmara incident and the death of Turkish activists in the hands of the Israeli Defence Forces (IDF) (Mufti 2014). The activists attempted to break the Israeli embargo and deliver aid to Gaza in May 2010. The Israeli government branded the activists as terrorists and linked them to the Turkish government. The Turkish response was a condemnation of Israel in international forums and a cease in diplomatic relations (Uzer 2013, 100–102). A rapprochement brokered by the Obama administration based on the prospect of a natural gas pipeline taking Israeli gas to Europe through Turkey proved to be short-lived (Efron 2018, 11, 34). The Israeli recognition to a Kurdish state in 2017, the Turkish response to deadly Gaza Strip protests in 2018 and Erdogan's fierce opposition to the US recognition of Jerusalem as Israel's capital have furthered the division (Heller 2017; BBC 2018).

The revisionist Turkish foreign policy has damaged Turkish-Egyptian ties as well. The Islamist turn of Erdogan seemed to strengthen the country's relations with Egypt since it coincided with the Arab Uprisings of 2011 and the downfall of Hosni Mubarak. Islamic political parties and groups spearheaded the uprising in Egypt; hence, Erdogan received a hero's welcome in his three days state visit in Cairo in September 2011. This represented the highpoint for Turkish influence in the region and Davutoğlu's "zero problems with neighbours" policy. Furthermore, the electoral victory of the Muslim Brotherhood and Mohammed Morsi as Egypt's new President brought ideological alignment between Ankara and Cairo.

However, Morsi's reign was short-lived being deposed by a military coup d'etat. His downfall led to a break in Egypt-Turkey relations with President Erdogan vehemently opposing the new government in

Cairo led by General Fatah al Sisi in support of the Muslim Brotherhood (Kouskouvelis and Zarras 2019). The inflexibility showcased by the Turkish elites regarding the change of leadership in Egypt in conjunction with Turkey's aspiration to lead Sunni Muslims across the globe meant that Egypt, a predominantly Sunni Muslim state that has always seen itself as a leading Arab and Muslim nation, felt increasingly threatened by Turkish foreign policy in the region (Kouskouvelis and Zarras 2019). Finally, the personal animosity between Presidents Erdogan and Sisi exacerbated tensions.

The strenuous relations with Egypt and Israel have made Turkish relations with the US uneasy. Both Egypt and Israel serve as pillars and critical partners of US foreign policy in the Eastern Mediterranean and the Middle East (Zahariadis 2015). Besides, the purchase of the S-400 Russian anti-aircraft missile system by the Turkish military has led to the banning of Turkey from the F-35 fighter jet programme while indicating the closer relations between Ankara and the Kremlin (Ahval 2019). This Russo-Turkish cooperation at the expense of US interests was exhibited in the aftermath of the withdrawal of US troops from Kurdish controlled regions in Syria (BBC 2019). Despite pleas from its trans-Atlantic partner not to invade the region, which were followed by threats of sanctions, Turkey moved ahead with the invasion (BBC 2019). The progress of Turkish troops was only halted after Erdogan and Vladimir Putin reached an agreement which allowed Turkish troops to retain control of the areas they seized while Syrian and Russian forces would oversee the withdrawal of Kurdish forces from the Turkish controlled strip (BBC 2019). The deal illustrated Turkey's move further away from the US while at the same time it enabled Russia to emerge once more as the principal power broker in the region.

Turkish revisionism has led US policymakers to alter their stance against their ally with soft balancing being the strategy of choice through the imposition of sanctions. Despite the efforts of the Trump administration to minimise the friction between the two sides, both the Republicans and the Democrats have been adamant in imposing sanctions on Turkey. The provisions of the 2020 National Defence Authorization Act (NDAA) apart from removing Turkey from the F-35 programme have also targeted companies and entities linked to the TurkStream pipeline that will supply Europe with Russian gas via Turkey (Ahval 2019). In October, the US House of Representatives also passed with overwhelming bipartisan support bills that would hamper Turkey's ability to import arms from if enacted by the President (Edmondson 2019). Additionally, the "Promoting American National Security and Preventing the Resurgence of ISIS Act of 2019" has been introduced in the US Senate with bipartisan support which if enacted will also impose restrictions to US arms sales to Turkey along with sanctions to political entities and government officials of the Turkish government (Risch 2019).

Turkey, Cyprus and the Trilaterals: Paving the Way for Closer US-Cypriot Relations

At the same time, Turkey is building up its armed forces through extensive investment in its homegrown military industry with particular emphasis on its navy (Kurç 2017). The expansion of the Turkish navy is a crucial pillar of Turkish grand strategy in the twenty-first century and interlinked with the hydrocarbon discoveries in the Eastern Mediterranean according to Cem Güdeniz, a retired Turkish admiral (Tziarras 2019b). Turkish aspirations in the region are becoming clear under the Blue Homeland doctrine (Tziarras 2019b). The synonymous military drill of 2019 undertaken by the Turkish navy included concurrent naval exercises in three theatres—the Aegean, the Black Sea and the Eastern Mediterranean (Kasapoglu 2019). Turkish military planners seek to establish Turkey as the region's stronger maritime force (Kasapoglu 2019).

Turkey's turn to the sea is exhibited through its gunboat diplomacy in the region in conjunction with the developments related to hydrocarbon exploitation in the Eastern Mediterranean. Turkish research vessels protected by the Turkish navy have been conducting gas explorations within Cyprus's EEZ and have even obstructed a drillship leased by the Italian oil firm ENI to conduct scheduled drillings approved by the Cypriot government (Kambas 2018). In another move which challenges both Greece and Egypt, President Erdogan has signed deals with the Government of National Accord (GNA) in Libya demarcating their EEZs and has even sent military support in Tripoli against the forces of the Libyan National Army (LNA), under General Khalifa Haftar (Gall 2020; Johnson 2019). The demarcation deal in particular cuts through areas in which both Greece and Egypt consider parts of their EEZs (Kathimerini 2019).

Turkish actions in the region were bound to be met by a response, especially at a time when the stakes regarding energy exploitation are so high. Within this fluctuating geopolitical environment, Cyprus and

Greece have managed to construct meaningful partnerships with regional states like Israel and Egypt (Karagiannis 2016). Initially, Cyprus demarcated its EEZ with these two states. Hydrocarbon discoveries and Turkey's aggression allowed Cyprus along with Greece to develop closer relations with these states and construct trilateral partnerships in the region. Hydrocarbons allowed the RoC to change the patterns of its interaction with Israel and Egypt. In parallel to Turkey's revisionist policy, the trilateral partnerships took off and with them the prospect of closer relations between the US and the RoC.

From the perspective of the RoC foreign policy, hydrocarbon discoveries along with Turkey's revisionism provided an opportunity for Nicosia to forge closer relations with regional states (Tziarras 2019a). According to former Foreign Minister Nikos Christodoulides, up to the country's accession to the EU and the hydrocarbon discoveries in the Eastern Mediterranean, the RoC's foreign policy was "monothematic", catering for the Cyprus Problem and Turkey, but this has been altered and hydrocarbons "facilitated this shift" (Christodoulides 2018). Initially, the RoC moved forward to demarcate its EEZ with Egypt in 2003 and Israel in 2010. Subsequently, the RoC's choice to involve Noble Energy and Delek within its EEZ, two firms that have close relations with the Israeli state and its hydrocarbon exploitation was a choice made with "geostrategic criteria" (Stavrinos 2018). In a similar move, the RoC and Egypt signed an agreement in September 2018 for the construction of an underwater pipeline that would take natural gas to the Egyptian LNG facility in Idku (Psyllides 2018). In this respect the RoC was able to exploit the geopolitical opportunity presented by the break in Turkish-Israeli and Turkey-Egypt relations, taking steps towards increased cooperation in energy development vis-à-vis a common threat. The consolidation of these two trilateral partnerships has been critical in reshaping the power dynamics in the Eastern Mediterranean that would eventually allow closer relations between the US and the RoC.

The trilateral partnership between Greece, Cyprus and Israel is by far the more developed of the two. The demarcation agreement between Cyprus and Israel in 2010 and the breakdown of relations between Turkey and Israel created the impetus for increasing cooperation. The visits of George Papandreou in Israel and Benjamin Netanyahu in Athens highlighted this shift (Tziampiris 2014, 92–94). Soon after the Mavi Marmara incident leaders from the three countries were quick to exchange visits at the highest level seeking to make the most of this geopolitical opportunity at the expense of Turkey. The three states have also committed to the construction of an Eastern Mediterranean pipeline that will take Cypriot and Israeli gas to Europe through Greece (Nedos 2020). Although the project has been under consideration since 2016, the signing of a Memorandum of Understanding between Turkey and the GNA prompted a direct response by the three partners. This response took the form of an agreement for the creation of the pipeline signed in January 2020 (Nedos 2020). Despite the scepticism regarding the viability of the endeavour, the will of the three partners to push things towards a direction that makes them largely independent from any other regional players showcases their deepening cooperation. Finally, in military terms, Search and Rescue form the central area of cooperation with the conduct of joint exercises by the three partners while both Cyprus and Greece have acquired Israeli arms (Hadjipavlis 2018).

Although not as developed as the trilateral with Israel, the trilateral with Egypt is vital for the RoC's foreign policy in the Eastern Mediterranean and beyond. The RoC can count on a leading state in the Arab and Muslim worlds to promote its position against the recognition of the TRNC. Like Israel, both Greece and Cyprus have increased their defence cooperation with Egypt through Search and Rescue and other military exercises. For Egypt, the trilateral provides a platform to represent its interests in the EU through Greece and Cyprus; something acknowledged by President Sisi and the Egyptian leadership (Cyprus News Agency 2019a). Additionally, the agreement signed by the RoC for the construction of a pipeline from the Cypriot EEZ to Idku has since been followed by a deal between the Cypriot government and Noble Energy, Delek and Shell, the three parties responsible for the exploitation of the Aphrodite field in the Cypriot EEZ. The deal grants an exploitation license to the three firms involved in the Aphrodite field to export natural gas to Egypt (Hazou 2019). The liquefied natural gas from Idku will be used primarily for the needs of the Egyptian gas markets with the possibility of exports also on the table. The deal, worth approximately $9.3 billion, represents a new page in the bilateral relations between Egypt and Cyprus, creating vested Egyptian interests in the security of RoC's EEZ (Hazou 2019).

US-RoC Relations

The development of these two trilaterals and the problematic bilateral ties between Turkey and the US along with the energy developments in the Eastern Mediterranean have created a favourable international circumstance enabling closer relations between the US and Cyprus. All three countries with which the RoC has engaged in deepening cooperation through the trilaterals are key US allies in the Eastern Mediterranean region. Greece is a NATO member; Israel has an organic relationship with the US and Egypt is one of the pillars of US policy in the Middle East (Zahariadis 2015; Alterman et al. 2018; Chorev et al. 2019).

The View from Washington

For US policymakers, the prospect of the Eastern Mediterranean becoming an energy hub that could potentially supply the EU is deemed as increasingly important (Rubio 2019). One of the critical US strategic objectives in Europe is to lessen the ability of Russia to use its dominant position in the European energy markets to influence EU politics. As Wigell and Vihma (2016) argue, Russia was quite efficient in making use of its "gas weapon" to advance its interests and position vis-à-vis the EU prior to the war in Ukraine through selective accommodation of EU members like Germany. US lawmakers and the country's foreign policy apparatus is looking for ways to counter Russia's influence. The recent sanctions on the Nord Stream 2 pipeline illustrate this foreign policy approach (Sevastopulo et al. 2019). If adequate amounts of natural gas are discovered, dependency of the EU on Russian pipe gas could decrease; hence, it is in the interest of the US to see the Eastern Mediterranean becoming an energy-producing region. After all, American oil firms like Noble Energy and Exxon Mobil have already invested in Cyprus's EEZ and the region more generally.

As the region's energy potential was becoming apparent along with the RoC's centrality to developments due to the island's geographical location, the US developed a keen interest in the negotiations for the settlement of the Cyprus Problem. Initially, the US played an active role in the latest round of talks for the settlement of the Cyprus Problem that culminated in the Crans Montana Summit in 2017 (Kaskanis 2014; Sigmalive 2015). A solution to the Cyprus Problem would solve one of the perpetual diplomatic issues affecting US-Turkey relations and end the constant threat of a Greco-Turkish conflict. A solution would also allow for better NATO-EU cooperation by addressing the "participation problem" arising from the inability of NATO and the EU to enforce the Berlin Plus agreements that would enable closer and more integral cooperation between the two organisations (Janigian 2017). In the aftermath of the RoC's accession to the EU, both Cyprus and Turkey vetoed against other's participation, the RoC from the EU's side and Turkey from the part of NATO, thus leading to ineffective cooperation between the two international bodies (Janigian 2017). A solution to the Cyprus Problem would also pave the way for the creation of a gas pipeline from the Eastern Mediterranean to Europe through Turkey, which is considered as the cheapest monetisation option of Eastern Mediterranean gas.

The failure of the latest round of negotiations to the Cyprus Problem along with Turkey's defiance of the US in the region has led the US to promote other partnerships in the region. In this respect, the Cyprus-Israel-Greece trilateral has been brought to the forefront of US foreign policy in the Eastern Mediterranean. The participation of then US Secretary of State Mike Pompeo in the 2019 trilateral summit between Greece, Cyprus and Israel was a clear indicator. A joint declaration by all four parties declared "Secretary Pompeo underlined U.S. support for the trilateral mechanism established by Israel, Greece, and Cyprus, noting the importance of increased cooperation" (U.S. Embassy in Cyprus 2019). This 3 + 1 formation (Israel, Greece, Cyprus and the US) made its appearance in the 1st meetings of the Energy Ministries of the four countries in Athens, in August 2019 (Reuters 2019). In the words of US State Department officials, the RoC is a "force for stability, democracy, and prosperity, and a valued U.S. partner in the important Eastern Mediterranean region" (U.S. Department of State 2019).

Apart from visits and statements, US support for the RoC has begun taking a more concrete form through critical legislative acts in Washington. As mentioned above, the US has partially lifted the arms embargo in place since 1987 thus enabling the RoC to acquire defence equipment from the US, pertinent to some conditions as part of the Congress' 2020 National Defence Authorization Act for 2020 (Cyprus News Agency 2019b). Additionally, Senators Marco Rubio and Bob Menendez through the Eastern Mediterranean Peace and Security Act seek to reshape US strategy in the Eastern Mediterranean, making energy and the Cyprus-Greece-Israel trilateral the focal points (Rubio and Menendez 2019). According to the bill, the US views the Eastern Mediterranean as crucial for the diversification of Europe's energy dependence on Russia (Rubio and Menendez 2019). The bill is also a response to what US policymakers perceive as Russia's "malign influence" in the region (Rubio and Menendez 2019). Moreover, the bill recognises the RoC's right to the development of hydrocarbons within its EEZ, which is also in line with US interests in the area.

The Cypriot FPE and the US

Throughout the whole process, the Anastasiades administration in Cyprus has been eager to better its relations with Washington and become a critical partner for US interests in the Eastern Mediterranean. Given the problematic history between the two parties, this apparent shift in attitudes has been enabled by the liberal and pro-Western outlook of the RoC policymakers since 2013. The RoC's foreign policy decision-making process is centred around the person of the President, who has the exclusive prerogative of conducting policy in the international domain according to the constitution. The Ministry of Foreign Affairs is in turn responsible for the diplomatic corps of the country and the enactment of the country's foreign policy with its minister being influential in the conduct of international affairs on behalf of the state.

In the case of President Nicos Anastasiades, we find a politician educated in the UK and with clear pro-Western tendencies. He is an adamant supporter of the EU and the trilateral partnerships which his party views as "alliances" that will "fortify" Cyprus in the Eastern Mediterranean (Neofytou 2019; RIK 2019). Another key figure here in the current administration is Minister of Foreign Affairs Nikos Christodoulides, who began his career initially as the head of the President's diplomatic office before moving into the post of Minster of Foreign Affairs. Christodoulides studied in the US and has been in favour of the RoC playing a bridging role between the EU and the West, on the one hand, and the Middle East, on the other. He is thus an individual who has supported the RoC's alignment with the US. In this respect both the President and the Minister of Foreign Affairs are in favour of a closer relationship with the US.

Importantly, Anastasiades' party, the Democratic Rally (DISY), is arguably the only political party within the RoC political spectrum that has levelled little or no criticism against the US throughout its history—particularly with regard to the Cyprus Problem. DISY was the only party that was in favour of the US-Canadian plan of 1978 for the solution of the Cyprus Problem. Similarly, under Anastasiades' leadership, DISY supported the 2004 Annan Plan for Cyprus which was backed by the US. Besides, as leader of the opposition, he was heavily critical of the former President Demetris Christofias' decision not to apply for the RoC's participation in NATO's Partnership for Peace (PfP) programme, which is viewed as a track that will lead to NATO membership. Ahead of the 2013 Presidential election, Anastasiades campaigned with the promise apply for participation in PfP (Kambas and Babington 2013).

The Emergence of a Strategic Partnership

The aforementioned factors have allowed the US and the RoC to rejuvenate their relations. The lifting of the arms embargo on Cyprus, the sanctions on Turkey as well as the pro-RoC stance of the US in its gas dispute with Turkey illustrate the employment of a soft balancing strategy against Turkey by the US. The US, the party with the upper hand in this bilateral relationship, does not view Turkey as an existential threat; thus, it can afford to resort to a soft balancing strategy, already exhibited by the sanctions of the US Congress on Turkey. In line with that strategy, it has chosen to elevate its relationship with the RoC to the extent that it approximates that of a strategic partnership.

Consistent with this chapter's theoretical approach is the fact that the US is following a two-pronged strategy concerning Turkey. The first part aims to inflict cost on Turkey's interests through sanctions, but also through the construction of a strategic partnership with a regional adversary of Turkey. This is done in the hope that Turkey will recognise the increasing cost and fall back in line. If that fails, then the US having built a strategic partnership with the RoC can choose to enhance that relationship and in conjunction with its other alliances in the region pursue a harder balancing act against Turkey, should Washington deems it necessary. For its part, being the weaker part of the relationship, the RoC can enjoy the support of a global superpower, therefore accepting any help it can get against Turkish aggression. Of course, it would prefer a formal alliance since for Cyprus, Turkey is an existential threat. However, it does not have the material capacity to dictate the kind of relationship it desires and, as a result, any kind of closer relationship would be beneficial.

The relationship cannot yet be deemed as a full strategic partnership since no periodic meetings or joint military exercises between the two parties have been arranged. However, the foundations have been set and to a considerable extent it is up to the island state whether the relationship would be cultivated to that level. First, under certain conditions, the RoC now has access to US defence equipment, and this will provide a military element in the relationship. Second, the preference of the US to engage Greece-Cyprus-Israel can provide the RoC with the opportunity to push for increased involvement of the US in the dealings of the group, including in Search and Rescue operations.

The Limits of the Relationship

One should note that there are limitations to US-RoC relations. Three factors should be taken into consideration. The first, again, concerns leader images and perceptions. The focus here is placed on the leftist AKEL and its perception of the US which is in direct opposition to the pathway pursued by Anastasiades and DISY. The second is related to Russia's position on the RoC in matters of economy and defence. The third factor is the importance of Turkey for the US and NATO which concerns the scenario where the US would prefer a reinforced relationship with Turkey rather than with the RoC. Finally, the fourth limitation is linked to the possibility that the Eastern Mediterranean might not become such an important region for the EU's energy security. That would diminish the region's significance for the US policy calculations.

The AKEL Factor

AKEL is the oldest political party in Cyprus with a history dating back in the 1920s, and it is the largest party on the island along with DISY often attracting approximately a third of the electorate. To this day, the party proclaims that it is Marxist-Leninist organisation even though it has helped figures like liberal George Vassiliou and the conservative Tassos Papadopoulos to ascend to the position of President. Historically, the party has enjoyed close ties with Moscow and much of the party's leadership has been educated in the Eastern Bloc during the Cold War. The party's anti-Americanism runs deep and stems primarily from its Marxist-Leninist ideology and the conviction that the US played a pivotal role in the tragic events of July 1974(AKEL 2020, 2019).

AKEL found itself in power in the 2008–2013 period when the Party's General Secretary, Demetris Christofias, was elected President. Christofias studied in Moscow during the 1970s, at the height of the Cold War where he nurtured an anti-American worldview in which the US along with collaborators like Israel and other NATO states, were imperialist forces. Despite the party's pro-Palestinian sentiments and its Euroscepticism, Christofias proved to be a flexible leader in the international domain (Kouskouvelis 2016; Christou and Kyris 2017). He oversaw the signing of the EEZ demarcation agreement between Israel and the RoC that culminated in Noble's drilling in 2011, verifying the existence of natural gas in Cyprus' EEZ. He also took advantage of the geopolitical circumstances in the aftermath of the drilling and the Mavi Marmara flotilla incident to organise the first trilateral summit with the leaders of Israel and Greece with Netanyahu becoming the first Israeli Prime Minister to visit Cyprus (Tziarras 2019a). Additionally, Christofias oversaw the further Europeanisation of the RoC's Foreign Policy with all the ministries under his administration, creating European policy departments (Christou and Kyris 2017). Besides, he was also the head of state during the RoC's presidency of the EU in 2012.

Nonetheless, Christofias' flexibility ended when it came to deepening US-RoC relations. In February 2011 the Cypriot Parliament adopted a resolution to instruct the President, who has the sole prerogative of conducting foreign policy, to begin the application process for Cypriot membership to NATO's PfP programme. However, Christofias chose not to act on the resolution, dismissing it instead (Constantinou 2013). As members of AKEL argued in defence of the President, becoming a member in a NATO programme would mean supporting NATO's imperialist policies across the globe and an organisation that was responsible for the events of 1974 (Athanasiou 2013). Therefore, although under his tenure foreign policy was "westernised" even further, it did not make a decisive move towards an enhanced relationship with the US or NATO. Instead, Christofias and AKEL continued to view both as imperialist entities treating them with mistrust. The role of AKEL within the country's political landscape is such that it can find itself in power once more either through a coalition government or with a candidate from its own ranks, like Christofias. In such a scenario, it is quite likely that the party's anti-Americanism might stand in the way of better relations with the US and NATO.

Russian Influence

The RoC has substantial financial and economic ties with Russia and Russian businesses. First and foremost, the island is a tax haven for Russian individuals and companies. The competitive corporate tax regime on the island along with the position of the RoC as an EU member state creates an ideal entry point for Russian firms in the European markets (Smith 2018). According to statistics by the Bank of Russia released in 2019, Russian Foreign Direct Investment (FDI) stock in the RoC stands at approximately $175 billion while Cypriot FDI stock in Russia stands at almost $125 billion (Aris 2019). The RoC FDI stock in the Russian economy, if one accounts for the small size of the Cypriot economy, is Russian money circled through a financial tax haven. Moreover, since the 2013 financial crisis, Russian investment in the RoC has been driven to a large extent by the RoC government scheme that grants citizenship to individuals willing to invest €2 million in specific sectors of the economy and particularly in real estate (Smith 2018).

Russia has also been profoundly influential in the RoC through economic, military and diplomatic means. In the prelude to the country's financial crisis, Russia granted Nicosia with a loan worth $3.3 billion in 2011. The loan was extended in 2013 to alleviate the burden of the sovereign debt crisis (Reuters 2013). As Alterman et al. (2018, 8) point out, the loan and the extension were a recognition of the RoC's importance for Russian businesses and "conversely, as a way to repatriate Russian money under the guise of foreign investment in Russia". In military terms, the Cypriot government has chosen Russia for some of the most sophisticated systems in the RoC National Guard's arsenal like the T-80 main battle tank, the Mi-35 attack helicopter and the Buk anti-aircraft batteries. The inability to buy arms from the US along with the competitive prices of Russian armaments has led Cyprus to Russia. Through the acquisition of weapons, Russia has gained influence in Cyprus by creating a dependency in the Greek Cypriot armed forces. Also, the two countries have agreements through which Russian military vessels can access Cypriot ports for refuelling and servicing (Reuters 2015). Finally, Russia has provided vital diplomatic support to the RoC by supporting Nicosia's positions on the Cyprus Problem in the UNSC, where it has consistently supported the renewal of UN peacekeeping force (UNFICYP) mandate (Melakopides 2018).

Arguably the Russia-RoC relationship raises obstacles to deepening ties between the US and the RoC. If Nicosia wants to enjoy a deeper cooperation with the US, it will have to distance itself from Russia. This has been made clear in the 2020 National Defence Authorisation Act that enabled the RoC to access US arms and military aid. According to the Act's provisions, the RoC can buy US arms as long as it cooperates with the US in combatting money-laundering, and it denies access to Russian vessels to Cypriot ports for servicing and refuelling (Inhofe 2019, 468–469).

Turkey's Importance

Despite Turkey's revisionism under the AKP and Erdogan, the country remains a NATO member with valuable US assets on its ground and, as already noted, US actions against Turkey are partially aiming to re-establish Turkey's position as a US ally. The NATO base in Incirlik has been crucial for US operations in the Middle East and to this day it houses nuclear weapons. Besides, Turkey remains the 2nd largest military force within NATO, and the US will do everything in their power to restore their relationship to its previous standards. Therefore, for the US, its ties with Turkey are far more significant than any association with the RoC and given the right opportunity they could be normalised. If President Erdogan is replaced by a Kemalist administration or an individual with a pro-Western orientation, then Turkey could once more become a trusted partner of the US, to the detriment of US-Cypriot relations.

The Limits of Eastern Mediterranean Hydrocarbons

US policymakers are focusing on the Eastern Mediterranean in part because of the region's hydrocarbon potential that could lessen Europe's dependence on Russian gas and influence. This is an influential factor in US-RoC relations as the proposed Eastern Mediterranean Energy and Security Partnership Act of 2019 illustrates (Rubio and Menendez 2019). However, the Eastern Mediterranean does not seem to be able to reduce the dependency of the EU on Russian gas to a considerable extent. In 2018, Russian gas amounted to 40.5% of the EU's natural gas needs; however, the Eastern Mediterranean would only be able to cover a fraction of this need (Eurostat 2019). In the same year, Russia's Gazprom exported 202 billion cubic meters (bcm) of natural gas to Europe (Gazprom 2019).

In contrast, the EastMed pipeline will have the capacity when and if it becomes operational to transport up to 10 bcm of natural gas to Europe (Hazou 2020). One should also consider that through Turkstream, operational since January 2020, and the Nord Stream 2 pipeline, Russia will have the ability to circumvent Ukraine and Poland reducing its gas flows through those countries (Günther 2019). This will provide further stability to its gas exports to Europe with Gazprom being able to export 200.8 bcm of natural gas through non-Ukrainian routes, thus, enhancing Russia's predominance in European gas markets (Günther 2019). Finally, Eastern Mediterranean gas will have to compete with Russian and Norwegian pipe gas along with Qatari LNG exports which can provide much lower prices to European markets than those the EastMed pipeline could offer in the future (Butler 2019). Hence, it would be challenging to see Eastern Mediterranean gas becoming vital to European gas markets and, more importantly, an alternative to Russian gas.

Conclusion: US-Cypriot Relations, the Product of a "Mature" Cypriot Foreign Policy?

US-RoC relations approximate the level of a strategic partnership but are not at that level yet. The Eastern Mediterranean's hydrocarbon potential along with the RoC's ability to exploit systemic opportunities to form trilateral partnerships with key US allies in the region, like Israel and Egypt, as a result of Turkey's revisionism, has provided an opportunity for deeper US-RoC relations. US policymakers view the Eastern Mediterranean as an increasingly important region that could help Europe reduce its dependence on Russian gas. At the same time, Turkey's distancing from the West has prompted the US to look for alternative partners in the region, like the RoC, as part of a broader soft balancing strategy against Turkey that has included the imposition of economic sanctions. Simultaneously, RoC President Nicos Anastasiades, an firmly pro-Western individual, had no objections to closer relations with the US, unlike his communist predecessor Demetris Christofias. In essence, the opportunity provided by regional developments in the Eastern Mediterranean was grasped by a pro-Western RoC leadership. Nonetheless, this relationship could be constrained by the possibility of an AKEL government in the future, the decades-long influence of Russia on the island, the importance of Turkey for the US and the limited capacity of Eastern Mediterranean hydrocarbons to shift Europe's gas markets away from Russian influence.

In this respect, it can be argued that this relationship is not the result of a mature foreign policy strategy from the RoC's part. A mature foreign policy strategy would encompass well-reasoned and defined goals in line with the capacities and capabilities of the state in question accepting the limits placed on the state's power. RoC political parties, except AKEL, support closer US-RoC relations but at the same time seek further Russian influence on the island. These are contradictory goals showcasing the lack of a clearly defined strategy and international orientation.

The first step for a closer US-RoC relationship would be the full lifting of the US arms embargo. That would enable the two states to establish a military relationship, possibly a strategic partnership, and, if the US wishes, a formal alliance. However, Russia's influence has been persistent even in the days of pro-Western Anastasiades. The Russian navy can use Cypriot ports for refuelling and servicing and the government's citizenship by investment scheme has primarily benefited Russian oligarchs. Additionally, despite being an ardent supporter of the PfP during his time in opposition, Anastasiades' government has yet to apply for a PfP membership. The centrist parties EDEK and DIKO voted in favour of a PfP membership in 2011, thus supposedly supporting a better relationship between the RoC and the US. However, at the same time, they have asked for Russia's mobilisation in the Cyprus Problem to prevent a solution based on a Bizonal Bicommunal Federation, the type of solution envisaged by AKEL, the ruling DISY and the US (Melakopides 2017). These moves highlight that the RoC leadership and the political centre on the island do not have a clear idea of the kind of relationship they would want with the US. They do not have well-reasoned and defined goals. Uncertainty about desired objectives begets inability to strategise.

Beyond the lack of well-reasoned and defined goals, RoC decision-makers seem to overestimate the state's material capacity and capabilities, and especially its hydrocarbon potential. The Eastern Mediterranean's gas cannot become a game-changer for European markets and their dependency on Russia. Therefore, its importance for Washington will be diminished once its full potential (or lack thereof) is revealed. Once that happens, it is likely that the importance the US ascribes to its relationship with the RoC will also lessen. Generally, the current revamped relationship between the two parties is the result of systemic opportunities in conjunction with favourable leader images and perceptions. Notwithstanding, a closer relationship would necessitate that the RoC leadership understands that its value and foreign policy cannot be solely based on energy and that it will need to find ways to reduce Russian influence in Cyprus.

REFERENCES

Adamides, Constantinos, and Odysseas Christou. 2016. "Beyond Hegemony: Cyprus, Energy Securitisation, and the Emergence of New Regional Security Complexes." In *The Eastern Mediterranean in Transition: Multipolarity, Politics and Power*, edited by Spyridon N. Litsas and Aristotle Tziampiris. New York: Routledge.

Ahval. 2019. "Trump Signs Defence Spending Bill Imposing Sanctions on Turkey." Ahval News. https://ahvalnews.com/us-turkey/trump-signs-defence-spending-bill-imposing-sanctions-turkey.

AKEL. 2019. "Ιστορία ΚΚΚ-ΑΚΕΛ." Accessed January 2, 2020. https://www.akel.org.cy/istoria-kkk-akel/#.XhdiL0czZPY [In Greek].

AKEL. 2020. "Δήλωση Εκπροσώπου Τύπου ΑΚΕΛ Στέφανου Στεφάνου για τις εξελίξεις στη Μέση Ανατολή." AKEL. Accessed January 3, 2020. https://www.akel.org.cy/2020/01/09/ekselikseis-mesi-anatoli/#.XhdgSEczZPY [In Greek].

Alterman, Jon B., Heather A. Conley, Haim Malka, and Donatienne Ruy. 2018. *Restoring the Eastern Mediterranean as a U.S. Strategic Anchor*. Washington, DC: Center for Strategic International Studies.

Aris, Ben. 2019. "Which Country Is the Biggest FDI Investor into Russia? It's Cyprus... Not." Accessed January 2. https://www.intellinews.com/which-country-is-the-biggest-fdi-investor-into-russia-it-s-cyprus-not-165554/.

Aslim, Ilkoy. 2016. "The Soviet Union and Cyprus in 1974 Events." *Athens Journal of History* 2 (4): 249–262.

Athanasiou, Thanasis. 2013. "Συνεταιρισμός για την Ειρήνη: Ανάγκη ή προθάλαμος του ΝΑΤΟ." Sigmalive. Accessed January 3, 2020. https://www.sigmalive.com/news/politics/32316/synetairismos-gia-tin-eirini-anagki-i-prothalamos-tou-nato [In Greek].

Ball, George W., and Lawrence Freedman. 1982. *The Past Has Another Pattern: Memoirs*. New York: Norton.

BBC. 2018. "Gaza-Israel Violence: Netanyahu and Erdogan in War of Words." BBC. Accessed December 23, 2019. https://www.bbc.com/news/world-middle-east-43611859.

BBC. 2019. "Turkey Syria Offensive: Erdogan and Putin Strike Deal Over Kurds." BBC. Accessed December 23, 2019. https://www.bbc.com/news/world-middle-east-50138121.

Butler, Nick. 2019. "Eastern Mediterranean Gas Seeks a Buyer." *Financial Times*. Accessed January 5, 2020. https://www.ft.com/content/ef1036f0-fb06-11e9-98fd-4d6c20050229.

Buzan, Barry, and Ole Wæver. 2003. *Regions and Powers: The Structure of International Security, Cambridge Studies in International Relations 91.* Cambridge: Cambridge University Press.

Buzan, Barry, International Institute for Strategic Studies, Ole Wæver, Jaap de Wilde, and Lawrence Freedman. 1998. *Security: A New Framework for Analysis.* Boulder, CO: Lynne Rienner.

Chorev, Shaul, Douglas J. Feith, Dr. Seth Cropsey, Jack Dorsett, and Gary Roughead. 2019. "The Eastern Mediterranean in the New Era of Major-Power Competition: Prospects for U.S.-Israeli Cooperation." Hudson Institute.

Christodoulides, Nicos. 2018. Interviewed by the author. Nicosia. June 17.

Christou, George, and George Kyris. 2017. "The Impact of the Eurozone Crisis on National Foreign Policy: Enhancing Europeanization in the Case of Cyprus*." *JCMS: Journal of Common Market Studies* 55 (6): 1290–1305. https://doi.org/10.1111/jcms.12557.

Constantinou, Gus. 2013. "Partners for Peace?: Cyprus, NATO and the EU." NATO Association of Canada. Accessed January 4, 2020. http://natoassociation.ca/partners-for-peace-cyprus-nato-and-the-eu/.

Coufoudakis, Van. 1976. "U.S. Foreign Policy and the Cyprus Question: An Interpretation." *Millennium* 5 (3): 245–268. https://doi.org/10.1177/03058298760050030201.

Cyprus News Agency. 2019a. "President Sisi thanks Cyprus for its contribution in the establishment of EU-Egypt relations." Accessed December 23, 2019. http://www.cna.org.cy/WebNews-en.aspx?a=060b21903b594657aa31bd1e4f532dae.

Cyprus News Agency. 2019b. "US Congress to lift arms embargo on Cyprus." Accessed December 23, 2019. http://www.cna.org.cy/WebNews-en.aspx?a=cc4947cebbd04d968430ff4fc6fb5bf5.

Davutoglu, Ahmet. 2010a. "Turkey's Zero-Problems Foreign Policy." Accessed December 23, 2019. https://foreignpolicy.com/2010/05/20/turkeys-zero-problems-foreign-policy/.

Davutoglu, Ahmet. 2010b. *Το Στρατηγικό Βάθος: Η Διεθνής Θέση της Τουρκίας.* Athens: Piotita Publications. Original edition, Stratejik Derinlik: Türkiye'nin Uluslararası Konumu [In Greek].

Edmondson, Cattie. 2019. "In Another Bipartisan Rebuke of Trump, House Votes for Sanctions Against Turkey." *New York Times.* Accessed December 23, 2020. https://www.nytimes.com/2019/10/29/us/politics/house-turkey-sanctions.html.

Efron, Shira. 2018. The Future of Israeli-Turkish Relations. *Rand Cooperation.* Accessed December 28, 2021. https://doi.org/10.7249/RR2445.

Eurostat. 2019. "EU Imports of Energy Products—Recent Developments." Eurostat. Accessed January 3, 2020. https://ec.europa.eu/eurostat/statis

tics-explained/index.php/EU_imports_of_energy_products_-_recent_develo pments#Main_suppliers_of_natural_gas_and_petroleum_oils_to_the_EU.
Gall, Carlotta. 2020. "Turkey, Flexing Its Muscles, Will Send Troops to Libya." *New York Times*. Accessed January 3, 2020. https://www.nytimes.com/2020/01/02/world/europe/erdogan-turkey-libya.html.
Gazprom. 2019. "Gas supplies to Europe." Gazprom. Accessed January 4, 2020. http://www.gazpromexport.ru/en/statistics/.
Gerges, Fawaz A. 2016. *ISIS A History*. REV—Rev. ed. Princeton University Press.
Güney, Aylin. 2004. "The USA's Role in Mediating the Cyprus Conflict: A Story of Success or Failure?" *Security Dialogue* 35 (1): 27–42. https://doi.org/10.1177/0967010604042534.
Günther, Maik. 2019. "What Nord Stream 2 Means for Europe." Atlantic Council. Accessed January 5, 2020. https://www.atlanticcouncil.org/blogs/ukrainealert/what-nord-stream-2-means-for-europe/.
Hadjipavlis, Panayiotis. Interviewed by the author. Nicosia, June 29, 2018.
Harrison, Ross. 2019. "U.S. Foreign Policy Towards the Middle East: Pumping Air into a Punctured Tire." *Arab Centre for Research and Policy Studies*. Accessed December 28, 2021. https://www.dohainstitute.org/en/Lists/ACRPS-PDFDocumentLibrary/US-Foreign-Policy-Towards-the-Middle-East-Pumping-Air-into-a-Punctured-Tire.pdf
Hazou, Elias. 2019. "Lakkotrypis: Another Milestone in Cyprus' Energy Programme." *Cyprus Mail*. Accessed December 22. https://cyprus-mail.com/2019/11/07/lakkotrypis-another-milestone-in-cypruss-energy-programme/.
Hazou, Elias. 2020. "'Historic' Deal Signed in Athens for EastMed Pipeline (Update 2)." *Cyprus Mail*. Accessed January 2, 2020. https://cyprus-mail.com/2020/01/02/historic-deal-signed-in-athens-for-eastmed-pipeline/.
He, Kai, and Huiyun Feng. 2008. "If Not Soft Balancing, Then What? Reconsidering Soft Balancing and U.S. Policy Toward China." *Security Studies* 17 (2): 363–395. https://doi.org/10.1080/09636410802098776.
Heller, Jeffrey. 2017. "Israel Endorses Independent Kurdish State." Reuters. Accessed December 23, 2019. https://www.reuters.com/article/us-mideast-crisis-kurds-israel/israel-endorses-independent-kurdish-state-idUSKCN1B00QZ.
Hitchens, Christopher. 1984. *Cyprus*. London: Quartet.
Hurrell, Andrew. 2007. "One World? Many Worlds? The Place of Regions in the Study of International Society." *International Affairs (Royal Institute of International Affairs 1944–)* 83 (1): 127–146.
Inbar, Efraim, and Shmuer Sandler. 2001. "The Importance of Cyprus." *Middle East Quarterly* 8 (2).

Inhofe, James M. 2019. *National Defense Authorization Act of Fiscal Year 2020*. Edited by US Senate. Washington, DC: US Senate. https://www.congress.gov/bill/116th-congress/senate-bill/1790.

Janigian, Alan M. 2017. "The Cypriot-Turkish Conflict and NATO-European Union Cooperation." Naval Postgraduate School.

Johnson, Keith. 2019. "Newly Aggressive Turkey Forges Alliance With Libya." Foreign Policy. Accessed January 2, 2020. https://foreignpolicy.com/2019/12/23/turkey-libya-alliance-aggressive-mideterranean/.

Johnson, Lyndon B., and Inonu Ismet. 1966. "President Johnson and Prime Minister Inonu: Correspondence Between President Johnson and Prime Minister Inonu, June 1964, as Released by the White House, January 15, 1966." *Middle East Journal* 20 (3): 386–393.

Joseph, Joseph S. 1997. *Cyprus Ethnic Conflict and International Politics: From Independence to the Threshold of the European Union*. Basingstoke and New York: Macmillan and St. Martin's Press. https://ebookcentral.proquest.com/lib/kcl/detail.action?docID=736416.

Kambas, Michelle. 2018. "Standoff in High Seas as Cyprus Says Turkey Blocks Gas Drill Ship." Reuters. Accessed December 23, 2019. https://www.reuters.com/article/us-cyprus-natgas-turkey-ship/standoff-in-high-seas-as-cyprus-says-turkey-blocks-gas-drill-ship-idUSKBN1FV0X5.

Kambas, Michelle, and Deepa Babington. 2013. "After Election Win, Anastasiades Faces Cyprus Bailout Quagmire." Reuters. Accessed January 2, 2020. https://www.reuters.com/article/us-cyprus/after-election-win-anastasiades-faces-cyprus-bailout-quagmire-idUSBRE91N00220130224.

Karagiannis, Emmanuel. 2016. "Shifting East Mediterranean Alliances." *Middle East Quarterly* 23 (2).

Kasapoglu, Kan. 2019. "'The Blue Homeland': Turkey's Largest Naval Drill." Accessed December 23, 2019. https://www.aa.com.tr/en/analysis/-the-blue-homeland-turkey-s-largest-naval-drill/1404267.

Kaskanis, Giorgos. 2014. "Στην Κύπρος σήμερα ο Τζο Μπάιντεν." Deutsche Welle. Accessed December 23, 2019. https://p.dw.com/p/1C37g [In Greek].

Kathimerini. 2019. "Israel Opposes Turkey-Libya Maritime Border Accord." *Kathimerini*. Accessed December 25, 2019. http://www.ekathimerini.com/247872/article/ekathimerini/news/israel-opposes-turkey-libya-maritime-border-accord.

Kirschbaum, Mark, and Jessica Robertson. 2010. "Nile Delta Natural-Gas Potential is Significant." U.S. Geological Survey. Accessed December 24, 2019. https://archive.usgs.gov/archive/sites/soundwaves.usgs.gov/2010/07/research.html.

Kouskouvelis, Ilias. 2016. "'Smart' Leadership in a Small State: the Case of Cyprus." In *The Eastern Mediterranean in Transition: Multipolarity, Power* and *Politics*, edited by Spyridon N. Litsas and Aristotle Tziampiris. London: Ashgate Publishing.

Kouskouvelis, Ilias, and Konstantinos Zarras. 2019. "Cairo and Riyadh, Vying for Leadership." *Middle East Quarterly* 26 (2).

Kurç, Çağlar. 2017. "Between Defence Autarky and Dependency: The Dynamics of Turkish Defence Industrialization." *Defence Studies* 17 (3): 260–281. https://doi.org/10.1080/14702436.2017.1350107.

Melakopides, Costas. 2017. "On the 'Special' Nature of the Russia–Cyprus Relationship." Russia in Global Affairs. Accessed January 3, 2020. https://eng.globalaffairs.ru/book/On-the-Special-Nature-of-the-RussiaCyprus-Relationship--18786.

Melakopides, Costas. 2018. *Russia-Cyprus Relations: A Pragmatic Idealist Perspective*. Basingstoke, Hampshire: Palgrave Macmillan.

Mirbagheri, Farid. 1998. *Cyprus and International Peacekeeping, 1964–1986*. London: C. Hurst.

Mufti, Malik. 2014. "The AK Party's Islamic Realist Political Vision: Theory and Practice." *Politics and Governance* 2 (2): 28–42. https://doi.org/10.17645/pag.v2i2.48.

Nedos, Vassilis. 2020. "Leaders of Greece, Israel, Cyprus Ink Deal for Pipeline, Sending Out Multiple Messages." *Kathimerini*. Accessed January 3. http://www.ekathimerini.com/248071/article/ekathimerini/news/leaders-of-grece-israel-cyprus-ink-deal-for-pipeline-sending-out-multiple-messages.

Neofytou, Averof. 2019. "Η Κύπρος θα συνεχίσει να χτίζει συμμαχίες αξιοποιώντας τα συμφέροντα και τις συνέργειες που αναδύονται από την ενεργειακή προοπτική της χώρας. (2)." DI.SY. Accessed January 3, 2020. https://www.disy.org.cy/nea/paremvaseis/1020-averof-i-kypros-tha-synexisei-na-xtizei-symmaxies-aksiopoiontas-ta-symferonta-kai-tis-synergeies-pou-anadyontai-apo-tin-energeiaki-prooptiki-tis-xoras-3 [In Greek].

Norton, Augustus Richard. 1992. "The Soviet Union and Cyprus." In *Cyprus: A Regional Conflict and Its Resolution*, edited by Norma Salem. London: Palgrave Macmillan.

Pape, Robert A. 2005. "Soft Balancing Against the United States." *International Security* 30 (1): 7–45.

Paul, T. V. 2005. "Soft Balancing in the Age of U.S. Primacy." *International Security* 30 (1): 46–71.

Paul, T. V. 2012. *International Relations Theory and Regional Transformation*. Cambridge and New York: Cambridge University Press. https://ebookcentral.proquest.com/lib/kcl/detail.action?docID=866889.

Paul, T. V. 2018. *Restraining Great Powers: Soft Balancing from Empires to the Global Era*.

Psyllides, George. 2018. "Cyprus, Egypt sign Gas Pipeline Agreement." *Cyprus Mail.* https://cyprus-mail.com/2018/09/19/cyprus-egypt-sign-gas-pipeline-agreement/.

Ratner, Michear. 2016. *Natural Gas Discoveries in the Eastern Mediterranean.* Washington, DC: US Congress.

Reuters. 2013. "Russia Extends Cypriot Loan by 2 Years, Cuts Interest: Troika Document." Reuters. Accessed January 2. https://www.reuters.com/article/us-russia-cyprus/russia-extends-cypriot-loan-by-2-years-cuts-interest-troika-document-idUSBRE9450AK20130506.

Reuters. 2015. "Russia, Cyprus Sign Military Deal on Use of Mediterranean Ports." Reuters. Accessed January 3, 2020. https://www.reuters.com/article/us-russia-cyprus-military/russia-cyprus-sign-military-deal-on-use-of-mediterranean-ports-idUSKBN0LU1EW20150226.

Reuters. 2019. "Greece, Israel, U.S., Cyprus to Boost Energy Cooperation." Reuters. Accessed January 3, 2020. https://www.reuters.com/article/us-greece-energy-eastmed/greece-israel-u-s-cyprus-to-boost-energy-cooperation-idUSKCN1UX1EP.

RIK. 2019. "ΥΠΕΞ: Οι τριμερείς συνεργασίες έχουν θωρακίσει την ΚΔ." RIK News. Accessed January 3, 2020. http://riknews.com.cy/index.php/news/politiki/item/90657-ypeks-oi-trimereis-synergasies-exoun-thorakisei-tin-kd.

Risch, Jim. 2019. *To Promote United States National Security and Prevent.* Edited by US Senate. Washington, DC: US Senate.

Rubio, Marco. 2019. "Rubio, Menendez Introduce Eastern Mediterranean Security and Energy Partnership Act of 2019." Accessed December 19, 2019. https://www.rubio.senate.gov/public/index.cfm/2019/4/rubio-menendez-introduce-eastern-mediterranean-security-and-energy-partnership-act-of-2019.

Rubio, Marco, and Bob Menendez. 2019. *Eastern Mediterranean Energy and Security Partnership Act of 2019.* Washington, DC: US Senate.

Saltzman, Ilai Z. 2012. "Soft Balancing as Foreign Policy: Assessing American Strategy Toward Japan in the Interwar Period." *Foreign Policy Analysis* 8 (2): 131–150.

Schenk, Chris, and Jessica Robertson. 2010. "Natural-Gas Potential Assessed in Eastern Mediterranean." U.S. Geological Survey. Accessed December 25, 2019. https://archive.usgs.gov/archive/sites/soundwaves.usgs.gov/2010/05/research3.html.

Schweller, Randall L. 1994. "Bandwagoning for Profit: Bringing the Revisionist State Back In." *International Security* 19 (1): 72–107.

Sevastopulo, Demetri, Henry Foy, and Nastassia Astrasheuskaya. 2019. "US Lawmakers Agree Bill to Force Trump on Nord Stream 2 Sanctions." *Financial Times.* Accessed December 26, 2019. https://www.ft.com/content/3a0fde0c-1b10-11ea-97df-cc63de1d73f4.

Sigmalive. 2015. "Lavrov and Kerry in Nicosia to look at the Cyprus Problem." Sigmalive. Accessed December 23, 2019. https://www.sigmalive.com/en/news/politics/138223/lavrov-and-kerry-in-nicosia-to-look-at-cyprus-problem.

Smith, Helena. 2018. "Welcome to Limasolgrad: The City Getting Rich on Russian Money." *Guardian*. Accessed December 23, 2019. https://www.theguardian.com/world/2018/feb/17/welcome-to-limassolgrad-the-city-getting-rich-on-russian-money.

Stavrinos Michalis. Interviewed by the author. Nicosia. July 2, 2018.

Stivachtis, Yannis A. 2019. "Eastern Mediterranean: A New Region? Theoretical Considerations". In *The New Eastern Mediterranean: Theory, Politics and States in a Volatile Era*, edited by Aristotle Tziampiris and Spyridon N. Litsas, 45–59. Cham: Springer.

Tziampiris, Aristotle. 2019. "The New Eastern Mediterranean as a Regional Subsystem." In *The New Eastern Mediterranean: Theory, Politics and States in a Volatile Era*, edited by Aristotle Tziampiris and Spyridon N. Litsas, 1–30. Cham: Springer.

Tziampiris, Aristotlle. 2014. *The Emergence of Israeli-Greek Cooperation*. Cham: Springer.

Tziarras, Zenonas. 2018. *The Eastern Mediterranean: Between Power Struggles and Regionalist Aspirations*. Nicosia: PRIO Cyprus Centre.

Tziarras, Zenonas. 2019a. "Cyprus' Foreign Policy in the Eastern Mediterranean and the Trilateral Partnerships: A Neoclassical Realist Approach." In *The New Geopolitics of the Eastern Mediterranean: Trilateral Partnerships and Regional Security*, edited by Zenonas Tziarras, 53–72. Nicosia: PRIO Cyprus Centre.

Tziarras, Zenonas. 2019b. Οι «Δυόμισι Πόλεμοι» και η Άσκηση «Mavi Vatan»: Στρατηγική Κουλτούρα και το νέο Στάδιο της Τουρκικής Στρατηγικής. ELIAMEP.In Greek.

U.S. Department of State. 2019. *Senior State Department Officials Previewing Secretary Pompeo's Travel to Ukraine, Belarus, Kazakhstan, Uzbekistan, and Cyprus*. edited by U.S. Department of State. Washington, DC: U.S. Department of State.

U.S. Embassy in Cyprus. 2019. "Joint Declaration Between Cyprus, Greece, Israel, and the United States After the Sixth Trilateral Summit." U.S. Embassy in Cyprus. Accessed January 3, 2020. https://cy.usembassy.gov/joint-declaration-between-cyprus-greece-israel-and-the-united-states-after-the-sixth-trilateral-summit/.

Uzer, Umut. 2013. "Turkish-Israeli Relations: Their Rise and Fall." *Middle East Policy* 20 (1): 97–110. https://doi.org/10.1111/mepo.12007.

Walker, Joshua W. 2011. "Introduction: The Sources of Turkish Grand Strategy—'Strategic Depth' and 'Zero-Problems' in Context." In *Turkey's Global Strategy*, edited by Nicholas Kitchen. London: LSE Ideas.

Walt, Stephen M. 2015. "ISIS as a Revolutionary State: New Twist on an Old Story." *Foreign Affairs* 94 (6): 42–51.

Ward, Andrew. 2018. "Geopolitical Rivalries Cloud Prospects for Mediterranean Gas Finds." *Financial Times*. Accessed November 5, 2019. https://www.ft.com/content/f6adee5c-f126-11e7-b220-857e26d1aca4.

Wigell, Mikael, and Antto Vihma. 2016. "Geopolitics Versus Geoeconomics: The Case of Russia's Geostrategy and Its Effects on the EU." *International Affairs* 92 (3): 605–627. https://doi.org/10.1111/1468-2346.12600.

Zahariadis, Nikolaos. 2015. "Penelope Unravelling: The Obama Administration's Policy in the Eastern Mediterranean." In *The Eastern Mediterranean in Transition: Multipolarity, Politics and Power*, edited by Spyridon N. Litsas and Aristotle Tziampiris, 79–91. Surrey: Ashgate Publishing.

CHAPTER 6

Russia's Place in the Foreign Policy of the Republic of Cyprus: Will "Pragmatic Idealism" Survive in the 2020s?

Costas Melakopides

INTRODUCTION

Russia's elevated place in Cypriot affairs has been recognized by "(Political) Realism" ever since the 1950s. Realism conceived Moscow's interests in Cyprus exclusively in geopolitical and geostrategic terms, associated with its Cold War role as an East–West "apple of discord" or "bone of contention" (e.g., Adams and Cottrell 1968; Ball 1982; Stergiou 2007). But Realist conceptual categories and their methodological implications constrained a priori its analyses to power, national interest, military antagonism and conflict. Paradigmatic is George Ball's (1982, 342) blunt admission regarding the 1964 Cyprus crisis (added emphasis): "Viewed

C. Melakopides (✉)
Department of Social and Political Sciences, University of Cyprus, Nicosia, Cyprus
e-mail: comel@ucy.ac.cy

© The Author(s), under exclusive license to Springer Nature Switzerland AG 2022
Z. Tziarras (ed.), *The Foreign Policy of the Republic of Cyprus*, Reform and Transition in the Mediterranean,
https://doi.org/10.1007/978-3-030-91177-5_6

from Washington, the issue was clear enough. Cyprus was *a* strategically important piece of real estate at issue between two NATO partners: Greece and Turkey. We needed to keep it under NATO control".

Inevitably, such "realism" has ignored other dimensions of Soviet/Russian-Cypriot relations, associated with the two peoples' centuries-old historical, religious, cultural, emotional and concomitant affinities and bonds. Hence my decision to apply the methodological synthesis of "Pragmatic Idealism" (Melakopides 2008a, b), which revealed a crucial reality: that whereas the Western (i.e., British, American and NATO) treatment of Cyprus amounted repeatedly to victimization, Moscow, by offering Cyprus sustained protection and manifold support during the Cold War, cultivated a special relationship, premised on a cohabitation of interests and values, that I have called "Latent Pragmatic Idealism" (Melakopides 2018a, b).

The Cold War's end ushered in years of bilateral flourishing. Inter alia, Russia emerged as a primary defender of Republic of Cyprus (RoC) interests and needs, thereby establishing itself as an effective counterweight to Western errors and sins, while serving simultaneously its own interests. In other words, Moscow's Cyprus policies were emanating *primarily but not* exclusively from Russia's "national interests": for they respected international legal principles and ethical norms being also inspired by the aforementioned affinities and bonds. Thus, Russia-RoC relations between 1992 and the mid-2010s deserve *a fortiori* to be called "Pragmatic Idealist".

During the 2010s, however, the "special" relationship is traumatized by the tempestuous Eastern Mediterranean geopolitical developments, including the notorious Russia-Turkey strategic embrace, the energetic "return" of the United States (US), promising hydrocarbon deposits in Cyprus' Exclusive Economic Zone (EEZ), and Turkey's expansionist ambitions. This labyrinthine geopolitical landscape, where Turkish President, Recep Tayyip Erdogan, poses as protagonist, should be surveyed before we pronounce on the probable future of bilateral "pragmatic idealism".

This chapter, then, after recalling Cyprus' post-World War II (WWII) vicissitudes and their effects on Russia-Cyprus relations, will record the accumulated mutual benefits, place Russia-Cyprus relations in today's fluid geopolitical setting and submit cautious predictions of future bilateral tendencies coupled with a preliminary assessment of the RoC's foreign policy "maturity"—as per the central theme of this volume.

CYPRUS-RUSSIA RELATIONS DURING THE COLD WAR

Cyprus won (controversial) independence from British colonialism through a painful national liberation struggle (1955–1959). Its externally imposed Constitution overtly favoured the Turkish Cypriot minority (18% versus the 80% of Greek Cypriots), causing the Greek Cypriot (GC) majority's profound disappointment and anger towards the United Kingdom (UK) and the US.

Contrariwise, Moscow emerged as a "natural" ally, simultaneously defending the Cypriots and serving its geopolitical goals. In fact, Moscow's geopolitical and diplomatic interest in Cyprus began even before the August 1960 establishment of the Republic, since Moscow's support for the rights of the GC majority first manifested itself in the mid-1950s. The GCs, being politically more active, and inspired by the December 1952 United Nations (UN) General Assembly Resolution on self-determination, asked Athens to represent them at the UN. However, despite the global decolonization momentum and the monumental Greek sacrifices during WWII, London adamantly refused to set Cyprus free. Assisted by Washington, whose "containment" of the USSR was intensifying, the agenda of the 1954 UN General Assembly excluded the Cyprus issue. Besides the UK and the US, three more NATO members voted against Greece's appeal. The USSR sided with the Cypriots.

The Adventurous Birth of the Republic

The GCs began their "national liberation" struggle on 1 April 1955. London replied with *divide et impera*, openly favouring the Turkish Cypriots (TCs). As Vassilis Fouskas (2009, 16) wrote, "Britain, facing the Greek Cypriots' ferocious anti-colonial uprising, pitted the Turks against the Greeks by setting up auxiliary police totally composed of Turkish Cypriots [who] tortured Greek Cypriots under the blissful eye of British lieutenants". And as British author William Mallinson has lamented (2005, 23), "At a time when all Greek-speaking political parties were banned, the British authorities allowed the Turkish Cypriots to establish a political party called "Cyprus is Turkish". Although many members of EOKA were hanged and imprisoned, very few members of Volkan, a Turkish Cypriot terrorist group, were even tried". Similarly, in a masterly essay for the *London Review of Books*, Perry Anderson (2008, 7–16) added in dismay:

The standard repertoire of repression was applied. Makarios was deported. Demonstrations were banned, schools closed, trade-unions outlawed. Communists were locked up, EOKA suspects hanged. Curfews, raids, beatings, executions were the background against which, a year later, Cyprus supplied the air-deck for the Suez expedition.

EOKA's military success ultimately produced Cyprus' quasi-liberation: for the new Republic inherited truncated freedoms and two British Sovereign Bases Areas. O'Malley and Craig (1999, 78) characterized the "independence agreements" as "fatally flawed"; for the "imported" Constitution,

> was doomed from the start to promote divisions which eventually led to bloodshed. It had been devised by outside powers, bartering over their own political and defence interests on the island, and not by the people who had to live there, and resulted in neither real independence and unity nor a workable system of government.

The RoC was born in this manner on 16 August 1960. Moscow recognized it two days later. The predicted domestic instability erupted in December 1963. Faced with crippling governmental malfunctioning, President Archbishop Makarios III proposed constitutional improvements. The TCs responded by rebelling, thereby forcing the UN to send a Peacekeeping Force that remains on the Island ever since.

UN Security Council (UNSC) Resolution 186 of March 1964, establishing UNFICYP, legitimized the Nicosia government and falsified Turkey's traditional narrative: inter alia, that the TCs were "victimized" by the Greek majority, "ejected" from the Nicosia administration and "forced" to hide in enclaves, because the Greeks had "hijacked" the newborn Republic. And yet, Ankara, alone in the world, refuses to date to recognize the Republic.

Former Cypriot Foreign Minister, Dr Erato Kozakou-Marcoullis, has emphasized Moscow's decisive role, recalling that "some countries reacted negatively" to Resolution 186, because it stated that the UNFICYP would be,

> acting with the approval of the Government of the Republic of Cyprus...
> [B]ut the Soviet Union stood by us and by this very important wording... the international community through the Security Council recognizes the Government of Cyprus as representing the whole Republic of Cyprus and

all the people of Cyprus. Therefore, Moscow's support was vital at a very critical moment. (Melakopides 2018a, b, 55)

On 8 July 1964, as Adams and Cottrell reported, Nikita Khrushchev "again warned against a Turkish invasion of Cyprus, charging that this would cause a dangerous chain reaction"; he also repeated his demands for "withdrawal of British troops from Cyprus and an end of all Western intervention in the political affairs of the island" (Adams and Cottrell 1968, 37). Then, in mid-August, Khrushchev declared yet again that Moscow could not be indifferent to the threat of conflict south of its borders. Quoting *Pravda's* 17 August 1964 issue, Adams and Cottrell (1968, 38–39) wrote:

> [Khrushchev] charged that the Turkish air attacks on Cyprus were part of an 'imperialist plot' led by the US and Great Britain. He warned that Turkey could not 'drop bombs on Cyprus…with impunity' and that the harm inflicted on others may act as a boomerang.

Already, therefore, the "special relationship" was dawning. Moscow's pro-Nicosia logic was premised already on *pragmatic* grounds, including Soviet anxiety to prevent NATO hegemony over Cyprus; hopes to remove the British bases if Cyprus could not be removed from the West; the ambition to establish its credentials as a superpower; and the cultivation of strong political ties with the fully pro-Soviet Cypriot communist party AKEL.

Such *Realpolitik* or "pragmatic" considerations, while certainly valid, do not suffice to account fully for Moscow's pro-Nicosia policies. By ostracizing a priori the *normative dimension*, Realist analyses commit the fallacy of *petitio principii* or begging the question, through the "authoritarian" exclusion of most value judgements: about legal norms, ethical values, and all humane considerations (such as solidarity and friendship). Pragmatic Idealism avoids this fallacy, thereby doing justice to the historical record, which can reveal declarations, decisions and actions demonstrating Moscow's camaraderie and tangible support for Cyprus, in contrast to the US-UK-NATO triangle that viewed Cyprus cynically throughout the Cold War.

Two Conflicting Approaches

Telling facts that reveal Cyprus' Cold War victimization by Western errors, crimes and sins include, London's secret approval of Makarios' Constitutional proposals that gave an alibi to the TC rebellion; sustained machinations essentially aiming at the Republic's partition; the US-inspired 1967–1974 Colonels' dictatorship in Greece; Washington's proven disregard of the Greek junta's preparations for the anti-Makarios coup; the implicit green light to the first (July 1974) Turkish invasion; Henry Kissinger's demonstrable encouragement of Turkey's second (August 1974) invasion (Mallinson 2005); the ruthless violation of the Cypriots' human rights by the unending Turkish occupation; and the hypocritical "commitment to resolve" the Cyprus problem under UN auspices (Melakopides 2018a, b, 44–72). This catalogue of tragic sins and crimes suffices to explain the resulting Greek Cypriot alienation from Washington and London. Christopher Hitchens, the British author who adopted a normative analysis of the 1974 Turkish invasion, shared the GCs' sentiments: (Hitchens 1997, 166): "acquiescence in injustice is not 'realism'. Once the injustice has been set down and described, and called by its right name, acquiescence in it becomes impossible. That is why one writes about Cyprus in sorrow but more -much mote- in anger".

Moscow, on the other hand, exploiting the aforementioned Western record, cultivated consistently its image and prestige, by extending to Cyprus moral and material expressions of support (Melakopides 2018a, b, 58–60). It declared immediately the will to provide the Republic with military hardware desperately needed to handle Turkey's threats and provocations; the USSR supplied various weapons systems but also moral support and material assistance, as did Czechoslovakia and East Germany; Nikita Khrushchev kept warning Ankara against its threatened invasions, beginning in summer 1964; Moscow opposed diachronically the Western designs to partition Cyprus; against NATO's self-serving fixations, it systematically demanded settling the Cyprus problem by an International Conference according to International Law and offered young Cypriots generous scholarships to attend Soviet universities (Stergiou 2007, 121–128). Moscow, therefore, utilized effectively the ample space provided by Western anti-Cyprus acts and omissions, to serve its strategic goals. Simultaneously, it defended Cyprus' security interests and political needs according to international legal norms, ethical values and humane solidarity, thereby substantiating the pragmatic idealist hypothesis.

There is, however, one stereotypical realist objection to a sympathetic reading of Moscow's Cyprus policies: namely, Moscow's "neutrality" during Turkey's 1974 invasion. While accepting the reality of this neutrality, Pragmatic Idealism may reply as follows. First, Moscow's stance represents an instance of self-regarding (strategic) pragmatism, arguably far less "sinful" than the parallel Western realism. Second, our analysis acknowledges by definition the *synthesis* of pragmatism and idealism, never claiming that all decisions and actions of pragmatic idealist actors always exhibit both dimensions. Third, Pragmatic Idealism, unique in bringing to light the entire idealist spectrum of Moscow-Cyprus relations, could not be falsified by one or two, apparent or even real, objections. Finally, this realist objection seems condemned to the macabre implication that, for the sake of Cyprus, Moscow should have risked a global conflagration.

1992–2017: Golden Age of Pragmatic Idealism

The end of the Cold War, by moderating the strategic anxieties of the two camps, encouraged the expansion of the idealist dimensions of Russia-Cyprus relations. They included cultural, religious, "spiritual", ethical and emotional bonds, that strengthened simultaneously not only the traditional historical, political and diplomatic affinities and ties, but also their manifold mutual interests and tangible benefits. Reasons of space necessitate that our discussion should adopt a laconic character.

Telling Examples of Normative Affinities

Ambassador Georgi L. Muradov's (2000) *Russia-Cyprus: Our Common Way* contains valuable arguments and illustrations of ideas, decisions, values, sentiments and judgements shared by Cypriots and Russians. Thus, asked "whether Hellenism and the Russian people have additional connecting features besides religion", he replied (Muradov, 134):

> Certainly! I think they also have the same mentality, as peoples, but also the same ethical spirit. Of course, since times past, there is the economic, the political and the cultural connection. I am talking of the ancient years when the first Tsars or the princes were getting married to Greek women.

Invited to discuss whether the Greeks—of both Cyprus and Greece—appreciate and enjoy Russia's great cultural tradition, he observed:

> [B]oth in Greece and in Cyprus, the Russian culture has great effect and impact. It is popular! In literature, in music, and the other arts. I realize this when I see the Russian folklore groups performing in Cyprus. They literally enjoy an apotheosis. And this proves that the connection of our peoples has deep roots which go back in centuries.

When the CyBC interviewer noted the deep Hellenic gratitude for Russia's literary heritage, Muradov (2000, 123) responded in an "idealist" manner:

> Thank you very much. I believe that our two civilizations are very much interconnected. Mentality, Tradition, Orthodoxy unite us as peoples very closely. And I must say that culture provides peoples with the same ethics, and I see that the evaluations, the values of Cypriots and Greeks, of Hellenism generally and of the Russians, are almost the same. I am talking about the values of today's world.

International Law provides a crucial demonstration of Russian-Hellenic normative affinity. Besides Muradov's own condemnation of the NATO bombing of Serbia on pragmatic idealist (i.e., legal and humanitarian) grounds, Argyrios Pisiotis (2001, 412) has emphasized that Moscow, like Hellenism, favours legal solutions to international problems. The Law of the Sea Convention and the Cyprus question constitute paradigm cases. Moscow's "stated preference for a 'legal' solution to the bilateral problems that caused the Imia confrontation" (Pisiotis 2001, 412), was identical with Athens' position. By supporting international legal solutions to the Greek-Turkish disputes, Russia revealed (a) opposition to the Anglo-American preference for "political dialogue" between the two "NATO partners"—which manifestly favoured Turkey—and (b) antagonism to Ankara's traditional position, which arguably fears that international law will pronounce against it whereas a bilateral dialogue might entail Greek concessions.

Security and Defence

These dimensions occupied an elevated place in Russia's Cyprus policies ever since the birth of the Republic. In fact, Moscow became the major, and periodically the only, provider of Cyprus' defence equipment. However, the courageous purchase of the S-300 missiles for its air defence may qualify as a case of bilateral pragmatic idealism: serving Russian commercial interests but also shared values, including the RoC's moral duty to defend itself against endless Turkish threats. Ankara had long been threatening Cyprus and lobbying against the missiles' installation. When Moscow signalled its decision to deliver the missiles, "Turkey threatened to strike the Russian vessels carrying the missiles to Cyprus. Moscow described the Turkish threats as an outright provocation and a *casus belli*" (Stergiou 2001: 125). Ambassador Muradov stated to Turkey's *Anadolou* news agency that "if Turkey were to attack any ship carrying S-300 missiles to Cyprus via the Turkish Straits, this would be cause for war" (*Hurriyet Daily News* 1997).

Some days later, Ambassador Muradov restated Moscow's *casus belli* threat and endorsed once again the RoC—and International Law—position on the essence of the Cyprus Problem: "The current situation in Cyprus did not result from the deal to purchase the missiles but from the 1974 Turkish invasion and the continued occupation of the island's northern third" (Cyprus News Agency 1997). In this connection, Yannakis Omirou (2014), when President of the RoC Parliament, defended Moscow's principled and sustained support for Cyprus, through diplomatic, political and defence means. He also revealed that, while Minister of Defence, his Russian counterpart, Marshall Sergeef, had handed him in Moscow a message from Boris Yeltsin to President Glafkos Clerides: "We are ready to send two frigates to the Port of Limassol one week before the arrival of the missiles. The frigates will possess anti-air systems which will cover not only Cyprus but also the entire Mediterranean. Then we'll see if the Turks would dare to attack!" (Omirou 2014).

Russia's April 2004 UN Veto

Moscow's protection of the RoC was demonstrated anew in April 2004, through its UNSC veto. The first such veto in 10 years was prompted by the notorious Annan Plan (Melakopides 2018a, b: 78–80). Secretary General, Kofi Annan, had been urging the UNSC to adopt a resolution on proposed Cypriot security arrangements should the Cypriots vote for "reunification". Given, however, that opinion surveys had long established the Greeks' massive rejection of this plan—as "lopsided", "utterly unfair" and hence "unworkable"—the UN Secretariat's pressure on the GCs was manifestly unethical. Therefore, Russia's Deputy Ambassador to the UN, Gennady Gatilov, vetoed the attempt to influence unfairly the forthcoming referenda, declaring: "The [referenda] must take place freely, without any interference or pressure from outside" (quoted in Melakopides 2018a, b: 78–80).

Once again, therefore, Moscow defended the GCs' legal, political and human rights that were being violated anew by the Anglo-American fixation to treat the RoC as "a strategic piece of real estate". Needless to repeat, Russia's motivation was not exclusively idealistic; but our discussion aims to show the *pragmatic idealist synthesis* which was all the Greek Cypriots hoped for.

Characteristic Russian Statements and Declarations

Throughout 1992–2017, the Russia-Cyprus political dialogue was constant and productive, as were the mutual visits by their presidents, foreign ministers and other officials—from the parliamentary level to that of local government. Cypriot statesmen and officials kept expressing Nicosia's gratitude to Moscow for its consistent support. Russian officials and policymakers frequently celebrated the "special" character of the bilateral relationship, including common interests, shared international law principles and values, the "spiritual affinities" and the historical and "spiritual" bonds between Cyprus and Russia. Verbal actions should be taken seriously, especially when performed by a foreign minister with Sergey Lavrov's gravitas, and because his conception of Russia-RoC relations is repeatedly conveyed in pragmatic idealist terms. For example,

> At the basis of our traditionally friendly relations with the Republic of Cyprus lie strong historical and spiritual bonds...What brings us closer to each other is the common understanding of the necessity to be guided in international relations by universal principles and legal norms. (Russian Foreign Ministry 2007)

Similarly, Ambassador Muradov, in a 2000 interview with a Turkish Cypriot newspaper, stated quite boldly:

> I want to tell the Turkish Cypriots openly: the recognition of an independent state, which was created in a military way with the help from

the armed forces of a foreign country, regardless under what pretext this military action was done, is impossible and unacceptable in the modern world". (Muradov 2000, 171)

Analogous was Russian FM Spokesman, Andrey Nesterenko's, declaration during a September 2009 media briefing: "It goes without saying that Russia was never going to recognize the so-called 'Turkish Republic of Northern Cyprus" (*Russia Today* 2009).

Two years later, when Turkey was deploying gunboat diplomacy in Cyprus' EEZ, Ambassador Vyacheslav Shumskyi defended the Republic's rights according to the Law of the Sea, by stating that "this is totally in accordance with international law and with the EU regulations, so there is no doubt about that" (quoted in Melakopides 2018a, b, 157). Idealistic verbal actions kept being combined with pragmatic idealist non-verbal actions (primarily *legal and ethical* decisions and initiatives) during the Russophile years of President Tassos Papadopoulos (2003–2008). At the local administration level, for instance, it was celebrated through the Nicosia-Moscow cooperation agreement, reached in February 2005, "with a view to boosting and consolidating the good relations between the two capitals" (*Financial Mirror* 2005). It covered the exchange of community services in various fields, including construction of infrastructure projects, preservation of historic monuments in both towns and protection of the environment", through the "exchange of expertise, delegations and technology to achieve this goal".

On the highest level, President Dimitris Christofias' November 2008 state visit to Moscow produced solid results. Presidents Dmitry Medvedev and Christofias signed a Joint Declaration entitled "On Further Intensification of the Relations of Friendship and Comprehensive Cooperation between the Republic of Cyprus and the Russian Federation". Beyond political cooperation, the declaration covered many additional dimensions: from economic relations to cooperation of local authorities, continuing military-technical cooperation, collaboration in addressing "new threats and challenges" (such as terrorism and other criminal phenomena), ending with a long section on "Cultural, Religious and Humanitarian Fields". This section's language validates our methodological choice: "The Sides confirm that the development of bilateral cooperation in the humanitarian field has a strong foundation with regard to historic, cultural and religious closeness of the peoples of the two States" (see, Melakopides 2018a, b, 183n27).

Tourism and Investments

Russian tourism to Cyprus represents a major bridge between Russian-Cypriot pragmatism and idealism, since, besides tangible economic significance, it demonstrates the special inter-people affinity and friendship. The rise in Russian tourist arrivals to Cyprus has been impressive: from 130,000 in 2000, they reached around 181,000 in 2008 and 224,000 arrivals in 2010, placing Russia among the island's top sources of holidaymakers (Melakopides 2018a, b, 84). In early 2012, representatives of the Cyprus Tourism Organization (KOT) visiting Moscow expected Russian tourists that year to exceed 400,000 and announced that seven more Russian airports would be added for tourists to Cyprus, resulting in flights from a total of 16 cities (Melakopides 2018a, b, 84).

Argyrios Pisiotis' (2001, 421) observations about Russian tourism to Greece and Cyprus in the 1990s also reflect the pragmatic idealist framework, because Russian tourism's revival applied also to spiritual tourism. This category of tourism was taking place along "the traditional routes which nineteenth century Russian pilgrims followed to Greece": that is, Moscow-Odessa and then by ship to Constantinople, Thessaloniki, Mount Athos, Athens and Palestine.

From the spiritual back to the pragmatic, it is quite remarkable that small Cyprus steadily kept its position among the top three states investing in the Russian economy. According to the Russian State Statistics Committee, Cyprus kept the first place in 2001, representing 16.3% of total foreign investment income, followed by the US (11.2%) and Great Britain (10.9%). In August 2010, the total Cypriot cumulative investment in Russia amounted to US$52 billion, of which 38 billion consisted of Foreign Direct Investments (FDI) (Melakopides 2018a, b, 82). To be sure, these funds were mostly of Russian origin and returning to Russia using the favourable terms of Cypriot legislation. This, however, was not the only reason for Russian businessmen's interest in Cyprus. The Republic's attractiveness was also caused by (1) full membership in the European Union (EU) since 2004; (2) being a regional and world business centre; (3) political stability and safety; and (4) mutually established friendly attitudes.

On Mutual Friendly Attitudes

The reality of the fourth dimension is pronounced regularly and enthusiastically. For instance, Natalia Kardash (2010), Editor and publisher of the Limassol-founded weekly, *Vestnik Kipra*, made a powerful anthropocentric argument regarding the RoC's attraction for both Russian businessmen and ordinary Russians. In a November 2010 Conference on Russia-Cyprus relations, she replied to the question "Why do Russians Choose Cyprus?" as follows:

> [T]he most important reason is people. Cypriots like Russians. Russian people feel very comfortable here. There are many countries with good weather and similar business conditions. But Cyprus –I know it for sure- is the best country in Europe if you take into consideration how people treat Russians here...Many people say that in Cyprus they feel that they live a full life, they learn to enjoy every day.

According to her study, around 50,000 Russians were then living in Cyprus, about 46% of whom were visitors, earning money abroad and spending it in the Republic. The rest were counted as follows: Russian businessmen and their families, 26%; employees of local and international companies, 13%; wives of Cypriot citizens, 11%; and Russian students welcomed at various Cypriot universities, 4%. Additionally, 2010 data demonstrated the progressive incorporation of Russians in Cypriot life: Russian-speaking children number between 25,000–30,000; four Russian schools operate in the Republic; "there are more than 10 educational centres where children go in the afternoon"; and about 20 music and dancing schools use Russian as the main language (Kardash 2010).

Fully analogous was Ambassador Muradov's relevant opinion. Asked in February 1999 "Why are Russia and Cyprus so close?" Georgi Muradov, after mentioning their well-developed treaties and legal agreements, added,

> the good climate, political stability...favourable tax policy towards foreign companies and the sophisticated banking and business infrastructure. The geographical proximity of Russia and Cyprus also plays an important role, but for us it is more important that Cyprus is a traditionally friendly country, spiritually close to us and connected by strong historical ties. (Muradov 2000, 177)

Incidentally, following Ms Kardash's celebration of Russia-Cyprus bonding, I asked distinguished Russian academic, Dr Nadia Arbatova, if she would endorse my "pragmatic idealism" hypothesis. She replied confidently, "Yes!". After all, she had just concluded her own geopolitical analysis (Arbatova 2010) as follows: "Russia and Cyprus are natural allies!"

The pragmatic idealist synthesis was further confirmed in October 2010, during Dmitry Medvedev's official Nicosia visit. The 15 bilateral agreements signed at the time would, in Medvedev's words, "create a solid foundation for the future business development". In fact, the new tax deal, preventing double taxation, could enhance the positive conditions already in place, so that Medvedev could state that "Cyprus is perceived by our businessmen as a very convenient platform to make investments" (*Moscow Times* 2010).

Admittedly, Cypriots were primarily awaiting assurances that Russia-Cyprus relations would remain unaffected by the strengthening Turkey-Russia material embrace. Therefore, they welcomed Russian president's assurance that Moscow's growing commercial and political relations with Turkey "do not pose a threat" to Cyprus: "Our relations will remain just as friendly and mutually beneficial, and Russia will not change its position regarding the Cyprus question. This position is that Cyprus must be a single sovereign state with two communities...We will continue to work towards this goal" (*Moscow Times* 2010).

In 2011, Turkey attempted anew to intimidate Nicosia through verbal abuse and gunboat diplomacy. As we know, Ambassador Shumsky expressed Moscow's "absolutely clear" defence of the Republic's rights in its EEZ according to UNCLOS, directly condemning Ankara's bullying. But the international and EU financial crisis had also reached Cyprus' shores by mid-2011, rendering difficult the country's borrowing in international markets. When President Christofias requested assistance, Moscow responded without delay, promising a generous loan of 2.5 billion euro at an interest rate of 4.5%. And during the Cyprus-Russia Friendship Association's 50th anniversary meeting in Nicosia, in November 2011, Georgi Muradov, representing the Russian Foreign Ministry, read out a message from Sergei Lavrov. Six words in this message reflected what I have submitted as the essence of the bilateral relationship: "Russia is interested in close and fruitful cooperation with Cyprus on the basis of sincere friendship, mutual sympathy and common interests" (ITAR-TASS 2011).

A Summary of Mutual Benefits

The list of bilateral benefits, accumulated during 1992–2017, may begin by what Cypriots treasured first: the strong sense of political security and diplomatic solidarity provided by Moscow at the UNSC and bilaterally, through declarations, decisions and actions. Second, Cyprus was grateful because Moscow's verbal actions affirming the legality of the Republic contradicted cynical Anglo-American *Realpolitik* and Ankara's ongoing belligerence. Therefore, Moscow remained a principal reminder of the RoC's traumatized sovereignty and territorial integrity, whereas wily Western creative initiatives about the Cyprus problem, essentially aimed at exculpating Turkey. Third, the purely pragmatic benefits included Russia's energetic financial platform in Cyprus, with serious banking and real estate investments, plus Moscow's demonstrated readiness to assist Cyprus during the international financial crisis. Fourth, Russian tourism was established as a solid provider of valuable income and authentic camaraderie. Finally, Cypriots could count on sincere people-to-people friendship and mutual sympathy to strengthen interstate and inter-governmental political bonding resulting in further mutual benefits.

Moscow, in turn, could enjoy the political association with a grateful friend and natural ally, appreciating the RoC's pro-Russia voice in international fora, and primarily in Brussels, where one could hear the devious assertion, "Cyprus is Russia's Trojan Horse". Second, Russia benefited by the RoC's status as a top channel for massive investments. Indeed, by 2010, Cyprus' FDI to Russia reached USD 61.961 million, followed by the Netherlands (40.383m), Luxembourg (35.167m) and Germany (USD27.825m) (Melakopides 2018a, b: 91). Third, Russia expanded via Cyprus its economic presence within the EU, while Russian investors acquired a strong foothold in Cypriot real estate, banking and other services. Fourth, the RoC became a safe and exciting tourist destination, for both general and "spiritual" Russian tourism. The relevant figures are quite impressive, especially when we compare the 148,740 Russian arrivals of 2009 to the 334,083 in 2011. Fifth, Russia's pragmatic idealist treatment of Cyprus, with demonstrable respect for legal principles and ethical values, could be used to strengthen Russian soft power. Last but not least, Moscow had counted on Cypriot understanding and assistance in the Eastern Mediterranean and appreciated Nicosia's efforts to contain Russophobia in the EU.

Enter Anastasiades

Dimitris Christofias cultivated RoC-Russia bonding in true pragmatic idealist manner. But he decided against seeking re-election, arguably after his failure to perceive the coming economic crisis and because of the human and socio-economic tragedy of the July 2011 explosion at Mari, for which he was primarily blamed by the state-appointed investigator (Melakopides 2018a, b, 92–93). As for his final relations with Moscow, Christofias himself complained that Vladimir Putin avoided at the end even "to come to the phone" (Politis 2013). Nikos Anastasiades, who won the presidential election of February 2013 supported by his right-wing DISY party, promised a foreign policy balanced vis-à-vis both superpowers. Regarding Moscow's Cyprus record, Anastasiades always expressed Cypriot "gratitude", for consistent diplomatic and political support, economic cooperation, Russian tourism and the strong cultural and religious bonds. In March 2013, when the Eurogroup-imposed bail-in caused panic in Cyprus, Nicosia sent immediately Finance Minister Michalis Sarris to Moscow. His return with empty hands could be attributed to the cooling in the Putin-Christofias chemistry, the disconcerting image of the RoC's economy under "Brussels' attack", and Moscow's unwillingness to risk another friction with the EU.

Because EU-caused, the traumatic bail-in did not create a Moscow-Nicosia crisis, but rather confirmed the "special" relationship: first, only few Russian investors left Cyprus and those who stayed seemed to endorse the Russian proverb, "better an old friend than two new ones". Second, Russian trust was reportedly premised on the RoC's high-quality expertise in legal, financial, logistical, banking and associated matters. Third, during his spring 2013 Moscow visit, then Minister of Defence, Fotis Fotiou, perceived Moscow's desire to continue using Limassol port facilities for its military vessels cruising the Eastern Mediterranean, as they were doing during the ongoing Syrian war (ITAR-TASS 2013). Fourth, in late summer 2013, Moscow lowered the interest rate of the 2011 loan, extending its payment by some years. Finally, increasing numbers of Russian "return tourists" reaffirmed the established mutual sympathy while also providing Cyprus vital economic relief.

Anastasiades Under Pressure

Progressively, however, Nikos Anastasiades, notwithstanding his Russophile rhetoric, appeared to be courting Washington. But his being subjected to unconscionable Western pressures prevented the identification of his authentic inclinations. Still, the pressures concerned the settlement of the Cyprus problem, economic insecurity and the promising Cypriot hydrocarbon deposits. In all three, the idiosyncratic—to put it euphemistically—American Ambassador, John M. Koenig, usurped the role of first fiddle. For instance, during a September 2013 Conference, extroverted Koenig advertised passionately "the present ideal opportunity" to resolve the Cyprus problem, given Anastasiades' electoral victory.

Anastasiades had favoured openly the Anglo-American Annan Plan which the GCs triumphantly rejected, and Moscow had opposed by the famous 2004 veto. Now, he was ready to restart bi-communal negotiations along analogous lines, apparently oblivious to the dark realities in Erdogan's Ankara and in Cyprus' regional geopolitics. But the foreign pressures became so asphyxiating that Anastasiades exploded on national television, on 15 January 2015. Accumulated grounds for his outburst might have included post facto recognition of Victoria Nuland's trap regarding the 11 February 2014 Joint Declaration with TC leader Derviş Eroğlu that imposed a toxic framework for bi-communal negotiations; John Koenig's 11 May 2014 interview with *Phileleftheros* entitled, "You should trust Turkey more"; Joe Biden's advertised as "historic" visit that left Nicosia empty-handed; Turkey's October 2014 renewed violations of international law in Cyprus' EEZ; and various other cases of manipulation and deception against the RoC and its president, with discredited UN Secretary General Special Advisor, Espen Barth Eide, as protagonist.

Furious, Anastasiades asserted that he "was taken for granted" because of his 2004 support for the Annan Plan; and that, unwilling to disturb their relations with Turkey, the Americans expected him to make all the concessions. Hence, daily *Phileleftheros*' title: "Anastasiades got angry: Shots against the UN Secretary General and the United States" (Melakopides 2018a, b, 188n57). Meanwhile, whereas Washington and London reacted to Turkey's new aggression in the Cypriot EEZ by a lukewarm (pseudo-)condemnation, Moscow's strong denunciation emphasized: "Unilateral actions and the show of force are unacceptable, because they are threatening to worsen the situation not only in Cypriot affairs but also in the broader region of the Eastern Mediterranean" (Melakopides 2018a, b, 121).

Anastasiades Goes to Moscow

Thereupon, Anastasiades turned to Russia. Declaring again the special bilateral relations, Anastasiades arranged an official visit to Vladimir Putin. His February 2015 visit was quite successful as attested by Cypriot and Russian media. The latter chose such titles as "Russian warships allowed at ports of Cyprus for humanitarian purposes"; "Cyprus opposes sanctions against Russia"; and "Ever more politicians in Europe see negative results of sanctions—Cyprus' president" (see, Melakopides 2018a, b, 163). The three-day visit gave the opportunity to the two presidents and Premier Medvedev, to Foreign Ministers Ioannis Kasoulides and Sergey Lavrov and to Energy Minister George Lakkotrypis to reassert the relationship's excellent level and to enrich the long list of Protocols and Treaties with 11 new Agreements (RoC Foreign Ministry 2015).

Back in Nicosia, respectable columnist and author, Costas Venizelos, underlined the visit's positive results and implications. Among them, that "Moscow perceived positively Cyprus' axis with Egypt and the one with Israel and favours the cooperation of the three states of the region"; that Moscow's interest in energy issues is oriented towards investing in shares from companies already active in Cyprus' EEZ; and that Moscow's primary interest appears to be geostrategic, with energy issues operating in a supporting role, something that fits Nicosia's own calculations and desires. Venizelos also noted Anastasiades' request that President Putin may talk directly to Erdogan regarding Cyprus. As for the military agreement, he clarified that the Russian navy's right to use the Limassol port could not harm the RoC's relations with its other partners (Venizelos 2015).

Some more months of fruitful pragmatic idealism followed Anastasiades' Moscow visit. Rhetorically, there was constant bilateral confirmation of Sergey Lavrov's tripartite formula ("common interests, sincere friendship, and historical-cultural bonds"). Pragmatically, constructive results continued in diplomacy, politics, economy, trade, culture and tourism, while various high-level visits were successfully exchanged. The RoC was even attempting to reduce European Russophobia, as noted and appreciated by Moscow and its Nicosia Embassy. Ambassador Osadchyi kept reiterating that, "if asked", Russia was ready to help in the fair solution of the country's problem. Anastasiades' next trip to Moscow with a business agenda in October 2017 also proved successful. The Russian festivals in Limassol were attended by enthusiastic crowds. Russians living on the Island created a new political party called "I, the citizen". And a magnificent new Russian Orthodox Church was inaugurated near Nicosia.

Russian Popularity in Cyprus

Greek Cypriots kept favouring warm bilateral relations with Russia and wished for even stronger ties. Formal opinion research on these relations has been sporadic. Considering, however, the principal authors of Cyprus' vicissitudes—i.e., Washington, London, Ankara and increasingly the UN Secretariat—one could discern that most GCs appreciated thoroughly Russia's traditional role as the RoC's most powerful political and diplomatic counterweight. This intuition was enhanced by the steady recognition of Moscow's positive role by analysts, opinion makers and the Centrist political elites. Thus, anecdotal evidence had crystallized that GCs' affection and hopes are certainly oriented towards Moscow (Petasis and Mallinson 2017).

This perception was verified by opinion research in mid-December 2015 as reported by the *Cyprus Mail*:

> Almost three out of four Cypriots would welcome the provision of military facilities to Russia by Cyprus…Over half of those polled island-wide on December 16 and 17 said the government should seek closer ties with Moscow." In addition, "Three out five said they would feel safer if there was a Russian military presence on the island[…].Seven out of ten Cypriots were open to offering military facilities to Russian forces fighting against terrorism, with 37 per cent going as far as saying Cyprus should give them a base. (Jean Christou 2015)

Similarly, a bi-communal project subtitled, "Ideas for a new Security Architecture" (Philis 2016), interviewed GCs and TCs on possible Cyprus "futures". Most revealing were the answers regarding the Potential Guarantor States. Among the TCs, 69% responded that Turkey would be "satisfactory or desirable", placing it on top, while the least "satisfactory or desirable" was Russia, supported by only 10% of TCs. Russia, moreover, was voted "unacceptable" by 68% of the responding TCs.

Contrariwise, Russia was favoured by 53% of the GC respondents, who placed it on top of all alternatives. Unsurprisingly, Turkey was the most "unacceptable" (84%), followed by the UK (70%) and the US (51%). In addition, while Russia was "unacceptable" to only 32% of the GCs, 16% of them found Russia "tolerable". Therefore, adding the latter to the 53% of "satisfactory or desirable" reaches a total of 69%, compared to a mere 49% for the US and 30% for the UK.

Meanwhile, Nicosia's foreign policy deepened its trilateral relations with Israel, Greece and Egypt, with designs to include eventually Lebanon, Jordan and various Gulf States. Although the trilateral agreements, and the high-level meetings in Nicosia, Cairo, Jerusalem and Athens, emphasized as their aim regional peace and security via energy collaboration without any hostility against other parties, these emerging quasi-alliances (Tziarras 2016) were manifestly motivated by Turkey's arrogance and hostility *contra omnes*. Simultaneously, Nicosia kept cultivating cordial and productive relations with Paris, having established solid political support at the UNSC and numerous bilateral defence agreements since the 1960s. Nonetheless, in Cypriot hearts and minds, Russia remained the counterweight *par excellence* to Turkey's bellicosity. Given the unending "treacheries" by Washington, London, the UN, and even the EU, Cypriot political elites, opinion makers and large sectors of civil society had been expecting Russia to defend the Republic from Ankara's constant threats and provocations. Except for rhetorical support, however, Moscow now seemed unwilling or unable to effectively assume this role.

2017–2021: Pragmatic Idealism Tested

Erdogan's Role

Since the mid-2010s, Ankara's chauvinistic antagonism with Cyprus and Greece assumed frenzied proportions. Trapped in the Syrian minefield, facing escalating domestic problems, and isolated in the Eastern Mediterranean, Erdogan never abandoned his megalomaniacal ambition to impose a neo-Ottoman regional hegemony, risking the legendary costs of overexpansion. Inter alia, he orchestrates toxic verbal attacks, daily against Nicosia and Athens and frequently against Cairo and Tel Aviv. Simultaneously, Ankara employed provocative hybrid warfare, in the Cypriot EEZ and the Aegean Sea: violating Greece's FIR and airspace, flying over inhabited islands and ramming Greek Coast Guard vessels gravely risking human lives (Melakopides 2018c). The anti-Hellenic verbal attacks are accompanied by skilfully crafted distortions of historical facts and legal norms that represent *strepsodikia* that is, chicanery or pettifoggery. Additionally, by inciting his domestic audiences in "patriotic" delirium, Erdogan became imprisoned in the public's resulting expectations to effectively confront Turkey's omni-present enemies. Moreover, in tandem with Foreign Ministry spokesman, Hami Aksoi, and various ministers, Erdogan appealed constantly to Turkey's rights and interests as though the two are conceptually and legally identical. Characteristically, he appealed to international law whenever Turkey proceeded to violate it. The ongoing invasion in the Cypriot EEZ is a paradigm case.

Less familiar readers should know that, in November 2019, again "in accordance with international law", Turkey performed a double legal violation by signing two "MoUs" with Tripoli, never legitimized by the Libyan Parliament. The first memorandum was signed to let Turkey violate the UN Libya arms embargo. The second one, claiming to bridge Turkey's and Libya's EEZs, constitutes a legal and geographical absurdity, by contradicting the United Nations Convention on the Law of the Sea (UNCLOS), being premised yet again on Turkey's outlandish assertion that Islands possess neither Continental Shelf nor an EEZ. Thus, this "agreement" has literally ignored or circumvented the sovereign rights of Crete, Rhodes and other Greek Islands, by sheer Turkish fiat. And although this memorandum was immediately condemned as "illegal" or "null and void" by Greece and Cyprus, as "provocative" by Washington, and as clearly untenable by the EU, Erdogan responded by threatening to drill for gas in the Cretan EEZ (Fredriksen and Tziarras 2020).

Such international troublemaking would be incomprehensible if one ignored, first, Erdogan's *sui generis* Machiavellian rationality; second, his neo-Ottoman fixed ideas, including his vision of the New Turkey and the Blue Homeland (Tziarras 2019); and third, the fact that Erdogan's neo-imperialism is encouraged by the policy of appeasement adopted by Cyprus, Greece and a Turkophobic and blackmailed international community (Melakopides RUDN 2018c). Erdogan's emerging Operational Code prevents him from accepting the constant invitations to join regional energy projects and to endorse UNCLOS. Instead, Turkey has opted for provoking primarily Cyprus and Greece, challenging the energy companies, ignoring EU demands to cease any drilling for hydrocarbons in Cyprus' EEZ and threatening daily to use military force under preposterous rationalizations.[1]

Erdogan, therefore, daily demonstrates contempt for the principles and norms of International Law and International Ethics, attempting to substitute for them an absurd or "neo-surrealistic" (as Greek Foreign Minister Nikos Dendias has quipped) Turkish conception of legality. Manifestly, the RoC is constantly being threatened by Erdogan's belligerent intimidation. Therefore, Nicosia has been awaiting well-deserved international support. With the UN Secretariat suspiciously apathetic, the support was ultimately expected from the EU and the Russian Federation.

Bilateral Disagreements and Complaints

Brussels, however, has long surrendered to Erdogan's blackmail, through his perennial threats to flood Europe with refugees and migrants. Regrettably, this fact, together with the powerful economic interests of Germany, Italy and Spain, explains why the EU's promised sanctions keep being postponed, despite Turkey's actualizing its threats in the Aegean Sea and at the Evros River in March 2020. But if Brussels' erstwhile "normative power" has thus evaporated, Moscow's response should not. Therefore, the GC public's disappointment at Russian protracted "neutrality" seems justified. And yet, Moscow may also complain that Nicosia's deepening relations with Washington bluntly contradict its alleged balance towards the two great powers. Therefore, Maria Zacharova's December 2018 allegation of US military infiltration, immediately criticized as hyperbolic, is proven today prophetic. The question, then, arises: Can we tell whose culpability is chronologically prior?

Schematically, besides the strategic grievance, Moscow finds quite disconcerting Nicosia's failure to resist Western demands to confront alleged Russian money laundering. For Cypriots, deeply disheartening are three issues: building the Akkuyu nuclear power plant just across their land; selling the S-400 system to Turkey; and above all, Russia's

---

[1] Among other things, Turkey asserts ad nauseam that its EEZ extends south of Cyprus; it rejects Cyprus' EEZ delineation agreements with Israel and Egypt, because it has not given its consent; and asserts that, according to international law, it represents the TCs' violated rights.

abstention from effective condemnation of Turkey's illegal and immoral actions against the Republic. Moscow's strategic disappointment appears rational and reasonable. The same complaint is regularly voiced by left-wing AKEL and RoC Centrist political elites, long accusing Anastasiades of turning to Moscow (only) when in need. But Nicosia might claim that its slide towards Washington is essentially defensive; that it followed chronologically Moscow's protracted passivity towards Ankara's anti-RoC provocations; and point to its obligation to protect the energy giants contractually engaged in its EEZ. Misplaced also seems Russia's money-laundering protestation, considering the West's capacity to punish Cyprus, as by the traumatic 2013 bail-in.

On reflection, Cypriots' three complaints appear valid. Since the Akkuyu area is manifestly seismogenic, Cypriot, Turkish, and European ecologists have condemned the nuclear plant as tremendously risky. Moreover, people fear Erdogan's potential development of nuclear weapons, given his relevant insinuations. Similarly, whereas the S-400 missiles are advertised as merely defensive, Cypriots are justified to doubt their innocence towards them. Finally, if Moscow's present coyness is juxtaposed to Russia's unwavering support for Cyprus in 2011 and 2014, one appreciates immediately the current *differentia specifica*.

The Regional and the Idiosyncratic Levels of Analysis

A sketch of Russia-US regional antagonism and glimpses at Vladimir Putin's Operational Code may facilitate answering our dilemmas. The antagonism was reactivated through Washington's Eastern Mediterranean re-engagement and is not unrelated to Ankara's behaviour. As a recent Report by the CSIS observes,

> One recent trend in US policy toward the Eastern Mediterranean is to develop new security and energy alliances with Greece, Cyprus, Egypt, Israel, Lebanon, and Jordan in order to circumvent reliance on Turkey. Russia's relationship and increasingly frequent interaction with Turkey fuels this search for policy alternatives. For Russia, closer ties with a core NATO ally create friction inside the Alliance, is confirmation of its status in the region, and is an antidote to Western efforts to isolate Russia politically.

Regarding the RoC, this US policy was clearly signalled through Mike Pompeo's participation in the 20 March 2019 Jerusalem Trilateral

Summit between Israel, Cyprus and Greece, and further strengthened by his September 2020 visit to Nicosia that Nicosia greeted with relief (US Embassy). As former RoC Foreign Minister Nikos Christodoulides stated, Pompeo expressed the US commitment and interest in the security and stability of the broader Eastern Mediterranean region, which in the RoC case included potential US help vis-a-vis Turkey, the RoC's participation in the American military training programme IMET, "the partial lifting of the US arms embargo on Cyprus", and "the establishment of a training facility, in Cyprus, which will be named 'Cyprus Centre for Land, Open Seas and Port Security (Cyclops)'" (*Cyprus Mail* 2020).

Washington's return was fortified formally by the Menendez-Rubio Bill, that also aimed to reshape regional US policy, by supporting the trilateral partnership of Cyprus, Greece and Israel through energy and defence cooperation. Initially advertised in Nicosia as Washington's decision to protect the RoC from Turkey's machinations, an amendment demanded that Nicosia should deny Russian military vessels access to ports for refuelling and servicing. President Anastasiades called the demand "unfortunate", as hurting "the independence and sovereignty of the Republic of Cyprus" (*Knews* 2019) But Vice-Admiral (ret.) Constantine Fitiris openly condemned the development as rendering the RoC a "consumable pawn" in American geostrategic games:

> So, what is the solution? We should refuse to "play" in this chessboard because, in the fluid situation in the Eastern Mediterranean, our cost will be far greater than our benefit. If we hurt our relations with Russia we will obviously lose its support in the Security Council and if, simultaneously, the US warm up again their relations with Turkey (which is quite likely!) then the situation will be very dangerous for the Republic of Cyprus...[since] of the permanent members at the Security Council, we always had the support of France, China and Russia (whereas) Britain and USA usually abstain from resolutions favourable to us. (Fitiris 2019)

In any event, some Cypriots perceive Moscow's apathy towards Erdogan's belligerence as tantamount to betrayal. But then, such perception might reveal narcissism and immaturity, if the GCs assumed that Moscow's RoC policy is somehow autonomous, divorced from Russia's and Putin's Grand Strategy. If, however, this strategy aims, primarily, at upsetting the US-Turkey-NATO alliance and aspires to Russia's recognition as an undoubted superpower, it follows that Moscow's current treatment of Cyprus could not be equal to the one preceding Washington's return to the Eastern Mediterranean.

The idiosyncratic level of analysis could also provide useful insights. Two studies about Putin's mind may suggest that Moscow could not be unaffected by Nicosia's occasional strategic oscillation and experimentation. The first study, by Nikita Khrushchev's great-granddaughter, Nina L. Khrushcheva, argues that Putin's foreign policy is strongly motivated by the need to restore the honour and pride of his "Great Nation":

> Putin maintains that Russia's problem today is not that we, the Russians, lack a vision for the future but that we have stopped being proud of our past, our Russian-ness, our difference from the West. 'When we were proud all was great', he said at the Valdai International Discussion Club meeting last September [2014]. While he may bemoan the death of the Soviet state, Putin's search for greatness extends even further back in history, to Byzantine statehood. (Khrushcheva 2014, 19)

Recalling that when Constantinople fell to the "encroaching Ottoman Empire in 1453, Russia declared itself the Byzantine successor", Khrushcheva (2014, 19) argues that this notion "Putin has put back into vogue today". Pride and honour feed Putin's very "definition" of "the Russian (and his own) psyche": "We are less pragmatic than other people, less calculating. But then we have a more generous heart. Perhaps this reflects the greatness of our country, its vast size", Khrushcheva adds (2014, 19).

If a generous heart would expect reciprocation, its absence could entail deep disappointment, which is precisely what Putin has experienced. For in the speech on the Crimean annexation, he explained how this wonderful and trusting character was maliciously betrayed: "Russia strived to engage in dialogue with our colleagues in the West. We are constantly proposing cooperation on all key issues; we want to strengthen our level of trust and for our relations to be equal, open, and fair. But we saw no reciprocal steps" (Khrushcheva 2014, 21–22).

She then illustrates concretely Putin's progressive discontents, beginning with a March 2000 BBC interview, when Putin had insisted that "Russia is part of the European culture. And I cannot imagine my own country in isolation from Europe and what we often call the civilized world. So it is hard for me to visualize NATO as an enemy" (Khrushcheva 2014, 21–22). Moreover, Putin cultivated personal relations with major Western leaders, "becoming buddies with then British Prime Minister Tony Blair, whom he saw five times in 2000, thus announcing Russia's European orientation. George W. Bush joined the circle of friends a few years later...Both religious Christians, the two leaders struck a bond" (Khrushcheva 2014, 21–22). Unfortunately for Putin's expectations, "In 2002, Bush and Blair took into NATO seven countries, including the Baltic states. Because he was ignored in this historical reshuffling, Putin felt personally betrayed. As Blair candidly admitted in his memoir, 'Vladimir later came to believe that the Americans did not give him his due place'" (Khrushcheva 2014, 22).

It thus transpires that Putin's national pride coexists with a strong personal pride that seems to inhere his psychological makeup. Therefore, just as he could not forgive the malicious games played against Russia and himself by major international actors, he could hardly tolerate that Nicosia's recent Moscow policies, after hesitation and indecision, culminated in the Americanophile geopolitical embrace. John J. Mearsheimer also approached Putin's strategic mind in an impressive essay on the 2014 Ukraine crisis, that demonstrated how a sophisticated neo-realist can proffer persuasive theses by suppressing ethno-centric impulses. Mearsheimer establishes the sustained Western provocations at Russia's very borders, in both Ukraine and Georgia, the methodical propaganda, and the illegal and unethical actions aiming at aborting Kiev's Russophile decisions, to incorporate Ukraine in the EU and NATO (Mearsheimer 2014). Mearsheimer argues that Russia's August 2008 invasion of Georgia "should have dispelled any remaining doubts about Putin's determination to prevent Georgia and Ukraine from joining NATO" (Mearsheimer 2014, 3). There followed the fighting between the Georgian government and the South Ossetian separatists, and Russia's taking control of Abkhazia and South Ossetia. Therefore, "Moscow had made its point. Yet despite this clear warning, NATO never publicly abandoned its goal of bringing Georgia and Ukraine into the alliance. And NATO expansion continued marching forward, with Albania and Croatia becoming members in 2009" (Mearsheimer 2014, 3).

Before moving to Yanukovych's ouster, Mearsheimer handles the EU's "marching eastward", through the Eastern Partnership initiative, and the West's "efforts to spread Western values and promote democracy in

Ukraine and other post-Soviet states, a plan that often entails funding pro-Western individuals and organizations". Hence Victoria Nuland's 2013 estimation that,

> the United States had invested more than $5 billion since 1991 to help Ukraine achieve "the future it deserves". As part of that effort, the U.S. government had bankrolled the National Endowment for Democracy …[that] has funded more than 60 projects aimed at promoting civil society in Ukraine, and the NED's president, Carl Gershman, has called that country "the biggest prize". (Mearsheimer 2014, 4)

Mearsheimer also quotes Gershman's September 2013 cynical statement in the *Washington Post* that "Ukraine's choice to join Europe will accelerate the demise of the ideology of Russian imperialism that Putin represents". He added: "Russians, too, face a choice, and Putin may find himself on the losing end not just in the near abroad but within Russia itself" (Mearsheimer 2014, 4). In a paradigmatically honest evaluation of antagonistic strategic proclivities, he adds: "When Russian leaders look at Western social engineering in Ukraine, they worry that their country might be next. And such fears are hardly groundless" (Mearsheimer 2014, 4). Mearsheimer's diagnosis includes that "Putin is playing hardball", but "Putin's actions should be easy to comprehend"; because, since "Ukraine serves as a buffer state of enormous strategic importance to Russia [,] no Russian leader would tolerate a military alliance that was Moscow's mortal enemy until recently moving into Ukraine" (Mearsheimer 2014, 5). Therefore,

> Washington may not like Moscow's position, but it should understand the logic behind it. This is Geopolitics 101: great powers are always sensitive to potential threats near their home territory. After all, the United States does not tolerate distant great powers deploying military forces anywhere in the Western Hemisphere, much less on its borders. (Mearsheimer 2014, 5–6)

Finally, regarding the ensuing blame game, Mearsheimer dismissed Angela Merkel's implication "that Putin was irrational", offering his personal assessment: "Although Putin no doubt has autocratic tendencies, no evidence supports the charge that he is mentally unbalanced. On the contrary: he is a first-class strategist who should be feared and respected by anyone challenging him on foreign policy" (Mearsheimer 2014, 8).

Putin, of course, could not be the only decision-maker of Russian foreign policy, given primarily the experience, *gravitas* and role of Sergey Lavrov. Moreover, as regards Cyprus, we should endorse Ambassador Vladimir Lukin's conception, that post-Soviet Russian foreign policy is "a multi-entrance diplomacy" (*monogopod'ezdnaya diplomatiya*). Accordingly, "the whole host of interest groups and lobbies (including business interests, energy companies, powerful 'oligarchs', Russian Orthodox Church, etc.) are pursuing their own 'foreign policies'…" (Torbakov 2010).

Even so, Putin is certainly a *primus inter pares* and, drawing on Khrushcheva and Mearsheimer, we may deduce that his operational code exhibits strong emotional and clear rational dimensions, synthesized to produce decisions fortified by personal pride, that intend to serve national honour. Their execution proceeds after mature and precise—i.e., rational—consideration of ends and means. Applied to post-2017 Russia-RoC relations, Putin's synthesis represents decision-making that retains traditional Philhellenic/Philocypriot components but is determined primarily by Moscow's broader strategic goals and Nicosia's occasional oscillation and experimentation.

Parallel Affirmation of "Pragmatic Idealism"?

How far does this convoluted picture undermine traditional bilateral pragmatic idealism? Intriguingly, the answer is thoroughly affected by Moscow's and Nicosia's sustained refusal to endanger their relations, as revealed below. Thus, Nikos Christodoulides, lecturing on the RoC foreign policy in early 2019, called Russia-RoC relations "excellent" (Christodoulides 2019). To my question, "How can we call them 'excellent' after Ms Zacharova's recent warning?", he confidently replied: "'Excellent' does not mean we cannot have disagreements". Also in early 2019, Russian Ambassador Nebenzia, during the Security Council discussion about UNFICYP, firmly supported the RoC's positions against renewed Anglo-American machinations (UNSC 2019). Ambassador Osadchiy, who had skilfully defused the feared crisis following Zacharova's austere warning (*Cyprus Mail* 2018), asserted Moscow's legal commitments to the RoC. Angry at the self-declared "foreign minister" of the illicit "Turkish Republic of Northern Cyprus", who claimed to have met "officially" the Russian diplomat, Osadchiy responded: "Mr Ozersay, you know very well that the Russian Federation recognizes only the Republic of Cyprus" (Andreou 2019).

Anastasiades himself constantly emphasized the RoC's gratitude to Moscow. In June 2019, addressing the 14th Cyprus-Russia Festival in Limassol, he celebrated the two countries' "deep and diachronically historical, political, cultural and religious bonds"; he added his and President Putin's conviction that "the common goal remains the identification of new ways of mutually beneficial cooperation and the strengthening of the existing synergies" (RoC PIO 2019a). Six months later, General Director of the RoC Ministry of Foreign Affairs, Ambassador Tasos Tzionis, received assurances in Moscow of double Russian support: for the UN-sponsored resolution of the Cyprus problem and for Cyprus' rights in its EEZ (*In-Cyprus* 2019).

Igor Torbakov, an expert on Russian foreign policy, invited to comment on the recent bilateral idiosyncrasies, wrote:

> Indeed, these days "pragmatism" and "idealism" -- two pillars of a "special" Russia-Cyprus relationship -- appear to be out of balance, with the former seemingly eclipsing the latter. But it is also true that both sides would rather prefer to return to the status quo ante, whereby "pragmatism" and "idealism" reinforce each other instead of working at cross purposes. My little piece of advice to the Russian side would be as follows: in its relations with Nicosia, Moscow has to absolutely eschew overbearing and heavy-handed behaviour...The last thing the Cypriots want is a sense of being owned by a new master who thinks he has the right to lord it over them. (Torbakov 2019)

The privileged status of bilateral relations was confirmed anew during Christodoulides' February 2019 Moscow visit, when he stated that "the bilateral relations are at a very satisfactory level" and that they agreed "to work together, in concrete actions, for the further development of these relations in a number of subjects of common interest". Christodoulides expressed,

> the appreciation of the Republic of Cyprus for the diachronic stance of the Russian Federation, especially in the framework of the UN Security Council, [its] clear position on the abolition of the anachronistic system of guarantees of 1960, as well as the need for the unobstructed continuation of the UNFICYP's presence, for as long as the present unacceptable state of affairs continues. (RoC PIO 2019b)

Lavrov's own language was faithful to his traditional (pragmatic idealist) formulations:

> Cyprus is Russia's important and long-time partner in Europe. Our cooperation hinges on long-standing bonds of friendship and mutual sympathy, the spiritual and cultural affinity of our nations and serves to enhance security and stability in the East Mediterranean region and on the entire European continent. (Russian Foreign Ministry 2019)

He then added: "We are satisfied to note positive trends in all areas of bilateral cooperation" and, by endorsing explicitly Nicosia's recent proposals about guarantees, he contradicted implicitly Ankara's proverbial arrogance:

> the current system of the island's external security guarantees no longer meets modern realities and the Republic's current international status. We firmly believe that the UN Security Council's guarantees should become the most effective method for maintaining the security, sovereignty and territorial integrity of a united Cyprus. (Russian Foreign Ministry 2019)

In a 2019 essay, three Russian professors propounded a highly positive account of diachronic Moscow-Nicosia relations, endorsing many pragmatic idealist theses, including that,

> ...the ties between the USSR and Cyprus turned out to be even more intense and diverse than similar ties of the superpower with many other States at the time. After 1991, relations between Russia and Cyprus have been developing based on their traditional alliance. Russia's position with regard to the Cyprus conflict remained unchanged, and the ultimate goal was a unified State in terms that satisfy the Cypriot side. Cyprus, in turn, criticizes the west's anti-Russian sanctions, despite being a member of the EU. (Nikitina et al. 2019, 181)

Their essay ended thus: "No matter how pragmatic, Russian relations with Cyprus have remained friendly for decades despite the changing international environment" (Nikitina et al. 2019, 196).

It thus transpires that such methodologically neutral or unbiased historical analyses can reach valid conclusions, often corresponding to pragmatic idealist ones. Contrariwise, the fixations of old-fashioned Realism inevitably led to omissions, and even distortions, of the empirical record, thereby allowing subjectivism to determine outcomes. Such an example is a paper by Spyridon Litsas. Litsas' His strategic preoccupation with the sensitive region, his concern lest the US interests are defeated by Russia's Machiavellian "infiltration", and his limited knowledge of the idiosyncratic Russia-RoC relationship, result in a discussion that cannot acknowledge—literally—even one positive moment in this relationship since the 1960s. To this end, instead of recognizing the grounds for the GCs' pro-Russia sympathies, he opts exclusively for accusing them of anti-British and anti-American bias (Litsas 2019, 184):

> On the one hand, the British presence on the island from 1878 until 1960 and the troubles that occurred between 1955 and 1959 have established an anti-British political culture among Greek Cypriots… On the other hand, the Turkish invasions in 1974 and the conspiracy theory that these had been orchestrated by Washington, in particular by Secretary of State Henry Kissinger himself, have established a widespread anti-American sentiment… intensified due to the American support to the well-known Annan Plan for resolving the Cyprus question in 2004.

If "Colonial occupation" is called "British presence"; if the GC "national liberation struggle" is merely called "troubles"; and if Washington's and Henry Kissinger's role in Turkey's invasions of 1974 have to be whitewashed as "conspiracy theory", then the least one could say is that here we have a glaring example of the poverty of Realism in handling Russia-RoC relations.

To return to our account of recent verbal and non-verbal actions by Nicosia and Moscow, we should recognize the significance of Russian ambassador to Athens, Andrey Maslov's, 2020. Ambassador Maslov declared emphatically Moscow's respect and support for the provisions of UNCLOS regarding the right of islands to an EEZ and Continental Shelf:

> The only beacon for us here is International Law. The coastal zone, the continental shelf, the EEZ of the islands, the prohibition of the threats or the use of force are self-evident things. If one is interested in [knowing] the corresponding legal framework, it is sufficient to read the UN Convention on the Law of the Sea of 1982, e.g. Article 121 on Islands. (Maslov 2020)

Manifestly, Ambassador Maslov not only reiterated Moscow's consistent position on UNCLOS but also explicitly endorsed its implications in favour of Greece and Cyprus and against Ankara's associated legal, political and geopolitical provocations in the entire Eastern Mediterranean. Nicosia itself dispelled the melodramatic Cypriot fears that Moscow's stance might mean betrayal. In September 2020, it awarded Sergey Lavrov the Grand Cross of the Order of Makarios III. Lavrov himself dispelled such fears by emphasizing, inter alia, that the bilateral relations, established 60 years ago, "have been developing progressively, meeting the mutual desire of our peoples to interact, relying on our common historical and spiritual roots" (Russian Foreign Ministry 2020a).

An intriguing initiative was Lavrov's invitation to meet the leaders of the main Cypriot political parties. His decision may have arisen from a mere interest in hearing their views about regional developments and the Cyprus issue. But it may well have been prompted by the knowledge that the traditional Western proclivities regarding a settlement in Cyprus find the GCs permanently suspicious, as proven by the outcome of the 2004 referendum. Be that as it may, Lavrov noted that "the roots of relations between our nations go back hundreds of years". He also added: "Regardless of the outcome of the elections, we have always found common ground during the past 60 years. In addition, we have developed mutually beneficial ties in many spheres, including the economy and culture. The spiritual affinity of our nations is an important component as well" (Russian Foreign Ministry 2020b). Finally, during a news conference on 8 September 2020, Sergey Lavrov's comments on the harmonious bilateral cooperation culminated as follows: "Today we were gratified to say that during those years [since 1960] we have made substantial progress in key areas of cooperation. These include various fields of interstate relations from the economy to culture. At present, we can describe our relations with Cyprus as excellent" (Russian Foreign Ministry 2020a).

Towards Tentative Conclusions

Sergey Lavrov effectively renewed Moscow's broad commitment to special relations with the RoC. Simultaneously, except for matters of security, RoC-Russia bonding was served by the conservative RoC government, favoured openly by left-wing and Centrist political elites and strongly supported by the public, as we have seen. Meanwhile, disturbed by the Erdogan-Putin multiple embraces, some analysts describe Erdogan as exploiting Moscow to satisfy his geopolitical megalomania being also a willing instrument of Moscow's perceived high strategy to upset US-Turkey relations, to entice Turkey away from its formal NATO commitments, to defend its energy and defence related investments in Turkey and to undermine the West's Eastern Mediterranean energy projects. *Ceteris paribus*, if this conception is verified, Moscow's neutrality towards Turkey's bellicosity might survive ad infinitum. Contrariwise, other voices insist that the opportunistic Russia-Turkey honeymoon will be short-lived, given (a) the long and bloody history of Russo-Turkish wars, (b) their profound geostrategic disagreements (Crimea, Cyprus, Libya, Montreux, Syria, Ukraine) and (c) Erdogan's Machiavellian personality and worldview that generate decisions and actions causing palpable *Hubris*, bound to provoke Moscow's *Nemesis*. By implication, when Moscow becomes exhausted by Erdogan's ruses, associated with his geopolitical megalomania, the Hellenic World will be thoroughly relieved.

Although predictions are not compulsory in foreign policy analysis, I venture to suggest that future RoC-Russia relations will maintain energetic diplomatic and political association, economic and commercial cooperation, strong cultural and spiritual ties, and flourishing tourism. Moreover, Russia cannot possibly betray the RoC, given (1) their accumulated mutual benefits; (2) Moscow's need to safeguard its prestige through policy consistency required by soft power (Melakopides 2020); (3) the over-50,000 Russians choosing to live and thrive on the Island; (4) the hundreds of thousands of Russian visitors and repeat tourists opting for Cyprus vacations and "spiritual tourism"; and (5) Moscow's need to sustain grateful Cyprus' support in international fora, including the EU, and especially in Russophobic times.

As regards foreign policy maturity, considering that the RoC is universally recognized as a Western state (albeit closely associated with non-Western great powers such as China, and especially Russia); and since its predicament necessitated constructing urgently a security architecture; Nicosia arguably responded pragmatically to Washington's latest promises of geopolitical protection, cultivating simultaneously both its expanding regional quasi-alliances and its treasured relations with Moscow and the Russian people. This argument may amount to recognizing the RoC's foreign policy maturity, implying that Nicosia assessed rationally its existential and security needs. And yet, given the mind-boggling regional geopolitical fluidity; considering Washington's post-Trump Turkey-related dilemmas; and, finally, given Ankara's "eo-surrealistic" interpretation of International Law, it may be advisable to suspend judgements on maturity until tangible proof of Washington's fulfilling its implied assurances to the RoC and after the denouement of the unfolding Washington-Ankara-Moscow saga.

References

Adams, W. Thomas, and Cottrell, J. Alvin. 1968. *Cyprus Between East and West*. Washington: Johns Hopkins University Press.

Anderson, Perry. 2008. "The Divisions of Cyprus." *London Review of Books* 30 (8).

Andreou, Evi. 2019. "Russian Ambassador Accuses Ozersay of Trying to Discredit Him." *Cyprus Mail*, 24 May. https://cyprus-mail.com/2019/05/24/russian-ambassador-accuses-ozersay-of-trying-to-discredit-him/.

Arbatova, Nadia. 2010. "Russia and Cyprus in the Context of Regional and European Security." University of Nicosia Conference, 2 November.

Ball, George. 1982. *The Past Has Another Pattern*. New York: Norton.

Christodoulides, Nikos. 2019. "Lecture on Cypriot Foreign Policy." *ERPIC*, Nicosia, 23 January.

Christou, Jean. 2015. "Poll: Majority Would Favour Granting Military Facilities to Russia." *Cyprus Mail*, 20 December, https://cyprus-mail.com/2015/12/20/poll-majority-would-favour-granting-military-facilities-to-russia/.

Cyprus Mail. 2018. "Russia Ambassador Says Recent Spat Involves US Not Cyprus." 10 December. https://dikdurus.com/russia-ambassador-says-recent-spat-involves-us-not-cyprus/3596/.

Cyprus Mail. 2020. "Christodoulides Happy with Outcome of Pompeo Visit, FM Says." 13 September. https://cyprus-mail.com/2020/09/13/cyprus-happy-with-outcome-of-pompeo-visit-fm-says/.

Cyprus News Agency. 1997. "Russia Warns Turkey." 26 November.

Financial Mirror. 2005. "Nicosia-Moscow Set to Sign Cooperation Agreement." 21 February. https://www.financialmirror.com/2005/02/20/nicosia-moscow-set-to-sign-cooperation-agreement/.

Fitiris, Constantinos. 2019. "Σχέσεις ΗΠΑ – Κυπριακής Δημοκρατίας: Πικρές Αλήθειες" [US-Cyprus Relations: Bitter Truths]. *Sigmalive*, 29 June. https://www.sigmalive.com/news/opinions_sigmalive/575704/sxeseis-hpa-kypriakis-dimokratias-pikres-alitheies.

Fouskas, Vassilis K., and Alex O. Tackie. 2009. *Cyprus: The Post-Imperial Constitution*. London: Pluto Press.

Fredriksen, Sigvart Nordhov, and Zenonas Tziarras. 2020. *The Libya Conflict and Its Security Implications for the Broader Region, Re-imagining the Eastern Mediterranean Series: PCC Report, 4*. Nicosia: PRIO Cyprus Centre.

Hitchens, Christopher. 1997. *Hostage to History: Cyprus from the Ottomans to Kissinger*. London and New York: Verso.

Hurriyet Daily News. 1997. "Russia Threatens Retaliation Over S-300 Missiles." 10 November.

In-Cyprus. 2019. "Russia Reaffirms Support to Cyprus' Sovereign Rights." 15 October, https://in-cyprus.philenews.com/Russia-reaffirms-support-to-cyprus-sovereign-rights/.

ITAR-TASS News Agency. 2011. "Russia Interested in Close Cooperation with Cyprus—Russian ForMin." 9 November.

ITAR-TASS News Agency. 2013 "Piotr Velicky Nuclear Missile Cruiser to Make Portcall to Limassol." 27 December.

Kardash, Natalia. 2010. "Russian Community in Cyprus: Advantages and Challenges." Conference Paper, University of Nicosia, 2 November.

Khrushcheva, Nina. 2014. "Inside Vladimir Putin's Mind: Looking Back in Anger." *World Affairs* 177 (2): 17–24.

Knews. 2019. "Amendments to Menendez-Rubio bill 'Unfortunate.'" 27 June.

Litsas, Spyridon N. 2019. "The Russian Foreign Policy in the Eastern Mediterranean: A Sui-generis Revisionism." In *The New Eastern Mediterranean: Theory, Politics, and States in a Volatile Era*, edited by S. N. Litsas and A. Tziambiris. Cham: Springer.

Mallinson, William. 2005. *Cyprus: A Modern History.* London: I. B. Tauris.

Maslov, Andrey. 2020. "Ρώσος πρέσβης Αντρέι Μάσλοβ: Τα νησιά έχουν υφαλοκρηπίδα και AOZ" [Russian Ambassador Andrey Maslov: The Islands Have Continental Shelf and EEZ]. *Proto Thema*, 14 June. www.protothema.gr/politics/article/1016573/rosos-presvis-adrei-maslov-ta-nisia-ehoun

Mearsheimer, John J. 2014. "Why the Ukraine Crisis Is the West's Fault: The Liberal Delusions That Provoked Putin." *Foreign Affairs.*

Melakopides, Costas. 2018a. *Russia-Cyprus Relations: A Pragmatic Idealist Perspective.* London: Palgrave.

Melakopides, Costas. 2018b. "How Rational Is President Erdogan's Policy Against Cyprus and Greece: A Case Study." *Russian International Affairs Council (RIAC)*, 8 May. https://russiancouncil.ru/en/analytics-and-comments/columns/military-and-security/how-rational-is-president-erdogan-s-policy-against-cyprus-and-greece-a-case-study/.

Melakopides, Costas. 2018c. "Brief Remarks on President R.T. Erdogan and His Allies' Methodical Use of Logical Fallacies." *RUDN Journal of Political Science* 20 (3).

Melakopides, Costas. 2020. "Multi-Vector Management of Soft Power Policies: Will Russian Soft Power Be Victimized by the Moscow-Erdogan Association?" *RUDN Journal of Public Administration* 7 (4): 361–370.

Moscow Times. 2010. "Medvedev Resolves Cyprus Taxation." 8 October.

Muradov, Georgi L. 2000. *Russia-Cyprus: Our Common Way.* Nicosia: S. Satellite Publication.

Nikitina, Yulia, Denis Kuznetsov, and Leili Rustamova. 2019. "Diplomatic Relations Between Cyprus and the Soviet Union/Russia: From Cold War Games to Friendship and Comprehensive Cooperation." *The Cyprus Review* 31 (3).

O'Malley, Brendan, and Ian Craig. 1999. *The Cyprus Conspiracy: America, Espionage and the Turkish Invasion*. London: I. B. Tauris.

Omirou, Yiannakis. 2014. "Η στάση της Ρωσίας έναντι της Κύπρου και μια μαρτυρία" [Russia's Stance Towards Cyprus and a Revelation]. *Phileleftheros*, 29 October. https://archive.philenews.com/el-gr/f-me-apopsi-eponymes-gnomes/385/225274/i-stasi-tis-rosias-enanti-tis-kyprou-kai-mia-martyria.

Petasis, Aris, and William Mallinson. 2017. "Without Russia It's Only Hobson's Choice for Cyprus." Defend Democracy Press, 10 February. https://forum.agora-dialogue.com/2017/02/10/without-russia-its-only-hobsons-choice-for-cyprus/.

Philis, George. 2016. "Research Project on Security." *In-Cyprus*, 17 December. www.newsincyprus.com/news/50188/research-project-on-security.

Pisiotis, Argyrios. 2001. "Greece and Turkey in the Concentric Circles of Russian Post-Cold War Foreign Policy" [In Greek]. In *Greece and Turkey After the End of the Cold War* [In Greek], edited by Christodoulos Yialourides and Panayiotis Tsakonas. Athens: Caratzas.

Politis. 2013. "Παράπονα του Δημήτρη Χριστόφια: Ο Πούτιν δεν μου έβγαινε ούτε στο τηλέφωνο" [Complaints by Dimitris Christofias: Putin Did Not Even Come to the Phone]. 25 March.

RoC Foreign Ministry. 2015. "The Republic of Cyprus and the Russian Federation Signed a Number of Agreements and Memoranda of Understanding." 25 February.

RoC PIO. 2019a. "Address by the President of the Republic Mr Nicos Anastasiades at the 14 Cyprus-Russian Festival." 2 June. https://www.pio.gov.cy/en/press-releases-article.html?id=7955#flat.

RoC PIO. 2019b. "Δηλώσεις Υπουργού Εξωτερικών κ. Νίκου Χριστοδουλίδη και του Ρώσου Υπουργού Εξωτερικών κ. Sergey Lavrov, στη Μόσχα" [Statements by Foreign Minister Mr Nikos Christodoulides and Russian Minister of Foreign Affairs Mr Sergey Lavrov in Moscow]. 22 February. www.pio.gov.cy/ανακοινωθέντα-άρθρο.html?id=6215#flat.

Russia Today. 2009. "Russia-Japan: Towards Reaching a Compromise." 18 September.

Russian Foreign Ministry. 2007. Press Release. 26 December.

Russian Foreign Ministry. 2019. "Foreign Minister Sergey Lavrov's Remarks at a Joint News Conference Following Talks with Minister of Foreign Affairs of the Republic of Cyprus Nikos Christodoulides." 22 February. https://russische-botschaft.ru/de/2021/01/20/foreign-minister-sergey-lavrovs-remarks-and-answers-to-media-questions-at-a-news-conference-on-the-results-of-russian-diplomacy-in-2020-moscow-january-18-2021/.

Russian Foreign Ministry. 2020a. "Foreign Minister Sergey Lavrov's Remarks at the News Conference Following Talks with Foreign Minister of the Republic of Cyprus Nikos Christodoulides." September 8. https://www.mid.ru/en/ press_service/minister_speeches/-/asset_publisher/7OvQR5KJWVmR/con tent/id/4327926.

Russian Foreign Ministry. 2020b. "Foreign Minister Sergey Lavrov's Opening Remarks at a Meeting with the Leaders of the main Cypriot Political Parties." September 8. https://www.mid.ru/en/foreign_policy/news/-/asset_publis her/cKNonkJE02Bw/content/id/4327969.

Stergiou, Andreas. 2001. "Les Russes a Chypre dans l'apres-Guerre froide." *Outre-Terre: Revue europeenne de geopolique* 27.

Stergiou, Andreas. 2007. "Soviet Policy Toward Cyprus." *The Cyprus Review* 19 (2).

Torbakov, Igor. 2010. Correspondence with the author, 15 September.

Torbakov, Igor. 2019. Correspondence with the author, 18 February.

Tziarras, Zenonas. 2016. "Israel-Cyprus-Greece: A 'Comfortable' Quasi-Alliance." *Mediterranean Politics* 21 (3): 407–427.

Tziarras, Zenonas. 2019. "Οι 'Δυόμισι Πόλεμοι' και η Άσκηση 'Mavi Vatan': Στρατηγική Κουλτούρα και το Νέο Στάδιο της Τουρκικής Στρατηγικής" [The 'Two and a Half Wars' and the 'Mavi Vatan' Drill: Strategic Culture and the New Phase in Turkish Strategy]. *ELIAMEP Working Paper* (103/2019).

UNSC. 2019. 8453rd meeting, S/PV.8453, 30 January.

Venizelos, Costas. 2014. "Russian 'Canons' Against Turkey" [In Greek]. *Phileleftheros*, 10 October.

Venizelos, Costas. 2015. "Selling Natural Gas Creates New Conditions: The Cyprus-Egypt Agreement Creates Fait Accompli" [In Greek]. *Phileleftheros*, 22 February.

PART III

A Newly-Discovered Identity in the Eastern Mediterranean?

CHAPTER 7

Assessing Maturity in the RoC's Eastern Mediterranean Foreign Policy

Ioannis-Sotirios Ioannou

INTRODUCTION

Defining the foreign policy of a modern state is a complex process. One of the most concise and accurate definitions can be traced as far back as the nineteenth century, describing foreign policy as the 'general objectives that guide the activities and relationships of one state in its interactions with other states' (von Ranke, 1871). This is a simple but working definition that can facilitate the analysis of the foreign policy of the Republic of Cyprus (RoC), a state just over 60 years old. This paper examines the latest trends in the RoC's foreign policy through the lens of foreign policy maturity. It seeks to define what a mature foreign policy is and look at what can be further done to upgrade the RoC's role in the region—the broader Eastern Mediterranean. Regional developments, especially during the 2010s, have shown that there is a long way to go before the RoC's foreign policy can be described as 'mature'.

I.-S. Ioannou (✉)
Zenonas Tziarras, PRIO Cyprus Centre, Nicosia, Cyprus

© The Author(s), under exclusive license to Springer Nature Switzerland AG 2022
Z. Tziarras (ed.), *The Foreign Policy of the Republic of Cyprus*, Reform and Transition in the Mediterranean,
https://doi.org/10.1007/978-3-030-91177-5_7

The institutional dimension, namely the constitutional basis of foreign policy and its relation to other public policies, is here considered as primary for a mature foreign policy. Against this background, it is argued that the RoC's foreign policy is, still, to a great extent immature because it lacks institutional foundations. As long as the RoC's foreign policy-making lacks institutional, political and practical capacities, we cannot be talking of a mature foreign policy. In the concluding section, the paper makes certain recommendations about steps that could be taken towards a more mature foreign policy with a focus on diplomatic culture, institutionalisation and policymaking.

Foreign Policy Maturity and a Historical Background

If defining the foreign policy of a state is a complex process, the evaluation of whether a national foreign policy can be considered mature is also a complex task. Apart from its other aspects, the RoC's foreign policy should be also seen as the country's primary means for tackling the effects of the Cyprus Problem (Kranidiotis 1984, 2000). Indeed, diplomacy is the main tool for enacting foreign policy through actions such as the conduct of war, the formation of international alliances, participation in international and regional organisations and international trade (von Ranke, 1871). As noted by Gikas (2002, 2004a, 2004b, 2005a, 2005b), foreign policy—as an exercise in diplomacy—consists of Law and Diplomacy, Foreign Relations Law, Constitutional Diplomacy and the German term of External Competence (*Auswartige Gewalt*). In the case of the RoC, Constitutional Diplomacy cannot be used in a foreign policy assessment given that because of the Cyprus Problem the Turkish-Cypriots are institutionally absent from the policymaking and implementation process since 1963. At the same time, foreign policymaking in the RoC is largely affected by the Constitution which provides an inadequate legal framework mainly focused on the structure and functions of the Ministry of Foreign Affairs. The paradox here is the fact that Cyprus' Constitution is, since 1963, working under the 'law of necessity', a de facto legal framework that does not allow the constitutional capturing of the RoC's foreign policy. The current law that determines the functionality of the RoC Ministry of Foreign Affairs remains, legally speaking, static without a proper update in the last decades; a reality that cannot change without a proper constitutional amendment, and the clear determination of the RoC's key foreign policy strategic objectives under legislation.

The RoC's accession to the European Union (EU) in 2004 helped the country's foreign policy to evolve—and to a certain extent, mature—by rendering it part of EU policy (Chrysostomides 2005). In this sense, 2004 was a milestone year for Cyprus and the Cyprus Problem. The period between 2004 and the RoC's presidency of the European Council (EC) during the second half of 2012—the first presidency held by Cyprus—can be seen as the second stage of maturation in the RoC's foreign policy. During the 1950s, 1960s and 1970s, international diplomatic efforts regarding Cypriot affairs were mainly pursued by the 'national centre' in Athens, on the basis of the doctrine that 'Athens decides, Nicosia acquiesces' (Kranidiotis 2000, Vlachos 1980). In the 1980s and 1990s this doctrine shifted to 'Nicosia decides, Athens acquiesces' (Kranidiotis 1993) thus making way for the gradual independence of the RoC's foreign policy. This period could be seen as the first phase of maturation in the RoC's foreign policy.

With the Cyprus Problem still unresolved, the question that arises is whether the RoC has failed on a diplomatic level due to its inability to reach a deal with the Turkish-Cypriots, the guarantor powers (Greece, Turkey and the United Kingdom, UK) and the international community. Despite ethnic divisions and the de facto military occupation of 37 per cent of Cyprus by Turkey, the RoC remains economically robust and a full member-state of the EU, with operations that during the 2010s expanded to the field of energy as well. However, when it comes to foreign policy its limitations lie not only in the fact that the Cyprus Problem remains unresolved but also in how it perceives the process of foreign policymaking and implementation.

Over time, these weaknesses have become evident in an number of areas: (a) the RoC has been unable to inflict enough political or economic cost on Turkey by way of contributing to the peaceful reunification of the island; (b) the RoC does not sufficiently utilise its role as an honest broker (Crysostomidis 2012) by capitalising on its EU membership and approaching the countries of the region (Eastern Mediterranean, Middle East and North Africa); and (c) the RoC does not understand foreign policy as an External Competence (Gikas 2003), thus lacking adequate expertise regarding, e.g. Turkey, the broader Middle East region and cultural diplomacy. Moreover, it lacks the institutional make up that will not only be a part of relevant legislation on the functions of the Ministry of Foreign Affairs, but also embedded in its Constitution.

The RoC's accession to the EU coincided with the rejection of the Annan Plan by the Greek-Cypriot community, ushering in a new period for the Cyprus Problem at the international and communal level. At the same time, the RoC's accession to the EU with the Cyprus Problem unsolved ended the Turkish myth that such a development would constitute a *casus belli* (cause of war). Without a doubt, the Turkish obsession in the 1980s and 1990s with preventing the accession of Cyprus to the EU without a settlement to the conflict was a long-term diplomatic tactic that the RoC's foreign policy had to face and tackle. This was ultimately overcome thanks to the way Nicosia conducted its foreign policy by setting accession as a strategic goal and thanks to the diplomacy pursued by Athens and Nicosia.

The entry to the EU brought about a new framework of principles and policies that transformed the RoC's public and foreign policy. It transformed Cypriot politics, at least at an institutional level, into European politics and connected it to the principles and interests of the European family of nations. The harmonisation and integration of all public policy (including foreign policy) of the RoC with European policy has been a dynamic process that is still ongoing. From this perspective, respecting and abiding by EU principles is necessary for the success of the RoC foreign policy (Crysostomides 2012). When it comes to the RoC's foreign policy within the context of the EU, Nicosia is obliged not only to harmonise with and abide by the EU *acquis communautaire* but also to unremittingly follow a principled stance towards the EU and its enlargement—including Turkey—independently of the problems and complications arising from Ankara's stance on the Cyprus Problem. The 2004–2012 period signalled the passage of the RoC's foreign policy to an age of maturation—yet not necessarily maturity.

Looking at the country's foreign policy prior to 1974, during the first attempts of newly founded RoC at diplomacy, reveals a paradox that still exists today: the Cyprus Problem is still the main issue on the agenda. It first started as a question of self-determination which later turned into an ethnic conflict, eventually leading to the Turkish invasion of 1974. The Cyprus Problem continues to dominate the country's contemporary foreign policy across all fields. There are ideological aspects to this paradox. The presidency of Archbishop Makarios III coincided with two troubled decades of the Cold War (1960s and 1970s) during which early

RoC foreign policy identified with the Non-aligned Movement, instead of participating in either the Western alliance (NATO) or the Warsaw Pact (Clerides 1992).

From 1960 to 1977 the RoC was constantly trying to strike a balance between the West, the Soviet Union and the Non-aligned Movement in an effort to pursue a multilevel foreign policy (Kotzias 2010). The legacy of this ideology and political practice seems to be at play to this day as governments in the 1990s and in the twenty-first century have been also talking of a multilevel foreign policy. Although the entry of the RoC to the EU marked a transition towards a foreign policy based on European principles, because of the complexities of the Cyprus Problem foreign policy is still conducted in a particular way on multiple levels—with Cyprus maintaining excellent relations with Russia after the Cold War. Yet, the occasional inability of the RoC to effectively balance between the West and Russia, while maintaining good diplomatic relations with other countries, points to a degree of foreign policy immaturity. This weakness is salient whenever Cyprus becomes the centre of negative international attention because of its special ties with controversial Russian economic circles (Financial Times 2020).

In examining foreign policy maturity, one should also consider the lessons learnt from past mistakes. The RoC foreign policy remains quite particular due to the conditions created by the Cyprus Problem. However, important events during the 2010s such as the explosion at the Mari naval base, the ongoing war in Syria and the developments in the RoC's Exclusive Economic Zone (EEZ) including Turkey's hostile activities, illuminate important—albeit not catastrophic—mistakes of RoC diplomacy. Unlike the EU, the troubled regional system of the Eastern Mediterranean and the Middle East is not conducive to a foreign policy that can bring long-term benefits for Cyprus. Benefits, that is, that would include tangible results as analysed later in this paper. The 2010s changed the region dramatically creating the conditions for the reshaping of the long-term benefits for the RoC.

There are currently two dominant ideological perceptions in the RoC with regard to foreign policy, associated with the country's two largest political parties, the right-wing DISY and the leftist AKEL, respectively (Stergiou & Richter 2006). The characteristics of these parties raise obstacles to what Gikas (2003) defines as foreign policymaking and foreign policy implementation. For example, a holistic discussion on whether the RoC can participate or be integrated into NATO is not yet mature not only because of Turkey's stance on the issue but also because of domestic political dynamics. One example is DISY and Nicos Anastasiades' pledge prior to his election in 2013 to apply for accession to the Partnership for Peace (PfP), a clear step towards NATO accession. Anastasiades' government never followed through after his election. AKEL's consistent opposition to the idea of the RoC entering transatlantic institutions is indicative of the absence of an honest public discussion about the future of any RoC-NATO relationship.

Another challenge to the RoC's foreign policy comes from Turkey. Perhaps inevitably, the RoC foreign policy revolves around the Cyprus Problem and Turkey, consuming much of the Nicosia's energy, not leaving much space for other issues to enter the foreign policy agenda. Moreover, given that the Cyprus Problem is historically connected with Greek foreign policy (Joseph 2006) the ethnic ties of Greek-Cypriots and Turkish-Cypriots with their respective motherlands directly implicate both Greece and Turkey. As a result, outside actors are brought into Cypriot internal matters. This was evident in what followed the collapse of the Crans Montana talks in 2017, when a great debate emerged about the role of Greek, Turkish and British actors during the talks—with the Greek Minister of Foreign Affairs, Nikos Kotzias, being accused of his handlings by part of the Greek-Cypriot Press (Kyriakou 2020).

The internal and external aspects of the Cyprus Problem, the international and regional environment, as well as the structure of the RoC diplomacy, have shaped the country's foreign policy in various ways over the past few decades. However, the EU introduced new dynamics and trends that overtime created the conditions for a more mature foreign policy. Cyprus is nearing the completion of two decades as a full EU member-state and is therefore in a process of maturation when it comes to its European orientation. The question is whether its foreign policy could also be seen as maturing to the extent of (a) rendering Cyprus a powerful small state in the Eastern Mediterranean and on the EU-Middle East 'border'; (b) becoming a catalyst towards the solution of the Cyprus Problem and the normalisation of EU-Turkey relations; and (c) creating the necessary preconditions for the RoC to become a state with excellent political, economic and energy relations with all states in the region on the basis of mutual interests, honest brokerage and cooperation on geopolitical and energy issues. The next section elaborates on the RoC's foreign policy in the new geopolitical environment of the Eastern Mediterranean.

The RoC in a New Regional Environment

Cyprus sits in the middle of a volatile triangle containing three main subsystems: (a) North Africa, where Libya is a pole of instability (see, e.g., Ioannou and Tziarras 2020), (b) the Eastern Mediterranean where Turkey is the dominant power and illegally occupies RoC territory and (c) the Middle East where the continuing conflict in Syria, the instability in Lebanon and the regional rivalry between Saudi Arabia and Iran produce further destabilisation. Cyprus is also a special case because (a) it is under de facto military occupation, (b) it is a full member-state of the EU and (c) it is not a NATO member. Moreover, it has a high concentration of military presence within its limited geographic space: the Turkish occupation forces, the Greek-Cypriot army (i.e. National Guard), the Turkish-Cypriot army, the Greek army, UNFICYP and forces from the UK. Lastly, American, Russian, French, Israeli military forces as well as forces from other EU states often use the ports and airports of Cyprus. The RoC's complex geopolitical and strategic situation was complicated even further during the 2010s after the breakout of the Arab uprisings and ensuing developments.

Seeking a Role

The period of upheaval that begun in 2011 in the Middle East and Northern Africa has been characterised, among others, as Arab Spring or Arab Spring and Winter (Lynch, 2012). This series of political, social and economic changes had as a consequence the Syrian war as well as the rise of a new form of Islamic extremism, that of Daesh or ISIS (Weis and Hassan, 2015). The RoC foreign policy was suddenly faced with great regional instability and insecurity. New challenges (and opportunities) arose prompting the RoC's search for a new role. At the same time, the way in which Turkey attempted to use its model of democracy as a vehicle to increase its influence in the region (Tziarras 2013) was one of the main challenges the RoC had to face, especially in the period between 2011 and 2014, given the positive bilateral relations it historically enjoyed with countries of the region.

Cyprus proximity to the theatre of operations in western Syria upgraded its role and acted as a reminder of its geographical and geopolitical importance. The strikes conducted by western countries in Syria in April 2018 confirmed that as the British Bases in Akrotiri were becoming a springboard for British fighter planes operating against regime targets in Syria (Business Insider 2019). The new role that the RoC's foreign policy has sought to play after 2011 has been characterised by multiple methods of diplomatic conduct, some mistakes as well as challenges that remain open to this day. The search for this new role has been mainly expressed through a series of trilateral summits with Israel, Egypt and Greece—the so-called diplomacy of trilateral partnerships (Tziarras 2016, 2019). As elaborated below, one of the main shortcomings in the RoC's regional foreign policy is what we could call the 'Syrian gap'—the RoC's inability to play a more active role in Syria. Moreover, the most important open challenge is securing and protecting Cyprus from the side effects of the continuous changes that take place in the Eastern Mediterranean and the Middle East. In this respect, the aspect of regional energy security and cooperation is of particular importance and should be examined separately.

Searching for alliances

The 2011 violent overthrow of Hosni Mubarak in Egypt—a country with which the RoC has had excellent relations (apart from the 1978 to 1984 period)—led to the rise of the Islamist Mohammed Morsi to power. Morsi's ascendance and the process of political transition in Egypt created fertile ground for Turkey to seek to expand its influence in the country. For the RoC this was important because of Turkey's attempts to push Egypt to question the EEZ delineation agreement it signed with Nicosia in 2003 (and came into effect in 2004). By exercising political and ideological influence on Morsi's Muslim Brotherhood, Turkey attempted to damage Egyptian-Cypriot relations. Turkey's efforts to export its model of democracy and governance were part of this new regional approach that created, however, suspicions even within the Morsi government.

As can be seen in interviews conducted by the author with RoC diplomats[1] during that time, RoC diplomacy attempted both officially and unofficially to take corrective measures between March and June 2013, to prevent Egypt from backing down from the bilateral EEZ delineation deal. The RoC leadership clearly understood that these types of challenges

---

[1] Between 2013 and 2020 the author covered the diplomatic aspects of the Cyprus Problem and the talks on the Cyprus Problem conducting seven (7) interviews with RoC diplomats which shall remain anonymous. The names are in the possession of the author.

would recur often in the new regional environment. Morsi's overthrow by General Abdel Fattah al-Sisi in 2013 created a new window of opportunity for the RoC's foreign policy. Combined with the strengthening of Cypriot-Israeli relations since 2011 that came as a result of the deterioration of Turkish-Israeli relations and the prospect of energy cooperation, the developments in Egypt created opportunities in the RoC's search for regional alliances.

The diplomacy of trilateral partnerships with Greece and Israel, and Greece and Egypt, respectively, that started in 2014 continues to this day, and more countries have joined an extended network of cooperation. One example is Jordan, which opened its Cyprus embassy late in 2016. The foreign policy principles that can be found in the joint statements of the four countries point to: (a) a principled approach based on the United Nations Security Council (UNSC) resolutions (such as no. 550, 186, 789) for dealing with open regional matters such as Syria and Libya; (b) expressed support for the Cyprus peace process; (c) a common stance against extremism and terrorism, with the ISIS being the primary concern; and (d) cooperation in sectors such as economy, trade and tourism (Egypt Today 2020).

Strengthening relations with both Egypt and Israel is a challenge for the RoC foreign policy given the geopolitical weight of these countries in the area. The entire region's security architecture has changed radically after the normalisation of Egypt-Israel relations in 1979. What seems to have changed after 2004 is the way the two countries see the RoC as a member-state of the EU. This creates a window of opportunity for the RoC to indeed become an honest broker or mediator between the EU and Egypt and Israel. This, however, is an issue that needs delicate handling considering the criticism often expressed in European capitals regarding the Sisi government in Egypt and Israel's policies towards the Palestinians.

Given that the RoC has through the years supported the Palestinian Authority in the Arab–Israeli conflict, the strengthening of RoC-Israel relations signified a shift to pragmatism and, therefore, a degree of maturity in the RoC foreign policy. The cooperation between the RoC and Israel started after the events of the Mavi Marmara incident of 2010 between Israel and Turkey and the ensuing downgrading of Turkish-Israeli relations. A few years later, the Cypriot-Israeli relationship was upgraded in the field of defence, with Israel selling watercraft, medical supplies (during the COVID-19 pandemic) as well as weaponry to the

RoC, even as the armies of the two countries conducted joint military exercises on both Cypriot and Israeli soil (The Greek Observer 2017). The February 2018 crisis in the RoC's EEZ, when the Turkish navy actively blocked an ENI drillship from drilling on behalf of the RoC, stirred an academic and political discussion regarding the improvement of the RoC's relations with Israel and Egypt. The status of the partnerships in question cannot currently be described as an alliance in traditional terms (see, Haglund 1991; Tziarras 2016), but rather as a concerted effort to upgrade relations among neighbouring countries, aiming at economic, political and energy cooperation. The next section examines manifestations of foreign policy (im)maturity, particularly as regards the aspects of policy and institutions, with a focus on crises of foreign policy, energy policy and state institutions.

ELEMENTS OF (IM)MATURITY—INSTITUTIONS AND POLICY
External Relations Crises: Libya, Lebanon, Syria

There are three main cases of foreign policy crises in the Eastern Mediterranean that demonstrate elements of immaturity but also some glimpses of maturation in the RoC's foreign policy. The crisis in Libya, a country with excellent relations with the RoC during the Muammar Gaddafi years, was one of the cases that demonstrated the connections between the politico-economic dimensions of the Arab uprisings and the RoC's interests. In Libya, where Cypriot construction companies do business, the lives of RoC citizens after 2011 were endangered in two instances (Simerini 2014). The RoC diplomacy displayed a high level of professionalism in crisis management by safely repatriating 23 workers and working for the release of another two that were kidnapped. At the same time, because Libyan religious authorities run the Omeriye Mosque, the largest mosque in the RoC controlled territories, it had remained without an officially appointed imam due to the events of the war after 2011. Contrary to the case of the repatriation of Cypriots, this issue was not seriously handled by RoC authorities. An opportunity was thus lost to explore the dynamics in the RoC-Libya relationship and restore the proper operation of the mosque in a way that would also exclude any infiltration from extremists—a plausible scenario given the large number of Arab communities in Nicosia (Ioannou 2015).

In 2017 another crisis broke out in Lebanon between the government and Prime Minister Saad al-Hariri when the latter announced his resignation during a visit in Saudi Arabia. Amidst the crisis, the RoC managed to establish diplomatic backchannels between different political actors in Lebanon and finally played a constructive role in the de-escalation of the country's domestic crisis (Cyprus Mail 2017). If this foreign policy activism was consistent and organised on the RoC's part, it could entail a true regional role for the RoC, including the ability to act as an honest broker in coordination with the EU. But this is not often the case. What is more, Lebanon remains a challenge for the RoC, especially under the light of the ongoing, economic crisis in the country.

The case of Syria is rather an example of immaturity in the RoC's foreign policy. While Turkey has played a central role in the region since 2011, the breakout of the Arab uprisings and the war in Syria, often arming and ideologically guiding extremist groups connected not only with ISIS but also with a series of other Salafist-jihadi armed groups, Nicosia has been conspicuously absent from seeking an active diplomatic role in the Syrian crisis. This issue is not about whether the country is ideologically positioned for or against the Bashar al-Assad regime, but about the need for a pragmatic policy given that Cyprus and Syria share decades of diplomatic bilateral relations and excellent economic and cultural relations. The RoC has failed to play the role of an honest broker on behalf of the EU in Syria or to try mobilising the EU to the end of de-escalating the crisis. On the other hand, the Czech Republic has been the most active out of the 27 members of the EU. A country over 3.200 kms away from Syria not only takes a leading role as a mediator but also takes humanitarian initiatives while representing the US in Damascus—after Washington's decision to withdraw its diplomats—through its own embassy. The RoC has tried to make similar steps, moving the seat of its embassy to Beirut in Lebanon, while Ireland, Austria and Romania have remained active in Damascus despite the years of war (Greek City Times 2021). Eventually, in mid-2020, the RoC, along with Italy and Greece, decided to fully reopen their embassies in Damascus.

Against this background, the Syria conflict has highlighted a gap in the RoC's foreign policy. This gap has had other implications for the RoC's regional policies, as seen in two indicative events. First, the diplomatic complications met by the RoC in dealing with a vessel named Monchegorsk, which was carrying a cargo that ended up at the Mari nautical base and later exploded (Polignosi 2013). Second, the intermediary role Cyprus had in the destruction of the Assad regime's chemical weapons cache by the OPCW (BBC 2013). The first indicates the RoC's weaknesses whereas the second shows signs of maturation in the RoC foreign policy and the results it can achieve when working with the EU and other international organisations in which it participates. But both incidents demonstrate that the RoC has neither a realistic strategic objective regarding the outcome of the Syria conflict, nor a clear position on whether Assad should remain in power or whether there should be a political transition. Moreover, in Syria the RoC has failed (a) to effectively deal with the migrant flows, which often come from the sea (Sigmalive 2015) and potential extremist elements that might infiltrate Cyprus, not least through the occupied territories; and (b) to diplomatically capitalise the fact that Turkey intervened multiple times in Syria in violation of the country's sovereignty and is accused of fuelling Islamic extremism.

One of the RoC's main foreign policy weaknesses, more generally, is that it does not use its EU capacity to pursue diplomatic initiatives. We saw this happening in other cases as well such as Iran and Saudi Arabia. Iran is a country with which the RoC has excellent relations, while Saudi Arabia is a country with which the RoC has been in the process of upgrading relations since 2016. For example, the RoC could contribute to an EU-supported Iran-Saudi Arabia dialogue in the post-2020 Abraham Accords context. It is a great opportunity for the RoC to utilise its positive relations with the two countries, represent the EU and provide the latter with an opportunity for a more active foreign policy. The Israeli government often points out that Israel is the only democratic state in the region. This statement is not untrue. However, one could also say that after 1974 the RoC is the only democratic state in the region that is *also* a full member-state of the EU. After 2004 this reality has become a valuable asset for the RoC given that, despite the Turkish occupation, the island is still economically prosperous, generally stable and secure, as well as democratic. These are assets that the RoC needs to put in better use for a more mature and effective foreign policy.

Overall, the outcome of the Syria war is expected to bring about significant changes in the regional system, with important implication for Turkey among others. If the RoC fails in its efforts for a resolution to the Cyprus Problem, the new regional structure might also end up including a divided island with a hard border between the RoC and Turkey itself. This would in turn have various repercussions for the RoC's security and aspects such as the demographic balances in the occupied areas. A more active foreign policy with clear objectives regarding Syria would help the RoC (a) to acquire a leading diplomatic role on Middle East and Eastern Mediterranean affairs inside the EU, (b) to seek more involvement in terms of trade and investments amidst the post-war transitional period in Syria and (c) to more effectively implement a security policy within the Syrian communities residing in Cyprus in terms of tackling potential threats from Islamic militancy or terrorism, organised crime and intra-Syrian problems.

Energy

After 2011 Cyprus entered a period of intense developments in the energy sector. Big international companies have expressed an interest in the Cypriot EEZ and the hydrocarbon reserves of the Eastern Mediterranean more generally. The discovery of the 'Leviathan' gas field in Israel's EEZ (The New York Times 2010) and of the 'Zohr' field in Egypt's EEZ created the prospects for the Eastern Mediterranean to become (a) a union of regional energy cooperation and (b) a diversification option for Europe's energy security. The RoC's energy challenge, in terms of finding and exploiting hydrocarbon resources, foreign policy challenge. Between 2011 and 2018 Turkey openly and practically resisted the RoC's energy potential. In February 2018 the Turkish navy interrupted the work of vessel Saipem 12,000 which was conducting research on behalf of Italian company ENI. The RoC launched a diplomatic campaign against Turkey's actions took trying to garner support from international organisations (including the EU) and neighbouring states, in the lead up to the Turkey-EU summit in Varna (Euractiv 2018).

However, the RoC diplomacy was immediately criticised in the local press and analyses as populist. Especially after the authorities of the non-recognised 'Turkish Republic of Northern Cyprus' (TRNC) had consultations with ENI. After the direct communication between the Italian company and so-called TRNC Minister of Foreign Affairs, Kudret Ozersay, the latter travelled to Rome and had extensive meetings with Italian officials (Kibris Postasi 2018). The company denied that these meetings took place, but the events created the impression among the RoC public opinion that there was no mechanism to deal with such crises, to take the necessary measures and most importantly to pre-empt Turkish actions. Since 2011 the RoC has not managed to create coherent and long-term strategy regarding hydrocarbons. Despite synergies with Israel, Egypt and other regional states, the RoC does not have a clear vision on the development and exploitation of hydrocarbon reserves. Indeed, the issue of hydrocarbons may be first and foremost a matter of commercial feasibility and competition. The problem however is that the RoC has not laid out a strategy with clear aims regarding, for example, (a) energy security, (b) commercial options (LNG, pipelines) and (c) the country's contribution to the EU's energy security. This process of energy policy-making has to be part of the state's wider foreign policymaking and have a good degree of coherence and continuity. As of 2021, Turkey, under Turkish Petroleum Company (TPAO), conducted six exploration drillings in areas within and outside the declared EEZ of the RoC.

National Security, Foreign Policy and State Institutions

The particularly tense regional environment has led the RoC to work towards the development of a security culture and the improvement of its security apparatus more generally. However, relevant institutions are not yet properly integrated into the country's decision-making mechanisms, which points to another element of immaturity. One example was the creation of the Council for Geostrategic Studies (Sigmalive 2014) that would function as an advisory organ comprised of academics and experts. This was the first attempt to create a think tank directly attached to the RoC presidency. By 2018, however, not only did this organ not develop into an institutionalised think tank at the service of the Ministry of Foreign Affairs, but its mandate was not renewed by the President. At the same time, the Cyprus Intelligence Service (CIS) acquired a legal status as late as 2016, with a law passed by the House of Representatives. The aim was for CIS to function transparently and legally for the first time since its establishment in 1970. As 2021, however, and despite the provision of law N. 75(I)/2016) (CyLaw 2016) regarding the hiring of specialised civilians, the CIS has not fully transitioned into a modern intelligence agency, with civilian experts, to the image of other such agencies abroad. And yet, the CIS is still the main institution to provide foreign policy decision makers with intelligence and analysis.

When it comes to homeland security, despite being low on the target list of international Islamic terrorism during 2014–2018, Cyprus and specifically the British Sovereign Base Areas on the island were used for operations conducted by the international coalition against ISIS in

Syria and Iraq or Assad regime targets (Saul 2014). During that time, the Cyprus Problem was still the prism through which the government analysed regional developments, not least because the RoC's institutional structures are largely restricted to that and with little capacity to deal with broader geopolitical issues. For example, the National Council, a body where party leaders participate in consultations closed to the public, is the main body where political groups try to reach a common understanding and a unified stance on the national issue. But there has not been any substantial discussion about the prospect of turning the National Council into a broader and institutionalised body on matters of foreign policy and national strategy akin to a National Security Council (NSC) or even the Greek Government Council on Foreign Affairs and Defence (KYSEA), in which decisions on foreign policy can be taken on the highest level (Dokos and Tsakonas 2020).

On the institutional aspect of foreign policy, it is also worth mentioning that the RoC does not have a diplomatic academy to aid with the selection, training, assessment and placement of future diplomats. Staffing the Ministry of Foreign Affairs is a process in the hands of the Public Service Commission according to the relevant legislation on the assessment of candidates to be appointed to the public service. This process essentially equates the complex functions of diplomacy and foreign policy practice with those of any other public employee. Moreover, the fact that the RoC Ministry of Foreign Affairs has been consistently short on resources and staff is the root cause of phenomena such as (a) diplomatic missions in foreign countries being understaffed, (b) recycling of available diplomatic personnel and (c) gaps in administration after retirement. The fact that the different governments have not prioritised the establishment of a diplomatic academy is indicative of immaturity vis-a-vis the need for an institutionalised framework for foreign policymaking.

Overall, the RoC is searching for a new geopolitical role, alliances and a proactive foreign policy that will serve both the aim of resolving the Cyprus Problem and limiting its geopolitical implications, given that the country is part of a particularly fluid geopolitical environment. The RoC's deepening ties with Egypt and Israel are a first historic attempt in acquiring some regional influence through relations with non-EU states. The prospect of the RoC playing a positive and constructive role in efforts for regional integration in the Eastern Mediterranean adds value to its foreign policy. However, given the disruptive activities of Turkey, the unresolved Cyprus Problem and the rapid changes in the region, the RoC foreign policy needs to find ways of capitalising opportunities and having results.

Prior to the RoC's accession to the EU, Ankara stated that such an eventuality without the resolution of the Cyprus Problem would be a *casus belli*. In the light of recent developments in the RoC's EEZ, Turkey is bringing back that argument to insinuate that developing Cypriot hydrocarbons without solving the Cyprus Problem will be cause for tension and will lead to acts that will prevent energy plans from being carried out. The management of this unstable geopolitical environment and especially Turkey's behaviour could benefit from: (a) upgrading the role of the Ministry of Foreign Affairs beyond that of a traditional bureaucracy; (b) increasing diplomatic personnel abroad at least in the Eastern Mediterranean; (c) creating the legal framework for institutionalised consultation bodies (e.g. think tanks) specialised in matters such as Turkey, the Middle East, terrorism, energy security, etc.; (d) establishing a National Council for Foreign Relations and Crisis Management—whose members will not be selected based on party affiliation—under specific legislation; (e) creating a diplomatic academy; and finally (f) from upgrading security services by hiring civil staff.

Conclusions: The Way Forward for the RoC Foreign Policy

The next few decades—or even years—will be critical for the outcome of the Cyprus Problem. Beyond its resolution, three other scenarios are also plausible: (a) the perpetuation of the status quo and the de facto partition, (b) the full integration of the 'TRNC' into Turkey and the creation of a hard RoC-Turkey border on the ground, and (c) the upgrade and incremental recognition of the 'TRNC' which would gradually lead to the creation of two states in Cyprus—with or without a comprehensive settlement. The RoC's foreign policy needs to further mature urgently. This should be a priority as the Cyprus Problem remains open and poses an existential challenge to the RoC. Only a dynamic, proactive and goal-driven foreign policy can face these challenges. A mature foreign policy would add tremendous value to 'the only democratic and EU member-state in the area'.

The period after 2004 was one of transition, during which the RoC's foreign policy consolidated its European orientation. It broke away from the conditions that defined it prior to 1974 and 2004, and became part of shifting regional dynamics, not least by improving its relations with neighbouring states. But due to lack of institutions that would codify its external role and mission, as well as other difficulties, the RoC foreign policy can occasionally be quite counter-productive, consumed by the Cyprus Problem. To talk about the maturation of the RoC foreign policy is to talk about the need to develop principles, diplomatic tools and strategic culture in the context of a vision of the RoC as a leading small power in the region. This would render Cyprus the 'key' that could unlock a new relationship between the region and the EU. How could the RoC seek this role in the years to come? Some ideas are briefly listed below.

There is a need to reconsider the mode of operations of the Ministry of Foreign Affairs, the institutional aspect of foreign policy, by adopting legislation, and revisiting organisational structures and mission, to the extent possible. This would include the redefining of the mandate of foreign diplomatic missions as well as the means of economic and cultural diplomacy. The aim would be to develop regional expertise, with a focus on Turkey and the Middle East, beyond the geographical confines of Europe. Moreover, the RoC would have to draft a National Security Strategy and connect it both to the technocratic level and relevant institutions such as a Diplomatic Academy and a think tank on strategic and energy issues that would be staffed with academics and civilian experts. It is also necessary to relieve the Public Service Commission from the duty of selecting and assessing future diplomats so that the process is more specific to and helpful for the Ministry of Foreign Affairs. The selection process needs to be transparent so that pressure from political parties and the role of ideological inclinations are eliminated.

The gradual reshaping of the Ministry of Foreign Affairs to an institution with its own legal framework, separate budget and mission has to also be embedded in the Constitution. Regardless of prospects or developments in the Cyprus Problem, the new strategy should prioritise the opening of new diplomatic missions on the basis of geographic proximity. It is paradoxical that from 2011 to 2020, the RoC had an embassy in Portugal but not in Syria—a country much more crucial for the RoC's security and regional affairs. In 2019, the Ministry of Foreign Affairs adopted a gender equality policy and economic diplomacy as tools for a more modern foreign policy approach. These are steps in the right direction but need to be systematic, continuous and strengthened. Furthermore, given Cyprus' geographic location and new foreign policy activism, it is also necessary to ensure that future shapers of the RoC foreign policy will be trained in Turkish, Arabic and Hebrew. The Ministry of Foreign Affairs should also pioneer educational programmes and initiatives in primary and secondary schools to cultivate a broad understanding of the country's modern diplomatic history and the Cyprus Problem in the new generations.

Lastly, it is important that both the Ministry of Foreign Affairs and a prospective NSC are independent from party mechanisms and bureaucracies. This would signify a significant improvement and indicate the further maturation of foreign policy, given that micropolitics get often in the way of processes such as the secondment of diplomats or the staffing of embassies. From this perspective, the maturation of foreign policy is linked with the maturation of public policy, not only in terms of pursuing the objectives and the interests of the state but also when it comes to the democratic standards of a state (Kotzias 2004). Can the RoC foreign policy reach maturity during the first half of the twenty-first century? This is an existential question given both the reality of occupation and the fluid regional conditions. It can, however, start to be addressed through systematic efforts for its improvement, with a view of a better regional and international role for the RoC.

References

BBC. 2013. "Syria urged to step up efforts to ship chemical weapons", 29 December. Accessed 5 June 2020, https://www.bbc.com/news/world-middle-east-25539451.

Business Insider. 2019. "The British Air Force Just Sent its New F-35s on Their First Mission", 25 June. Accessed 5 May 2020, https://www.businessinsider.com/uk-f-35-fighters-fly-missions-from-cyprus-over-syria-iraq-2019-6.

Chrysostomides, Kypros. 2005. *Διεκδίκηση Ενωμένης Πατρίδας* [Claiming a United Homeland]. Kastaniotis: Athens.

Chrysostomides, Kypros. 2012. *Ανοικτά Ζητήματα* [Open Issues]. Kastaniotis: Athens.

Clerides, Glafkos. 1992. *Cyprus: My Deposition* [In Greek]. Nicosia: Alithia.

Cyprus Mail. 2017. "Hariri makes brief stopover in Cyprus on way back to Lebanon", 21 November. Accessed 4 May 2020, https://cyprus-mail.com/2017/11/21/lebanons-saad-hariri-makes-brief-visit-island/.

CY Law. 2016. Ο περί της Κυπριακής Υπηρεσίας Πληροφοριών (ΚΥΠ) Νόμος του 2016 (Ν. 75(Ι)/2016). Accessed 2 March 2020, http://www.cylaw.org/nomoi/indexes/2016_1_75.html.

Dokos, Thanos and Tsakonas, Panagiotis. 2020. *Ο δρόμος είναι τα βήματά μας: Οδικός Χάρτης Εθνικής Ασφάλειας για την Ελλάδα του Μέλλοντος* [Our steps are the way: National Security roadmap for the Greece of the future]. Athens: Sideris.

Egypt Today. 2020. "Nicosia to host 8th Cyprus-Greece-Egypt Trilateral Summit, Wednesday", 19 October. Accessed 4 June 2021, https://www.egy pttoday.com/Article/1/93257/Nicosia-to-host-8th-Cyprus-Greece-Egypt-Trilateral-Summit-Wednesday.

Euractiv. 2018. EU-Turkey Varna summit becomes conditional, 23 February. Accessed 2 March 2020, https://www.euractiv.com/section/global-europe/news/eu-turkey-varna-summit-becomes-conditional/.

Financial Times. 2020. "Moscow on the Med: Cyprus and its Russians", 14 May. Accessed 7 June 2021, https://www.ft.com/content/67918012-9403-11ea-abcd-371e24b679ed.

Gikas, Vasilis. 2002. *Παγκοσμιοποίηση και εθνική ασφάλεια: Η θεσμική διάσταση* [Globalization and National Security: The Institutional Aspect]. Sakkoulas: Athens.

Gikas, Vasileios. 2003. *The National Council of Foreign Policy* [In Greek]. Athens: Sakkoulas.

Gikas, Vasilis. 2004a. *Η εξωτερική αρμοδιότητα και η νομική θεμελίωση των εξωτερικών υποθέσεων του κράτους* [The external competence and the legal foundation of the external affairs of the state]. Sakkoulas: Athens.

Gikas, Vasilis. 2004b. *Το εθνικό συμβούλιο εξωτερικής πολιτικής* [The National Council on Foreign Policy]. Sakkoulas: Athens.

Gikas, Vasilis. 2005a. *Δίκαιο και θεσμοί της εξωτερικής πολιτικής* [Foreign policy law and institutions]. Stamoulis: Athens.

Gikas, Vasilis. 2005b. *Επικοινωνιακή Διπλωματία* [Communicative Diplomacy]. Sakkoulas: Athens.

Greek City Times. 2021. "Greece officially reopens embassy in Syria, Cyprus in the coming weeks", 24 June. Accessed 8 July 2021, https://greekcitytimes.com/2021/06/24/greece-reopens-embassy-syria/.

Ioannou, Ioannis-Sotirios. 2015. *The External Security of Cyprus: Challenges and Potential Threats*. The Europe Levant Observatory, Diplomatic Academy, Nicosia: University of Nicosia.

Ioannou, Ioannis-Sotirios and Zenonas Tziarras. 2020. What Peace for Syria? Spheres of Influence, the Sunni Opposition and the Day After, Re-imagining the Eastern Mediterranean Series: PCC Report, 5. Nicosia: PRIO Cyprus Centre.

Haglund, G. David. 1991. *Alliance Within the Alliance? Franco-German Military Cooperation and the European Pillar of Defense*. London: Routledge.

Joseph, Joseph. 2006. "Η επιρροή των εθνοτικών διασυνδέσεων στις συνθήκες συγκρούσεων: Το τρίγωνο Ελλάδας-Τουρκίας-Κύπρου" [The influence of

ethnic interconnections to conflict: The Greece-Turkey-Cyprus triangle]. In *Το Κυπριακό με το βλέμμα των ξένων* [The Cyprus Dispute as seen by non-Cypriot scholars], 64–97. Roes: Athens.
Kotzias, Nikos. 2004. *Το ενεργητικό δημοκρατικό κράτος* [The pro-active democratic state]. Kastaniotis: Athens.
Kotzias, Nikos. 2010. Η εξωτερική πολιτική της Ελλάδας στον 21ο αιώνα [The Greek foreign policy in the 21st century]. Kastaniotis: Athens.
Kibris Postasi. 2018. "3. Parseldeki haklarımı terk etmeyeceğim", 26 April. Accessed 10 April 2019, https://www.kibrispostasi.com/c58-GUNEY_KIB RIS/n249586-eni-ceosu-3-parseldeki-haklarimi-terk-etmeyecegim-26042018.
Kranidiotes, Giannos. 1984. *Το Κυπριακό Πρόβλημα* [Cyprus Problem]. Themelio: Athens.
Kranidiotes, Giannos 1993. *Προτάσεις για μια ευρωπαϊκή πολιτική* [Proposals for a European policy]. Sakkoulas: Athens.
Kranidiotes Giannos. 2000. *Η ελληνική εξωτερική πολιτική* [Greek Foreign Policy]. Sideris: Athens.
Kyriakou, Nikolas. 2020. "Περί Κοτζιά και Κραν Μοντανά" [On Kotzias and Crans Montana], *Politis*, 30 October. Accessed 12 June 2021, https://pol itis.com.cy/apopseis/peri-kotzia-kai-kran-montana-apo-ton-nikola-kyriakoy/.
Lynch, Marc. 2012. *The Arab Uprising: The Unfinished Revolutions of the New Middle East.* New York: PublicAffairs.
Stergiou, Andreas and Richter Heinz. 2006. *Το Κυπριακό με το βλέμμα των ξένων* [The Cyprus Dispute as seen by non-Cypriot scholars]. Roes: Athens.
The Greek Observer. 2017. "The Armed forces of Cyprus and Israel conduct the exercise Onesilos-Gedeon", 20 March. Accessed 2 March 2020, https://thegreekobserver.com/blog/2017/03/20/armed-forces-cyp rus-israel-conduct-exercise-onesilos-gedeon/.
The New York Times. 2010. "Gas Field Confirmed Off Coast of Israel", 30 December. Accessed 2 March 2020, https://www.nytimes.com/2010/12/ 31/world/middleeast/31leviathan.html.
Tziarras, Zenonas. 2013. "Turkey-Egypt: Turkish Model, Political Culture and Regional Power Struggle", *Strategy International*, SI Research Paper, no.4/2013.
Tziarras, Zenonas. 2016. Israel-Cyprus-Greece: A 'Comfortable' Quasi-Alliance. *Mediterranean Politics* 21 (3): 407–427.
Tziarras, Zenonas. ed. 2019. The new Geopolitics of the Eastern Mediterranean: Trilateral Partnerships and Regional Security, *Re-Imagining the Eastern Mediterranean Report Series: PCC Report*, 3. Nicosia: PRIO Cyprus Centre.
Polignosi. [2013] 2020. "Μαρί-Έκρηξη". Accessed 7 May 2020, http://www. polignosi.com/cgibin/hweb?-A=36230&-V=limmata.
Vlachos, Aggelos. 1980. *10 Χρόνια Κυπριακού* [10 years with Cyprus Problem]. Hestia: Athens.

Von Ranke, Leopold. [1871] 2018. *Die deutschen Mächte und der Fürstenbund*. Forgotten Books: France.
Weis, Michael, and Hassan Hassan. 2015. *ISIS: Inside the Army of Terror*. New York: Regan Arts.
Simerini. 2014. "Αποχώρησαν σχεδόν όλοι οι Κύπριοι που βρίσκονταν στη Λιβύη" [Almost all Cypriots located in Libya left], 1 August. Accessed 10 March 2018, https://simerini.sigmalive.com/article/2014/8/1/apokhoresan-skhedon-oloi-oi-kuprioi-pou-briskontan-ste-libue/.
Sigmalive. 2014. "Συμβούλιο Γεωστρατηγικών Μελετών" [Council of Geostrategic Studies], 17 September. Accessed 21 April 2020, http://www.sigmalive.com/news/local/162264/diorismos-melon-tou-symvouliou-geostratigikon-meleton.
Sigmalive. 2015. "400 πρόσφυγες ζήτησαν άσυλο στην Κύπρο το Β' τρίμηνο", 18 September. Accessed 4 March 2019, https://www.sigmalive.com/news/local/268041/400-prosfyges-zitisan-asylo-stin-kypro-to-v-trimino.
Saul, Heather. 2014. "Tornado jets took off from RAF Akrotiri in Cyprus on Saturday morning", *Independent*, 27 September. Accessed 4 April 2020, https://www.independent.co.uk/news/world/middle-east/iraq-air-strikes-raf-tornado-jets-begin-first-combat-mission-against-isis-9759475.html.

CHAPTER 8

The Eastern Mediterranean Disputes in the RoC's Foreign Policy: A Socio-Psychological Account

Emine Eminel Sülün

INTRODUCTION

Do states have an image of self? Is self a social structure, composed of expectations? Do these expectations provide meaning and orientation to states' actions in international affairs? This chapter seeks to explain how the image of herself provides a meaningful reference point for a state in its foreign policy decisions and its interactions with other states within the international system. Earlier studies have addressed the influence of identity politics on conflict resolution (Loizides 2015), or the Green Line as an emblem of ontological insecurity in Cyprus (Innes 2017). This chapter, on the other hand, specifies the exact sources of insecurities and anxieties related to foreign affairs and role-self inconsistencies in the RoC's neighbourhood role. There is a need to revisit the interplay between

E. E. Sülün (✉)
Near East University, Nicosia, Cyprus
e-mail: emine.sulun@neu.edu.tr

© The Author(s), under exclusive license to Springer Nature Switzerland AG 2022
Z. Tziarras (ed.), *The Foreign Policy of the Republic of Cyprus*, Reform and Transition in the Mediterranean,
https://doi.org/10.1007/978-3-030-91177-5_8

the RoC's neighbourhood role, its foreign policy strategies and anxieties related to the region as developments regarding the Exclusive Economic Zone (EEZ) delimitation and hydrocarbons explorations since 2011 have fundamentally altered the dynamics in its external environment. Owing to overlapping maritime zones regarding claims over continental shelf limits and EEZs in the region, Turkey has been questioning the sovereign rights of the RoC to explore hydrocarbons around Cyprus while the island is still divided. In a similar vein, Turkish Cypriot leadership is insisting on equal rights for the Turkish Cypriot community for prospective natural resource wealth. Conflicting sovereignty claims in the region and the challenges in maritime territorial delimitation are among the difficulties the RoC has been facing. Nonetheless, it can be argued that the ambiguity regarding the boundaries and territorial claims in the Aegean and the Eastern Mediterranean contexts is also providing an opportunity for the RoC to have a critical self-reflection addressing its insecurities related to its external environment. To elucidate this argument further, this chapter looks to the RoC's Eastern Mediterranean policy in the light of recent EEZ and exploration disputes in the region, and the RoC's responses to these crises from a socio-psychological perspective.

This chapter is a qualitative case study which has drawn most of its materials and arguments from careful readings of public documents; namely official documents released by official institutions and statements by official representatives, as well as the review of literature on the RoC's relations with its Eastern Mediterranean neighbourhood. Subsequent sections deal with the conceptual and theoretical discussions on OSL and IRT and their relationship to the IR literature, and how the crisis and the RoC's reactions can be read through these. Finally, the chapter draws conclusions about the RoC's role-playing capacities in its neighbourhood from 2011 onwards.

The IR, Ontological Security Literature, and Interactionist Role Theory

How can we theorize about ontological (in)security—a security of being—of international actors? Anthony Giddens (1991), who famously took the term 'ontological security' from the prominent psychoanalyst R.D. Laing (1965), explains the ways individuals and groups in the modern world have become increasingly anxious of their ontological security. Giddens (1991, 40) describes that we all seek a protective cocoon, and we find this in established norms and routines. International actors, like individuals, also have ontological security needs. There are routines which help international actors in their attempts of dealing with uncertainties and basic ontological challenges that emerge through their interactions with other actors in the international affairs.

How do these routines and self-conceptions are established? Following the OSL, it is important to begin with an understanding of the link between identity and security in the sense that stable identity narratives in challenging conditions are indispensable for ontological security (Rumelili and Adisonmez 2020, 28). In a similar vein, earlier social constructivist and post-structuralists studies have addressed a realization of identity, reproduction of it, and the need for otherization (Rumelili 2014a; Rumelili 2014b). The concept of ontological security, on a different note, discusses socio-psychological origins of these processes at the actors' level. It is the ontological security needs that determine an identity's relationship with the other and the otherization process. This means that ontological security may not necessarily depend on the otherization process as suggested by post-structuralist accounts (Connolly 1991, 64–66), but it rather provides some socio-psychological explanations about how and why otherization might happen (Rumelili and Adisonmez 2020, 30). To put it briefly, self-concepts and self-images are formed throughout the continuous interactions with the internal, external, and the other.

The ontological security concept discusses the ways in which a self-image is realized, undergoes a process of transformation, and engages in a process of otherization in order to reproduce its own self-image from a socio-psychological perspective (Rumelili and Adisonmez 2020, 28). All actors need a stable sense of who they are, an 'identity', to act; for example, to have goals, assess environments, make choices (Mitzen 2006a, 272). Holding cognitive and behavioural certainty through routines help actors to recognize what they can expect and lead them to systematically relate ends to means. Since ends are constitutive of identity, if actors cannot pursue their ends, this would render their identity insecure (Mitzen 2006b, 342; Mitzen 2006a, 273). At the level of instincts, we are aware that there are many dangers in everyday life. As expressed by Giddens (1991, 36) "chaos lurks" behind seemingly comfortable routines and "this chaos is not just disorganization, but the loss of a sense of the very reality of things and of other persons." Ontological insecurity is an uncomfortable feeling about not being able to cognitively confront the threat environment, and therefore not being able to survive in this world.

In world politics, security is conventionally physical. Yet ontological security, as described from an identity perspective, has implications for international affairs as well (Mitzen 2006a, 273; Huysmans 1998; McSweeney, 1999; Manners 2002; Mitzen 2006b, 341). Over this, scholars within the discipline of IR have discussed ideas related to the significance of cognitive consistency and biographical continuity in an uncertain international environment (Mitzen 2006a; Mitzen 2006b; Roe 2008; Steele 2005; Steele 2008; Berenskoetter and Giegerich 2010). Some of these scholars have conceptualized states as ontological security seekers in their relations with others in international society (Mitzen 2006a; Mitzen 2006b; Zarakol 2010; Lupovici 2016). Different from the intersubjectivity emphasis in these, others have pointed out the important role of self-fulfilling autobiographical narratives for states in their attempts of defining their self-identity (Steele 2005; Steele 2008; Krolikowski 2008; Subotić 2016). Yet others have challenged the idea of state personhood possessing ontological status herself (Krolikowski 2008). In a similar vein, the idea that states are in need of ontological security, just like individuals, has been also criticized (Roe 2008; Mälksoo 2015; Rossdale 2015).[1]

Despite the recent unit of analysis debate within the OSL, ontological security as a concept has become increasingly enlightening for the growing research agenda on insecurities and anxieties (on trauma Kinnvall 2012; on migration Huysmans 2006; on terrorism Solomon 2012; on peace and conflict studies Rumelili 2015a; Rumelili 2015b). Another debate has been on the search for different modes of ontological security which suggests that states can seek ontological security not only in problematic but also in healthy and constructive ways (Browning 2016; Browning 2018, 2019; Steele 2013, 2019). Critically, there are also more recent works which problematize a stabilized sense of self and address the dangers of such a closure (Steele 2019; Browning 2016; Browning 2019; Kinnvall 2018; Vieira 2018). There is a growing emphasis on engaging in self-critical and self-reflective practices instead of pursuing "a pipe dream of a perfectly securable identity" (Mälksoo 2015, 226). These studies, according to Klose (2020, 855), seem to move the OSL closer to the IRT, which provides another socio-psychological perspective to the IR literature.

---

[1] Mälksoo (2015) and Rossdale (2015) even question the assumption that individuals are in need of ontological security.

How do international actors satisfy their ontological security needs? On that matter, the IRT offers a potential in complementing the OSL in its endeavour of theorizing the ontological (in)security of international actors (Klose 2020, 853). Related to this, the main contention of IRT is that ontological security needs can be fulfilled as international actors express and validate their identity (self-image) in society by the making and playing of roles, and the casting of other actors into certain roles matching with one's image of self (Klose 2020, 852). A stable and comforting image of self (ontological security) which is generated by role-making, role-playing, and alter-casting then provides some meaning and orientation for international actor's actions in society. In essence, the ability to generate ontological security is tied to role-making, role-playing, and alter-casting (Klose 2020, 852).

Like the OSL, the IRT literature, through its role-theoretical lens, looks at the ways in which actors develop a self in society (Mead 1934; Wendt 1992; Wendt 1999; Harnisch, Frank, Maull 2011; Harnisch 2012; Klose 2018; Klose 2019; McCourt 2011; McCourt 2014; Wehner 2015; Wehner and Thies 2014).[2] From that perspective, an international actor emerges from the development of an image of itself, together with the making and playing of roles. Through these roles, an actor expresses and stabilizes its own self-image in social interaction. The 'I' and 'me' become elements of a social process that allows identities to emerge. Through role-making and alter-casting, individual actors realize their image of self. Especially, alter-casting is a critical mechanism for the expression and stabilization of an actor's image of self in society in the sense that it is actors who attempt to get significant others to perform roles resembling their self-image in society (Harnisch 2016, 15–16; McCourt 2011, 1607; McCourt 2014, 33). These can be regarded as critical processes of self-realization and equally problematic ones since they are related to the capacity of an actor to take-up societal roles which can validate its image of self and its capacity to cast others into equally matching or counter roles. Actors have differing capacities depending on their material and social resources, together with their creativity and the social expectations of others (Klose 2018, 1149; Klose 2019, 430).

---

[2] The IRT literature is extensively based on the ideas developed by well-known social psychologist George Herbert Mead. The literature is also based on ideas of constructivist theory of international politics mostly articulated by Alexander Wendt.

Following the IRT, individual actors take part in the emergence of the social structures that come to represent their image of 'self'. Societal roles performed by international actors constitute core elements of social societal structures. It is along these lines where 'role' as a concept establishes its meaning in the context of the emergence, preservation, and transformation of the social structures (Harnisch 2016, 5). Within these structures, disconnects between one's self-image and societal roles can create an identity crisis that can be described as severe ontological security challenges. Actors, under these conditions, are expected to develop an ontological resilience (Klose 2020, 852): self-critical and creative re-imagination and re-assertion of a self in social societal structures. Building on these ideas, the IRT perspective on ontological security is employed for analysing how the RoC's ontological security has been both strengthened and challenged in its Eastern Mediterranean neighbourhood in the last decades.[3]

Eastern Mediterranean Disputes and the RoC's Foreign Policy

This section looks at how the RoC's ontological security is tied to its role-making and role-playing in its external environment. It follows with a brief description of the RoC's self-understanding within the context of its neighbourhood and then looks at recent crisis related to the energy and maritime policy in the region.

The RoC in Its Region

What are the components of a self-understanding with an ontological security-enhancing quality or, in other terms, a self-validating effect for the RoC since its independence in 1960? One of the components of this self-understanding is the perception of Turkey or, in other words, the way Turkey is portrayed in the region. Considering the foreign policy strategies which the RoC has adopted over the last sixty years or so, one can say that the preservation of its existence—i.e. survival—as an undisputedly

---

[3] See Klose (2020) for the case study of the European Union's (EU) ontological security in relation to its neighbourhood drawn on IRT perspective on ontological security.

sovereign state has been a very strong motivation. The RoC's neighbourhood policy in the region has enabled it to strengthen its ontological security from time to time since the RoC's subjective sense of self has not been at odds with the way it is perceived by the states in its neighbourhood, except Turkey. Its self-perceived role has, to a certain extent, allowed the RoC to define and fix a particular vision of its 'self' (and its external environment) in the interaction with its neighbouring others.

However, Turkey has a destructive effect on this self-perceived role. The RoC has experienced persistent political problems with Turkey mainly within the context of the Cyprus problem. The Zurich and London Agreements of 1959 were supposed to provide a peaceful settlement of the Cyprus problem; however, ethnic conflict ensued and the island de facto partitioned in 1974. Since then, the RoC has developed a heightened understanding of the Eastern Mediterranean as a strategic region. Laing (1965, 41) holds that having a firm core of ontological security evolves around some self-validating data of experience for individuals such as feeling real, alive, whole, set apart from the rest of the world. Otherwise, one's identity and autonomy can be in question. In the same spirit, feeling "as spatially co-extensive with the body" (Laing 1965, 41) has a powerful self-validating effect.

The RoC has viewed itself as having a vital geopolitical significance, especially when conflicts extending from the Middle East to the Persian Gulf are considered (Tsardanidis and Nicolau 1999, 171). However the notion that its territorial integrity has been in question with respect to the Cyprus problem has created distortions in this self-validating effect. As Laing (1965, 42–43) states:

> If the individual cannot take the realness, aliveness, autonomy, and identity of himself and others for granted, then he has to become absorbed in contriving ways of trying to be real, of keeping himself or others alive, of preserving his identity, in efforts, as he will often put it, to prevent himself losing his self.

The partition of the island which was followed by the insertion of Turkish troops in 1974 has led the RoC to channel most of its foreign policy efforts to get the attention and the support of the international community for a withdrawal of Turkish troops. Since then, the main foreign policy objective has been to attain a state of affairs that is as close to its previous set of parameters as possible. One can argue that, for a consolidation of a self-understanding as an undisputed sovereign state until reaching such a desired constitutional and territorial settlement, the RoC has chosen to ignore the various potential roles Turkey could play in the region. This can be seen as a necessary arrangement to feel real and alive.

Another component of a self-understanding which has an ontological security-enhancing quality in that respect is the EU membership of the RoC. This has a very powerful self-validating effect. It has channelled the impulses and expectations of the RoC to feel alive, beyond the ones particularly driven by its perception of Turkey. As Giddens (1991, 53) states, self-identity "is not something that is just given, as a result of the continuities of the individual's action-system, but something that has to be routinely created and sustained in the reflexive activities of the individual." The RoC has set a number of foreign policy goals and objectives for itself essentially in relation to its position in its close neighbourhood, in the context of the European Union (EU).[4] These objectives have not been mutually exclusive with its position on the Cyprus problem and its problematic relationship with Turkey. But the very fact that, in 1994, the European Commission affirmed that the solution of the Cyprus problem was not linked to the RoC's membership to the Union has substantially helped Nicosia to choose to ignore those linkages rather than consider them carefully. The comforting and stable image of 'self' as an autonomous unit is confirmed within the context of the EU. It is possible to argue that the RoC has pursued parallel foreign policy strategies since 1974 (Tsardanidis and Nicolau 1999, 172); parallel strategies which, at varying degrees, all share the objective of pulling together enough diplomatic pressure on Turkey. The comforting and stable image of 'self' as an autonomous unit in a foreign policy arena has also given the RoC a sensation of having been recognized outside of the context of the Cyprus problem. Driven by both the domestic impulses and prevailing external expectations as an EU member state, the RoC has developed an aspiration to perform a more significant role in its Eastern Mediterranean neighbourhood over the years. Related to these, one might need to take

---

[4] See the website of the Republic of Cyprus (RoC), Ministry of Foreign Affairs, (https://mfa.gov.cy/goals-and-objectives/) which includes useful information on foreign policy goals and objectives.

a closer look at how a vision of being a member of the EU in a strategically peculiar geography, at the intersection of conflicts in the Middle East, has shaped the RoC's self-image.

This brings us to the third component of self-understanding that has an ontological security-enhancing quality for the RoC in the same context. This point can be better understood when juxtaposed to the RoC's potential role within the framework of the Southern Dimension of the European Neighbourhood Policy, which has been critical in building a self-vision in the framework of what can be called a European orientation. Since 2004, with full membership in the EU, the RoC has acquired a greater motivation and power to utilize its regional position to assure sanctions and other forms of pressure vis-a-vis Turkey. To illustrate, several restrictive measures were imposed by the European Council (EC) in November 2019 in response to Turkey's drilling activities in the Eastern Mediterranean, reaffirming the EU's solidarity with the RoC (European Council 2019). These might be seen as some societal roles to express and solidify a regional self-vision in the Eastern Mediterranean while fundamental questions continuously dominate talks on how to create a bi-zonal bi-communal federal system in Cyprus.

The development and performance of certain societal roles also connect an actors' self to, and shape at the same time, international social structures. Regarding the Eastern Mediterranean, it can be argued that the RoC has carved out a regional role for its 'self' by casting others into certain roles and creating a regional structure in the process. In this view, the RoC has sought to realize its 'self' through the development of a role in the Eastern Mediterranean, and this role has become more institutionalized through its neighbourhood policy (Anastasiades 2014). Related to this role, the former Minister of Foreign Affairs, Erato Kozakou-Marcoullis (2012) once said:

> As a member of the European Union, the furthest member to the east and to the south, we intend to contribute to promoting and injecting the policies of the Union in our southern neighbourhood and to serving as a conduit for our neighbors in Brussels and among our European partners.

International EEZ agreements signed with Egypt and Israel are particularly important in that respect. A more recent example is certainly the Eastern Mediterranean Gas Forum (EMGF) and the RoC's active participation in the development of alliances within the context of the forum.

It can be said that hydrocarbon discoveries in the region generated a new situation and new dynamics. The Eastern Mediterranean appears to be more relevant for both bilateral and multilateral relations in that context (Natural Gas Europe 2011; Mavroyiannis 2014; Coats 2014a; Coats 2014b). The regional geostrategic role of the RoC was also transformed with the hydrocarbon discoveries and prospects around the island. "Cyprus is poised to become a key player, transforming the Eastern Mediterranean into a new global hub for natural gas," said Joe Biden, who at the time was then United States (US) Vice President, to underscore Cyprus' potential to become key gas supplier to Europe (NDTV 2014). For the RoC, energy was also seen as a foundation for the improvement of geo-economic relations with other regional states such as Israel, Egypt, Jordan, Lebanon, and Palestine. As Klose (2020, 862) highlights:

> The successful casting of others into commensurate roles has allowed actors to express and solidify its 'self' (and vision for society), which in turn has become tied to the (more or less routinized) social practices that structure its relations with 'neighboring' states.

Bilateral relations with the neighbouring countries are growing with an emphasis put on the RoC being "the closest EU Member State to the region that enjoys excellent relations with neighbouring countries and has a good understanding of this part of the world."[5]

It can be argued that the RoC's portrayal of itself as the bridge between the EU and the region is an act of casting others into corresponding roles. The RoC has sought to cast its neighbours into close and stable partners, with whom it can essentially cooperate with in enhancing security especially in the field of energy. Especially after 2010, through EEZ delimitations and hydrocarbons exploration activities, the RoC has sought more proactive diplomacy in enhancing cooperation with the states in the region such as Israel and Egypt. In this vein, several bilateral and trilateral memorandums of understanding have been signed among the RoC,

---

[5] The website of the Republic of Cyprus (RoC), Ministry of Foreign Affairs, (https://mfa.gov.cy/goals-and-objectives/).

Greece, Egypt, and Israel. The Cairo Joint Declaration of Egypt, Greece, and the RoC in October 2019 is only one example.

In accordance with its 'self-image' as an undisputed sovereign state, one can say that the RoC needs to cast its neighbours (Israel, Egypt, Greece, the EU) into states who continuously question Turkey's military presence in Cyprus, the Turkish position vis-à-vis the Cyprus problem and a number of other security challenges facing the region. To this end, it seems that the RoC has offered neighbouring states incentives/motivations. For example, access to its licensing blocks for explorations (see, ENI of Italy, TOTAL of France, Exxon Mobil of the US, Qatar Petroleum of Qatar); EEZ agreements (e.g. with Egypt and Israel); and defence alliances in the field of energy and maritime security—such an alliance between the RoC and France was reactivated in 2020 (Financial Mirror 2020). In return, the RoC expected a demonstratable commitment by these actors to support the RoC's on the Cyprus problem. In the same context, it can be argued that the motivation provided to the EU has been the RoC's capacity to meet the energy needs of broader Europe. As an indication of the widespread view that extraction/existence of hydrocarbons has the potential of contributing to Europe's energy security in future, former RoC Minister of Agriculture, Natural Resources and Environment Nicos Kouyialis once said, "the Cypriot natural gas is essentially the European Union natural gas" (Coats 2014c).

Growing trilateral relations over the years can also be seen as part of the RoC's foreign policy endeavour of casting its neighbours into close and stable partners. The 2019 summit between Greece, Cyprus, and Egypt in Cairo, for instance, clearly calls for respecting the sovereign rights of the RoC for the security and stability of the region (In-Cyprus 2019). At the trilateral summit, Greek Prime Minister Kyriakos Mitsotakis indicated the former US Secretary of State Mike Pompeo's support for the sovereign rights of the RoC in its EEZ (In-Cyprus 2019). Moreover, RoC President Nicos Anastasiades stressed that cooperation in the energy sector can be seen as a catalyst for wider regional cooperation in the Eastern Mediterranean, adding that "Turkey's unilateral and unacceptable actions are far from these principles, while at the same time are threatening stability, peace and security in the already turbulent Eastern Mediterranean" (In-Cyprus 2019). It is through such practices that the RoC has been able to express and solidify its image of 'self' (as an actor aiming to restore international law in the region) in a specific social structure of the international society and seek the solidarity of the international community and the EU against the Turkish challenge.

As discussed above, the RoC's perception of its role in the region has enhanced its (provision of) ontological security (a comforting and stable image of 'self'). The question is whether this mode of thinking is providing a problematical guidance for the RoC's foreign policy in the Eastern Mediterranean? One of the problems related to a mode of thinking which provides ontological security for international actors would be that the self-role they cast for themselves can be compromised by role contestation and/or internal contradictions (Klose 2020, 862). Turkey and the lack of a political settlement for the Cyprus problem continuously challenge the self-image of the RoC in the region and create internal inconsistencies. One such example is that the RoC has not declared any EEZ blocks in the north of the island as that is currently not possible. At the same time, this reality challenges the the RoC's comforting and stable image of self. Any dialogue with Turkey may equally challenge the ontological security-enhancing mode of thinking of the RoC.

The RoC's ability to realize its 'self' as an undisputed sovereign state in its neighbourhood has been challenged mostly against the background of regional cooperation schemes (e.g. exporting Eastern Mediterranean natural gas via the TANAP-TAP pipelines) and/or on issues holding important regional dimensions (e.g. EEZ delimitation). It is argued that an image of self in the region and the international arena can be expressed and stabilized by a state's neighbourhood role. Yet the same neighbourhood role creates a social context within which that self-image can be unsettled. In more recent years, the endeavour of playing a greater role in the region led the RoC to engage in maritime delimitation and hydrocarbon exploration activities more ambitiously and, in this vein, Turkey to contest these developments more assertively. A closer look at the recent crisis in the RoC's neighbourhood can be helpful in laying down these challenges further.

Energy and Maritime Crises

During the 2010s, the Eastern Mediterranean has acquired an upgraded role within the field of energy geopolitics both in the context of European energy security concerns (diversification of the energy supply routes) and discovered energy resources in the region (EIA 2013). With respect to the former, both the TANAP pipeline project which transports natural gas from the Shah Deniz II field in the Caspian Sea through Turkey, and the Trans Adriatic Pipeline (TAP) are indicative. Yet, the delimitation of maritime boundaries in the region is problematic and this creates a number of important disputes related to the matters of maritime zones (e.g. between Turkey and Cyprus, or Lebanon and Israel). More critically, these energy and maritime delimitation-related crises have added new dimensions to the existing confrontations and conflicts such as the Cyprus problem, the Arab–Israeli conflict, and even resurface the Greek-Turkish differences particularly in the Aegean Sea. While maritime delimitation issues are pending, any actions such as licensing hydrocarbon explorations, or drilling and exploitation activities have resulted in geopolitical tensions, in the region.

In the light of hydrocarbon discoveries, Cyprus, Israel, Greece, and Turkey, they all cast an important role for themselves especially within the European energy corridor framework, either as an alternative energy supplier or an alternative transit route (Chrysochou and Dalaklis 2019). In the pursuit of having EEZ agreements with neighbouring countries, the RoC signed bilateral agreements with Egypt and Israel. A similar agreement was reached with Lebanon in 2007; however, the Parliament of Lebanon has never ratified the agreement due to political tensions and boundary disputes surrounding the country. The RoC, starting from the 2000s, has systematically built on its capacity of hydrocarbon exploration with the help of the recognition and demarcation of maritime boundaries based on the equidistance/median line principle. Each of these EEZ agreements helped the RoC to secure its self-image more. Israel has also considered Cyprus as a transit point for the transportation of Israeli gas to Europe via the EastMed Pipeline (Navon 2019).[6] Regardless of whether there will be Liquefied Natural Gas (LNG) tankers traffic, or pipelines laying across the region, any of these need a strategic relationship between

---

[6] There are increasing pipeline security issues in the region. The Cypriot-Israeli gas can be transported to Europe via the Arab Gas Pipeline and Turkey, but this option is quite difficult because of the heightened regional volatility. A pipeline from Cyprus to Turkey and then to Europe is politically unthinkable given the Cyprus problem. Exporting Israeli gas directly to Turkey or the liquefaction of natural gas at terminals in Damietta and Idku (in Egypt) and its shipment as LNG to the world seems also quite complicated. The EastMed Pipeline appears to be plausible but economically less feasible compared to other options.

Israel, Cyprus, Egypt, Greece, and the EU. Especially, given the notion that the discovery of giant Zohr gas field in Egypt by ENI has added a new dimension to all these calculations as Egypt can now play a bigger role in supplying natural gas to international markets.[7]

In addition to these, it is important to add the memorandum of understanding (MoU) on the delimitation of maritime jurisdiction areas in the Mediterranean signed between Turkey and Libya (Government of National Accord, GNA) in November 2019. The MoU is based on the equity principle, and—through a second MoU—it expands security and military cooperation at the same time. Regarding the former MoU, Turkish Foreign Minister Mevlut Cavusoglu states that, "this means protecting Turkey's rights deriving from international law" (quoted in Butler and Gumrukcu, 2019).For Greek Foreign Minister Nikos Dendias, the MoU "ignores something that is blatantly obvious, which is that between those two countries there is the large geographical land mass of Crete" (quoted in Butler and Gumrukcu 2019). Egypt condemned the deal as "illegal and not binding or affecting the interests and the rights of any third parties" (quoted in Butler and Gumrukcu 2019). In a similar vein, the government in eastern Libya deemed the maritime accord as illegitimate. As the MoU seemingly cuts off Crete's southeastern maritime zone, the most critical impact of the deal would be on the prospects of the EastMed Pipeline project. Another equally important agreement was signed in August 2020, between Egypt and Greece delimiting an EEZ in the Eastern Mediterranean between the two countries (Reuters 2020a). The agreement seemingly aimed at nullifying the agreement between Turkey and the internationally recognized government of Libya. The accord between Egypt and Greece was signed at a time when the tension in the region were already high over a range of issues from seismic survey plans of Turkey to overflights in the Aegean Sea (Oil and Gas 360 2020; Gumrukcu and Erkoyun 2020; In-Cyprus 2020; Reuters 2020b; Ekathimerini 2020b; Ekathimerini 2020a).

As detailed above, ambiguity regarding the boundaries and territorial claims in the region creates difficulties for the RoC in projecting its self-image while constantly being challenged by Turkey. The RoC holds:

---

[7] The Zohr field is managed by the ENI. ENI also has licenses on three blocks of Cyprus and major shares at the liquefaction terminal in Damietta, Egypt. When all these factors put together, there is a view that Israel's future exporting role may be reduced in relation to that of Egypt.

A vision of transforming the Eastern Mediterranean region into a model of cooperation and development by means of energy diplomacy, which is closely linked to maritime policy...[hydrocarbons] acting as a catalyst to build stability, security, and peace in the Eastern Mediterranean region.[8]

In this context, energy-related regional initiatives through transnational, bilateral, or trilateral agreements are indispensable elements of the RoC's neighbourhood policy. Evidently, the RoC aspires to project European principles, values, and policies in its relations with the neighbouring countries especially through fostering respect for the Law of the Sea. Yet, there are anxieties related to its self-image and its role that can be discerned in its responses to Turkey's drilling activities and to the Turkish Cypriot authorities' call for the bi-communal development of hydrocarbons offshore Cyprus.

RoC Responses to the Hydrocarbons Crisis and a Self-Critical Adjustment

It seems that the RoC has formed a cooperative relationship with Israel, Egypt, and Greece with regard to its offshore energy activities (Sideris 2017; Press and Information Office Ministry of Interior Republic of Cyprus 2021); it has complied with the International Law of the Sea and has respected international customary and conventional practice.[9] Yet, Turkey's fundamentally different view of maritime delimitation has created difficulties for the RoC in its effort to approach maritime and sovereignty issues in the region. In many *notes verbales* and press releases, Turkey disputed the RoC's EEZ agreements with the argument that the RoC cannot jointly represent both the Turkish Cypriots and Greek Cypriots, and because there are overlapping zones with the Turkish maritime claims in the region (Republic of Turkey Ministry of Foreign Affairs 2020, 2011). A delimitation agreement between Cyprus and Greece based on the equidistance/median line principle would limit Turkey in the Gulf of Antalya (Chrysochou and Dalaklis 2019, 160).

---

[8] Cited from the website of the Republic of Cyprus (RoC), Ministry of Foreign Affairs, (https://mfa.gov.cy/themes/) which includes useful information on some of the most central themes of Cyprus foreign policy.

[9] The RoC Law Act 64(I)/ 2004 establishes and proclaims an EEZ for Cyprus.

There have been numerous diplomatic and legal reactions by the RoC against Turkish objections including calling the EU to impose sanctions in response to Turkey's actions of hydrocarbon explorations in the Eastern Mediterranean. This call can be viewed within the framework of one of the main pillars of the RoC's foreign policy, which is the development of alliances within the EU (In-Cyprus 2018). When in June 2020 the High Representative of the EU for Foreign Affairs and Security Policy, Josep Borrell, paid a visit to the RoC in the midst of crisis related to the exploration and drilling operations of Turkey in disputed areas, he underlined the EU's firm support of the RoC's sovereign rights, while adding "you have difficult relations with Turkey in general, these relations are currently facing important and difficult challenges" (European Union External Action Service 2020).

In the same statement, Borell stressed the importance of improving the relations with Turkey through dialogue and negotiations, highlighting that the EU "should try to be good neighbors and that is why the European Union was invented, to foster good neighbor's relations" (European Union External Action Service 2020). Nonetheless, Turkey's exclusion from the existing cooperation schemes has an important function in ontological terms for the RoC. It can be argued that its self-image and routines are sustained in changing regional dynamics when Turkey is non-existent in the regional cooperation scheme. However, there can be a paradigmatic shift on the issues of delimitation of maritime boundaries and energy development in the region in a positive manner if relations with Turkey can be rejuvenated and reconceptualized. Self-role disconnects inhibit the RoC to substantially address these challenges, but a more creative self-reflection can create new channels of cooperation in the region. Related to that, one can ask whether the RoC can show an ability of creative self-reflection in the face of EEZ and exploration crisis in its neighbourhood. How can the RoC cope with these crises for self-critical adjustment?

Given the protracted nature of the Cyprus conflict, strengthening, and promoting its legitimacy as an international political actor have been the RoC's foreign policy priorities. Paradoxically, they have generated self-role disconnects in its neighbourhood policy. It can be argued that this paradox can also generate a process of creative self-reflection through the revision of strategic positions and policies, in the context of the political settlement of the Cyprus problem. Such a revision may suggest an ontological resilience: "ability to constructively engage with – and recover from – ontological security challenges" (Klose 2020, 867).

Contextual framework of the conflict, and the changing nature of the parties' strategic priorities have been shaping the intercommunal talks in Cyprus since 1970s. While engaging more with the regional (the EU, Southern European and Middle Eastern contexts), and the international (not least international energy companies) level, the RoC has stayed firm on its strategic positions and policies, regarding the political settlement of the Cyprus problem. As the effects of the 1974 de facto partition of the island have been remarkable on multiple levels, in its sub-regional and socio-psychological setting, the conflict bears what is broadly dubbed as "double minority complex" (Michael 2007). Michael (2007, 589) also emphasizes that the ethnic divide in Cyprus suffers from a "double (in)security" dilemma preoccupying both communities and their motherlands. This explains why the conflict has been an integral part of the bilateral relations between Greece and Turkey. Yet addressing what has been described as ontological security challenges of the RoC in its neighbourhood relations entails revisiting its strategies and priorities at different levels than the sub-regional setting (Cyprus-Greece-Turkey relations) given the recent developments in the region.

In what can be called a process of creative self-reflection, the RoC can come to a new understanding of its regional setting, by considering Turkey as an actor in its external environment with whom the maritime boundaries can be negotiated with.

Conclusion

Turkish claims and objections have, to a certain extent, unsettled the vision of the RoC's 'self' in the interaction with its neighbouring others. These role-self disconnects challenge the RoC's driven attempts at asserting a greater role in the region such as being an important pillar of the southern dimension of the European Neighbourhood Policy and most importantly an important contributor to the Southern Gas Corridor with the planned EastMed Pipeline. Turkey's restrictions and contestations on these matters challenge the RoC's role-play and alter-casting strategies since they question the RoC's self-image as an undisputed sovereign state in its neighbourhood.

Following these crises, the RoC barely attempted to re-establish a consistency between its role-play in the region and its self-image. Recovering from ontological security challenges requires an engagement in a reflective review of a 'self'-image. The disconnect between the two can be rethought through a careful revisiting of the Cyprus problem. In this context, it can be argued that the Cyprus peace talks have been the milieu in which the RoC had the chance to engage in a creative review of self-image. Since 2011, regional dynamics and events have shaped the RoC's role-playing capacities in its neighbourhood together with domestic and external role expectations in a certain way. The continuing disconnects between the self-image and role-play in its neighbourhood suggest that there is a need for a pragmatic revisiting of the Cyprus problem to create channels of dialogue with Turkey and the Turkish Cypriot authorities. Otherwise, the RoC will struggle more to realize its neighbourhood policy in the Eastern Mediterranean. A renewed foreign policy strategy which will consider the need for a pragmatic approach on that matter will provide a much needed coherence between the self-image and role-play in this case. A renewed vision on the Cyprus peace talks may offer a new foreign policy strategy with an opening for adjusting the RoC's self-expectations and role aspirations to dynamics and events in the RoC's regional milieu.

References

Anastasiades, Nicos. 2014. The True Story about the Geopolitical Role of Cyprus: David or Goliath? Speech delivered at London School of Economics and Political Science, 16 January. Retrieved 27 December 2021 from https://www.youtube.com/watch?v=w5GmNfaEQJk

Berenskoetter, Felix, and Bastian Giegerich. 2010. "From NATO to ESDP: A Social Constructivist Analysis of German Strategic Adjustment After the End of the Cold War." *Security Studies* 19 (3): 407–452.

Browning, Christopher. 2016. "Ethics and ontological security". In *Ethical Security Studies: A New Research Agenda*, edited by Jonna Nyman and Anthony Burke, 160–174. Routledge.

Browning, Christopher. 2018. "'Je suis en terrasse': Political Violence, Civilizational Politics, and the Everyday Courage to Be." *Political Psychology* 39 (2): 243–261.

Browning, Christopher. 2019. "Brexit populism and fantasies of fulfilment." *Cambridge Review of International Affairs* 32 (3): 222–244.

Butler, Daren, and Gumrukcu, Tuvan. 2019, November 28. "Turkey signs maritime boundaries deal with Libya amid exploration row." *Reuters*. Retrieved from https://www.reuters.com/article/us-turkey-libya-idUSKBN1Y213I.

Chrysochou, Georgios and Dalaklis, Dimitrios. 2019. "Offshore Energy Exploration Activities and the Exclusive Economic Zone Regime: A Case Study of the Eastern Mediterranean Basin." In *Wealth and Miseries of the Oceans: Conservation, Resources and Borders*, edited by Patrick Chaumette and Gaetan Balan, 137–173. GOMILEX.
Coats, Christopher. 2014a, February 19. "The Diplomatic Potential of Eastern Mediterranean Gas." *Forbes*, Retrieved 9 March 2021 from http://www.forbes.com/sites/christophercoats/2014/02/19/the-diplomatic-potential-of-eastern-mediterranean-gas/.
Coats, Christopher. 2014b, July 16. "What Does the U.S. See in Cypriot Natural Gas?" *Forbes*, Retrieved 9 March 2021 from https://www.forbes.com/sites/christophercoats/2014/07/16/what-does-the-u-s-see-in-cypriot-natural-gas/?sh=66f893ee6780.
Coats, Christopher. 2014c, May 14. "Does Cyprus Hold the Key to Europe's Energy Woes?" *Forbes*. Retrieved 9 March 2021 from http://www.forbes.com/sites/christophercoats/2014/05/14/does-cyprus-hold-the-key-to-europes-energy-woes/.
Connolly, William. E. 1991. *Identity/Difference: Democratic Negotiations of Political Paradox*. Ithaca: Cornell University Press.
Ekathimerini. 2020a. New Turkish Overflights Over Eastern Aegean. 12 April. https://www.ekathimerini.com/news/251625/new-turkish-overflights-over-eastern-aegean/. Accessed 28 July 2021.
Ekathimerini. 2020b. Turkey extends 'seismic survey' East Med NAVTEX to Thursday. 23 August. https://www.ekathimerini.com/news/256154/turkey-extends-seismic-survey-east-med-navtex-to-thursday/. Accessed 28 July 2021.
European Union External Action Service. 2020. Cyprus: Remarks by HR/VP Josep Borrell after his meeting with Minister of Foreign Affairs Nikos Christodoulides. 25 June. https://eeas.europa.eu/headquarters/headquarters-homepage/81570/cyprus-remarks-hrvp-josep-borrell-after-his-meeting-minister-foreign-affairs-nikos-en. Accessed 28 July 2021.
EIA. 2013, August 15. Eastern Mediterranean Region, Retrieved 9 March 2021 from http://www.eia.gov/beta/international/.
European Council. 2019, October 17. European Council conclusions on Turkey, illegal drilling activities and MH17. Retrieved 3 April 2021 from https://www.consilium.europa.eu/en/press/press-releases/2019/10/17/european-council-conclusions-on-turkey-illegal-drilling-activities-and-mh17/.
Financial Mirror. 2020. Cyprus, France Defense Alliance Enters New Era. 6 August. https://www.financialmirror.com/2020/08/06/cyprus-france-defence-alliance-enters-new-era/. Accessed 21 August 2020.
Giddens, Anthony. 1991. *Modernity and Self-Identity: Self and Society in the Late Modern Age*. Stanford University Press.

Gumrukcu, Tuvan and Erkoyun, Ezgi. 2020, November 23. Turkey Extends Seismic Survey in Contested Waters in Eastern Mediterranean. *OE*. Retrieved from https://www.oedigital.com/news/483409-turkey-extends-seismic-survey-in-contested-waters-in-eastern-mediterranean.

Harnisch, Sebastian. 2012. "Conceptualizing in the Minefield: Role Theory and Foreign Policy Learning." *Foreign Policy Analysis* 8 (1): 47–69.

Harnisch, Sebastian. 2016. "Role Theory and the Study of Chinese Foreign Policy." In *China's International Roles: Challenging or Supporting International Order?*, edited by Sebastian Harnisch, Sebastian Bersick and Jörn-Carsten Gottwald, 3–22. Routledge.

Harnisch, Sebastian, Cornelia Frank, and Hanns W. Maull. eds. 2011. *Role Theory in International Relations: Approaches and Analyses*. Routledge.

Huysmans, Jef. 1998. "Security! What do you Mean? From Concept to Thick Signifier." *European Journal of International Relations* 4 (2): 226–255.

Huysmans, Jef. 2006. *The Politics of Insecurity: Fear, Migration and Asylum in the EU*. Routledge.

In-Cyprus. 2018. Cyprus FM Analyses the Three Main Pillars of Foreign Policy Priorities. 30 July. https://in-cyprus.philenews.com/cyprus-fm-analyses-the-three-main-pillars-of-foreign-policy-priorities/. Accessed 28 July 2021.

In-Cyprus. 2019. Trilateral Summit in Cairo calls for an immediate end to Turkey's illegal actions in Cyprus' EEZ. 8 October. https://in-cyprus.philenews.com/trilateral-summit-in-cairo-calls-for-an-immediate-end-to-turkeys-illegal-actions-in-cyprus-eez/. Accessed 8 March 2021.

In-Cyprus. 2020. Turkey to conduct seismic survey in eastern Mediterranean. 12 October. https://in-cyprus.philenews.com/turkey-to-conduct-seismic-survey-in-eastern-mediterranean/. Accessed 28 July 2021.

Innes, Alexandria. J. 2017. "Mobile Diasporas, Postcolonial Identities: The Green Line in Cyprus." *Postcolonial Studies* 20 (3): 353–369.

Kinnvall, Catarina. 2012. "European Trauma: Governance and the Psychological Moment." *Alternatives* 37 (3): 266–281.

Kinnvall, Catarina. 2018. "Ontological Insecurities and Postcolonial Imaginaries: The Emotional Appeal of Populism." *Humanity & Society* 42 (4): 523–543.

Klose, Stephan. 2018. "Theorizing the EU's Actorness: Towards an Interactionist Role Theory Framework." *JCMS: Journal of Common Market Studies* 56 (5): 1144–1160.

Klose, Stephan. 2019. "The Emergence and Evolution of an External Actor's Regional Role: An Interactionist Role Theory Perspective." *Cooperation and Conflict* 54 (3): 426–441.

Klose, Stephan. 2020. "Interactionist Role Theory Meets Ontological Security Studies: An Exploration of Synergies Between Socio-Psychological Approaches to the Study of International Relations." *European Journal of International Relations* 26 (3): 851–874.

Kozakou-Marcoullis, Erato. 2012, May 10. "New Challenges and Prospects in the Eastern Mediterranean: The Cyprus Perspective." Speech delivered at Paasikivi Society Think Tank, Helsinki. Retrieved 18 October 2015 from http://www.mfa.gov.cy/mfa/embassies/embassy_stockholm.nsf/C9D624 8F7F554078C1257A45002F3C9A/%24file/Address%20by%20the%20Mini ster%20of%20Foreign%20Affairs%20Dr%20Erato%20Kozakou-Marcoullis% 20in%20Helsinki%2010%205%202012.pdf.

Krolikowski, Alanna. M. 2008. "State Personhood in Ontological Security Theories of International Relations and Chinese Nationalism: A Sceptical View." *Chinese Journal of International Politics* 2 (1): 109–133.

Laing, Robert. 1965. *The Divided Self: An Existential Study in Sanity and Madness*. Penguin UK.

Loizides, Neophytos, G. 2015. "Ethnic Nationalism and the Production of Ontological Security in Cyprus." In *Conflict Resolution and Ontological Security Peace Anxieties*, edited by Bahar Rumelili, 71–97. Routledge.

Lupovici, Amir. 2016. *The Power of Deterrence*. Cambridge: Cambridge University Press.

Mälksoo, Maria. 2015. "'Memory must be Defended': Beyond the Politics of Mnemonical Security." *Security Dialogue* 46 (3): 221–237.

Manners, Ian. 2002. "'Normative Power Europe': A Contradiction in Terms?" *Journal of Cutaneous Medicine and Surgery: Incorporating Medical and Surgical Dermatology* 40 (2): 235–258.

Mavroyiannis, Andreas D. 2014. "The Geopolitical Role of Cyprus in the Wider Context of the European Union." *The Mediterranean Quarterly* 25: 1.

Mead, George H. 1934. *Mind, Self and Society*, vol. 111. Chicago: University of Chicago Press.

McCourt, David M. 2011. "Role-Playing and Identity Affirmation in International Politics: Britain's Reinvasion of the Falklands 1982." *Review of International Studies*, 1599–1621.

McCourt, David M. 2014. *Britain and World Power Since 1945: Constructing a Nation's Role in International Politics*. University of Michigan Press.

McSweeney, Bill. 1999. *Security, Identity and Interests: A Sociology of International Relations* (No. 69). Cambridge University Press.

Michael, Michalis S. 2007. The Cyprus Peace Talks: A Critical Appraisal. *Journal of Peace Research* 44 (5): 587–604.

Mitzen, Jennifer. 2006a. Anchoring Europe's Civilizing Identity: Habits, Capabilities and Ontological Security. *Journal of European Public Policy* 13 (2): 270–285.

Mitzen, Jennifer. 2006b. Ontological Security in World Politics: State Identity and the Security Dilemma. *European Journal of International Relations* 12 (3): 341–370.

Natural Gas Europe. 2011. Christofias: Cyprus will Press on with Gas Exploration. 22 November. http://www.naturalgaseurope.com/christofias-cyprus-will-press-on-with-gas-exploration-3633. Accessed 9 March 2021.

Navon, Emmanuel. 2019, February 18. "The New Emerging Energy Hub in the Eastern Mediterranean." *Natural Gas World*. Retrieved from https://www.naturalgasworld.com/the-new-emerging-energy-hub-in-the-eastern-mediterranean-ggp-not-ready-67401.

NDTV. 2014. Cyprus May Become Global Natural-Gas Hub: Joe Biden. 22 May. http://www.ndtv.com/world-news/cyprus-may-become-global-natural-gas-hub-joe-biden-563417. Accessed 9 March 2021.

Oil and Gas 360. 2020. Turkey to Carry Out Seismic Survey in Eastern Mediterranean. 12 October. https://www.oilandgas360.com/turkey-to-carry-out-seismic-survey-in-eastern-mediterranean/. Accessed 28 July 2021.

Press and Information Office Ministry of Interior Republic of Cyprus. 2021. The President of the Republic Met with the President of Israel. 14 February. https://www.pio.gov.cy/en/press-releases-article.html?id=18442#flat. Accessed 28 July 2021.

Republic of Turkey Ministry of Foreign Affairs. 2020. "Our Preference in Eastern Mediterranean is Diplomacy without Preconditions" published in Kathimerini. 15 September. http://www.mfa.gov.tr/sayin-bakanimizin-kathimerini-makalesi-15-9-2020.en.mfa. Accessed 28 July 2021.

Republic of Turkey Ministry of Foreign Affairs. 2011. Statement by Prime Minister Erdogan following the signing of continental shelf delimitation agreement between Turkey and the Turkish Republic of Northern Cyprus New York. 21 September. http://www.mfa.gov.tr/statement-by-prime-minister-erdogan-following-the-signing-of-continental-shelfdelimitation-agreement-between-turkey-and-thetur.en.mfa. Accessed 9 March 2021.

Reuters. 2020a. Egypt and Greece Sign Agreement on Exclusive Economic Zone. 6 August. https://www.reuters.com/article/us-egypt-greece-idUSKCN252216. Accessed 28 July 2021.

Reuters. 2020b. Egypt says Turkish seismic survey plans could encroach on its waters. 1 August. https://www.reuters.com/article/uk-egypt-turkey-idUKKBN24X42F. Accessed 28 July 2021.

Roe, Paul. 2008. "The 'Value' of Positive Security." *Review of International Studies* 34 (4): 777–794.

Rossdale, Chris. 2015. Enclosing Critique: The Limits of Ontological Security. *International Political Sociology* 9: 369–386.

Rumelili, Bahar. 2014a. "İnşacılık/Konstrüktivizm." In *Küresel Siyasete Giriş: Kavramlar, Teoriler ve Süreçler,* edited by Evren Balta, 151–173. İstanbul, İletişim Yayınlari.

Rumelili, Bahar. 2014b. "Kimlik". *Uluslararası İlişkilere Giriş,* edited by Şaban Kardaş ve Ali Balcı, 260–265. İstanbul, Küre Yayınları.

Rumelili, Bahar, ed. 2015a. *Conflict Resolution and Ontological Security: Peace Anxieties.* London: Routledge.

Rumelili, Bahar. 2015b. "Identity and De-Securitization: The Pitfalls of Conflating Ontological and Physical Security." *Journal of International Relations and Development* 18: 52–74.

Rumelili, Bahar, and Umut Can Adisonmez. 2020. "A New Paradigm on the Identity-Security Nexus in International Relations: Ontological Security Theory." *Uluslararasi Iliskiler-International Relations* 17 (66): 23–39.

Sideris, Spiros. 2017, December 5. "Energy Ministers of Cyprus, Greece and Israel and the Italian Ambassador in Cyprus sign MoU on EastMed pipeline Project." *IBNA.* Retrieved from https://balkaneu.com/energy-ministers-of-cyprus-greece-and-israel-and-the-italian-ambassador-in-cyprus-sign-mou-on-eastmed-pipeline-project/.

Solomon, Ty. 2012. "'I wasn't angry, because I couldn't believe it was happening': Affect and discourse in responses to 9/11." *Review of International Studies* 38 (4): 907–928.

Steele, Brent J. 2005. "Ontological Security and the Power of Self-Identity: British Neutrality and the American Civil War." *Review of International Studies* 31 (3): 519–540.

Steele, Brent J. 2008. *Ontological Security in International Relations: Self-Identity and the IR State.* Routledge.

Steele, Brent J. 2013. *Alternative Accountabilities in Global Politics: The Scars of Violence.* New York and London: Routledge, Interventions Series.

Steele, Brent J. 2019. "Welcome Home! Routines, Ontological Insecurity and the Politics of US Military Reunion Videos." *Cambridge Review of International Affairs* 32 (3): 322–343.

Subotić, Jelena. 2016. "Narrative, Ontological Security, and Foreign Policy Change." *Foreign Policy Analysis* 12 (4): 610–627.

Tsardanidis, Charalambos and Yannis Nicolau. 1999. "Cyprus Foreign and Security Policy: Options and Challenges." In *The Foreign Policies of the European Union's Mediterranean States and Applicant Countries in the 1990s,* 171–194. London: Palgrave Macmillan.

Vieira, Marco. 2018. "(Re-) imagining the 'self' of Ontological Security: The Case of Brazil's Ambivalent Postcolonial Subjectivity." *Millennium* 46 (2): 142–164.

Wendt, Alexander. 1992. "Anarchy is What States Make of It: The Social Construction of Power Politics." *International Organization* 46 (2): 391–425.

Wendt, Alexander. 1999. *Social Theory of International Politics* (Vol. 67). Cambridge University Press.

Wehner, Leslie E. 2015. "Role Expectations as Foreign Policy: South American Secondary Powers' Expectations of Brazil as a Regional Power". *Foreign Policy Analysis* 11 (4): 435–455.

Wehner, Leslie E., and Cameron G. Thies. 2014. "Role Theory, Narratives, and Interpretation: The Domestic Contestation of Roles." *International Studies Review* 16 (3): 411–436.

Zarakol, Ayşe. 2010. "Ontological (In) Security and State Denial of Historical Crimes: Turkey and Japan." *International Relations* 24 (1): 3–23.

CHAPTER 9

Towards a Foreign Policy Actor? Turkish Cypriot Perceptions of Cyprus in European Affairs and the Eastern Mediterranean

Nur Köprülü

Introduction

Writing on the foreign policy of Cyprus from the perspective of Turkish Cypriots seems to be ironic in principle; we call it the 'Cyprus Issue' or 'Cyprus Problem'. The island of Cyprus, that used to be under British colonial rule, was granted independence in 1960 following the 1959 signing of the London and Zurich Agreements. The Constitution of the new Republic of Cyprus (RoC) was ratified on 16 August 1960 and proclaimed the state of Cyprus 'an independent and sovereign Republic with a presidential regime, the President being Greek and the Vice-President being Turk elected by the Greek and the Turkish Communities of Cyprus respectively as hereinafter in this Constitution provided'

N. Köprülü (✉)
Department of Political Science, Near East University, Nicosia, Cyprus
e-mail: nur.koprulu@neu.edu.tr

© The Author(s), under exclusive license to Springer Nature Switzerland AG 2022
Z. Tziarras (ed.), *The Foreign Policy of the Republic of Cyprus*, Reform and Transition in the Mediterranean,
https://doi.org/10.1007/978-3-030-91177-5_9

(Constitution of the RoC, Article 1). The new republic codified the existence of two founding communities of the island—i.e. the Greek Cypriot and Turkish Cypriot communities—but lasted only three years, with the common republic's power-sharing model ending in 1963.

A series of attempts to resolve the Cyprus Issue via bi-communal talks have been unsuccessful in bringing a federal solution based on the political equality of each community. The most recent attempt was made under the auspices of the United Nations (UN) in 2017 with the Conference on Cyprus in Crans Montana, Switzerland; it eventually failed to achieve a comprehensive settlement. Having said that, the RoC has been engaged in the international system ever since the break-up of the republic, and specifically in European and Eastern Mediterranean affairs since its 2004 accession to the European Union (EU), while also reaching beyond its traditional Third World alignment by cultivating ties with 'new' Transatlantic (i.e. the United States, US) partners.

Since the early 2010s, gas explorations and discoveries in the Eastern Mediterranean Sea have caused new energy and security policies among the littoral states to become intertwined with the perennial conflicts of the region. The discovery of hydrocarbons in the Eastern Mediterranean and the competing interests of regional, as well as global state and non-state actors in the region, have opened the Pandora's Box of the still-unsettled Cyprus Problem, along with other chronic problems of the region such as the Arab–Israeli Dispute. The merging of old and new problems among littoral states has culminated in a dispute over the delineation of maritime boundaries and the transport route for the hydrocarbon reserves. The dispute over the energy resources in the region has four key aspects: exploration, drilling and transportation of natural resources, but the more importantly the delineation of maritime boundaries among Cyprus, Turkey, Greece, Israel, Egypt, Syria, Lebanon and Libya. Indeed, the tension has recently been heightened, drawing the attention of extra-regional actors such as the European Union (EU) and the US.

In line with the overarching framework of this volume, this chapter aims to highlight the new patterns of behaviour that have accompanied the RoC's foreign policy, which in some circumstances extend far beyond the limits of the Cyprus Problem. The next section will address the perceptions and interpretations of Turkish Cypriots residing on the northern part of the island towards the proactive foreign policy choices of the RoC. As a corollary, the perception of Turkish Cypriots regarding this course of action by the parent state (RoC), and how it intersects with the regional power equation—which has been undergoing a critical shift since the onset of the 2011 Arab Uprisings—will also be underscored.

THE ISLAND OF CYPRUS AND THE EU: A TURKISH CYPRIOT PERSPECTIVE

One of the most decisive foreign policy developments in the history of the RoC is indisputably its accession to the EU in 2004. As one of the primary countries adhering to the Non-Aligned Movement during the heyday of the Cold War, Archbishop Makarios III, as President of the RoC, practised a foreign policy that aligned with Third World countries. Towards the end of the Cold War, however, Cyprus joined the ranks of those countries knocking on the EU's door (with the Treaty of Maastricht the European Community was renamed as the EU in 1992) in 1990, under the Giorgos Vasiliou presidency. In this regard, as Nikos Christodoulides—former Minister of Foreign Affairs of the RoC—postulated, Cyprus' accession to the EU was 'the most pivotal moment in Cyprus' modern history and certainly one of its greatest diplomatic successes' (RoCMFA 2020).

Negotiations spanned nearly a decade and culminated in Cyprus becoming a full member state of the EU, but it did so without a comprehensive settlement being reached on the island's de facto division since 1963 along the so-called Green Line (which extends 180 km through the capital city Nicosia). Since 1963, the southern part of the island, led by the Greek Cypriot community, overrides the authority and the northern part of the island—which Turkish Cypriot leadership declared the Turkish Republic of Northern Cyprus (TRNC) in 1983, a state that has since been recognized only by Turkey.

During and after the application process by the RoC, the Turkish Cypriot political elites—specifically Rauf R. Denktaş, the President of the TRNC—rejected the RoC's accession to the EU as illegal. Denktaş stated in 1999, following a Helsinki Summit meeting, that

> We continue to strongly oppose, on the basis of law and international agreement, the process conducted by the EU with the Greek Cypriot side, under the title of "Cyprus", which is only one of the two parties in the island, in contravention of all norms of justice and the realities. The EU's support for an overall settlement between two equal parties, on the one

hand, and its treatment of one of the parties as eligible to negotiate in the name of Cyprus, on the other, is a contradiction that forces the limits of logic and justice. (TurkeyMFA 1999)

Despite efforts by the Turkish Cypriot leadership and the Turkish authorities, Cyprus joined the EU on 1 May 2004 as one of 10 new member states. The RoC's signing of the Accession Treaty on behalf of the whole island (Casaglia 2019, 39) was characterized as monopolizing the accession negotiations by the Turkish Cypriots and the representation of Cyprus to EU organs such as the European Parliament (EP) and the European Commission has been another matter of contention among the Turkish Cypriots elites hitherto. The comments of Fikri Toros—former president of the Turkish Cypriot Chamber of Commerce and a current member of the TRNC parliament—illustrate one of the key dynamics shaping the perception of Turkish Cypriot political elites towards accession: 'the Greek Cypriot side opted to broaden their isolationist policies towards the Turkish Cypriots with occupation of six seats by the RoC in the Parliament' (interview with Toros 2020). His view was that one-third—or two out of the total six seats in the EP—should have been either kept vacant pending a comprehensive settlement of the Cyprus Issue or filled by 'two Turkish Cypriot delegates as observers without voting rights, and this would be a prudent representation of Cyprus, if not perfect' in the EU's organizational structure (interview with Toros 2020).

It is imperative to state here that the problematic nature of relations between Cyprus and the EU was viewed by Turkish Cypriot elites as a *sui generis* issue due to the absence of Turkish Cypriots from the process entirely. Although the EU strongly backed the UN-sponsored Annan Plan, which was put to referendum on both sides on 24 April 2004, it was rejected by the Greek Cypriots with 76% of the electorate, nullifying the 64% 'Yes' vote of Turkish Cypriots. The failure of the Annan Plan did not lead to the suspension of the RoC's integration with the EU, because settlement of the decades-old dispute had not been endorsed as a prerequisite for the island's full membership. This being the case, relations between the EU and the island's two co-owner communities have been essentially 'exclusionary' for one of them since their inauguration (Demetriou 2005). Nonetheless, Turkish Cypriots' 'Yes' vote on the Annan Plan was intended to have been a step towards resolving the Cyprus Problem (EURACTIV 2013). Turkish Cypriots also expected that:

> EU membership for the whole of the island means [...] increased freedoms, prosperity and security [...] it means the end of our [Turkish Cypriots] isolation from the rest of the world (The Common Vision 2002).

The Accession Treaty that the RoC signed with the EU was drafted

> as if the RoC has jurisdiction over the island entirely, but their jurisdiction north of the Green Line is obstructed by Turkish intervention in the northern island – which is not exactly a true reflection of the situation as it is recorded in UN resolutions... however, there is a political issue between the two communities which traces back to the 1963 inter-communal conflicts", said Toros (interview with Toros 2020).

Within this context, the official position of the Union towards the northern part of the island is as follows:

> Despite joining the EU as a de facto divided island, the whole of Cyprus is EU territory. Turkish Cypriots who have, or are eligible for, EU travel documents are EU citizens. EU law is suspended in areas where the Cypriot government (Government of the Republic) does not exercise effective control. Cyprus has two official languages: Greek and Turkish; only Greek is an official EU language. (EU 2020)

The *acquis communautaire* (henceforth 'the *acquis*') was thereby suspended in the northern part of the island on the basis that it is not under the 'effective control' of the RoC (EU 2020a). Herman Van Rompuy, who held the EU Presidency in 2013, stated at the opening ceremony of his presidency that, 'As long as Cyprus is divided, in a way, Europe will be divided. Indeed, until today, almost half of the country sees no full application of EU law, Turkish-Cypriots do not take part in EU decision-making and their interaction with Brussels, albeit greater than before, continues to be limited', referring to the presidency of Cyprus during the period of 1 July–31 December 2012 (EURACTIV 2013).

Since the early days of the RoC's membership, EU officials and organs adopted a *sui generis* position towards its Turkish Cypriot community, which has received special treatment by the organization as a result. For example, the EU endorsed three significant Regulations to enable the Turkish Cypriot community to remain close to Europe and integrated into the Union despite the suspension of the *acquis* in the north. These regulations are, the Green Line Regulation (GRL), Financial Aid Regulation and Direct Trade Regulation. The first two have been in force since accession in 2004. Motivated by its policy towards the Turkish Cypriot community, the European Commission also proposed to enable 'Turkish Cypriots to trade directly with EU countries' with the aim of emboldening the neighbouring Turkey's accession, but this proposal eventually failed to be enacted (Collinsworth 2010).

In addition, the Union launched a Task Force for the Turkish Cypriot Community under the mandate of the European Commission in charge of implementing the EU Aid Programme for Turkish Cypriots, as well as assisting the Turkish Cypriot community to 'prepare for the reunification of Cyprus' (EU 2020). The Commission then moved the Task Force, first under the auspices of REGIO, then to the EU's 'Secretariat General's Structural Reform Support Service (SRSS) in 2016, which coordinates all the Commission's efforts in facilitating the process for the reunification of Cyprus' (EU 2020). The reason for the transfer stemmed from the Greek Cypriots' 'recognition phobia' of the TRNC.

Hence, the island of Cyprus as a whole is *de jure* EU territory, but de facto has never been in the EU as a whole. In accordance with the EU's official policy towards the north, the *acquis* is suspended in the northern part of the island, 'where the Government of Cyprus does not exercise effective control, EU legislation is suspended in line with protocol 10 of the 2003 accession treaty' (EU 2020). Since the RoC's EU accession, major developments have occurred consistently, including the EU's paralysing neutrality on the Cyprus Issue. Due to the influence of Greece, and because of the RoC's full membership, the EU's ability to influence the issue has been regarded as not adequate. Indeed, in Casaglia's (2019, 38) words, 'the EU is not merely seen as a neutral actor involved in the Cypriot conflict; rather, its role can be understood as affecting the situation at the political and social levels'.

Another spill over effect of the RoC's accession is that the EU has been critiqued for not implementing the Direct Trade Regulation, which would have enabled Turkish Cypriots to trade with EU member states and thereby end their isolation from the international community (interview with Toros 2020). In addition, Turkish, one of the official languages of the RoC, has not been listed as an official language of the EU despite the island's full membership (EURACTIV 2017). This issue has been one of the driving forces behind the decision of Niyazi Kızılyürek—a Turkish Cypriot academic residing in the southern part of the country—to run in the EP elections in June 2019. He has become the first Turkish Cypriot from a Greek Cypriot political party (AKEL, a communist party) to be elected by crossvoting from both the Greek and Turkish Cypriot electorates, and to be represented among Cyprus' six seats in the parliament. A key aim of Kızılyürek's platform is achieving recognition of Turkish as one of the EU's official languages (Cyprus Mail 2019).

The Cyprus Issue has always been central among Turkish Cypriots. The failure of the Annan Plan and the accession of Cyprus to the EU have, however, altered its significance, not just because expectations regarding reunification following accession were reduced, but also because of increased disappointment among the people about the EU's normative/soft power actorness around the issue. According to a 2009 Eurobarometer survey, 55% of Turkish Cypriots considered 'the economic situation in their community to be bad" (Eurobarometer 2009), which also suggests that Turkish Cypriots consider the economic situation and not the Cyprus Problem to be among the most important issues facing the country. Regarding trust of the EU and its organs, 50% of the respondents "trust the EU, compared to 40% who say the opposite' (Philenews 2020).

Cyprus is a small EU state that receives special treatment in European affairs. The Cyprus Problem itself still overrides all other policy areas of the RoC. As Neil Nuget argues, the Cyprus Problem 'dominates much of its political focus and because it is the member state 'most geographically distanced from Brussels'" (Nugent 2006, 61). Furthermore, the prolonged unsettlement of the problem and the persisting "unresolved status of Turkish Cypriots' within the EU, as well as the existence of the TRNC, obscure 'the positioning of Northern Cyprus in any of the EU's various concentric circles' (Casaglia 2019, 46).

THE EASTERN MEDITERRANEAN PARADOX: WHY DOES IT MATTER FOR TURKISH CYPRIOTS?

Over the last two decades, the discovery of hydrocarbon reserves across the East Mediterranean has raised regional tensions that have been accompanied by the continued lack of resolution to the Cyprus Problem, as well as the perennial conflicts over the Aegean Sea between Turkey and

Greece. The conflict over the delineation of the Exclusive Economic Zone (EEZ) over the Eastern Mediterranean Sea traces back to the agreement between the RoC and Egypt in 2003 over the delimitation of their maritime zones. The RoC finalized another agreement with Lebanon in 2007, though it has not yet been ratified by the Lebanese Parliament. Turkey played a decisive role in requesting from the Lebanese government 'not to do so' (Altunışık 2020). Crucially, Turkish Cypriots and Turkey have asked the UN to suspend these attempts until a comprehensive settlement to the Cyprus question has been realized; no such suspension has been enacted, however.

The gas explorations and discoveries across the Eastern Mediterranean have since alarmed the littoral states—Cyprus, Turkey, Egypt, Israel and Greece—leading to their divergence, and to the formation of new blocs and increased polarization. The gas discoveries first began in the early 2000s in Israel, followed by Cyprus in 2011. Two offshore gas fields in Israel—Tamar in 2009 and Leviathan in 2010—were found to be among the largest natural gas reserves in the region, containing nearly 320 and 600 bcm of natural gas, respectively (Biresselioğlu 2019, 122). Along with the discovery of the Zohr field off Egypt in 2015, these developments have drastically altered the energy and geopolitical landscape in the region, with implications that reach far beyond the borders of these fields. In short, the issue of gas exploration has in recent years led the region down a path of competition over the permission rights for exploring and drilling around the Eastern Mediterranean, and for the delineation of EEZs, notably around the island of Cyprus.

In fact, the longstanding discussion on power sharing between the Turkish and Greek Cypriot community, and its continued unsettlement, lies at the heart of the hydrocarbon dispute in the region. As mentioned, since the collapse of the common republic and the deployment of the United Nations Peacekeeping Forces in Cyprus (UNFICYP) in 1964, the island has been divided into its northern and southern parts along the so-called Green Line. This division became entrenched with the Turkish intervention in 1974. After peace talks failed, the Turkish Cypriot parliament in the northern part of the island proclaimed its independence in 1983 and declared the establishment of the TRNC. The TRNC today lacks international recognition, being recognized only by Turkey. Since the break-up of the common republic, the RoC retains its full membership in the UN, and continues to represent the island as a whole in the international system, thereby theoretically representing the rights of the Turkish Cypriot community without its input.

When the RoC first began to conduct agreements for the delineation of the maritime zones with Egypt in 2003 and gas explorations in 2011, Turkish Cypriots opposed these actions due to the unilateral decision-making of the RoC, without agreement from the RoC's other founding community. As a result, the core of the Cyprus Problem, which is power sharing between the two founding communities, comes to the fore once again. While the RoC has claimed a 'sovereign right' to take decisions on its own with regard to energy, Turkey has rejected any such activities that moved forward without the consent of Turkish Cypriots as 'equitable', and none of these three parties have since agreed on what constitutes 'equitable'. For instance, in Fikri Toros' words,

> The RoC did this again on their own, as if they were the only stakeholders of the republic; by overseeing the rights of Turkish Cypriots, they have also chosen to oversee the political dispute on the island. The political dispute is in regard to sovereignty. Sovereignty on the island as well as sovereignty in the waters surrounding the island. They oversaw the political dispute and they relied solely on the international. International law does not predominantly prevail in areas where there is political conflict … They persistently considered there to be no Cyprus Problem, only a problem of occupation … This was an exclusionist policy towards the Turkish Cypriots. A blind eye approach to the core of the Cyprus Issue (interview with Toros 2020).

While the Turkish Cypriots, as well as the Turkish authorities, demand to be involved in decision-making with energy companies such as the Italian company ENI, the Greek Cypriots claim sovereignty over the whole island, and are sceptical about allowing Turkish Cypriots into the decision-making processes, which would at the end of the day endorse the de facto division of the island. Furthermore, the Greek Cypriot administration also fears any attempt to allow the Turkish Cypriots a seat at the table, which may lead to the recognition of the TRNC ('recognition phobia').

Following the RoC's gas exploration activities, the Turkish Cypriot authorities made an offer to the Greek Cypriot government on 24 September 2011 through the UN Secretary General to either mutually 'suspend all hydrocarbon exploration activity until an urgently needed comprehensive settlement is reached, or to form a joint "ad hoc" committee, with participation from the UN, that would be responsible for the joint operation of all hydrocarbon activity' (Olgun 2019). However, the explorations continued. During this period of time, one of the paramount manifestations of the perceptions and course of action taken by the Turkish Cypriot political elites can be illustrated through the actions of Kudret Özersay, the former chief negotiator of the Office of the President, and the former Foreign Minister of the TRNC. Özersay is the key architect of the agreement over delimiting the Continental Shelf (CS) between Turkey and the TRNC, signed in 2011, which was harshly opposed by the Greek Cypriots. Under this agreement, the TRNC has licensed the Turkish Petroleum Corporation (TPAO) for exploration and drilling activities in the areas that fall under the TRNC's sovereignty (BBC News Türkçe 2011). Özersay stated that

> The year 2011 is a paradigm change point. We were protesting before. We signed the Continental Shelf Delimitation Agreement with Turkey in 2011. We delineated the maritime borders between TRNC and Turkish Republic. Thus, we have established a balance in the field in terms of licensing, seismic research and exploration... It is necessary to hold an international conference where the relevant actors will come together. Then, a way out has to be found through dialogue and negotiation (quoted in Çubukçu 2019).

Özersay stated that, 'The TRNC will drill in the licensed areas we gave the Turkish Petroleum in the past. Nobody can deny that the Turkish Cypriot nation has the right among the mentioned areas ... Thus, just as the Greek Cypriot side is drilling with the licenses it gives to companies, we will also drill through licenses we give to Turkish Petroleum' (Hürriyet Daily News 2020). In addition, the Foreign Ministry Office of the TRNC denounced '"excessive rhetoric" as well as its [the Greek Cypriot administration's] "hijacker" mind-set that rejects all proposals for cooperation' in early 2020 (Hürriyet Daily News 2020). In parallel with this policy, the Turkish Cypriot authorities, as well as Turkey, are determined to preclude any further exploration or drilling activities by the Greek Cypriots in the Blocks licensed to TPAO.

On 6 February 2018, this policy became apparent when Turkish authorities issued a notice to mariners (i.e. NAVTEX, FA78-0198), reserving for 'military training' an area to the southeast of Cyprus, including Block 3, which was licensed by the Greek Cypriot side to ENI.

In the view of Mustafa Ergün Olgun, also the former chief negotiator of the Turkish Cypriots, 'So far, the Greek Cypriot side has been in a protected "comfort zone" inside the box—the status quo. Depending on its severity, the "curse element" may now be challenging the status quo and could stimulate win–win solutions based on a "problem solving" approach' (Olgun 2019). Despite all the scenarios or expectations that the energy resources would act potentially as a catalyst for a 'broader agreement' (Aydıntaşbaş 2020) and foster reunification, the dispute over hydrocarbon reserves—which subsequently became interlocked with the old problems of the Eastern Mediterranean and Middle East—illustrates that we are presently far behind finding a solution to the Cyprus Problem. What is more, rising tensions in the region over the hydrocarbon reserves crystallized the newly emerging blocs in the Eastern Mediterranean, rather than prompting regional collaboration.

Turkey's Position

Over the past few years, the Eastern Mediterranean region has become one of the key foreign as well as security issues shaping Turkey's policy orientation. As mentioned, the maritime delimitation and ownership problem among the littoral states in the Eastern Mediterranean is central to the dynamics behind the regional quagmire. The major factors include divergences in the interests of littoral states and disagreement over safe transportation routes for the gas from these fields to Europe (Altunışık 2020). What is more, Turkey has been excluded from regional cooperation or partnership initiatives since the outbreak of the 2011 Arab Uprisings.

The so-called anti-Turkey bloc that has emerged comprises Egypt, Israel, Greece and the RoC; its emergence prompted Turkey to move forward with a maritime delimitation deal with the UN–recognized Government of National Accord (GNA) in Libya, led by President Fayez al-Sarraj, in late 2019. Although Turkey reached an agreement with Libya in 2019, the process for a possible cooperation between Ankara and Tripoli traces back to 2011 (Yaycı 2011). Thus, Ankara and Tripoli signed both the Delimitation of Maritime Jurisdiction Areas in the Mediterranean, and Security and Military Cooperation agreements. In accordance with the Turkish authorities' view, this move would provide Ankara 'a legal counter-claim to contest the Exclusive Economic Zones established by Greece's bilateral understandings with Egypt and Cyprus, upon which much of the development of the Eastern Mediterranean's offshore natural gas depends' (Tanchum 2020a, b 9).

The foremost source of controversy for the Turkish authorities is the unilateral drilling activities of the RoC. Besides this, Turkey argues that the RoC violates Turkey's CS in Blocks 1, 4, 5, 6 and 7, where some areas overlap with Turkey's jurisdiction. The first licence was granted by the RoC to Noble Energy Company in October 2008 for Block 12 (the Aphrodite field), which holds an estimated 4.2 trillion cubic feet of natural gas. Drilling activities began in September 2011 without consultation or agreement from the Turkish Cypriot community (Olgun 2019). As mentioned, following this move by the RoC, Turkey and Turkish Cypriots signed a maritime delimitation deal. In addition, from the view of the Turkish authorities, the international recognition of the Greek Cypriots under the RoC—and as its corollary the RoC's de facto oversight of Turkish Cypriot rights and interests, which resulted in it realizing drilling activities unilaterally.

The maritime dispute between Turkey and Greece dates back to the 1970s and is largely about whether islands—especially those closer to the Turkish coasts—can have a CS (and EEZ). Turkey, a non-signatory country of the United Nations Convention on the Law of the Sea (UNCLOS III), has historically argued that its mainland has the longest shore in the Eastern Mediterranean Sea and, therefore, it would not be fair for its maritime sovereign rights to be restricted by the CS and EEZ of Greek islands (as provided by UNCLOS, to which Greece is a signatory). In other words, Turkey claims that the Aegean Sea has a *sui generis* character and, therefore, the delimitation of the EEZs and Continental Shelves in this area should not be drawn according to the median line (equal distance) method; rather, an 'equitable' solution should be pursued through bilateral dialogue.

NEW MIDDLE EAST POWER BALANCES AND THEIR IMPACT ON THE EASTERN MEDITERRANEAN

Several developments in the region have led Turkey to be excluded from the matrix, particularly since the 2011 Arab Spring. The Arab Spring refers to a series of public protests across the Middle East and North Africa calling for economic and political change, which resulted from a huge increase in unemployment rates, as well as the ongoing struggle against corruption (Pace and Cavatorta 2012). The public rallies hit most countries in the region and in some of them, such as in Tunisia and Egypt, the authoritarian leaders were overthrown. However, the protests did not result in a linear increase in democratization, but rather redistributed the regional power equation.

Turkey under the Justice and Development Party (AKP) has been among the key countries supporting the public protests, stressing that the 'Arab Spring has increased the trend towards democratization in the region and symbolized the very fact that sovereignty belongs to the nations' (Hürriyet 2011; see also Oran 2013). For instance, Turkish President Recep Tayyip Erdoğan took the initiative to visit several Arab countries just as the uprisings were beginning. This proactive foreign policy increased as the protests escalated and included Islamist elements. Moreover, Turkey opted to back the rebel groups fighting against the Ba'ath regime led by Bashar al-Assad in Syria, and also showed support for the Muslim Brotherhood movement (*al-Ikhwan al-Muslimin*) in Egypt.

The dispute over gas explorations in the region has, thus, become interwoven with the new geopolitics that emerged particularly after 2013. The toppling of Hosni Mubarak in Egypt and the ascendancy of popularly elected Mohammad Morsi as the new President of the Egyptian Republic in 2012 led Turkey and Egypt to collaborate in various areas, such as supporting the Palestinian cause, as well as opposing the Ba'ath regime in Syria. Having said that, relations between Ankara and Cairo became severely strained after the July 2013 coup d'état that ousted Morsi and the Ikhwan in Egypt. With the elections in May 2014, General Abdel Fattah al-Sisi became the new President of Egypt, and one of the first moves of his rule was to ban the Ikhwan. This represented a watershed moment for the Ikhwan, as the al-Sisi regime also declared it a 'terrorist organization', as did the US, Saudi Arabia and the United Arab Emirates (UAE) (BBC News 2019). Turkey's ties with Egypt have been negatively affected by this power shift, triggering Turkey's isolation from the emerging regional partnerships. Thus, the power alternation in Egypt from Morsi to al-Sisi allowed for a closer cooperation between Cyprus and Greece (as well as Israel).

Ankara's strained relations with Cairo came on the heels of the deterioration of Turkey's relations with Israel, which suffered a setback after a heated dialogue between Turkish President Erdoğan and Israeli President Shimon Peres at the Davos World Economic Form Summit in 2009, against the background of the 2008 Gaza war (Guardian 2009). No doubt, these events explicitly demonstrated a deteriorating trajectory (which in fact goes back to 2004) that culminated in the 2010 Mavi Marmara incident. Amid the repercussions of these incidents an 'anti-Turkey' bloc began to emerge, becoming evident with the establishment of the Eastern Mediterranean Gas Forum (EMGF) in January 2019. The EMGF, that was pioneered by Egypt, comprises the RoC, Greece, Egypt, Israel, Jordan, the Palestinian Authority and Italy. It was founded to promote natural gas production in the Eastern Mediterranean, and to launch an energy hub aiming to transfer gas to Europe.

In the midst of all this, the RoC's unilateralism has been faced with several surprises. According to Fikri Toros, three critical developments have changed the power balance of the Eastern Mediterranean rivalry. These have taken the form of interventions by Turkey:

1. To protect Turkish Cypriot interests under the Constitution of Cyprus, which have been neglected deliberately;
2. To protect its own purportedly overlapping interests, specifically its opposition to the RoC's exclusion of Turkey from the regional political and energy equation;
3. To reach to a conclusion (a) under the prevailing global market conditions, (b) under the prevailing regulations against fossil fuels and (c) as a result of the incentives provided for renewable energy.

In this regard, Turkish Cypriot elites and Turkish authorities pursue a parallel approach in countering the position of the RoC regarding the situation over the Eastern Mediterranean (TurkeyMFA 2021). These factors affect the economic viability of regional ventures (interview with Toros 2020). In parallel, Turkish officials maintain that the explorations and drilling attempts in the Eastern Mediterranean that aim to restrict Turkey's activities in the region are not justified and are aimed at preventing Turkish Cypriots from utilizing the island's natural resources, too. According to Mevlüt Çavuşoğlu, Minister of Foreign Affairs of Turkey, 'Turkey does not recognize the unilateral and illegitimate exclusive economic zone claims of the Greek Cypriots', and noted that Turkey's activities in the region are in order for Turkish Cypriots and Turkey to exercise their 'own sovereign rights' (Alhas and Doğantekin 2019). Similarly, Fatih Dönmez, the Minister of Energy and Natural Resources of Turkey, has stressed that Turkey would maintain its activities and operations in its own CS, and that the TPAO 'would begin operations in areas under its licence after the process was completed' (Daily Sabah 2020).

In May 2020, Egypt, the UAE, Cyprus, Greece and France issued a joint statement denouncing the Turkish moves in the Eastern Mediterranean as 'provocative and illegal' (Saled 2020). In a statement issued following the National Security Council meeting held in June 2020, Turkish President Erdoğan stated that, 'The negative approaches of some actors, who met on common ground against Turkey's legitimate and legal steps in the Mediterranean, have been evaluated, and it is stated that the protection of our country's rights and interests on land, sea, and air will continue without compromise' (Daily Sabah 2020). Meanwhile, the spokesman of the Foreign Ministry Office, Hami Aksoy, also paid attention to Turkey's commitment to 'protect the rights of Turkey and Turkish Cypriots in the Eastern Mediterranean' and reiterated that the recent permit for additional oil exploration and drilling activities in the region is 'within the boundaries of the UN's continental shelf for Turkey' (Daily Sabah 2020). According to Turkish officials, Turkey's exploration activities are sited within its own CS.

The Egypt–Greece deal (signed in August 2020) was rejected by Turkey on the basis that it nullifies the maritime delimitation agreement between Ankara and Tripoli signed almost a year before (Saled 2020). A dispute over the delineation of the EEZ across the Eastern Mediterranean was subsequently triggered again by disputes between Turkey and Greece over the islands in the Aegean Sea. The mounting tensions specifically between Turkey and the RoC have exacerbated those between Turkey and the EU. Angela Merkel, the Chancellor of Germany of the time, played a crucial role during this period when she called Turkish President Erdoğan and Greek Prime Minister Kyriakos Mitsotakis to deescalate the tensions (Bryza 2020). Although some EU member states pursue a pro-RoC position vis-à-vis the Turkish moves in the region, in the view of some Turkish analysts, 'European countries feel it is a bad idea to alienate Turkey—and that Ankara's concerns about being frozen out of the eastern Mediterranean are not unwarranted. While paying lip service to European Union solidarity, they are reluctant to support crippling sanctions' (Ülgen and Adıntaşbaş 2020).

In Aslı Aydıntaşbaş' (2020) view, the regional competition over hydrocarbon reserves can also be seen as 'the convergence of the old and new disputes' between Turkey, Greece and Cyprus. Having said that, the new hydrocarbon discoveries off the coasts of Israel, Cyprus and Egypt were accompanied by the failure of the peace talks between Turkish and Greek Cypriots at Crans Montana in 2017, and were later exploited as a 'blessing' or a catalyst for the settlement of Cyprus, but were more of a 'curse' in the moment. For Zenonas Tziarras (2019, 5), another development that triggered tension was the AKP government's foreign policy, which created 'unprecedented (in)security linkages and connections among the "Middle Eastern" and "European" states of the Eastern Mediterranean, giving rise to a geopolitical space with distinct significance'. As Biresselioğlu postulates, 'The gas discoveries failed to create the hoped-for regional cooperation; instead, tensions in the region further increased...[;] there are four classes of disputes in the region: territorial, geopolitical, economic, and social' (2019, 121).

Conclusion

Following the RoC's accession, the EU in fact witnessed 'the most awkward enlargement' (EURACTIV 2013) since its foundation. Although the island as a whole was now considered EU territory, the *acquis* was suspended on the northern part of the island, which led North Cyprus to being treated as a special 'neighbour' to the Union. The key debate in the Turkish Cypriot community since 2004 regarding EU membership has been centred on the unfulfilled commitments by the EU, in particular the Direct Trade Regulation. In addition, the special status of the EUPSO—the EU Support Office in northern Nicosia established soon after accession—did not go beyond the limits of the persistent Cyprus Issue due to the contentious nature of recognition of the de facto state in the north, i.e. the TRNC.

With respect to the dispute over the Eastern Mediterranean, the RoC indisputably enjoys its legitimate status as representative of the whole island and has endorsed that the wealth to be gained from the natural resources surrounding the island of Cyprus will be shared with Turkish Cypriots. Meanwhile, the Turkish Cypriot leadership three times—in 2011, 2012 and 2019—proposed the establishment of a joint ad hoc committee to supervise exploitation of the natural resources offshore. Turkey also officially called for a regional conference of all Mediterranean littoral states. The key aspect of Turkish Cypriot and Turkish political elites behind the objection to the RoC's policies in the region stems from its 'unilateralism' in decision-making over natural resources, disregarding the Turkish Cypriot community's rights as co-owners of the island, and also resolving the Cyprus Issue based on the principle of political equality. Viewed from a regional equilibrium perspective, the RoC's foreign policy in strengthening its ties with regional actors—especially with Egypt, Israel, Jordan and the Palestinian Authority—has been facilitated by the breakdown of these countries' ties with Ankara in the post-2011 Arab Uprisings era. This chapter has, therefore, illustrated that despite Cyprus' increased role and proactive policy in both European and regional affairs since the beginning of the 2000s, the continued unsettlement of the Cyprus Issue restricts the RoC from fulfilling its primary goals and further pursue proactive policymaking.

References

Alhas, Ali Murat, and Vakkas Doğantekin. 2019. "Turkish FM Writes to EU, UNSC Members on E. Med. Drills," *Anadolu Agency*, 17 May 2019. Retrieved 7 July 2019, from https://www.aa.com.tr/en/europe/turkish-fm-writes-to-eu-unsc-members-on-e-meddrills/1481003.

Altunışık, Meliha Benli. 2020. "Tukey's Eastern Mediterranean Quagmire", *Middle East Institute*, 18 February 2020. Available at https://www.mei.edu/publications/turkeys-eastern-mediterranean-quagmire.

Aydıntaşbaş, Aslı. 2020. "Cyprus: A New Bargain on Energy", *European Council for Foreign Relations*, May 2020. Available at https://ecfr.eu/special/eastern_med/cyprus.

BBC News. 2019. "White House to Designate Muslim Brotherhood Terrorist Organization", 30 April 2019. Available at https://www.bbc.com/news/world-us-canada-48111594.

BBC News Türkçe. 2011. "Türkiye ve Kuzey Kıbrıs sondaj anlaşması imzaladı" (Turkey and North Cyprus Sign Drilling Agreement), 21 September 2011. Available at https://www.bbc.com/turkce/haberler/2011/09/110921_turkey_cyprus_deal.

Bireselioğlu, Mehmet Efe. 2019. "Clashing Interests in the Eastern Mediterranean: What About Turkey", *Insight Turkey*, 21(4): 115–134.

Bryza, Mathew. 2020. "Solving the Eastern Mediterranean Crisis Requires Compromise", Eastern Mediterranean Perspectives, The Atlantic Council. Available at https://www.atlanticcouncil.org/blogs/turkeysource/solving-the-eastern-mediterranean-crisis-requires-compromise/.

Casaglia, Anna. 2019. "Northern Cyprus as an 'Inner Neighbour': A Critical Analysis of European Union Enlargement in Cyprus", *European Urban and Regional Studies* 26(1): 37–49.

Constitution of the RoC. The Constitution of Republic of Cyprus. Available at www.law.gov.cy.
Collinsworth, Didem Akyel. 2010. "Eroglu's Victory a Challenge for Cyprus, Turkey and the EU", *Crisis Group*, 26 April 2010. Available at https://www.crisisgroup.org/europe-central-asia/western-europemediterranean/turkey/eroglu-s-victory-challenge-cyprus-turkey-and-eu.
Cyprus Mail. 2019. Evie Andreou, "Cypriot MEP Kizilyurek Pressing EU to Make Turkish an Official Language", 24 September 2019. Available at cypriot-mep-kizilyurek-pressing-eu-to-make-turkish-an-official-language.
Çubukçu, Mete. 2019. Pasaport–Documentary, Prepared by Mete Çubukçu, NTV, 9 December 2019. Available at https://www.youtube.com/watch?v=jpaW8f5LwLA.
Daily Sabah. 2020. "Turkey Reiterates Will to Keep Protecting Rights in East Med Without Compromise", 2 June 2020. Available at https://www.dailysabah.com/business/energy/turkey-reiterates-will-to-keep-protecting-rights-in-east-med-without-compromise.
Demetriou, Olga. 2005. "EU and the Cyprus Conflict: Perceptions of the Border and Europe in the Cyprus Conflict", *EU Border Conflicts Working Paper Series*, No. 18, Intercollege Cyprus and University of Birmingham.
EU. 2020. European Union's Official Website. Retrieved 1 December 2020. Available at https://europa.eu/european-union/about-eu/countries/member-countries/cyprus_en.
EU. 2020. "Representation in Cyprus: Turkish Cypriot Community". Available at https://ec.europa.eu/cyprus/about-us/turkish-cypriots_en.
EURACTIV. 2013. "The European Union and Cyprus: The Awkward Partnership", 2 April 2013. Available at https://www.euractiv.com/section/euro-finance/opinion/the-european-union-and-cyprus-the-awkward-partnership/.
EURACTIV. 2017. Sam Morgan, "Turkish Language Still Far Away from Official EU Status", 11 April 2017. Available at https://www.euractiv.com/section/languages-culture/news/official-eu-language-status-evades-turkish/.
Eurobarometer. 2009. "Eurobarometer 72 Public Opinion in the European Union". Available at https://ec.europa.eu/commfrontoffice/publicopinion/archives/eb/eb72/eb72_cy_en_exec.pdf.
Guardian. 2009. "Recep Erdogan Storms Out of Davos After Clash with Israeli President Over Gaza", 30 January 2009. Available at https://www.theguardian.com/world/2009/jan/30/turkish-prime-minister-gaza-davos.
Hürriyet. 2011. "Erdoğan: Arap Baharı demokrasiye geçişte ivme yarattı", 6 Aralık 2011. https://www.hurriyet.com.tr/gundem/erdogan-arap-bahari-demokrasiye-geciste-ivme-yaratti-19404022.
Hürriyet Daily News. 2020. "Turkey Will Continue Its Operations in Areas Where the TRNC Has Licensed the Turkish Petroleum Corporation",

20 January. https://www.hurriyetdailynews.com/turkish-cyprus-to-continue-drilling-in-licensed-areas-minister-says-151201.

Nugent, Neill. 2006. "Cyprus and the European Union: The Significance of Its Smallness and Both as an Applicant and a Member", *European Integration*, 28(1) 51–71, March 2006.

Olgun, Mustafa Ergün. 2019. "Can Hydrocarbons Catalyse New Out of the Box Thinking on Cyprus? A Turkish Cypriot Perspective", *Istituto Affari Internazionali* (IAI), 2019: 4–5.

Oran, Baskın. 2013. *Türk Dış Politikası Cilt: 3 (2001–2012): Kurtuluş Savaşından Bugüne Olgular, Belgeler, Yorumlar*. Ankara: İletşim Yayınları.

Pace, Michelle and Cavatorta Francesco. 2012. "The Arab Uprisings in Theoretical Perspective—An Introduction", *Mediterranean Politics* 17(2): 125–138.

PhileNews. 2020. https://in-cyprus.philenews.com/eurobarometer-cypriots-dis trust-political-parties-tend-to-trust-the-army-more-than-other-institutions/.

RoCMFA. 2020. "Cyprus Foreign Policy—The Way Forward". Available at https://mfa.gov.cy/interviews/2020/12/05/christodoulides-keynote-art icle-cyprus-foreign-policy-dec2020/.

Saled, Mohamed. 2020. "As EU Mulls Sanctions Against Turkey, East Med Allies to Begin Joint Drills", *Al-Monitor*, 30 November 2020. Available at https://www.al-monitor.com/pulse/originals/2020/11/egypt-greece-cyp rus-military-drills-turkey-eu-mediterranean.html#ixzz6fTwAP1us.

Tanchum, Michael. 2020a. "Eastern Mediterranean Energy and Regional Cooperation: 2021 Outlook", *IEMed*. https://www.iemed.org/publication/eas tern-mediterranean-energy-and-regional-cooperation-2021-outlook/

Tanchum, Michael. 2020b. "The Geopolitics of the Eastern Mediterranean Crisis: A Regional System Perspective on the Mediterranean's new Great Game", *Eastern Mediterranean in Unchartered Waters: Perspectives on Emerging Geopolitical RealitiesKonrad Adenauer Stiftung*. https://www.kas. de/documents/283907/10938219/Eastern+Mediterranean+in+Uncharted+ Waters_KAS+Turkey.pdf/6f554da1-93ac-bba6-6fd0-3c8738244d4b?version= 1.0&t=1607590823989

TurkeyMFA. 1999. "Statement by H. E. Mr. Rauf R. Denktaş, President of the Turkish Republic of Northern Cyprus Regarding the EU Helsinki Summit Conclusions, 11 December 1999". Available at http://www.mfa.gov.tr/sta tement-by-h_e_-mr_-rauf-r_-denktas_-president-of-the-turkish-republic-of-northern-cyprus-regarding-the-eu-helsinki-summit.en.mfa.

TurkeyMFA. 2021. "Greek Cypriot's Unilateral Activities in the Eastern Mediterranean". Available at http://www.mfa.gov.tr/greek-cypriot_s-unilateral-activi ties-in-the-eastern-mediterranean.en.mfa.

Tziarras, Zenonas. 2019. "The New Geopolitics of the Eastern Mediterranean—An Introduction". In *The New Geopolitics of the Eastern Mediterranean:*

Trilateral Partnerships and Regional Security, edited by Tziarras Zenonas. Reimagining the Eastern Mediterranean Series: PCC Report, 3. Nicosia: PRIO Cyprus Centre, 5–10.

Ülgen, Sinan and Aslı Aydıntaşbaş. 2020. "A Conflict Could Be Brewing in the Eastern Mediterranean. Here's How to Stop It", *Washington Post*, 17 September 2020. Available at https://carnegieeurope.eu/2020/09/17/conflict-could-be-brewing-in-eastern-mediterranean.-here-s-how-to-stop-it-pub-82759.

Yaycı, Cihat 2011. "Doğu Akdeniz'de Deniz Yetki Alanlarının Sınırlandırılmasında Libya'nın Rolü ve Etkisi", *Güvenlik Stratejileri Dergisi*, Cilt 7, Sayı 14.

PART IV

Foreign Policymaking, Institutional Capacities & Grand Strategic Concerns

CHAPTER 10

International Law and the Republic of Cyprus' Foreign Policy

Nicholas A. Ioannides

INTRODUCTION

International law has always been of critical importance for Cyprus even prior to the establishment of the Republic of Cyprus (RoC). As a matter of fact, the Cypriot people invoked the principle of self-determination to justify their revolution seeking liberation from the British colonial rule and union (*Enosis*) with Greece. Moreover, it was an offspring of international law, namely the United Nations Security Council (UNSC), which reaffirmed the legitimacy of the government of the RoC on the international plane when the Turkish Cypriots abandoned their posts in the governmental apparatus (UNSC Res 186/1964). Additionally, despite the Turkish military invasion of Cyprus in 1974 and the ensuing belligerent occupation of the northern part of the island, international law has safeguarded the territorial integrity and political independence of the RoC. In other words, international law ensures that the RoC

N. A. Ioannides (✉)
University of Nicosia, Nicosia, Cyprus
e-mail: ni@nioannides.com

© The Author(s), under exclusive license to Springer Nature Switzerland AG 2022
Z. Tziarras (ed.), *The Foreign Policy of the Republic of Cyprus*, Reform and Transition in the Mediterranean,
https://doi.org/10.1007/978-3-030-91177-5_10

remains the sole sovereign as regards the occupied areas of Cyprus, while the prolonged Turkish military presence therein does not generate any adverse legal consequences.[1] Against this background, the UNSC considered the secessionist entity installed by Turkey in the occupied areas to be non-valid and called on all states not to recognise it (UNSC Res 541/1983; UNSC Res 550/1984).

An important aspect of international law is dispute settlement by international judicial or arbitral bodies. The most renowned international judicial organ is the International Court of Justice (ICJ or 'the Court'), which is the principal judicial organ of the United Nations (UN). Although the most critical conundrum facing the RoC is the Turkish military invasion and belligerent occupation, unilateral recourse to the Court against Turkey is, in principle, not feasible given that the latter does not recognise the compulsory jurisdiction of the ICJ. In a similar vein, the RoC cannot file a case against the United Kingdom (UK) with respect to the continuing presence of the Sovereign Base Areas (SBAs) in Cyprus as the UK has excluded any dispute between itself and members of the Commonwealth from the Court's jurisdictional ambit.

Since contentious proceedings against Turkey and the UK are not, in principle,[2] possible, the RoC has appeared before the ICJ only twice in advisory proceedings (2010 *Kosovo Declaration of Independence* and 2019 *Chagos Archipelago* cases). In respect of the foregoing procedure, it should be pointed out that solely UN organs, mainly the UNSC and General Assembly, are entitled to ask the Court to give an advisory opinion on a matter of general interest for the international community falling within their competence.

Furthermore, over the last years, the RoC has taken to the sea endeavouring to avail itself of the offshore hydrocarbon bonanza. Thus, the RoC penned maritime delimitation agreements with its neighbouring states and has been carrying out maritime activities under the auspices

---

[1] *Ex iniuria ius non oritur.* See infra.

[2] Even if a state has not accepted the Court's compulsory jurisdiction by virtue of a declaration according to Article 36(2) ICJ Statute, it can still appear before the Court either by signing a special agreement (*compromis*) with another state; or, in case another state unilaterally files an application it may recognise the Court's jurisdiction for only that particular case (*forum prorogatum*); or if a multilateral treaty to which the interested states are parties envisages recourse to the ICJ in order to resolve a dispute arising from that treaty (compromissory clause).

of international law. However, Turkey has vehemently opposed the aforementioned activities on the part of the RoC and has put forward its own maritime claims. Once again, the pertinent international law framework provides the yardstick according to which the interested states' conduct should be scrutinised.

Bearing in mind the above, this chapter briefly examines the role of international law in the RoC's foreign policy. First, this chapter scrutinises the participation of the RoC in the *Kosovo Declaration of Independence* and the *Chagos Archipelago* advisory proceedings. Next, a brief analysis of the RoC's policy as regards the marine domain and the pertinent regional tensions is made. What this study reveals is that the RoC is a law-abiding state observing its international law obligations. What is noteworthy is that, albeit the RoC has primarily used international law to safeguard and advance its interests, in doing so it has also demonstrated an unequivocal willingness to contribute to the particular legal field's development, especially through its appearance before the Court. Therefore, it is argued that the RoC has shown maturity *vis-à-vis* international law given that it does not merely deem this branch of law a foreign policy 'tool'. What its stance towards international law evinces is that the RoC has invoked international law prudently and has been inclined to play a part in the evolution of the legal framework governing international relations.

ICJ JURISDICTION

According to Chapter 14 UN Charter, the ICJ is the principal judicial organ of the UN and all member states are 'ipso facto' parties to its Statute. However, that does not automatically confer jurisdiction to the Court to adjudicate disputes between UN member states. It is up to each state's discretion to accept the Court's compulsory jurisdiction.[3] This may be done through a unilateral declaration according to Article 36(2) ICJ Statute.[4] It should be noted that judgments in contentious

---

[3] That stems from the principle of sovereign equality among states (*par in parem non habet imperium*) according to which no state is entitled to impose its will over another.

[4] Article 36(2) ICJ Statue: 'The states parties to the present Statute may at any time declare that they recognise as compulsory ipso facto and without special agreement, in relation to any other state accepting the same obligation, the jurisdiction of the Court in all legal disputes concerning: (a) the interpretation of a treaty; (b) any question of international law; (c) the existence of any fact which, if established, would constitute a

cases are binding only on the parties to the particular case since the rule of precedent (*stare decisis*) is not applicable in international law (Article 59, ICJ Statute). At any rate, the Court does not significantly depart from its previous jurisprudence (*jurisprudence constante*).

As mentioned earlier, apart from adjudicating contentious cases, the ICJ may issue advisory opinions upon the request of a UN organ. Just like any case before it, the Court must ascertain whether it does have competence to examine the questions put to it and whether the request is admissible.[5] The procedural requirements are: (a) the request for an advisory opinion must be submitted either by the UNSC or the General Assembly or any other UN organ duly authorised to do so, (b) the submitted question(s) must be of a legal nature. Next, the Court examines the admissibility of the request. It should be borne in mind that even if the Court does, eventually, have jurisdiction to hand down the requested advisory opinion, it is not obliged to do so. The issuance of an advisory opinion remains at the Court's discretion, which must be satisfied that there are no serious reasons calling for rejection of the request.

THE ICJ ADVISORY OPINION ON THE DECLARATION OF INDEPENDENCE OF KOSOVO

In the wake of the NATO airstrikes against Serbia in 1999 (Simma 1999; Cassese 2005; Crawford 2019; Gray 2018), the Assembly of Kosovo adopted a declaration of independence on 17 February 2008 spurring Serbia's rigorous reaction.[6] As a result, the UN General Assembly, through Resolution 63/3, asked the ICJ to opine on the following question: 'Is the unilateral declaration of independence by the Provisional Institutions of Self-Government of Kosovo in accordance with international law?' (UNGA Res 63/3). Nevertheless, the Court did not give an adequate answer to the above question as it did not elaborate on the rules

---

breach of an international obligation; (d) the nature or extent of the reparation to be made for the breach of an international obligation'.

[5] According to the well-established principle 'Kompetenz-kompetenz', stipulating that only the adjudicating court may decide on the matter of its jurisdiction. Article 36(6) ICJ Statute.

[6] *Accordance with International Law of the Unilateral Declaration of Independence in respect of Kosovo* (Advisory Opinion) [2010] ICJ Rep 403, paras 37, 58–77.

governing secession. Even though the Court gave emphasis on the importance of territorial integrity, it eventually promulgated that international law does not prohibit unilateral declarations of independence.[7] In addition, the Court did not examine whether Kosovo fulfils the criteria under international law to be considered as a state[8]; whether there is a right to secession outside the realm of decolonisation; or if international law recognises the concept of 'remedial secession'.[9] Albeit it cannot be clearly deduced from the text of the Opinion, it seems that the Court implicitly accepted that Serbia's sovereignty over Kosovo has been temporarily suspended.[10]

The appearance of the RoC before the Court was a landmark moment owing to the fact that it was the first time ever the RoC participated in ICJ proceedings. Of course, the RoC attempted to demonstrate that the declaration of independence of Kosovo was not in accordance with international law. At the same time, it aimed at distinguishing the case of Kosovo from the Turkish occupation of Cyprus and the establishment of the so-called 'Turkish Republic of Northern Cyprus' ('TRNC').

From the outset, the RoC made clear that it took part in the proceedings because it deems the matter of unilateral declarations of independence very important and believes that the findings of the Court in the Kosovo case would be applicable in other disputes as well.[11] The RoC also paid particular attention to the notions of sovereignty and territorial integrity, which pertained to the examination of the Kosovo case.[12] With respect to the question put to the Court, the RoC held the view that the Provisional Institutions of Kosovo were not entitled to declare independence and the inhabitants of Kosovo do not qualify as a people having the right to self-determination; hence, Serbia has not lost sovereignty

---

[7] Ibid., paras 80–81, 84.

[8] Ibid., para 51.

[9] Ibid., paras 56, 82–83.

[10] Ibid., paras 97–100.

[11] *Accordance with International Law of the Unilateral Declaration of Independence in respect of Kosovo* (Request for Advisory Opinion) Written statement of the Republic of Cyprus (17 April 2009), para 2.

[12] Ibid., paras 82–90.

over Kosovo.[13] Unsurprisingly, the RoC rejected the concept of 'remedial secession'[14] and claimed that Kosovo does not fulfil the criteria under international law in order to attain statehood.[15] Lastly, the RoC supported that an entity resulting from a violation of international law rules i.e. unlawful use of force, cannot gain statehood.[16]

Eventually, although the Opinion was quite ambiguous, it contained important points in respect of the views of the RoC. In particular, paragraph 81 of the Opinion reads as follows:

> Several participants have invoked resolutions of the Security Council condemning particular declarations of independence: see, inter alia, Security Council resolutions 216 (1965) and 217 (1965), concerning Southern Rhodesia; *Security Council resolution 541 (1983), concerning northern Cyprus*; and Security Council resolution 787 (1992), concerning the Republika Srpska...*the illegality attached to the declarations of independence thus stemmed not from the unilateral character of these declarations as such, but from the fact that they were, or would have been, connected with the unlawful use of force* or other egregious violations of norms of general international law, in particular those of a peremptory character (*jus cogens*).[17]

The aforementioned excerpt fully satisfied the RoC as it distinguished the case of Kosovo from that of Cyprus, while it highlighted the cause of the installation of the secessionist entity in the occupied areas. The Court rightly opined that because the 'TRNC' was an offshoot of unlawful use of force it can never become a state since the relevant provision prohibiting use of force (Article 2(4) UN Charter) is a peremptory rule of international law (*ius cogens*) from which no derogation is permitted.[18]

---

[13] Ibid., paras 106–139.

[14] Ibid., paras 140–158. The term refers to situations where part of a population has suffered serious and systematic human rights violations and seeks secession from the central state in order to safeguard its rights.

[15] Ibid., paras 166–183.

[16] Ibid., paras 184–191.

[17] Kosovo Advisory Opinion (n 6) para 81 (emphasis added).

[18] *International Status of South-West Africa (Advisory Opinion)* [1950] ICJ Rep 128, p. 82; *Legal Consequences for States of the Continued Presence of South Africa in Namibia (South West Africa) notwithstanding Security Council Resolution 276 (1970)* (Advisory Opinion) [1971] ICJ Rep 16, paras 111–124; Declaration on Principles of International

Another relevant axiom is the one stipulating that a violation cannot generate law (*ex iniuria ius non oritur*).[19] Accordingly, the 'TRNC' cannot be recognised as a state (Crawford 2006), while the members of the international community are under an obligation not to recognise this unlawful situation; not to provide any assistance to the secessionist entity; and shall cooperate with a view to ending this illegality (ARSIWA, Articles 26, 40–41). The foregoing reference strengthens the wording of Security Council Resolutions 541/1983 and 550/1984 on the invalidity of the 'TRNC'.[20]

In general, it should be stressed that the references to Cyprus in the Advisory Opinion on Kosovo reaffirmed the positions of the RoC in respect of its territorial integrity and the consequences of the illegal Turkish invasion of Cyprus in 1974. Notwithstanding the fact that the Court did not pronounce on the substance of the submitted question, it, nevertheless, enhanced the RoC's arguments against the recognition of the 'TRNC'. At the same time, the legal arguments submitted by RoC during the proceedings gave the Court the opportunity to stress the superior status of the prohibition of use of force and consolidate the rule that the outcome of an unlawful use of force can never attain legitimacy.

Law concerning Friendly Relations and Cooperation among States in accordance with the Charter of the United Nations, UNGA Res 2625 (XXV) (24 October 1970) Annex, Principle 1; *Legal Consequences of the Construction of a Wall in the Occupied Palestinian Territory* (Advisory Opinion) [2004] ICJ Rep 136, paras 87, 146, 150, 159; *Jurisdictional Immunities of the State (Germany v Italy: Greece intervening)* (Judgment) [2012] ICJ Rep 99, para 93; 'The Stimson Note of January 7, 1932' (1932) 26 AJIL 342.

[19] *Gabčíkovo-Nagymaros Project (Hungary/Slovakia)* (Judgment) [1997] ICJ Rep 7, para 133; *Legal Status of Eastern Greenland* (Judgment) [1933] PCIJ Rep Series A/B No 53, p. 95, Dissenting Opinion of Judge Anzilotti; *Construction of a Wall* (n 18) para 74.

[20] Another reference to the Cyprus Problem was made in paragraph 114: '...the Security Council, in its resolution 1251 of 29 June 1999, reaffirmed its position that a "Cyprus settlement must be based on a State of Cyprus with *a single sovereignty and international personality and a single citizenship, with its independence and territorial integrity safeguarded*" (para. 11). The Security Council thus set out the specific conditions relating to the permanent status of Cyprus. (emphasis added)'.

The ICJ Advisory Opinion on the Legal Consequences of the Separation of the Chagos Archipelago from Mauritius in 1965

The island of Mauritius in the Indian Ocean was under UK sovereignty until 1968 when it gained independence.[21] Nevertheless, in 1965, the UK had separated the Chagos Archipelago from the territory of the Colony of Mauritius and turned it into a new entity, namely the British Indian Ocean Territory (BIOT). The BIOT is one of the 14 British Overseas Territories (BOTs) and the United States (US) has established a significant military base on the biggest island of the Archipelago (Diego Garcia) (Hendry and Dickson 2011; Allen 2014).[22] Following a period without any noteworthy developments, in 2004 Mauritius expressed its desire to leave the Commonwealth so as to be able to lodge a case to the ICJ against the UK. It is reminded that the latter had submitted a reservation to its declaration accepting the compulsory jurisdiction of the Court whereby it excluded from the jurisdiction of the Court any disputes with members of the Commonwealth.[23] Facing the risk of a case against it before the ICJ, the UK modified its previous declaration which now excludes disputes with both current and former members of the Commonwealth (Snoxell 2018).[24]

Despite the above, Mauritius attempted to evade the jurisdictional hurdles set by the UK by means of the 1982 United Nations Convention on the Law of the Sea (LOSC) dispute settlement mechanism. Mauritius

---

[21] *The Chagos Marine Protected Area Award (Mauritius v United Kingdom)* [2015] paras 56–60; *Legal Consequences of the Separation of the Chagos Archipelago from Mauritius in 1965* (Request for Advisory Opinion) Written Statement of the Republic of Mauritius (1 March 2018) paras 1.6, 2.1–2.48.

[22] The Chagos islanders were expelled from their homeland at the request of the USA: *Chagos Islanders v United Kingdom* App no 35622/04 (ECtHR, 11 December 2012).

[23] 'Mauritius may sue for Diego Garcia' *Guardian* (London, 7 July 2004), www.theguardian.com/world/2004/jul/07/politics.foreignpolicy.

[24] Declarations Recognising the Jurisdiction of the Court as Compulsory: United Kingdom of Great Britain and Northern Ireland (as at 22 February 2017) para 2(ii) 'any dispute with the government of any other country which is *or has been a Member of the Commonwealth*' (emphasis added), www.icj-cij.org/en/declarations/gb; on the previous UK declarations see Declarations recognising the jurisdiction of the Court as compulsory: United Kingdom of Great Britain and Northern Ireland, https://treaties.un.org/Pages/ViewDetails.aspx?src=TREATY&mtdsg_no=I-4&chapter=1&clang=_en#EndDec;

contested the UK's power to declare a Marine Protected Area (MPA) around the Chagos Archipelago as, so the Mauritian argument went, the UK is not the coastal state (Scovazzi 2014). The ad hoc Arbitral Tribunal constituted under Annex VII LOSC issued its Award in 2015. In a nutshell, the Tribunal did not examine Mauritius's first three claims as it resolved that they relate 'to land sovereignty', thus falling outside the jurisdiction of the Tribunal, since it is not a dispute concerning the interpretation or application of the LOSC (Boyle 1997; Buga 2012; Nguyen 2016).[25] What international case law illustrates is that when there is a sovereignty dispute over continental or insular territories, it is necessary for it to be resolved prior to the consideration of any maritime rights accruing from those areas and the delimitation of their maritime space (Qu 2016).[26] Be that as it may, the Tribunal accepted Mauritius's fourth claim and set forth that the establishment of the MPA was in breach of Mauritius's rights under Articles 2(3), 56(2) and 194(4) LOSC.[27]

Mauritius's endeavour to bring the case before an international dispute settlement body culminated in the adoption of resolution 71/292 by the UN General Assembly on 22 June 2017, whereby the latter decided to request an advisory opinion from the ICJ concerning the following questions:

> (a) 'Was the process of decolonization of Mauritius lawfully completed when Mauritius was granted independence in 1968, following the separation of the Chagos Archipelago from Mauritius and having regard to international law, including obligations reflected in General Assembly resolutions 1514 (XV) of 14 December 1960, 2066 (XX) of 16 December 1965, 2232 (XXI) of 20 December 1966 and 2357 (XXII) of 19 December 1967?';

---

[25] *Chagos Award* (n 21) paras 212–221; the LOSC does not include any provisions on settlement of disputes over terrestrial territories and it applies only when a state has an uncontested title over a territory from which maritime claims derive.

[26] *Land, Island and Maritime Frontier Dispute (El Salvador/Honduras: Nicaragua intervening)* [1992] ICJ Rep 351; *Land and Maritime Boundary between Cameroon and Nigeria (Cameroon v Nigeria: Equatorial Guinea intervening)* (Judgment) [2002] ICJ Rep 303; *Maritime Delimitation and Territorial Questions between Qatar and Bahrain (Qatar v Bahrain)* (Judgment) [2001] ICJ Rep 97; *Territorial and Maritime Dispute (Nicaragua v Colombia)* (Judgment) [2012] ICJ Rep 624.

[27] *Chagos Award* (n 21) para 547(B).

(b) 'What are the consequences under international law, including obligations reflected in the above-mentioned resolutions, arising from the continued administration by the United Kingdom of Great Britain and Northern Ireland of the Chagos Archipelago, including with respect to the inability of Mauritius to implement a programme for the resettlement on the Chagos Archipelago of its nationals, in particular those of Chagossian origin?' (UNGA Res 71/292).

With a view to addressing the foregoing questions, the Court scrutinised the pertinent legal framework.[28] As regards the first question, the ICJ noted that respect for the right to self-determination is one of the UN purposes and the matter of decolonisation falls within the ambit of the Organisation's functions.[29] Notably, the Court pronounced that UN General Assembly resolution 1514/1960 concerning decolonisation affirmed the customary character of the right to self-determination and territorial integrity of non-self-governing territories[30]; consequently, the right to self-determination had been crystallised as custom before 1960 thus covering a range of other colonial territories gaining independence earlier. The Court also stressed that the exercise of the right to self-determination 'must be the expression of the free and genuine will of the people concerned'.[31] Moreover, self-determination should be implemented over the entire territory of a non-self-governing territory since the right to territorial integrity forms a fundamental element of the right to self-determination. Therefore: 'It follows that any detachment by the administering Power of part of a non-self-governing territory, unless based on the freely expressed and genuine will of the people of the territory concerned, is contrary to the right to self-determination'.[32]

---

[28] Prior to that, the ICJ had found that it had jurisdiction to give the requested opinion and had referred to the facts concerning the detachment of the Chagos Archipelago from the Colony of Mauritius and the independence of the latter, while it resolved that there was no need for rephrasing the submitted questions: *Legal Consequences of the Separation of the Chagos Archipelago from Mauritius in 1965* (Advisory Opinion) [2019] paras 54–91, 92–131, 133–137.

[29] *Chagos Advisory Opinion* (n 28) paras 88, 146, 163–168.

[30] Ibid., paras 150–153.

[31] Ibid., para 157. This finding is in line with the Court's *jurisprudence constante*: *Western Sahara* (Advisory Opinion) [1975] ICJ Rep 12, para 55.

[32] *Chagos Advisory Opinion* (n 28) para 160; the UN General Assembly had long expressed its concerns over the practice of detachment of colonial territories for the

In another noteworthy point, the Court promulgated that 'heightened scrutiny should be given' as regards the consent provided when it comes to the detachment of territory while a people is still under colonial rule.[33] In other words, it is unlikely for the consent given by a colonial people to the colonial power to be genuine and free due to the inherent inequality between the two parties. Having said this, the Court put forward that the dismemberment of the Chagos Archipelago 'was not based on the free and genuine expression of the will of the people concerned', and hence the decolonisation of Mauritius was not lawfully completed.[34]

Moving on to the second question, the ICJ stressed that it must apply international law as it stands today (and not the rules in force at the time Mauritius's decolonisation took place).[35] As the Court had decided that the decolonisation of Mauritius was not lawfully completed, it, thus, found that the continued administration of the Chagos Archipelago by the UK constitutes a continuing wrongful act triggering the latter's international responsibility; hence, the UK must cease its unlawful conduct as soon as possible in order for decolonisation to be completed. The Court also added that it is up to the UN General Assembly to define the decolonisation process, while all states are under a duty to cooperate with the UN to this end since the right to self-determination generates obligations *erga omnes*.[36]

Even though the advisory opinion is not binding on states per se because it is given to the requesting UN organ (the General Assembly on this occasion), it is still a landmark. The Opinion was handed down with an overwhelming majority (13–1) concerning the substantive legal points and its wording is—unexpectedly—clear compared to previous opinions (i.e. Kosovo) where the Court avoided giving direct answers to the questions posed. In the aftermath of the Opinion, the matter returned to the

---

establishment of military bases and considered such actions to be a violation of Resolution 1514/1960. UNGA Resolutions 2066 (XX) (16 December 1965); 2232 (XXI) (20 December 1966); 2357 (XXII) (19 December 1967).

[33] This view contradicts the position held by the Tribunal in *Mauritius v UK* where the arrangement between the representatives of the colony of Mauritius and the UK was deemed to have been upgraded to an international treaty due to Mauritius's independence: *Chagos Award* (n 28) para 425.

[34] *Chagos Advisory Opinion* (n 28) paras 172, 174.

[35] Ibid para 175.

[36] Ibid paras 177–180.

General Assembly, which welcomed the outcome, endorsed the Court's findings demanding the UK's withdrawal from the Chagos Archipelago and called upon all states to cooperate with the UN to that end (UNGA Res 73/295).

Interestingly, the Court condoned several of the positions advocated by the RoC. In its oral pleadings, the RoC mentioned that as a former colony it stands alongside all the peoples that still struggle for self-determination.[37] It also argued that by withholding a part of the territory of a former colony, the colonial power is under a continuing obligation to effectively implement the principle of self-determination.[38] What is more, the RoC held the view that colonialism violates international law and that the right to self-determination is a peremptory norm (*ius cogens*) generating legal obligations for all states (*erga omnes*).[39]

Additionally, the RoC gave emphasis on the matter of territorial integrity and referred to the term 'incomplete decolonisation'.[40] The RoC argued that since there is a presumption in favour of independence of the territorial unit as whole, its dismemberment and retention of part of the territory by the colonial power is incompatible with the right to self-determination.[41] Genuine and free consent within the context of an agreement can be given only as between equal states.[42] However, consent cannot be deemed to have been freely given in situations where a state is established with its territory having already been dismembered, and especially in situations where the new state comes into existence subject to legal constraints on its ability to challenge such prior dismemberment.[43]

Lastly, the RoC supported that irrespective of whether self-determination and territorial integrity were concepts already upgraded to rules in 1965, what matters is that today they are non-derogable peremptory norms. Following this trail of thinking, even if the dismemberment of Mauritius was not prohibited under international law in 1965,

---

[37] *Legal Consequences of the Separation of the Chagos Archipelago from Mauritius in 1965* (Request for Advisory Opinion) Oral statement of the Republic of Cyprus (04 September 2018), 47.

[38] Ibid., 48, 53.

[39] Ibid., 48.

[40] Ibid., 52.

[41] Ibid., 52, 55.

[42] Ibid., 54.

[43] Ibid., 54–55.

the continuing retention of the Chagos Archipelago by the UK renders the decolonisation of Mauritius incomplete and obliges the colonial power to terminate its unlawful conduct, which triggers its international responsibility.[44]

Given that the Court has resolved that the decolonisation of Mauritius has not been lawfully completed, owing to the withholding of part of its territory by the former colonial power, it is likely that this finding would also be applicable to the case of the SBAs in Cyprus. Therefore, it can be argued that the UK is in breach of its obligation to complete the decolonisation of Cyprus. As mentioned above, the right to self-determination seems to be a peremptory norm and its violation gives rise to the international responsibility of the wrongdoer state (ARSIWA, Articles 40–41). Consequently, the UK is under an obligation to terminate its wrongful conduct towards the RoC and allow the Cypriot people to exercise its right to self-determination with respect to the whole of the island. For the UK to avoid its international responsibility, it should relinquish the SBAs' territory in favour of the RoC and enter into negotiations with the latter for the conclusion of a leasehold agreement concerning its military facilities.

As shown in the foregoing analysis, the RoC's contribution to the elaboration of the right to self-determination and the law on decolonisation was substantial. This finding strengthens the argument that the RoC is not only interested in fulfilling its own foreign policy tasks, but also attaches great significance to the progress of international law in general.

The Maritime Activities of the Republic of Cyprus

International law is also pivotal for the conduct of maritime activities in the Eastern Mediterranean Sea. It should be borne in mind that it is of utmost importance for the regional states to operate in accordance with the pertinent legal framework so as to effectively pursue their rights and interests. Thus, stimulated by the hydrocarbon discoveries, several Eastern Mediterranean states decided to collaborate within the purview of international law with a view to benefiting from the offshore oil and gas reserves discovered in the region. A fundamental prerequisite to do so is the delimitation of maritime boundaries. To date, three maritime

---

[44] Ibid., 57–59.

boundary delimitation agreements have been signed in the region. Egypt and the RoC were pioneers in maritime delimitation as in 2003 they concluded the first Exclusive Economic Zone (EEZ) delimitation agreement in the Mediterranean Sea.[45] Egypt and the RoC used the median line even though the former possesses a longer relevant coast compared with Cyprus.

Nonetheless, Turkey rejected the aforementioned agreement and laid claims for the sea waters between the Greek islands of the south-eastern Aegean Sea and Cyprus as part of its continental shelf, disregarding the rights of the Greek islands, as well as the capacity of Cyprus to generate maritime zones other than territorial sea. Turkey also published maps where its alleged maritime borders according to the median line abut those of Egypt (Erciyes 2012). As a consequence, the Turkish putative continental shelf limits partly overlap with blocks 1, 4, 5, 6 and 7 of Cyprus' continental shelf/EEZ and also partially coincide with segments of the Greek continental shelf. One of the arguments put forward by Turkey to persuade Egypt to abandon its EEZ delimitation with Cyprus is that Egypt has 'abolished' a maritime space of approximately 19.400 km^2 owing to the median line agreed with Cyprus (Çubukçuoğlu 2014; Yayci 2012).[46]

The Turkish contentions over the western sector,[47] but mainly over the southwestern part of the Cyprus' continental shelf/EEZ, in relation to which a maritime boundary delimitation and a framework agreement[48] between the RoC and Egypt are in force, contest the former's sovereign

---

[45] Agreement between the Republic of Cyprus and the Arab Republic of Egypt on the Delimitation of the Exclusive Economic Zone (signed 17 February 2003, entered into force 07 March 2004) 2488 UNTS 3.

[46] A Turkish author argues that both Israel and Lebanon should revisit their EEZ delimitation agreements with Cyprus as they are detrimental to their interests; Yayci holds the view that Turkey can conclude delimitation agreements with Egypt, Syria, Israel, Libya and Lebanon disregarding the island of Cyprus.

[47] There is no maritime boundary delimitation agreement either between Cyprus and Greece or Turkey concerning the maritime area between the Greek islands of the southeastern Aegean and Cyprus.

[48] Framework Agreement Between the Government of the Republic of Cyprus and the Government of the Arab Republic of Egypt Concerning the Development of Cross-Median Line Hydrocarbons Resources, Republic of Cyprus, Government Gazette No 4196 (signed 12 December 2013, entered into force 25 July 2014) p. 10703, www.mof.gov.cy/mof/gpo/gpo.nsf/All/A88D02909DC27F10C2257D20002C1DB5/$file/4196%2025%207%202014%20PARARTIMA%201o%20MEROS%20III%20.pdf.

rights under both conventional and customary international law. Significantly, the framework agreement and the fact that Egypt has awarded oil concessions respecting the median line with Cyprus have reaffirmed and consolidated the maritime boundary of the two states and, accordingly, any efforts towards a unilateral revocation of the delimitation agreement would be extremely difficult. Even if such an act does take place, it would be hard to affect the maritime boundary because of the 'doctrine of executed treaty provisions', which entails that 'once a boundary line has been established by treaty … its existence as a legal construction binding on the parties is no longer dependent on the continued existence of the treaty or the treaty provision which established it' (VCLT, Articles 62(2)(a), 70(1)).[49]

Based on the 'pilot agreement' with Egypt, the RoC penned another two delimitation agreements with Lebanon (2007)[50] and Israel (2010).[51] All three agreements are concise and comprise five articles each. Although the agreement with Lebanon has not entered into force, the western limit of its EEZ, as outlined by the coordinates the Lebanese authorities unilaterally deposited with the UN Secretary-General in 2010 and 2011,[52] are well-nigh identical to the median line agreed between Lebanon and Cyprus (Dörr 2012).[53]

By way of reaction to these developments, Turkey, from 2008 until 2012, granted concessions to the TPAO for areas Greece considers to be falling within its continental shelf, as well as for areas claimed by Cyprus

---

[49] International case law condones the view that Article 62(2)(a) VCLT applies to maritime boundaries as well: *Aegean Sea Continental Shelf Case (Greece v Turkey)* (Jurisdiction) [1978] ICJ Rep 3, para 85; *Arbitral Award of 31 July 1989 (Guinea-Bissau v Senegal)* (Judgment) [1991] ICJ Rep 53, para 63; *Bangladesh v India Award* [2014] para 216.

[50] Agreement between the Government of the Republic of Cyprus and the Government of the Republic of Lebanon on the Delimitation of the Exclusive Economic Zone (17 January 2007) (not in force). Reproduced in David A Colson and Robert W Smith (eds), *International Maritime Boundaries*, Vol VI (Martinus Nijhoff 2005–2011) 4452.

[51] Agreement between the Government of the Republic of Cyprus and the Government of the State of Israel on the Delimitation of the Exclusive Economic Zone (signed 17 December 2010, entered into force 25 February 2011) 2740 UNTS 55.

[52] Deposits by Lebanon, www.un.org/Depts/los/LEGISLATIONANDTREATIES/STATEFILES/LBN.htm.

[53] Even though the delimitation agreement is not in force, the parties are under an obligation 'not to defeat the object and purpose' of that treaty: VCLT art 18.

as part of its continental shelf/EEZ off its western coasts.[54] Furthermore, Turkey has repeatedly dispatched the government survey vessel 'Barbaros' since 2013 in maritime areas around the island of Cyprus. These activities have caused a vehement reaction by Cyprus, but Turkey continued surveys in the region throughout 2020. Having already made its intentions public, Turkey moved to the realisation of its hydrocarbon objectives and deployed two drilling vessels off the coasts of Cyprus, stirring further reactions. Hence, as of May 2020, the state-owned drilling vessels 'Fatih' and 'Yavuz' have performed six drillings within the RoC's continental shelf/EEZ, while the seismic vessels 'Barbaros' and 'Oruç Reis' have been deployed several times (Ioannides 2020).

In light of the above, the RoC, once again, resorted to international law in order to safeguard its rights. By means of a letter to the UN Secretary-General, the RoC officially invited Turkey to negotiations concerning the delimitation of their respective maritime zones (UNGA Doc. A/73/651). Moreover, following intense diplomatic attempts on the part of the RoC, the Council of the European Union (EU) adopted a Decision within the context of the Common Foreign and Security Policy (CFSP) 'concerning restrictive measures in view of Turkey's unauthorised drilling activities in the Eastern Mediterranean' and a Regulation implementing the Decision (Council Decision (CFSP) 2019/1894; Council Regulation (EU) 2019/1890). These acts paved the way for the imposition of sanctions against natural and legal persons involved in Turkey's illegal activities within Cyprus' maritime zones. This is a significant Decision given that the EU had never hitherto decided to take restrictive measures against a candidate member state. In November 2019, Cyprus transmitted a note verbale (dated 15 November 2019) to the Turkish Embassy in Athens, whereby it proposed the conclusion of a special agreement (*compromis*) envisaging joint submission of the two states' maritime dispute to the ICJ, asking the Court to delimit their respective maritime zones (it is reminded that Turkey does not recognise the compulsory jurisdiction of the Court).

---

[54] Official Gazette of the Republic of Turkey, No 27290 (16 July 2009) Decisions of the Council of Ministers 14002/2008, 14003/2008, 14004/2008, 14005/2008, www.resmigazete.gov.tr/main.aspx?home=http://www.resmigazete.gov.tr/eskiler/2009/07/20090716.htm&main=http://www.resmigazete.gov.tr/eskiler/2009/07/20090716.htm; Official Gazette of the Republic of Turkey, No 28276 (27 April 2012) Decisions of the Council of Ministers 2802/2012, 2968/2012, 2973/2012, 2974/2012, www.resmigazete.gov.tr/eskiler/2012/04/20120427.htm.

Irrespective of the above, Cyprus has announced that it will unilaterally have recourse to the ICJ invoking the latter's prorogated jurisdiction (*forum prorogatum*) by virtue of Article 38(5) ICJ Rules of the Court.[55] Put simply, the RoC intends to file an application and then wait for Turkey to provide its consent in order for the case to make it to the Court's docket. Even though this is unlikely to happen owing to Turkey's long-standing reluctance to appear before international dispute settlement bodies, it is still a very interesting development within the context of the Eastern Mediterranean saga. This unilateral application appears to be the culmination of the RoC's efforts to delimit its maritime boundaries with Turkey following an invitation for negotiations and a proposal for the conclusion of a special agreement for adjudication. Since both states rely on the rules of international law to put forward their assertions, the ICJ would be the most appropriate forum for the resolution of their dispute.

Once again, as this section illustrates, the RoC has acted within the realm of international law to both protect its interests and promote peaceful settlement of disputes. Notably, the maritime delimitation agreements struck in the Eastern Mediterranean may serve as a model of regional cooperation. At the same time, the attempt of the RoC to bring its maritime dispute with Turkey before the ICJ highlights its trust to international dispute settlement bodies and its long-standing belief that disputes should be resolved peacefully and in conformity with international law.

Conclusion

As discussed in this chapter, international law holds a prominent position in the RoC's foreign policy. This is not surprising bearing in mind that Cyprus is located in a turbulent region where the application of international law is indispensable in order to stymie/de-escalate tensions and establish a secure and stable environment. Thus, the RoC is a staunch supporter of peaceful settlement of disputes before international judicial bodies and shapes its foreign policy along the lines of international law.

The first appearance of the RoC at the ICJ was prompted by its interest in the legality of unilateral declarations of independence, owing to the

---

[55] 'Cyprus petitions The Hague to safeguard offshore rights', *Reuters*, 5 December 2019, www.reuters.com/article/us-cyprus-turkey-hague/cyprus-petitions-the-hague-to-safeguard-offshore-rights-idUSKBN1Y90TA.

'TRNC' conundrum. Although the Court did not provide the General Assembly with substantive guidance as regards the matter, the Advisory Opinion is quite significant for the RoC. For the Court explicitly referred to the secessionist entity in the occupied areas of Cyprus making it clear that it can never acquire statehood since it is the result of unlawful use of force on the part of Turkey. Therefore, it is argued that the participation of the RoC in the proceedings affirmed the importance of taking part in such cases to promote state interests since the Opinion has enhanced the RoC's argumentation with respect to the illegality of the 'TRNC'.

A few years later, the RoC actively participated in the proceedings regarding the legal status of the Chagos Archipelago championing the right to self-determination. Considering that the Court has resolved that the detachment of territory from a colony prior to its independence renders decolonisation incomplete, the continuing presence of the SBAs in Cyprus appears to be in breach of the right to self-determination of the Cypriot people giving rise to the UK's international responsibility. As a result, the UK is under an obligation to terminate its unlawful behaviour and accept a modification of the SBAs' legal regime for their presence not to violate international law.

In the aftermath of the discovery of offshore hydrocarbon reserves in the Eastern Mediterranean, the regional states decided to collaborate under the auspices of international law. The RoC took significant initiatives and signed three maritime delimitation agreements, while it commenced a host of maritime activities. Notwithstanding Turkey's aggressive conduct, the RoC remains committed to the pertinent international law framework and has become a beacon of legality and stability in the region.

Undoubtedly, the substantive participation of the RoC in two advisory proceedings before the ICJ and its achievements in terms of maritime affairs over the last years support the view that even small states may have a notable role in international relations insofar as they act in a consistent and systematic manner. That's exactly what Mauritius has achieved; following decades of contempt on the part of the UK and the international community, it managed to stir the discussion on self-determination anew and cause the issuance of a catapulting advisory opinion.

Furthermore, this chapter evinces that the RoC's approach to international law is not monolithic, namely it does not focus entirely on the protection and enhancement of its own interests. As illustrated above, the RoC has contributed to the elaboration of the rules governing the prohibition of use of force and the installation of secessionist entities in the wake of aggression; the rules on self-determination and decolonisation; and the rules pertinent to the performance of maritime activities. This stance reveals a mature attitude in the sense that the RoC seems to have perceived well its role in international relations and the making of international law. It is thus argued that through active participation in the shaping of international law the RoC may upgrade its political status in the international community. However, international law should not be deemed merely a foreign policy 'tool'. As a matter of fact, by demonstrating a sincere interest in the development of international law, the RoC has proved that, apart from the promotion of its positions, it is also keen on engaging in attempts to entrench international law with a view to facilitating the orderly conduct of international relations across the globe.

In any case, even though inequality and injustice have not vanished, international law has become a point of reference for all states. Despite the challenges facing the international community, we must admit that there has been a noteworthy progress in the creation and application of norms regulating state conduct in the international sphere. It is thus submitted that the cynical aphorism 'might makes right' has been diluted. Twenty-five centuries on, humankind has managed to contain states' unaccountability, up to a certain extent. Albeit the situation is far from ideal, one cannot deny that international law has improved our lives. It is our duty to intensify our efforts towards the achievement of a more humane standard of living for all human beings under the guidance of international law.

REFERENCES

ARTICLES

Allen, Stephen. 2014. *The Chagos Islanders and International Law.* Hart Publishing.

Boyle, Alan E. 1997. "Dispute Settlement and the Law of the Sea Convention: Problems of Fragmentation and Jurisdiction." *International and Comparative Law Quarterly* 46 (1): 37.

Buga, Irina. 2012. "Territorial Sovereignty Issues in Maritime Disputes: A Jurisdictional Dilemma for Law of the Sea Tribunals." *International Journal of Marine Coastal Law* 27 (1): 59–95.

Cassese, Antonio. 2005. *International Law.* 2nd ed, 44, 351. OUP.

Crawford, James. 2006. *The Creation of States in International Law*. 2nd ed, 144. OUP.
Crawford, James. 2019. *Brownlie's Principles of Public International Law*. 9th ed, 726–728. OUP.
Çubukçuoğlu, Serhat S. 2014. "Turkey's Exclusive Economic Zone in the Mediterranean Sea: The Case of Kastellorizo," *Master's Thesis, The Fletcher School of Law and Diplomacy 2014* (27, 32) www.academia.edu/9532225/Turkeys_EEZ_in_the_Mediterranean_Sea_The_Case_of_Kastellorizo.
Dörr, Oliver. 2012. "Article 18: Obligation Not to Defeat the Object and Purpose of a Treaty Prior to Its Entry into Force." In *Vienna Convention on the Law of Treaties: A Commentary*, edited by Oliver Dörr and Kirsten Schmalenbach, 226. Springer.
Erciyes, Çagatay. 2012. "Maritime Delimitation and Off-Shore Activities in the Eastern Mediterranean: Legal and Political Perspectives, Recent Developments." *Turkish Ministry of Foreign Affairs*.
Gray, Christine. 2018. "The Use of Force and the International Legal Order." In *The International Law*, edited by Malcolm D. Evans, 5th ed, 608. OUP.
Hendry, Ian, and Susan Dickson. 2011. *British Overseas Territories Law*, 301–305. Hart Publishing.
Ioannides, Nicholas A. 2020. "*Maritime Claims and Boundary Delimitation: Tensions and Trends in the Eastern Mediterranean Sea*." Routledge, Chapter 3.
Nguyen, Lan Ngoc. 2016. "The Chagos Marine Protected Area Arbitration: Has the Scope of LOSC Compulsory Jurisdiction Been Clarified?." *International Journal of Marine and Coastal Law* 31 (1): 120–143.
Qu, Wesheng. 2016. "The Issue of Jurisdiction Over Mixed Disputes in the Chagos Marine Protection Arbitration and Beyond." *Ocean Development and International Law* 47 (1): 40.
Scovazzi, Tullio. 2014. "Marine Protected Areas in Waters Beyond National Jurisdiction." In *30 Anos da assinatura da Convenção das Nações Unidas sobre o Direito do Mar: protecção do ambiente e o futura do direito do mar*, by Marta Chantal Ribeiro, 209–238. Coimbra Editora.
Simma, Bruno. 1999. "NATO, the UN and the Use of Force: Legal Aspects." *European Journal of International Law* 10: 1–22.
Snoxell, David. 2018. "An ICJ Advisory Opinion, Basis for a Negotiated Settlement on the Issues Concerning the Future of the Chagos Islanders and of the British Indian Ocean Territory." *Questions of International Law* 55 (3): 6–7.
Yayci, Cihat. 2012. "The Problem of Delimitation of Maritime Areas in Eastern Mediterranean and Turkey." *Bilge Strateji* 4 (6): 1–2.

United Nations Documents

UNSC Res 186/1964 (04 March 1964) UN Doc S/RES/186.

UNSC Res 541/1983 (18 November 1983) UN Doc S/RES/541.
UNSC Res 550/1984 (11 May 1984) UN Doc S/RES/550.
UNGA Res 63/3 (8 October 2008) UN Doc A/RES/63/3.
UNGA Res 71/292 (22 June 2017) UN Doc A/RES/71/292.
UNGA Res 73/295 (22 May 2019) UN Doc A/RES/73/295.

European Union Documents

Council Decision (CFSP) 2019/1894 of 11 November 2019. Concerning Restrictive Measures in View of Turkey's Unauthorised Drilling Activities in the Eastern Mediterranean [2019] OJ L 291/47.
Council Regulation (EU) 2019/1890 of 11 November 2019. Concerning Restrictive Measures in View of Turkey's Unauthorised Drilling Activities in the Eastern Mediterranean [2019] OJ L 291/3.

International Legislation

Articles on Responsibility of States for Internationally Wrongful Acts (adopted on November 2001).
Statute of the International Court of Justice (adopted on 26 June 1945).
Vienna Convention on the Law of Treaties (signed on 23 May 1969, entered into force on 27 January 1980).

CHAPTER 11

Gender Mainstreaming in the Foreign Policy of the Republic of Cyprus

Constantinos Adamides and Josie Christodoulou

[…] the equality rights, responsibilities and opportunities of women and men and girls and boys. Equality does not mean that women and men will become the same but that women's and men's rights, responsibilities and opportunities will not depend on whether they are born male or female. Gender equality implies that the interests, needs and priorities of both women and men are taken into consideration equality between women and men is seen both as a human rights issue and as a precondition for, and indicator of, sustainable people-centered development. (UN 2001)

With the above in mind, gender *inequality*, is based on social attributes, biases and perceptions associated with the biological sex of

C. Adamides (✉)
University of Nicosia, Nicosia, Cyprus
e-mail: adamides.c@unic.ac.cy

J. Christodoulou
Ministry of Foreign Affairs, Nicosia, Cyprus
e-mail: jchristodoulou@mfa.gov.cy

© The Author(s), under exclusive license to Springer Nature Switzerland AG 2022
Z. Tziarras (ed.), *The Foreign Policy of the Republic of Cyprus*, Reform and Transition in the Mediterranean,
https://doi.org/10.1007/978-3-030-91177-5_11

one being born female or male. As a result, gender becomes a determining factor in the 'what is expected, allowed and valued in a woman or a man in a given context' (UN 2001). Inevitably, perhaps, in most societies women and men are expected to have different responsibilities, decision-making opportunities as well as access to control over resources (UN 2001).

This expectation of responsibilities seems to be more profound in the realm of foreign policy, and this paper aims to explore the degree of maturity in this area using the Republic of Cyprus (RoC) as a case study. Specifically, it examines whether the RoC foreign policy aspiration is in line with the state's needs and interest in women's rights and gender equality through the strategy of mainstreaming gender. Thus, the scope of this work is threefold: The first is to highlight the past and current gender representation gap in the RoC foreign affairs structures and the efforts undertaken to rectify the problem. The second aim is to analyze how a more focused gender strategy across the board can also contribute to a state's foreign policy goals beyond the ones related to gender. Lastly, in a mirror image of the above, the paper focuses on how there can be foreign policy actions that can also contribute to the regional, European Union (EU) and global efforts for the advancement of women's rights.

Despite noticeable improvements in some regions, there is still systematic sexism—the idea that mainly women and girls are perceived as inferior because of their sex—which means that women still face multiple institutional and interpersonal discrimination and violence solely because of their sex. Therefore, any action towards the advancement of women's rights and the promotion of gender equality should be framed in a way that takes into consideration the historically unequal power relations between men and women. Strategies and tools were developed to promote equality, with the most prominent one being gender mainstreaming; the *process* of assessing the impact on women and men for any planned action, including legislation, policies and programmes, in every field and at all levels. Gender Mainstreaming is also a *strategy* as the goal is to make the issues and experiences of women and men part of an integrated dimension in the design, implementation, monitoring and evaluation of policies and programmes on political, economic and societal issues. Thus, the goal is to stop the perpetuation of inequality and enhance the equal benefits of women and men.

Gender Mainstreaming has become a priority for most European and international organizations, including the United Nations (UN), the EU, the Council of Europe and the Union for the Mediterranean. Indeed, as Sylvia Walby notes convincingly,

> Gender Mainstreaming often draws on transnational processes involving transnational networks and agencies and transformations of the discourse of universal human rights, challenging the traditional focus on national processes. [...]. Gender mainstreaming is a leading-edge example of the potential implications of globalizations for gender politics. (Walby 2011, 97)

The principle of gender mainstreaming was initially developed by feminist development practitioners in the 1970s and launched at the UN Conference on women in 1995 (Meyer and Prügl 1999). Since then, it has been adopted by the EU as a core part of its gender equality policy and with the 1997 Treaty of Amsterdam it has gained even more prominence. Preceding these efforts, the UN as the largest multilateral organization adopted a number of legal and other frameworks with the most important ones for the field being the Universal Declaration of Human Rights, the Convention on the Elimination of all forms of Discrimination Against Women CEDAW adopted in 1979 (CEDAW 1979), and the 1995 Beijing Declaration and Platform for Action (Beijing Declaration and Platform for Action 1995). These two tools, in most countries, form the legal basis for formulating national action plans and legislation for the rights of women, while at the same time they, and other similar UN conventions, highlight the need for international cooperation and transnational processes to maximize the impact. The public policy dimension is one of the areas that is still in need of more gender mainstreaming as the EU acknowledges in the EU Gender Action Plan (GAP III 2020). This is a Plan which provides the framework for the European Commission's (2020), the European External Action Services' (EEAS) and the EU Member States' (MS) approaches to gender equality through external action. Similarly, the European Parliament (EP) calls for gender equality in the EUs foreign and security policy (EP 2020).

Gender Equality should be mainstreamed in the state machinery with focus on, inter alia, employment opportunities, economic, justice, health and education related decisions, environmental policies, and, importantly, on foreign policy and diplomacy. This need is recognized and accepted in Cyprus, as in many other parts of the world. Indeed, Cyprus has joined a growing number of countries that have begun to institutionalize gender equality, with intensified efforts since the country's EU accession in 2004. A series of strategic National Action Plans on gender equality have been adopted and Gender Equality was further institutionalized with the appointment of Gender Equality Commissioner in 2013 and the adoption of more comprehensive legal and other tools. Despite the aforementioned efforts to make gender mainstreaming a 'horizontal' strategy in all state institutions, the issue was not set as a priority within the Ministry of Foreign Affairs (MFA), until very recently, as we discuss in the subsequent sections.

Women in the Foreign Policy Arena

There is little doubt that the world of foreign policy and diplomacy is a male-dominated realm. The under-representation of women is unquestionable; as of November 2020, there are only 20 female Heads of States and only 33 Ministers of Foreign Affairs and Secretaries of State. This unbalanced environment is largely the outcome of a strong and internalized perception that 'manliness' is an attribute to be valued in international politics. As the CEO of Grassroot Diplomat Talyn Rahman-Figueroa (2011) notes, in many parts of the world 'as a traditionally male domain, existing power structures within the diplomatic infrastructure remain to reinforce overt discriminatory practices, making it difficult for women to enter diplomacy at the highest position'. The absence of more women in the foreign policy decision-making apparatus is, inevitably, a major obstacle in achieving gender equality and parity through the strategy of gender mainstreaming. It is worth noting that the advancement of women's rights for the promotion of a global gender equality in international relations, multilateralism and foreign policy are very much presented as a new concept although it goes back centuries. As Aggestam and Town (2018a) argue women had a role in diplomacy and foreign policy affairs, until they were prohibited to do so. In their words,

> [...] women's immersion in diplomacy precedes their twentieth century roles as diplomats and diplomatic wives by several centuries. In fact, women occasionally served as diplomatic negotiators and were even appointed as ambassadors in Europe prior to the nineteenth century, before European bans emerged that prohibited women from holding formal state office. (Aggestam and Towns 2018b, 13)

Foreign policies often have security implications, especially in times of crises, and the absence of more women in the decision-making ranks has a significant impact as global economic, health and regional insecurity is affecting women and men in different ways with women being those who are hit the hardest. Wars and global health crises, like the Covid-19 pandemic and past epidemics, such as Ebola and Zika, have led to gross human rights abuses against women and girls in the worst-hit areas. This leads to the 'push back of women's rights' as UN Secretary-General, Antonio Guterres stated (UNSG 2019). Women, because of their different roles and positions in society, face different consequences from war, pandemics, economic crises, but also contribute differently to peacebuilding and recovery efforts. Despite that, traditional approaches to foreign and security policy are in essence gender blind and do not consider these differences on any real scale (Adebahr and Mittelhammer 2020), thus perpetuating an imbalance, which leads to incomplete political analyses and continued gender inequalities. This is also why the 1325 resolution of the United Nations Security Council (UNSC 2000) on Women, Peace and Security has such a critical role to play, for the development of more democratic and peaceful societies. In 2009, former US President, Barak Obama, was one of the first state leaders to take concrete actions towards reducing the imbalance in the foreign policy sector, when he appointed the first US Ambassador at Large for Global Women's Issues; this was the first appointment of its kind.

Since then, a growing number of states have institutionalized women's rights and gender equality in their foreign policy and security activities. Countries like Sweden went a step further by introducing a new approach and a new term: Feminist foreign policy. Sweden was the first country, in 2014, to announce the adoption of a Feminist Foreign Policy, a term which was then adopted by Mexico and partially adopted by Canada and France. As the Swedish Ministry of Foreign Affairs notes in its Handbook 'Sweden's feminist foreign policy 2019', the policy was considered necessary given the 'discrimination and systemic subordination' of women and girls around the world. The goal is to apply a 'systematic gender equality perspective throughout foreign policy'. The specific policy is considered to be a

> working method and a perspective that takes three Rs as its starting point and is based on a fourth R. The implication is that the Swedish Foreign Service, in all its parts, shall strive to strengthen all women's and girls'

Rights, Representation and Resources, based on the Reality in which they live. Sweden's feminist foreign policy is a transformative agenda that aims to change structures and enhance the visibility of women and girls as actors. (Handbook on Sweden's Feminist Foreign Policy 2019, 11)

Other countries followed Sweden's example and placed gender in the heart of their foreign policy, by introducing functions that will provide strategic guidance for more gender mainstreaming in the field. In 2010, the Seychelles established an Ambassador for Women and Children's Affairs. Similarly, in 2011, Australia appointed its first Ambassador for Women and Girls; a position now held by the fourth ambassador. The creation of similar roles is accelerating as Norway created a Special Envoy post for Women, Peace and Security, and Finland appointed an ambassador for gender equality. Similar positions were created by the United Kingdom (UK) in 2017 (Special Envoy for Gender Equality), by Iceland in 2018 (Special Envoy for Gender Equality), by Spain (Ambassador in a Special Mission for Gender Equality) and by Canada (Ambassador for Women, Peace, and Security). In 2019, the Netherlands expanded the mandate of its Ambassador for Sexual and Reproductive Health and Rights & HIV/AIDS to a broader ambassador post for women's rights and gender equality. In the RoC, the first dedicated appointment took place in 2019, when the Minister of Foreign Affairs, Nikos Christodoulides, appointed a gender advisor in an effort to place women's and girls' rights at the heart of foreign policy of the RoC. In February 2020, during the first High Level Conference on Women in Diplomacy, Minister Christodoulides underlined the importance of such initiatives, noting that 'to safeguard women's rights we need collective action. The responsibility for the promotion and acceleration of women's rights rests with all states, and therefore effective action should also be undertaken at the multilateral and foreign policy levels' (Christodoulides 2020).

On an EU level, the former EU High Representative of the EEAS, Federica Mogherini, appointed a Principle Advisor on Gender Equality and on the implementation of the UNSC Resolution (1325) on Women, Peace and Security to shape the external policy of the EU on women's and girls' rights. This is in line with the UN position that gender inequality can undermine peace and lead to conflict and violence, while equality between women and men enhances, among other things, socio-economic life and improves people's daily lives in all sectors. Similarly, in 2010, the UN created an office to work specifically on women and girls' rights widely known as UN Women and in 2012 the NATO Secretary-General appointed a first NATO Special Representative for Women, Peace and Security.

The overall aim of the aforementioned appointments is not only to advance gender equality in foreign and security policy, governments and international EU institutions in terms of numbers, but also to promote changes in leadership, policy and resource allocation, aiming at securing women rights, equality and equity. While in all cases the goal is the same, these initiatives vary significantly in terms of where they are housed within governments, how they are measured, and the extent to which they are implemented.

Women in the Ministry of Foreign Affairs of the RoC

The RoC, much like most former colonies, is a relatively new state and as such it was 're-born' as an independent state in a period when equal gender opportunities, at least in Europe, were considered to be of particular importance, as clearly noted in the European Convention of Human Rights (1951) and the European Social Charter (1961). Yet, much like in most other countries, at the time gender equality in the realm of diplomacy and foreign policy did not seem to be a priority.

The law for the establishment of a Foreign Service was passed almost immediately after the 'creation' of the new republic in 1960, and the Minister of Foreign Affairs had its first Minister, Spyros Kyprianou, on 7 September 1960 along with its first seven Ambassadors and Heads of Missions in Washington and the UN, London, Athens, Ankara, Moscow, Bonn and Cairo. Unsurprisingly, all were men, which reinforced the established perception that foreign policy is the 'responsibility of men'. As the MFA and the Diplomatic Corps needs grew, so did the need for more employees. Fast forward a few decades, the gender parity of incoming new civil servants at the MFA appears to remain rather unbalanced. As demonstrated in Table 11.1, during the 1983–2018 period out of the 161 new MFA civil servants hired, only 49, or 30%, were women, and only three times during this period women constituted 50% or more of the newly hired employees.

That said, the very small number of new employees during the period 1983–2018 (less than eight per year on average) may have a significant role to play in the male–female distribution as the numbers are not significant enough to generate concrete statistical conclusions, especially in the absence of data regarding the male–female number of candidates. In other words, if the candidates were mostly men, then, *ceteris paribus,* the expectation may very well be that, probabilistically speaking, new positions will be filled by more men than women. However, if the reverse is true—that is more women as candidates, but still more men as newly hired staff—then it would be a development that deserves much more attention and analysis. While the 'raw data' is important and highlight an imbalance, the potential impact of small numbers must be emphasized. Indeed, during this 35 years-period there was hiring only 21 times, and 33% of those times—that is seven years—the total number of new hires was four or less. Given the small numbers, it is hard to reach concrete conclusions for those years on why there were not enough women hired. The answer may simply be that it happened that more men were successful in the exams, especially if the candidate distribution was more male skewed. Whether this is due to dominant perceptions and unconscious biases that men are more suitable for these positions is discussed in greater detail below. It must be noted that the hiring process does not just depend on the anonymous written exams, as in addition to that, there is also an interview round for the top candidates.

It was not until 2010 that the MFA had, for the first time, a significant number of newcomers; 35 in total. That year 15 of the successful candidates, or 45%, were women, indicating a more balanced hiring compared to most of the previous years. In 2020, the data indicates that the overall male–female balance in the Foreign Affairs Service (HQ) is unsurprisingly in line with the historical hiring data; out of the 162 members in the Service, only 49 (or 30%) are women (MFA of the Republic of Cyprus 2020).

While the aforementioned information may have caveats due to the absence of historical data on the gender distribution of candidates, the historical information regarding the position of the Minister is crystal clear. As shown in Table 11.2, there were ten different individuals who served as Ministers of Foreign Affairs, with three of them serving two full or partial terms. Since the birth of the RoC in 1960 only one woman served as a Minister of Foreign Affairs, Erato Kouzakou-Markoullis. Similarly, the position of the MFA Permanent Secretary was never held by a woman.

What is more interesting with potentially more significant spill over effects on the RoC image is the distribution in the decision-making and leadership positions. In this paper, such positions are considered to be the Minister and the Permanent Secretary, Ambassadors, Heads of Divisions, the Directors of Departments and Heads of Units and the Heads of Missions. The 2020 distribution of the aforementioned categories shows that out of the 90 leadership positions—Heads of Division, Missions and Units plus the Minister and Permanent Secretary—only 20% are held by women (see Table 11.3). From those top positions, seven women serve as Heads of Missions as of the end of 2020.

These statistics are certainly noteworthy and potentially concerning, but the historical absence of more women in the top positions should, unfortunately, not be very surprising given that such positions are usually held by the most senior members of any Ministry, and in the case of

Table 11.1 Hiring statistics at the Ministry of Foreign Affairs 1983–2018

Year	Men	Women	Total	Women as % of Total Hirings
1983	1	0	1	0%
1984	6	1	7	14%
1987	1	0	1	0%
1989	6	0	6	0%
1990	2	0	2	0%
1991	5	1	6	17%
1992	2	0	2	0%
1993	3	1	4	25%
1996	10	2	12	17%
1997	4	4	8	50%
1998	2	4	6	67%
1999	6	3	9	33%
2001	9	1	10	10%
2002	5	2	7	29%
2003	6	2	8	25%
2005	4	5	9	56%
2006	9	4	13	31%
2008	2	1	3	33%
2009	9	2	11	18%
2010	18	15	33	45%
2018	2	1	3	33%
Total	112	49	161	30%

Source: Ministry of Foreign Affairs

Table 11.2 Ministers of foreign affairs RoC 1960–2020

Foreign Minister	1st Term	2nd Term
Spyros Kyprianou	1960–1972	
Ioannis Christofides	1972–1978	
Nicos A. Rolandis	1978–1983	
Georgios Iacovou	1983–1993	2003–2006
Alecos Michailides	1993–1997	
Ioannis Kasoulides	1997–2003	2013–2018
Giorgos Lillikas	2006–2007	
Erato Kozakou-Marcoullis	2007–2008	2011–2013
Markos Kyprianou	2008–2011	
Nicos Christodoulides	2018–Jan. 2022	

Source: Ministry of Foreign Affairs, Republic of Cyprus

Table 11.3 Decision-making/Leadership positions-2020

Position	Male	Female	Total
Head of Division (MFA HQ)	7 (58.3%)	5 (41.6%)	12
Director of Department/Head of Unit (MFA HQ)	16 (72.7%)	6 (27.3%)	22
Head of Mission Abroad	47 (87%)	7 (13%)	54
Foreign Affairs Service (HQ)	113 (69.7%)	49 (30.25%)	162

Source: Ministry of Foreign Affairs

the MFA the male–female parity in the early years (1980s and early 1990s) was very male skewed, which subsequently means that in 2020 the most senior members are more likely to be men. This image is currently changing as more women are serving as Heads of Divisions and Units. Furthermore, given that proportionately more women entered the MFA the last 20–25 years compared to the years before that, there are even more opportunities for women to serve at the highest positions of the Ministry.

The RoC is not unique in having a severely male inclined environment at the highest diplomatic ranks. A very interesting piece of work by Towns and Niklasson (2017) examined 7,000 ambassador appointments in 2014 in the top 50 states based on their GDP. Europe—excluding the Nordic countries—is limited to only 14% and North America region to 25% of women ambassadors. By 2018, things have not changed significantly;

globally, in 2018, only 15% of the Ambassadors were women. Germany, the economic backbone of the EU and one of the most advanced countries in the world, had only 14.5% female ambassadors; and that is the highest percentage on record until 2018.

Explaining the RoC Numbers: The Masculinity Variable

One 'reflex response' to this question would be that the RoC is not unique and it simply follows the European and global trend where there is under-representation of women in the specific more male-dominated field of diplomacy. As Cynthia Enloe (1990) argued over 30 years ago, the world of diplomacy is [or was at the time at least] considered to be a man's world, not least because men were considered to have both the necessary skillset and the resources required to promote the state's international status. Indeed, much of the feminist academic work in the field emphasize the link between masculinity and power in international relations. It is beyond the scope of this work to provide an overview of all the possible reasons why there are generally far fewer women than men in the highest ranks of diplomacy; rather the focus of this section is specifically on the link of masculinity and foreign policy and diplomacy as a potential explanatory factor for the case of Cyprus. The link between masculinity on one hand and foreign policy and diplomacy on the other, may have routes in the contemporary turbulent history of the Cyprus conflict, and more specifically how protection from the conflict-deriving existential threats appears to be the men's responsibility.

Since the first day of its 'inception', the RoC faced numerous serious political challenges and existential threats. It is still one of the most protracted conflicts in the world, albeit a 'comfortable' one given the absence of major violent incidences since the Turkish invasion in 1974 (Adamides and Constantinou 2012). The protracted nature of the conflict allowed for the development of extremely resilient conflict-perpetuating routines, which elevated and maintained the Problem at the centre of societal concerns and political discourses on an elite and media level (Adamides 2020). Unsurprisingly, the RoC considers the Problem to be, primarily and above everything else, an issue of invasion and occupation. There is, thus, a strong linkage with a threat from Turkey, and more specifically the Turkish military. Such military-related threats were—and perhaps to some extend still are—expected to be defended by actions that are traditionally carried out by men. However, given the realities on the ground, the physical defence from the aforementioned existential threat were inevitably linked to the need for 'political defence', especially if one takes into consideration the chaotic military power asymmetry between the RoC and Turkey.

Subsequently, to enhance both the actual defence, as well as the perception of security, the MFA and the majority of the diplomatic activities of the RoC focus on enhancing its relative defence position and power vis-à-vis Turkey. This 'constant defence' mentality is part of the political and societal routines which have been dominating the political and societal agendas for decades. As mentioned, the main actors involved in the political and military defence actions were, in the first decades at least, just men—given that there was (and still is) a male-dominated national guard as well as a group of diplomats and high-ranked male political elite—thus enhancing the perception that this 'job' is essentially for men to handle. The fact that Cypriot women did not participate in the global women's movements of the 1960s, not least because they experienced ethnic nationalism and militarism (Hadjipavlou and Mertan 2010), contributed to the domination of men in the foreign policy, diplomacy and more generally the public policy arena. Similarly, Vassiliadou (2002) argues that feminist ideology and activism at the local level was minimal, thus creating the perception of passivity and the reluctance to change the *status quo*.

There is little doubt that things have changed significantly since the 1960s, 1970s and 1980s, as most Cypriot women are now highly educated and are much more involved in the political realm. Indeed, there are currently more women than men enrolled in tertiary education in Cyprus, with the gross enrolment percentage being particularly high at 84.5% and 78% for women and men respectively for 2018 (UNESCO 2020). The enrolment percentage has had a constant increasing trend since 2010, with women numbers being consistently higher than those of men for the entire period (UNESCO 2020). With this in mind, education does not seem to be contributing variable for the current significant gender gap and the glass ceiling phenomenon in the sector under review. Whether more highly educated women will contribute to bridge the gap, or whether other variables, such as the aforementioned security-defence mentality nexus, will continue to maintain it, cannot be fully determined at this point due to lack of sufficient data.

Understanding Gender Inequality: Steps Towards the Right Direction

As already mentioned, one of the first concrete actions took place in 2019, with a top-down initiative to promote gender mainstream in the Ministry with the appointment of a gender advisor to the Minister. The appointment is part of the ongoing reform and restructuring of the Ministry of Foreign Affairs aiming to develop 'thematic pluralism', with gender equality being one of the fundamental goals of the Cypriot foreign policy (MFA of the Republic of Cyprus 2020). Towards this goal, a Framework of Action 'promoting equality between women and men: Gender Mainstreaming in Foreign Policy' has been adopted and approved by the Council of Ministers in October 2020. The main aim of the framework of action is to provide guidance on targeted actions to be implemented by the Ministry focusing specifically on the advancement of women's rights and the advancement of gender equality, within the context of the Cypriot foreign policy, and as part of the 'global strategic efforts to promote the rights of women and girls worldwide, in the European context and at the regional level' (MFA of the Republic of Cyprus 2020).

The drafting of the Framework was part of a holistic approach which included a series of consultations with the entire foreign service, civil society organizations working specifically for women's rights, while it also included discussions with most of the Heads of the political parties represented in the Cyprus Parliament. The aim of the consultations went beyond the drafting of a holistic framework; it also aimed at creating a strong notion of ownership of the process within the diplomatic service. Similarly, albeit in a more external dimension, there were numerous informal discussions with UN officials as well as with countries implementing a feminist foreign policy or those that use other strategic functions to mainstream gender within their own foreign policy.

From a policy standpoint, there is clear evidence that the Ministry of Foreign Affairs is reinventing, restructuring and re-budgeting in an effort to place the gender aspect at the heart of its policy. Towards that end, a specialized unit on gender mainstreaming has been established making gender a horizontal issue at the ministry by providing guidance for the objectives implementation as dictated in the Framework of Action. The Framework (2020) defines five concrete objectives through which targeted actions and initiatives are carried out at three levels: regional, EU and global. The five objectives, as outlined below, aim towards the implantation of the 12 critical areas of the aforementioned Beijing Platform for Action:

1. Strengthening bilateral and multilateral relations, with a view to promoting gender equality.
2. Gender mainstreaming in development cooperation, humanitarian aid and other forms of financial grants administered by the Ministry.
3. Enhancing dialogue with civil society and the private sector as well as with academic institutions and research organizations.
4. Raising awareness and communicating with society on updates in this area.
5. Gender mainstreaming in the operational planning and the activities of the diplomatic service, such as trainings on gender mainstreaming and how it can be utilized by the diplomatic service, as well as studies on the different needs and possible barriers of men and women in the diplomatic service.

This last objective is of crucial importance as its main aim is to shift cultural perceptions and attitudes including the equal treatment as an added value to the overall objectives of the framework of action.

The International Dimensions of Local Efforts

Issues of gender equality and women's rights are one of the top priorities of many regional and international organizations, and the RoC should not be voiceless; on the contrary, it has the opportunity to have a disproportionately loud voice by becoming an example-setter where possible. While this may appear as a far-fetched goal, it should be a strategic goal nonetheless. And a goal it is. Over the past few years, the RoC has been slowly but steadily strengthening its policy making voice in numerous multilateral fora and organizations, such as the UN, the EU and OSCE, by actively participating in the drafting of policy cantered documents, discussions and joint statements on issues pertinent to women's rights. For example, and in view of the backlash on women's rights in the area of sexual reproductive health and rights, the MFA joined 38 Ministers from around the world calling for coordinating actions on the global and national arena for the protection of sexual and reproductive health and Rights and promoting gender-responsiveness in the Covid-19 crisis through a joint statement (Reliefweb 2020a).

Such efforts only enhance the voice of the RoC in international fora, but also render the country as one of the actors, among others, that focus on issues of global concern. More importantly, from a foreign policy perspective, it is an opportunity to build bilateral and multilateral relations with like-minded states, and even demonstrate that the RoC Foreign Policy goes beyond the Cyprus Problem. Such activities could include the planning for the organization of side events within the margins of—for example—the Commission for Statues of Women or the UN General Assembly, on issues related to women's rights. Such events allow for more bilateral and multilateral collaborations as they develop the political commitments of countries to work towards a common goal. At the same time, they provide the platform to civil society actors from different countries including international, regional or EU organizations to present their work, which also creates new collaborations and synergies and broadens the prospect for strategic collaboration in the promotion of women's rights within the UN. Bilateral and multilateral collaborations can take different forms, such as the exchange of information and collaboration on a common issue of interest and the improvement of national policies for the advancement of women's rights and gender mainstream. This can also be done in a collaborative manner between the RoC and other EU, or UN members states in third countries. The Ministry has already undertaken the initiative for such actions in collaboration with like-minded states like Norway and Spain.

In this context, a strong voice in such fora is beneficial for a variety of reasons and goes beyond raising awareness and the provision of information to interested audiences. What makes such issues interesting from a foreign policy perspective is that the audience of such events is particularly diverse as it includes participation of state representatives, civil society organizations and policy makers. Thus, there are opportunities to build bilateral and multilateral relationships on issues that do not necessarily have a direct impact on the political efforts of the MFA vis-à-vis the Cyprus Problem. That said, these activities are likely to eventually have a spill over effect in other foreign policy areas as the closer relationships may be utilized outside the context of the initial collaboration focus. An indicative example, albeit with a different focus, of how there may be spill over from one specific context to broader issues, is the ever-closer bilateral relations between the RoC and Israel and Egypt. While certainly the decline of the Israeli-Turkish and Egypt-Turkish relations had a role to play, it was the prospects for collaboration in energy-related issues that led to the improvement of the bilateral and regional affairs, which subsequently had a major spill over impact in other foreign and defence areas, as well as in tourism, health and education (Tziarras 2019).

Part of the bilateral and multilateral efforts is actions that fall under the MFA developmental cooperation strategy. Within the economic capabilities of the country, the Ministry has taken on budgeting for small projects with expected significant impact on women's and girls' lives, and always in consultation with the recipient countries to ensure that the projects have an impact directly relevant to the policy needs of the target-state to advance women's rights and promote gender equality. Towards this end, the MFA supported projects in Jordan, Lebanon and Palestine. Specifically, in Jordan, the project focuses on the promotion of positive gender norms, roles and attitudes, and support for gender equality and women empowerment. In the case of Palestine, the MFA co-funded a project on women's political participation under the framework of Palestine gender strategy. Another set of actions within the Ministry is the financial investment to UN and other international, regional and European entities through voluntary contributions to further promote gender equality. Two indicative examples include the support to the Anna Lindh Foundation with a target audience of young women ages 18 to 30, for the purpose of building healthy relationships and enhancing gender equality in Egypt, Lebanon and Jordan and the voluntary support to UN for Training and Research, a project entitled 'Gender Empowerment Now! – Building Capacity to Mainstream Gender Equality and Women's Empowerment (GEWE) into Government Policy', which is currently implemented in Jordan and Lebanon.

Conclusions

There has been global progress on the promotion of women's and girl's rights over the past few decades. However, as UN Secretary-General noted, in recent times, a pushback against women's rights is observed. Indeed, the UN Secretary-General argued that 'now is the time to push back against the pushback'. (Reliefweb 2020b). We must also not forget that the world will benefit if women are secured, and if half the population is equally represented in key decision-making positions. Similarly, we must not forget that this should not just be a nice-sounding goal, but rather a strategic goal that can strengthen a state's foreign policy and subsequently the promotion of national interest; and indeed, gender equality is a national interest. This requires bold steps on a leadership and societal levels and transnational collaboration. It is also one area that small countries have the opportunity to have a disproportionately big impact; they can contribute to global goals, they can have a voice in international fora and build strong bilateral and multilateral relations with like-minded countries, and, in some cases, they can become best-practice cases for other states to follow their path.

The RoC has made some very positive steps, but there is still a long path ahead. The men-women numbers disparity, at least at the highest-level positions in the MFA is obviously unquestionable. Similarly, much is yet to be done to achieve true gender balance in the field of foreign policy and diplomacy and there are still challenges in achieving the gender mainstreaming goals. However, it would also be unfair to argue either that the RoC is unique in the EU or that it does not take positive steps that show signs of 'maturity'. There are systematic and continuous references to the policy by the Minister and concrete decisions and initiatives within the structures of the Ministry. There is also a strong policy direction through the inclusion of women's rights and gender equality in speeches, media and social media or other articles, and a clear intention and practice to prioritize the issue during visits and contacts and during international and regional meetings. The focus on developmental support projects, coupled with the regional contribution for the promotion of women's rights is mature foreign policy actions that enhance the Cypriot voice and influence abroad. Lastly, there are also signs of maturity because the actions taken reveal an understanding that focusing on gender equality within the foreign policy mechanisms does not come in opposition with the focus on the Cyprus Problem. On the contrary, it can provide opportunities for strengthening international relationships with multiple positive benefits for the country's national goals.

References

Adamides, Constantinos. 2020. *Securitization and Desecuritization Processes in Protracted Conflicts: The Case of Cyprus.* London: Palgrave Macmillan.

Adamides, Constantinos, and Costas M. Constantinou. 2012. "Comfortable Conflict and (Il)liberal Peace in Cyprus." In *Hybrid Forms of Peace: From*

Everyday Agency to Post-Liberalism, edited by Oliver P. Richmond and Audra Mitchell. London: Palgrave Macmillan, 242–259.

Adebahr, Cornenlius, and Barbara Mittelhammer. 2020. *A Feminist Foreign Policy to Deal with Iran? Assessing the EU's Options*, 23 November. Accessed 29 November 2020. https://carnegieeurope.eu/2020/11/23/feminist-foreign-policy-to-deal-with-iran-assessing-eu-s-options-pub-83251.

Aggestam, Karin, and Towns, Ann. 2018a. "Introduction: The Study of Gender, Diplomacy and Negotiation." In *Gendering Diplomacy and International Negotiation*, edited by Karin Aggestam and Ann Towns. Cham: Palgrave Macmillan.

Aggestam, Karin, and Ann Towns. 2018b. "The Gender Turn in Diplomacy: A New Research Agenda." *International Feminist Journal of Politics* 21 (1): 9–28.

Beijing Declaration and Platform for Action. 1995. *United Nations*. Accessed 28 November 2020. https://www.un.org/en/events/pastevents/pdfs/Beijing_Declaration_and_Platform_for_Action.pdf.

CEDAW. 1979. Convention on the Elimination of all Forms of Violence Against Women. *Office of the United Nations High Commissioner for Human Rights*. Accessed 2 December 2020. https://www.ohchr.org/en/professionalinterest/pages/cedaw.aspx.

Christodoulides, Nikos. 2020. Opening Address, Conference "Women in Diplomacy", 22 February. *Ministry of Foreign Affairs of the Republic of Cyprus*. Accessed 30 November 2020. Available at https://mfa.gov.cy/themes/.

Enloe, Cynthia. 1990. *Bananas, Beaches, and Bases: Making Feminist Sense of International Politics*. Oakland, CA: University of California Press.

European Commission. 2020. "Joint Communication to the European Parliament and the Council EU Gender Action Plan." *GAP III- An Ambitious Agenda for Gender Equality and Women's Empowerment in EU External Action*. Brussels 25 November 2020, JOIN (2020) 17 Final. Accessed 7 December 2020. https://ec.europa.eu/international-partnerships/system/files/join-2020-17-final_en.pdf.

European Convention of Human Rights. 1951. European Convention on Human Rights coe.int. Accessed 7 December 2020.

European Parliament. 2020. "Fostering Gender Equality in the EU's Foreign and Security Policy." *European Union*. 23 October. Accessed 1 December 2020. https://www.europarl.europa.eu/news/en/press-room/20201016IPR89563/fostering-gender-equality-in-the-eu-s-foreign-and-security-policy.

European Social Charter. 1961. Accessed 7 December 2020. https://www.coe.int/en/web/conventions/full-list/-/conventions/rms/090000168006b642.

GAP III. 2020. "Gender Action Plan III. Joint Communication to The European Parliament and the Council Eu Gender Action Plan (GAP) III—An Ambitious Agenda for Gender Equality and Women's Empowerment in EU External

Action." *European Union.* 25 November. Accessed 30 November 2020. https://ec.europa.eu/commission/presscorner/detail/en/IP_20_2184.

Hadjipavlou, Maria, and Mertan, Biran. 2010. "Cypriot Feminism: An Opportunity to Challenge Gender Inequalities and Promote Women's Rights and a Different Voice." *Cyprus Review* 22 (2): 247–268.

Handbook on Sweden's Feminist Foreign Policy. 2019. Government Offices of Sweden, Ministry of Foreign Affairs. Accessed 22 October 2020. Available at https://www.government.se/4ae557/contentassets/fc115607a4ad4bca91 3cd8d11c2339dc/handbook---swedens-feminist-foreign-policy.pdf.

Meyer, Mary K., and Elisabeth Prügl, eds. 1999. *Gender Politics in Global Governance.* Lanham, MD, Boulder, CO and New York, Oxford: Rowman & Littlefield.

MFA of the Republic of Cyprus. 2020. *Framework of Action "Promoting Equality Between Women and Men: Gender Mainstreaming in Foreign Policy"* 2019–2023.

Rahman, Talyn. 2011. "Women in Diplomacy: An Assessment of British Female Ambassadors in Overcoming Gender Hierarchy, 1990–2010." *American Diplomacy.* Accessed 8 December 2020. http://americandiplomacy.web.unc.edu/2011/04/women-in-diplomacy/.

Rahman-Figueroa, Talyn, "Women in Diplomacy" Grassroot Diplomat. Accessed 1 December 2020. Available at https://www.grassrootdiplomat.org/news/talyn-rahman-figueroa-women-in-diplomacy.

Reliefweb. 2020a. "Protecting Sexual and Reproductive Health and Rights and Promoting Gender-Responsiveness in the COVID-19 Crisis." 6 May. Accessed 2 December 2020. https://reliefweb.int/report/world/joint-press-statement-protecting-sexual-and-reproductive-health-and-rights-and.

Reliefweb. 2020b. "Press Release: Progress Towards Gender Equality Under Threat, World Leaders Warn as General Assembly Marks Twenty-Fifth Anniversary of Landmark Women's Rights Conference." 2 October. Accessed 3 December 2020. https://reliefweb.int/report/world/progress-towards-gender-equality-under-threat-world-leaders-warn-general-assembly-marks.

Towns, Ann, and Birgitta Niklasson. 2017. "Gender, International Status, and Ambassador Appointments." *Foreign Policy Analysis.* https://doi.org/10.1093/fpa/orw039.

Tziarras, Zenonas, ed. 2019. *The New Geopolitics of the Eastern Mediterranean: Trilateral Partnerships and Regional Security, Re-Imagining the Eastern Mediterranean Report Series: PCC Report 3.* Nicosia: PRIO Cyprus Centre.

UN. 2001. United Nations Entity for Gender Equality and the Empowerment of Women (UN WOMEN). Accessed 30 November 2020. Available at https://www.un.org/womenwatch/osagi/conceptsanddefinitions.htm.

UNESCO. 2020. "Institute for Statistics." Accessed 29 November 2020. Report Available at http://uis.unesco.org/en/country/cy?theme=education-and-literacy.
UNSC. 2000. "United Nations Security Council, Resolution 1325, S/RES/1325 (2000)." Accessed 26 November 2020. Available at https://documents-dds-ny.un.org/doc/UNDOC/GEN/N00/720/18/PDF/N0072018.pdf?OpenElement.
UNSG. 2019. "Antonio Gutteres, Remarks at the opening of the 63rd Session of the Commission on the Status of Women." Accessed 27 November 2020. Available at https://www.un.org/sg/en/content/sg/speeches/2019-03-11/csw-remarks-opening-of-63rd-session.
Vassiliadou, Myria. 2002. "Questioning Nationalism: The Patriarchal and National Struggles of Cypriot Women Within a European Context." *European Journal of Women's Studies* 9 (4): 459–482.
Walby, Sylvia. 2011. *The Future of Feminism*. Cambridge: Polity Press.

CHAPTER 12

The Republic of Cyprus in International and Regional Organizations: Towards a Mature Small State Status Seeking Strategy?

Revecca Pedi and Kalliopi Chainoglou

INTRODUCTION

During the last two decades, the foreign policy of the Republic of Cyprus (RoC) is underpinned by a turn from a monothematic exclusively focused on the Cyprus Problem agenda to a multidimensional strategy, aspiring to change the RoC's international standing (Tziarras's Introduction in this volume). The RoC's status seeking strategy is supported by two main pillars: first, the strengthening of RoC's ties with its neighbours and second the improvement of its relations with all the great powers. The small island state aspires to gain recognition as a 'good power' regionally and internationally, expand its net off supporters and partners and assume a greater role in the region (Pedi and Kouskouvelis 2019). A third and

R. Pedi (✉) · K. Chainoglou
Department of International and European Studies, University of Macedonia, Thessaloniki, Greece
e-mail: rpedi@uom.gr

© The Author(s), under exclusive license to Springer Nature Switzerland AG 2022
Z. Tziarras (ed.), *The Foreign Policy of the Republic of Cyprus*, Reform and Transition in the Mediterranean,
https://doi.org/10.1007/978-3-030-91177-5_12

less explored pillar of the RoC's status seeking strategy is the RoC's presence and actorness in International Organizations (IOs). In this chapter, we engage with the RoC's efforts to gain more visibility and raise its status within and through different IOs, to explore whether the RoC as a small state employs a mature status seeking strategy.

Small state status seeking can take many different forms, respond to various purposes and it is always dependent on the context in which it takes place (Long and Urdinez 2021; Schia and Jacob Sending 2015). Multilateral institutions constitute a unique arena for status seeking due to the specificities of power differentiation and rules abiding within IOs as well as because of the opportunities they provide for small states to assume special roles (Schia and Jacob Sending 2015). Small states have harnessed their membership in IOs to advance their immediate interests and even, at times, challenge great powers; they have also seen International Institutions as springboards for shaping new rules and norms, raising their prestige and meeting their status ambitions (see Corbett et al. 2019; Hurd 2005; Jaschik 2014; Mohammadzadeh 2017; Schia and Jacob Sending 2015; Thorhallsson and Margrét Eggertsdóttir 2020).

To this background, we draw on small state studies and establish a framework for the mature small state status seeking strategy. We combine literature on status seeking with studies on small states in IOs, taking into consideration this volume's approach on maturity, as it is set forth in the introduction by the editor. Building on this, we are particularly interested in the role(s) the RoC assumes within IOs, its means and ends, priorities and areas of activity as well as in the values and norms the small island state supports and sponsors.

The empirical analysis looks at three different multilateral institutional settings: the United Nations (UN), the Council of Europe (CoE) and the European Union (EU). For each case, we focus on particular aspects of the RoC's activity. Regarding the UN, we explore the RoC's voting history and overall participation in the UN and UN organs concerning the promotion of initiatives, including standard-setting efforts, in the field of cultural heritage and culture. Concerning the CoE, we investigate the period when the RoC held the Chairmanship of the Committee of Ministers. In the case of the EU, we assess the RoC's capacity to invest the available funds under the EU Aid Programme for the Turkish Cypriot in interventions aimed at increasing cooperation between the Turkish Cypriot and Greek Cypriot communities whilst protecting cultural heritage across the RoC and the occupied territories. For the empirical part, we rely on content analysis of primary resources (i.e., official EU/CoE/UN/RoC documents) and interviews we have conducted with politicians and diplomats. We chose the area of culture and cultural heritage protection as it is one of the main themes of the RoC's foreign policy in multilateral settings and one in which the RoC has invested considerable resources and efforts.

In what follows, we first elaborate on small state status seeking in multilateral settings and the concept of maturity to establish a framework for a mature small state status seeking strategy. Then, we investigate the RoC's presence and actorness in the three different institutional settings. We finally assess whether the RoC's status seeking strategy is a mature one.

SMALL STATE STATUS SEEKING, INTERNATIONAL ORGANIZATIONS AND MATURITY

Small State Status Seeking

Status is a social attribute, it is about gaining recognition in the eyes of others and therefore it concerns the collective perceptions about a state's rank in the hierarchy of states (Larson et al. 2014). Status can be even more significant to small states than to great powers, because of the lower material capabilities of the former (Neumann and de Carvalho 2015). Thus, status seeking which "refers to acts undertaken to maintain or better one's placement" constitutes an important enterprise for all small states; yet, the latter competes for a higher status with one another not with great powers (Neumann and de Carvalho 2015, 5). Due to their inferior capabilities, small states choose different means towards reaching a higher status from those of great powers, ideational, normative factors and low-key political agendas matter most to the former, whilst material capabilities and high politics are of importance to the latter (Wohlforth et al. 2017). The main goal of a small state status seeking strategy is to attract the attention and the recognition of the targeted great power and to be identified as a 'good power' and a useful ally, as great powers are those who grant status to lesser actors in the system (Larson et al. 2014; Neumann and Carvalho 2015).

In this sense, small states contribute to the maintenance of the system, according to the principles of a great power, or even to the sustentation of the great power itself (Wohlforth et al. 2017). Besides, gaining the appreciation of a great power or powers, small states embark on status seeking adventure in order to excel amongst their peers and be recognised as leaders at the regional level or regarding a specific area of action (Pedi and Kouskouvelis 2019). Status seeking can also be a bilateral affair between two lesser powers building a special relationship (Long and Urdinez 2021). Thus, small state status seeking is a phenomenon with a range of variations around a core aim which is no other than recognition. In this context, status seeking can be an end in itself (Schia and Jacob Sending 2015) but it can also be instrumental, as an increased status allows small states to advance their interests more effectively (Pedi and Kouskouvelis 2019).

Status Seeking in and Through International Organizations

Status seeking in and through IOs differs from status seeking through bilateral relations. Although getting attention and recognition continue to exist as a motive and status seeking remains a competitive enterprise, a logic of appropriateness matters for great powers and small states alike (Hurd 2005; Müller 2004). As Schia and Jacob Sending (2015, 73) suggest 'multilateral settings put a premium on behaviour that is in keeping with a commitment to the furtherance and expansion of the rules established by multilateral cooperation and organizations.' Instead of gaining the appreciation of a great power and maintaining the hegemon's status, serving the values of the IO and raising the status of the IO itself becomes a major goal for a small state seeking for status in multilateral settings; at times, these two goals can be mutually reinforcing. According to Schia and Jacob Sending (2015), it is the principle of sovereign equality that allows smaller states to raise their status in multilateral institutions. In addition, and beyond the principle of sovereign equality, multilateral settings also provide small states with ample room for cooperation and coalition building, to capitalise on the resources of others to 'punch above their weight' (Thorhallsson 2012).

Furthermore, sovereign equality allows lesser powers to assume high posts, such as the presidency or chairmanship of an IO and exploit its position to advance its status. In this context, Schia and Jacob Sending (2015, 73) underline that 'certain types of behaviour or role rather than certain types of resources can accord status.' Amongst such types of behaviour, the roles can be those of a facilitator, a helper, a mediator, an honest broker, a policy on norm entrepreneur, an expert and an agenda setter who acts in accordance with the processes and the values of an IO (Schia and Jacob Sending 2015; Pedi 2016). Small states assuming such roles, given the opportunity can raise their status by generating value, such as prosperity, stability, security, for themselves and others (Pedi and Sarri 2019). Value creation for others lies at the core of small state status seeking, as this is the type of behaviour that can classify a small state as a 'good power' (Pedi and Kouskouvelis 2019). Small state status seeking in multilateral settings can be decoupled from a state's immediate interests, as sometimes small states have an interest in status itself (Schia and Jacob Sending 2015).

Maturity and Status Seeking

According to the approach advanced by Tziarras in the introductory chapter of this volume 'a mature foreign policy could be generally defined as that which has clearly defined and set goals/aspirations that match a state's needs, interests and capabilities. Moreover, a mature foreign policy is one with a well weighted strategy, and for that a state needs the necessary institutions and policy-making mechanisms'. Combining this conceptualization of maturity in foreign policy with the fundamentals of a small state status seeking strategy, as the latter was presented above, we establish a framework for a mature small status seeking strategy in IOs consisting of three basic hypotheses:

First Hypothesis (H1): A small state with a mature status seeking strategy has clearly defined and set status seeking goals and a strategic plan to achieve them. This means that the former's status seeking strategy in multilateral settings is well defined, consistent and acknowledged by all the involved institutions and mechanisms. In addition, its goals and the strategic plan are compatible with the principles, the goals and the procedures of each IO in which the respective small state pursues a status seeking strategy. Therefore, it has a clear understanding of the context in which it acts and is able to identify opportunities when they rise.

Second Hypothesis (H2): A mature small state status seeking strategy matches the capabilities of the small state. According to this hypothesis, the small state holds all the necessary resources to implement its initiatives. In addition, it shows awareness of the specificities of smallness and power differentiation in multilateral settings. This hypothesis supposes that a small state with a mature status seeking strategy undertakes initiatives and assumes roles relevant to small state status seeking in multilateral settings, it acts as a facilitator and/or a helper, a mediator, an honest broker, a policy on norm entrepreneur, an expert and an agenda setter.

Third Hypothesis (H3): A mature small state status seeking strategy fits the needs of the respective small state and serves its interests, but it also creates value for others in the region and beyond. This hypothesis suggests that the priorities set by the small state and the initiatives it undertakes are related to the interests of the latter, but their impact exceeds a state's self-interest.

The Republic of Cyprus Champions Cultural Heritage Protection in and Through IOs

The RoC's foreign policy is characterised for its extensive participation in IOs and the use of diplomatic instruments in order to increase international visibility on the 1974 Turkish illegal invasion and occupation of the northern part of the RoC and other unlawful actions against the country's sovereignty (Kouskouvelis and Chainoglou 2018). The RoC's agenda in IOs is structured upon the consequences of the Turkish illegal invasion and occupation and the protection of cultural heritage has been initially seen through these lenses.

The RoC has consistently invested in 'culture' and 'cultural heritage' as part of its IOs agenda to attain its national objectives and hence preserve the country's core values concerning sovereignty, territorial integrity, preservation of the cultural identity of its population, economic prosperity as well as compliance with rules of international law. To this end, The RoC has engaged in numerous multilateral and bilateral partnerships in order to protect its culture and cultural heritage but has also embarked on novel initiatives 'in order to promote the protection of cultural heritage all over the world, utilising and bringing into play the experience accrued by the Republic's authorities in dealing with the consequences of the Turkish illegal occupation' (RoC 2021). With approximately 60,000 cultural objects stolen from the country, the RoC has capitalised on its experience with regard to the legal and social implications of destruction, damage, looting and trafficking of cultural heritage and its understanding as to why cultural heritage is fundamental to dialogue and reconciliation, identity, knowledge-sharing and development. Consequently, the RoC has championed the advancement of the protection of cultural heritage and the right to access and enjoy heritage within multilateral settings, such as the UN, the CoE and the EU.

A Firm Advocate of Culture and Cultural Heritage Protection in the UN

The RoC has used the UN to end the damage and destruction of cultural heritage and to identify new norms or clarify existing rules concerning the protection of cultural heritage. Within the UN, the RoC's stance is very much reflecting the spirit of the international conventions on the protection of the cultural heritage and the *opinio juris* on this area. Through its voting history and sponsorship of draft resolutions, the RoC has consistently condemned acts of vandalism and intentional attacks directed against historic, religious and cultural monuments, irrespective of whether such acts are taking place in the occupied territory of Cyprus or elsewhere, i.e. Syria, maintaining thus that any damage to cultural property belonging to any people whatsoever means damage to the cultural heritage of all mankind. And the RoC has also deplored the organised looting and trafficking of illegally exported cultural property and has called for an end to such violations of international law which provide a fertile ground for further international law violations and human rights abuses.

Being aware of how the destruction of cultural heritage can have an adverse and destructive effect not only on the cultural heritage of the island but also on the cultural heritage of mankind, the RoC has repeatedly reported the destruction of cultural heritage by Turkey in the occupied part of Cyprus. Hence, the RoC has *inter alia* protested against the illegal archaeological excavations by Turkey at Salamis and other archaeological places in the occupied territory; the destruction of approximately 243 religious sites in northern Cyprus; the desecration of Christian churches in the occupied villages in the district of Kyrenia; the plundering of religious-related cultural objects, such as icons and vessels and other cultural objects from the occupied territory; the damage caused to the castle of Saint Hilarion, one of the historic sites in Cyprus, through the use of explosives; and the destruction of cultural heritage by Turkish forces in the Karpas peninsula (RoC 2001a 2001b, 2001c, 2005, 2013a).

The RoC diplomatic efforts paid off when the UN Rapporteur in the field of Cultural Rights brought to the attention of the international community the issue of the destruction of cultural heritage and the systematic looting of cultural objects, both of which impede the exercise of the right to access and enjoy cultural heritage and endanger the rights of future generations of Cypriots. In particular, the UN Rapporteur referred to: (1) the lack of systematic documentation of all the destruction that has taken place, (2) the looting of cultural (and religious) object in the occupied territory, (3) the change of historical and cultural landscapes in all areas of Cyprus (including the changing of names of places, streets and villages in the occupied territory), as well as (4) the misuse and neglect of cultural heritage in the occupied territory (UN Rapporteur in the field of cultural rights on her mission to Cyprus, 2017a).

Furthermore, the RoC's actorness on cultural heritage has to a certain extent served within the UN as a springboard for filling the remaining gaps as to how the UN should frame cultural heritage in its law and policy. This is, for example, evidenced in the numerous resolutions (whether drafted, sponsored or voted for by the RoC) that have been adopted by the UN General Assembly and other UN bodies on matters pertaining to the protection of various forms of cultural heritage (including underwater heritage) and the repatriation and restitution of illegally exported cultural property to countries of origin (see Table 12.1, Column A) and the protection of cultural heritage and culture as an integral part of human rights (see Table 12.1, Columns B and C). The RoC's prioritisation is perhaps best illustrated with the long list of draft resolutions that it has sponsored within various UN bodies (see Table 12.1, Column D). Without the stern commitment of the RoC (and like-minded states) to the protection of culture and culture heritage within the UN, it might have been impossible to have in place the multifaceted and collaborative cultural heritage governance and regulatory framework which exists today under the UN auspices and which is also the point of reference for regional organisations (such as the EU and the CoE) on this subject area. Within this context, the RoC has in addition invested time and resources in repatriating cultural objects that have been pillaged during the Turkish invasion. Furthermore, the RoC's international actorness on cultural heritage has been matched with similar efforts at national level, i.e. by introducing legislative and other measures enabling the policing and monitoring of the existing cultural objects (i.e. through the digitization of cultural heritage).

Perhaps, the most proud moment for the RoC's actorness in the UN has been an initiative in Geneva for the adoption of the first-ever resolution of the UN Human Rights Council on Cultural Rights and the Protection of Cultural Heritage in September 2016 and its subsequent renewal in March 2018, which affirmed states' obligations to respect, promote and protect the right of everyone to take part in cultural life,

Table 12.1 UN resolutions related to the protection of culture and cultural heritage supported or sponsored by the RoC

A. General Assembly Cultural heritage related Resolutions	B. General Assembly Culture and Human Rights-related Resolutions	C. Human Rights Council Resolutions	D. Draft Resolutions
A/RES/75/239 (2021)	A/RES/75/193 (2020)	A/HRC/RES/37/17()	A/HRC/37/L.30 (2018)
A/RES/52/24 (1998)	A/RES/75/192 (2020)	A/HRC/RES/33/20()	A/73/L.54 (2018)
A/RES/50/56 (1996)	A/RES/75/191 (2020)		S/2017/242 (2017)
A/RES/48/15 (1993)	A/RES/75/179 (2020)		A/HRC/33/L.21 (2016)
A/RES/46/10 (1991)	A/RES/74/159 (2020)		A/70/L.28 (2015)
A/RES/44/18 (1989)	A/RES/73/344 (2019)		A/69/L.76 (2015)
A/RES/40/19 (1985)	A/RES/73/127 (2018)		A/69/L.71 (2015)
A/RES/38/34 (1984)	A/RES/72/229 (2018)		A/67/L.34 (2012)
	A/RES/44/130 (1990)		A/66/L.21 (2011)
	A/RES/41/187 (1987)		A/64/L.18/Add.1 (2009)
	A/RES/36/172I (1981)		A/64/L.17, (2009); A/64/L.17/Rev.1 (2009)
	A/RES/33/50 (1978)		A/61/L.15/Rev.1 (2006)
	A/RES/3148 (1973)		A/58/L.11/Rev.2/Add.1 (2003)
			A/55/L.81 (2001)
			A/55/L.79 (2001)
			A/54/L.31 (1999)
			A/48/L.15, (1993)
			A/46/L.11 (1991)
			E/1990/L.20 (1990)

Sources see, UN (1990–2018); UNGA (1973–2021); UNHRC (2016–2018)

including the ability to access and enjoy cultural heritage and it further urged all parties to armed conflicts to refrain from any unlawful military use or targeting of cultural property and calls for enhanced international cooperation in preventing looting and illicit trafficking of cultural objects (see Table 12.1, Column C). The RoC's pioneering efforts on the protection of cultural heritage at international level have also led to the establishment of the 'Group of Friends for the Protection of Cultural Heritage' along with Italy which aims at protecting cultural heritage, combating cultural goods trafficking and mobilising the international community with a view to implement the international legal framework on the protection of cultural heritage, and in particular the UN Security Council (UNSC) Resolution 2347 on the destruction and trafficking of cultural heritage by terrorist groups in situations of armed conflict (UNSC 2017).

A Fierce Promoter of Culture and Cultural Heritage Protection in the Council of Europe

The RoC's efforts on the protection of culture and cultural heritage at the UN level have been met by equivalent efforts at regional level, and primarily within the CoE. The RoC joined the CoE in 1961 and in 2016 the RoC assumed for the fifth time in the 55 years since its accession the Chairmanship of its Committee of Ministers. This was deemed an ideal opportunity for the RoC to bolster the principles and values protected and promoted by the CoE and for the RoC to leave its imprint on the normative work of the organisation in the field of human rights and cultural heritage. With the flag theme 'Reinforcing Democratic Security in Europe,' the RoC announced that it would focus on the following strategic priorities: (a) Rights and freedoms for all people without any discrimination, (b) Democratic citizenship and (c) Prevalence of the rule of law.

In setting out the priorities of the Cypriot Chairmanship and in line with its IOs agenda, the RoC declared that:

> The Cyprus Chairmanship attaches great importance to the protection of cultural heritage. Cypriot diplomacy has undertaken an international initiative to bolster the protection of cultural property from wanton destruction and the illicit trafficking of cultural goods, exploring innovative approaches

for the creation of synergies and the development of capacities for the effective protection of cultural heritage. Cyprus will do its utmost to promote the efforts of the Council of Europe to finalise *the new Convention on Offences related to Cultural Property* and to draw international attention and support for the pioneering work of the Organisation in this field. (RoC 2017a)

More than 30 official events were put forward to support the Cypriot Chairmanship's strategic priorities (RoC 2017a) and 21 cultural events were organised by the Cypriot chairmanship in order to introduce the Cypriot culture in Strasbourg, the seat of the CoE (RoC 2017a).

With the participation of high-level representatives from international organizations and national governments, as well as with the involvement of academic cultural policy experts, the RoC organised events aimed *inter alia* at strengthening cooperation to protect cultural heritage from wanton destruction and to prevent the illicit trafficking of cultural goods, including the so-called blood antiquities from conflict-affected territories. Some of the 2017 key events were, for example, the 18th Assembly of the Authors of the 'Compendium Database on Cultural Policy and Trends in Europe' (2017), the Intercultural Workshop on Democracy Organised by the Venice Commission, the International Conference on 'Developing a culture of co-operation when teaching and learning history,' the High Level Conference (launching event) for the promotion of the 'European Cultural Heritage Strategy for the twenty-first century,' and the International Conference 'Towards a new governance of diversity: building on successful local experiences.' All these events were strategically chosen to be hosted in Cyprus to raise the profile of the RoC both internally and externally and to raise visibility of the long-standing fact that the island remains forcibly divided.

Only a handful events were organised abroad, such as the High-level Segment in the framework of the Preparation of a new Convention on Offences relating to Cultural Property (Council of Europe 2017a) which took place in Strasbourg, the event on 'Strengthening international capacities for the protection of cultural property and for preventing the illicit trafficking of cultural goods' co-organised by the RoC and the United Kingdom (UK) House of Commons where representatives of national Governments and national parliaments discussed ways to promote the protection of cultural property in conflict-affected areas which took place in the UK, and the Seminar organised by the Cyprus Chairmanship of the

Committee of Ministers and International Institute for the Unification of Private Law (UNIDROIT) on 'Promoting and strengthening the international legal framework for the protection of cultural heritage,' which took place in New York.

Furthermore, the RoC strategically used these international events to spiral bridge-building with states and non-state actors with significant technical expertise and experience in the protection of cultural heritage and set up informal task forces in the field. Such has been the case with the an event on 28 February 2017, co-organised by the Missions of Cyprus and Italy to the UN and by the UNIDROIT at the UN headquarters, on promoting and strengthening the international legal framework for the protection of cultural heritage, and where it was announced the inauguration of an informal Task Force, open to all states wishing to participate, aimed at the promotion of the wider ratification of the 1995 UNIDROIT Convention (RoC 2017b; UN 2001a).

All these events were deemed by the RoC's Ministry of Foreign Affairs a unique opportunity to contribute to the *opinio juris* on the protection of cultural heritage and also gather support for the new Convention on offences related to Cultural Property. Moreover, similar efforts to raise awareness on the RoC's goal on the protection of cultural heritage were organised at national level—see for example, the 'Act for Heritage' two-day event which was organised by the Commissioner for Volunteerism and Non-Governmental Organisations of the RoC, in cooperation with the Ministry of Foreign Affairs of the RoC, the CoE and the European Commission Representation in Cyprus. The event aimed at the promotion of the Nicosia Convention and its universality, as well as enhancing cooperation of various national and international stakeholders on the issue of preventing offences relating to cultural property (RoC, Commissioner for Volunteerism and Non-Governmental Organisations 2019).

Under the Cypriot Chairmanship, a new Convention on Offences related to Cultural Property, envisaged to become the single international treaty focusing on criminal measures and sanctions on illicit activities in the field of cultural heritage, was opened up for signing at the 127th Session of the Committee of Ministers in Nicosia on 19 May 2017 (Council of Europe 2017b). Despite the RoC's Ministry of Foreign Affairs feverous efforts to gather support from member states of the CoE, only Armenia, Greece, San Marino and Portugal deposited their instruments of signature on the day of the opening of the treaty. However, the RoC being aware of the lack of widespread support on the part of the members of CoE, managed to convince the CoE to allow for the treaty to be signed also by non-member states of the CoE, including those states that participated in its elaboration such as Japan, Holy See and Mexico (see, Council of Europe 2018). Hence, Mexico became the first non-member state signing and ratifying a CoE legal instrument. Since 2017, Italy, Montenegro, Latvia, Slovenia, Ukraine and Russia have also signed the Convention. This success of the RoC's diplomacy is also echoed in the explanatory report of the Convention (Council of Europe 2017b, para. 13).

Uploading the Protection of Culture and Cultural Heritage in the EU's Agenda

The RoC's efforts on the protection of culture and cultural heritage at regional level have also been advanced within the EU. Under the Cypriot Chairmanship of the Council of the EU in 2012, RoC diplomacy displayed a number of successes consistent with its interest in culture and cultural heritage matters. The Cypriot Chairmanship's vision on Europe being 'filoxenos topos' was based partially on culture as a major factor for the enhancement of social cohesion and solidarity within Europe; hence the Cypriot Chairmanship proceeded for example, with (1) the adoption of the Council Resolution on the creation of an informal network of law enforcement authorities and expertise competent in the field of cultural goods for the purpose of preventing and combating crime against cultural goods by strengthening coordination at national level between law enforcement authorities and cultural authorities and private organisations (EU CULNET 2012); (2) a progress report for the work undertaken in the Council on the proposal for a Directive of the European Parliament and of the Council amending the scope of Directive 2003/98/EC on re-use of public sector information in order to also cover certain cultural institutions (namely museums, libraries and archives); (3) a Partial agreement in the Council on the Creative Europe programme; (4) Council conclusions on cultural governance as a tool in the hands of governments to deliver cultural policies and implement integrated policies, so as to place culture at the heart of the public policy agenda, and (5) a progress report on the proposal for a decision establishing a Union action for the European Capitals of Culture for the years 2020–2033 (RoC 2013b).

In addition, as a member state of the EU since 2004, the RoC has benefited from a range of programmes funded by the EU and a number of them has provided funding *inter alia* on cultural heritage and culture-related projects such as the Competitiveness and sustainable development 2014–2020 programme, URBACT Interreg 2014–2020, Interreg Greece-Cyprus 2014–2020, Interreg Med programme 2014–2020 and the EU's Aid Programme for the Turkish Cypriot community. As the EU has been supporting the RoC's two communities to work towards a final settlement and to end decades of division arising out of the de facto occupation of the northern territory and pave the way for reunification, one of the aims of the EU Aid programme has been to bring the two communities together by developing the economy of the Turkish Cypriot community. The programme is temporary in nature, aiming to facilitate the reunification of Cyprus in line with the Aid Regulation No 389/2006 and Council Regulation No 1311/2133. Between 2006 and 2020 under the EU's Aid Programme for the Turkish Cypriot community, €591 m has been allocated for projects aimed to improve infrastructure, support economic development, foster reconciliation within the two communities, bring the Turkish Cypriot community closer to the EU and help the Turkish Cypriot community prepare for the implementation of EU law once a comprehensive settlement of the Cyprus issue is agreed (EU 2020). On 25 August 2020, it was announced that a total of €31.6 m would be allocated for more projects in this line (EU Commission 2020b).

The programme provides *inter alia* for the protection of cultural heritage which is perceived an integral part of the on-going process of increasing mutual trust and broadening areas of reconciliation, cooperation and confidence-building between the Turkish Cypriot and Greek Cypriot communities. Instrumental to the success of this programme has been the work of the bi-communal Technical Committee on Cultural Heritage (this was set up in 2008 pursuant to an agreement reached between Greek Cypriots and Turkish Cypriots under the auspices of the UN). The bi-communal Technical Committee on Cultural Heritage which is dedicated to the island-wide restoration, physical protection and preservation of culturally symbolic and historically significant immovable cultural heritage of Cyprus, that is monuments, civil buildings, mosques and churches, is assisted in its work by an advisory board of heritage professionals and the UNDP, which assumes the neutral role of providing logistical and administration support to the Committee's conservation works and visibility efforts (UNDP Cyprus 2021).

The work of the Committee has been applauded for its non-political approach with regard to cultural heritage across Cyprus, including the occupied territory, which has consistently been found to include a 'strong bi-communal and public awareness component' (EU Commission 2020a, 33). This has for example been realised through the direct involvement of technical teams from both communities (architects, archaeologists, engineers, etc.) act, in time, as team- and confidence-building measures, allowing for increased exchange of experiences and the setting of a positive example of successful collaboration between Greek Cypriots and Turkish Cypriots. Since 2012 the EU has provided almost €20 m in support for island-wide preservations and restorations, with an 'impact on 66 conserved sites island-wide, increasing heritage-site visitation and intra-island exchanges, and engaging more than 6 000 Greek Cypriots and Turkish Cypriots, thus improving the perceptions of the general public vis-à-vis the other community' (EU Commission 2020a, 33). In 2020, the EU Commission allocated to the Technical Committee on Cultural Heritage €2.5 m with expected results to include: '(1) Completed conservation designs for at least 10 sites ready for future implementation; (2) completed conservation works for at least 8 sites; (3) at least four capacity-building and community-involvement events implemented; and (4) increased awareness amongst the general public and respect for the heritage sites of both communities in Cyprus' (EU Commission 2020a, 35).

Assessing the Maturity of the RoC's Status Seeking Strategy in and Through IOs

In this section, we build on the framework about the mature small state status seeking strategy and by using the aforementioned analysis on the RoC's actorness in the area of culture and cultural heritage protection, we assess the maturity of the RoC's status seeking strategy in and through IOs. Regarding our first hypothesis, we observe that the RoC has clearly stated that the protection of culture and cultural heritage constitutes one of its top priorities in multilateral settings. The RoC has been engaged in promoting the protection of culture and cultural heritage throughout the years in all the three main multilateral institutions in which it participates, and it has consistently launched initiatives aiming at shaping the *opinio juris* and norms/policy entrepreneurship in this area. The consistency in the RoC's actorness in the area of culture and cultural heritage protection in the UN, the EU and the CoE shows that its strategy is well defined, coherent and shared by all the involved RoC institutions and mechanisms. The enactment of domestic law concerning the protection of culture and cultural heritage provides further evidence for the argument that the RoC's policies are consistent. The management of EU funds devoted to the protection of culture and cultural heritage by both the Greek Cypriot and the Turkish Cypriot Communities reveal the RoC's ambition to fulfil its agenda both at home and abroad and adds to the claim about the consistency of the RoC's actorness.

In all the three cases, the RoC's goals and its actions are compatible with the principles, the goals and the procedures of each and every IO in which the RoC has pursued a status seeking strategy through its protection of culture and cultural heritage agenda. The small island state spares no effort to present itself as a guarantor of the principles and the values of the institutions within which it acts, and it justifies its activity in the area of protection of culture and cultural heritage accordingly. Last but not least, the plethora of Resolutions on the protection of culture and cultural heritage that the RoC has initiated or supported as well as the importance which the RoC attributed to the protection of culture and cultural heritage when it held the CoE's Chairmanship and the EU's Council Presidency reveal that the RoC has a clear understanding of the context in which it acts and is able to identify opportunities when they arise.

Regarding our second hypothesis, we suggest that the RoC is aware of the limitations and the benefits that accompany smallness in multilateral settings. Its status seeking strategy matches its capabilities. The series of Resolutions, Events and Campaigns that the RoC orchestrated show that the small island state holds all the necessary resources to implement its initiatives. The RoC has concentrated its efforts on the protection of culture and cultural heritage out of interest but also because it is a low-key issue in the international agenda, appropriate for small state advocacy. In this context, the RoC managed to be an agenda setter and policy/norm entrepreneur in all the three different multilateral contexts. The RoC's partnerships with the UK House of Commons and Italy as well as its cooperation with non-state actors show a clear understanding of the value of coalition building and of harnessing the resources of others.

In terms of the third hypothesis, it is evident that the RoC's involvement in the protection of culture and cultural heritage has its roots in the country's experiences and interests. Yet, the RoC has systematically been involved in drafting and supporting Resolutions on the protection of culture and cultural heritage whose core was beyond the RoC's immediate interests, i.e. the 'Draft Resolution on Saving the Cultural Heritage of Iraq,' (A/69/L.71 2015). In addition, initiatives such as those that Nicosia undertook during its Chairmanship of the EU Council, or the new Convention on Offences related to Cultural Property, in the context of the CoE Chairmanship, as well as its campaign for the adoption of the first-ever resolution of the UN Human Rights Council on Cultural Rights and the Protection of Cultural Heritage, have a broader impact and universal value that goes beyond the RoC's self-interest.

Therefore, the RoC's actorness in the domain of the protection of culture and cultural heritage satisfies all the three hypotheses for a mature small state status seeking strategy in multilateral settings. The RoC holds a clearly stated strategy in this area and means that corresponds to its ends and the status of a small state. Through its actorness in the area of the protection of culture and cultural heritage in multilateral settings, the RoC served its immediate interests but also increased its visibility as a good power and useful partner and as a result the small island state improved its status.

Conclusion

This chapter contributed an assessment of the RoC's status seeking strategy within and through regional and international organizations, relating it to the concept of maturity in international relations, as the latter is set forth in the introduction of this volume. We focused on the issue of the protection of culture and cultural heritage as it is one of the main themes of the RoC's actorness in multilateral settings and based on a framework consisting of three different hypotheses combining the fundamentals of small state status seeking with the concept of maturity, we argue that the RoC holds a mature small state status seeking strategy in multilateral settings. Although the RoC's activity in this area is directly related to the Cypriot Issue in terms of both experiences and interests, the small island state has accomplished to advance initiatives that go well beyond its own self-interest and better its position in multilateral settings.

References

COMPENDIUM OF CULTURAL POLICIES & TRENDS IN EUROPE. 2017. "Assembly of Stakeholders of the Council of Europe/ERICARTS." 30–31 March. https://www.ucy.ac.cy/frml/documents/Conferences/Program.Compendium2017.pdf.

Corbett, Jack, Xu Yi-Chong, and Patrick Weller. 2019. "Norm Entrepreneurship and Diffusion 'from Below' in International Organizations: How the Competent Performance of Vulnerability Generates Benefits for Small States." *Review of International Studies* 45 (4): 647–668.

Council of Europe. 2017a. Convention on Offences Relating to Cultural Property, CETS No.221. Nicosia. 19 May 2017.

Council of Europe. 2017b. Explanatory Report to the Council of Europe Convention on Offences Relating to Cultural Property. Nicosia. 19 May 2017.

Council of Europe. 2018. "Note on Convention on Offences Relating to Cultural Property—Accession by States Which Are Not Member States of the Council of Europe and Which Have Not Participated in the Elaboration of the Convention." November 2018. https://rm.coe.int/16808fe38b.

EU. 2020. "EU Aid Programme for the Turkish Cypriot Community, Directorate-General for Structural Reform Support (DG REFORM), 2006–2020." https://ec.europa.eu/info/funding-tenders/funding-opportunities/funding-programmes/overview-funding-programmes/aid-programme-turkish-cypriot-community_en#examples-of-funding-recipients.

EU Commission. 2020a. "Annex to COMMISSION IMPLEMENTING DECISION of 25.8.2020 on adopting an Action Programme for the Turkish Cypriot Community for the Year 2020 (Part II)." 25 August 2020. https://ec.europa.eu/info/publications/turkish-cypriot-community-aid-programme-financing-decision_en.

EU Commission. 2020b. "Commission Implementing Decision of 25.8.2020 on Adopting an Action Programme for the Turkish Cypriot Community for the Year 2020 (Part II), C(2020) 5698 final." https://ec.europa.eu/info/sites/info/files/1_en_act_part1_v3_2.pdf.

EU CULTNET. 2012. "EU Council Resolution on the Creation of an Informal Network of Law Enforcement Authorities and Expertise Competent in the Field of Cultural Goods for the Purpose of Preventing and Combating Crime Against Cultural Goods by Strengthening Coordination at National Level Between Law Enforcement Authorities and Cultural Authorities and Private Organisations, 14232/12. 4 October.

Hurd, Ian. 2005. "The Strategic Use of Liberal Internationalism: Libya and the UN Sanctions, 1992–2003." *International Organization* 59 (3): 495–526.

Jaschik, Kevin. 2014. "Small States and International Politics: Climate Change, the Maldives and Tuvalu." *International Politics* 51 (2): 272–293.

Kouskouvelis, Ilias, and Chainoglou, Kalliopi. 2018. "Against the Law: Turkey's Annexation Efforts in Occupied Cyprus." *Hague Yearbook of International Law* 29: 55–102.

Larson, Paul Welch Deborah, Thazha Varkey, and William Wohlforth. 2014. "Status and World Order." In *Status in World Politics*, edited by Thazha Varkey Paul, Deborah Welsch Larson and William Wohlforth, 3–29. New York: Cambridge University Press.

Long, Tom, and Francisco Urdinez. 2021. "Status at the Margins: Why Paraguay Recognizes Taiwan and Shuns China." *Foreign Policy Analysis* 17 (1): 1–22.

Mohammadzadeh, Babak. 2017. "Status and Foreign Policy Change in Small States: Qatar's Emergence in Perspective." *The International Spectator* 52 (2): 19–36.

Müller, Harald. 2004. "Arguing, Bargaining and All That: Communicative Action, Rationalist Theory and the Logic of Appropriateness in International Relations." *European Journal of International Relations* 10 (3): 395–435.

Neumann, Iver, and Benjamin De Carvalho. 2015. "Introduction Small States and Status." In *Small State Status Seeking Norway's Quest for International Standing*, edited by Benjamin De Carvalho and Iver Neumann, 1–21. Abingdon: Routledge.

Pedi, Revecca. 2016. "Theory of International Relations: Small States in the International System" (Unpublished PhD Thesis). University of Macedonia, Thessaloniki. Retrieved from https://www.didaktorika.gr/eadd/handle/10442/38599.

Pedi, Revecca, and Ilias Kouskouvelis. 2019. "Cyprus in the Eastern Mediterranean: A Small State Seeking for Status." In *The New Eastern Mediterranean Theory, Politics and States in a Volatile Era*, edited by Spyridon Litsas and Aristotle Tziampiris, 151–167. New York: Springer.

Pedi, Revecca, and Katerina Sarri. 2019. "From the Small But Smart State to the "Small and Entrepreneurial State": Introducing a Framework for Effective Small State Strategies within the EU and Beyond." *Baltic Journal of European Studies* 9 (1): 3–19.

RoC. 2001a. "Letter Dated 16 October 2001 from the Permanent Representative of Cyprus to the United Nations Office at Geneva addressed to the United Nations High Commissioner for Human Rights, E/CN.4/2002/124." 27 November 2001.

RoC. 2001b. "Letter dated 24 July 2001 from the Permanent Representative of Cyprus to the United Nations Office at Geneva addressed to the United Nations High Commissioner for Human Rights, E/CN.4/2002/12." 17 August.

RoC. 2001c. "Letter Dated 8 August 2001 from the Chargé D'affaires a.i. of the Permanent RoC. 2017. Chairmanship Activities." 22 November 2016–19 May 2017. https://www.coe.int/en/web/presidency/cyprus-other-activities.

RoC. 2005. "Letter Dated 30 September 2005 from the Permanent Representative of Cyprus to the United Nations Addressed to the Secretary-General, A/60/404–S/2005/622." 3 October.

RoC. 2013a. "Letter Dated 6 December 2013 from the Permanent Representative of Cyprus to the United Nations Addressed to the Secretary-General, A/68/647–S/2013/724." 9 December.

RoC. 2013b. "Working Towards a Better Europe-Results of the Cyprus Presidency of the Council of the EU 1 July–31 December 2012." 14 January. http://www.cy2012.eu/index.php/en/file/7hcUHnC8O2T2nxXo9+AUZw==.

RoC. 2017a. "Priorities of the Cyprus Chairmanship of the Committee of Ministers of the Council of Europe, 22 November 2016–19 May 2017." https://search.coe.int/cm/Pages/result_details.aspx?ObjectID=09000016806be078.

RoC. 2017b. "Programme des activites culturelles." https://rm.coe.int/CoERMPublicCommonSearchServices/DisplayDCTMContent?documentId=09000016806bf0bf.

RoC. 2019. "Commissioner for Volunteerism and Non-Governmental Organisations, Act for Heritage." 24–26 October 2019. https://www.coe.int/en/web/culture-and-heritage/act-for-heritage-?fbclid=IwAR2KTkepMOZbovlr9N9JJbqd3yg6b3fXlExb4puQL3K36ZlGtfg_9j83B6Q.

RoC. 2021. Protection of Cultural Heritage 2021. *Ministry of Foreign Affairs*. https://mfa.gov.cy/themes/.

Schia, Niels Nagelhus, and Jacob Sending, Ole. 2015. "Status and Sovereign Equality: Small Powers in Multilateral Settings." In *Small State Status Seeking Norway's Quest for International Standing*, edited by Benjamin de Carvalho and Iver B. Neumann, 73–85. Abingdon: Routledge.

Thorhallsson, B. 2012. "Small States in the UN Security Council: Means of Influence?" *The Hague Journal of Diplomacy*, 7 (2): 135–160.

Thorhallsson, Baldur, and Margrét Eggertsdóttir, Anna. 2020. "Small States in the UN Security Council: Austria's Quest to Maintain Status." *The Hague Journal of Diplomacy*. https://doi.org/10.1163/1871191X-BJA10017.

UN. 1990. "Draft Resolution, Revival of the Ancient Library of Alexandria, E/1990/L.20." 8 May 1990.

UN. 1991. "Draft Resolution, Return or Restitution of Cultural Property to the Countries of Origin, A/46/L.11." 21 October 1991.

UN. 1993. "Draft Resolution, Return or Restitution of Cultural Property to the Countries of Origin, A/48/L.15." 29 October 1993.

UN. 1999. "Draft Resolution, Oceans and the Law of the Sea, A/54/L.31." 16 November 1999.

UN. 2001a. "Draft Resolution, Protection of Religious Sites, A/55/L.81." 25 May 2001.

UN. 2001b. "Draft Resolution, the Destruction of Relics and Monuments in Afghanistan, A/55/L.79." 7 March 2001.
UN. 2001c. "Letter Dated 9 August 2001 from the Charge d'affaires a.i of Cyprus to the United Nations Addressed to the Secretary General (A/55/1026–S/2001/778)." https://www.cyprusun.org/?p=4221.
UN. 2003. "Draft Resolution, United Nations Year for Cultural Heritage, 2002, A/58/L.11/Rev.2/Add.1." 18 December 2003.
UN. 2006. "Draft Resolution, Return or Restitution of Cultural Property to the Countries of Origin, A/61/L.15/Rev.1." 30 November 2006.
UN. 2009a. "Draft Resolution, Oceans and the Law of the Sea, A/64/L.18/Add.1." 22 December 2009.
UN. 2009b. "Draft Resolution, Return or Restitution of Cultural Property to the Countries of Origin, A/64/L.17." 11 November 2009.
UN. 2009c. "Draft Resolution, Return or Restitution of Cultural Property to the Countries of Origin, A/64/L.17/Rev.1." 3 December 2009.
UN. 2011. "Draft Resolution, Oceans and the law of the sea, A/66/L.21." 28 November 2011.
UN. 2012. "Draft Resolution, Return or Restitution of Cultural Property to the Countries of Origin, A/67/L.34." 5 December 2012.
UN. 2015a. Draft Resolution, Return or Restitution of Cultural Property to the Countries of Origin, A/70/L.28." 4 December 2015.
UN. 2015b. "Draft Resolution, Saving the Cultural Heritage of Iraq, A/69/L.71." 21 May 2015.
UN. 2015c. "Draft Resolution, Threats to International Peace and Security Caused by Terrorist Acts by Al-Qaida and Associated Groups, S/2015/100." 12 February 2015.
UN. 2015d. "Draft Resolution, United Nations Alliance of Civilisations, A/69/L.76." 25 June 2015.
UN. 2016. "Draft Resolution, Cultural Rights and the Protection of Cultural Heritage, A/HRC/33/L.21." 27 September.
UN. 2017a. "Report of the UN Special Rapporteur in the Field of Cultural Rights on Her Mission to Cyprus, A/HRC/34/56/Add.1." 2 March.
UN. 2017b. "Draft Resolution, Destruction and trafficking of cultural heritage by terrorist groups in situations of armed conflict, S/2017/242." 24 March.
UN. 2018a. "Draft Resolution, Cultural Rights and the Protection of Cultural Heritage, A/HRC/37/L.30." 19 March.
UN. 2018b. "Draft Resolution, Return or Restitution of Cultural Property to the Countries of Origin, A/73/L.54." 10 December.
UNDP Cyprus. 2021. "Projects." https://www.cy.undp.org/content/cyprus/en/home/projects.html.
UNGA. 1973. "Resolution, Preservation and Further Development of Cultural Values, A/RES/3148(XXVIII)." 14 December.

UNGA. 1978. "Resolution, Protection, Restitution and Return of Cultural and Artistic Property as Part of the Preservation and Further Development of Cultural Value, A/RES/33/50." 14 December.
UNGA. 1981. "Resolution, Academic, Cultural and Sports Boycotts of South Africa, A/RES/36/172/I." 17 December.
UNGA. 1984. "Resolution, Return or Restitution of Cultural Property to the Countries of Origin, A/RES/38/34." 3 February.
UNGA. 1985. "Return or Restitution of Cultural Property to the Countries of Origin, A/RES/40/19." 27 November.
UNGA. 1987a. "Resolution, Proclamation of the World Decade for Cultural Development, A/RES/41/187." 29 January.
UNGA. 1987b. "Resolution, Return or Restitution of Cultural Property to the Countries of Origin Adopted on 22 October 1987, A/RES/42/7." 24 November.
UNGA. 1989. "Resolution, Return or Restitution of Cultural Property to the Countries of Origin, A/RES/44/18." 19 December.
UNGA. 1990. "Resolution, Indivisibility and Interdependence of Economic, Social, Cultural, Civil and Political Rights, A/RES/44/130." 26 February.
UNGA. 1991. "Resolution, Return or Restitution of Cultural Property to the Countries of Origin, A/RES/46/10." 20 December.
UNGA. 1993. "Resolution, Return or Restitution of Cultural Property to the Countries of Origin, A/RES/48/15." 11 November.
UNGA. 1996. "Resolution, Return or Restitution of Cultural Property to the Countries of Origin, A/RES/50/56." 2 February.
UNGA. 1998. "Resolution, Return or Restitution of Cultural Property to the Countries of Origin, A/RES/52/24." 23 January.
UNGA. 2015. "Resolution, United Nations Alliance of Civilisations, A/RES/69/312." 31 July.
UNGA. 2018a. "Resolution, Culture and Sustainable Development, A/RES/72/229." 19 January.
UNGA. 2018b. "Resolution, International Day of Multilateralism and Diplomacy for Peace, A/RES/73/127." 19 December.
UNGA. 2018c. "Resolution, Return or Restitution of Cultural Property to the Countries of Origin, A/RES/73/130." 24 December.
UNGA. 2019. "Resolution, Academy for Human Encounters and Dialogue, A/RES/73/344." 20 September.
UNGA. 2020a. "Resolution, Human Rights and Cultural Diversity, A/RES/74/159." 20 January.
UNGA. 2020b. "Resolution, Situation of Human Rights in the Islamic Republic of Iran, A/RES/75/191." 28 December.

UNGA. 2020c. "Resolution, Situation of Human Rights in the Autonomous Republic of Crimea and the City of Sevastopol, Ukraine, A/RES/75/192." 28 December.
UNGA. 2020d. "Resolution, Situation of Human Rights in the Syrian Arab Republic, A/RES/75/193." 28 December.
UNGA. 2020e. "Resolution, The Right to Food, A/RES/75/179." 28 December.
UNGA. 2021. "Resolution, Oceans and the Law of the Sea, A/RES/75/239." 5 January.
UNHRC. 2016. "Cultural Rights and the Protection of Cultural Heritage, A/HRC/RES/33/20." 6 October.
UNHRC. 2018. "Cultural Rights and the Protection of Cultural Heritage, A/HRC/RES/37/17." 9 April.
UNSC. 2017. "Resolution 2347, S/RES/2347 (2017)." 24 March.
Wohlforth, William, Benjamin De Carvalho, Halvard Leira, and Neumann, Iver. 2017. "Moral Authority and Status in International Relations: Good States and the Social Dimension of Status Seeking." *Review of International Studies* 44 (3): 526–546.

CHAPTER 13

Defence Diplomacy by the Republic of Cyprus: A Dynamic Policy in the Process of Maturation

Marinos Papaioakeim

Introduction

Whether based on quantitative or qualitative criteria, there can be little doubt that Cyprus falls under the category of small states.[1] Nevertheless, beyond the 'smallness', the Republic of Cyprus (RoC) has undertaken several initiatives in the framework of defence diplomacy. Its accession to the European Union (EU) in 2004, coupled with some other geopolitical developments, gave impetus to the activation of the country's defence diplomacy. Especially over the past decade the RoC has shown a great degree of dynamism in its defence foreign relations, although it still faces several challenges and has a long way to go for its defence diplomacy to

---

[1] For a more detailed analysis about small states, see: Thorhallsson (2006). The Size of States in the European Union: Theoretical and Conceptual Perspectives. *Journal of European Integration* 28 (1): 7–31.

M. Papaioakeim (✉)
University of Cyprus, Nicosia, Cyprus

© The Author(s), under exclusive license to Springer Nature Switzerland AG 2022
Z. Tziarras (ed.), *The Foreign Policy of the Republic of Cyprus*, Reform and Transition in the Mediterranean,
https://doi.org/10.1007/978-3-030-91177-5_13

become a mature policy. The issue of maturity in foreign policy particularly as it regards defence diplomacy is central to this paper the aim of which is twofold. On the one hand, it aims to present some initial thoughts about the issue of maturity in foreign policy, and particularly in defence diplomacy. On the other hand, it explores the defence diplomacy efforts of the RoC for the period between 2004 until 2020[2] and assesses the degree to which the policy has over the past 10 to 15 years matured.

The Concept of Defence Diplomacy

Although the use of soldiers or defence/military institutions can be recognised in many cases in the long history of diplomatic practice, the term of defence diplomacy first became known in modern discussions in 1998 with the United Kingdom's (UK) Strategic Defence Review (Ministry of Defence, United Kingdom 1998). The idea of modern defence diplomacy can be traced back to the aftermath of the Cold War, when western governments initiated specific defence programmes, such as the Partnership for Peace (PfP), which aimed to transform the large, USSR-style armed forces of the Eastern bloc states into western-style armies (Meixner 2005). In this effort, many western armed forces have cooperated with their counterparts from the ex-soviet states in various ways. By introducing training programmes and enabling the exchange of officers, western armies were used not only to transform the eastern militaries but also to reorient their strategic thinking. Having spent several decades as enemies, these programmes were used widely right after the Cold War to help mend the strategic and cultural rift between the East and the West. In describing the enlarged role that armed forces and military establishments had in supporting the diplomatic initiatives of their government, the UK Ministry of Defence coined the term *defence diplomacy* and defined it as "the varied activities undertaken by the Ministry of Defence (MoD) to dispel hostility, build and maintain trust, and assist in the development of democratically accountable armed forces, thereby making a significant contribution to conflict prevention and resolution" (Ministry of Defence, United Kingdom 1998).

---

[2] The selection of this specific chronological period is not a random choice. A remarkable shift towards comprehensive understanding and practice of defence diplomacy has happened since the accession to the EU in 2004.

The discussion on defence diplomacy has gradually entered academic debates and many scholars have engaged more actively in research about the concept. Andrew Cottey and Anthony Forster (2004, 7) were among the first scholars who attempt to examine defence diplomacy in a comprehensive manner, and they defined it as "peacetime cooperative use of armed forces and related infrastructure (primarily defence ministries) as a tool of foreign and security policy". Seng Tan and Bhubhindar Singh (2012, 221), who analysed the Asian states' experience in defence diplomacy, defined it as "the collective application of pacific and/or cooperative initiatives by national defence establishments and military practitioners for confidence building, trust creation, conflict prevention, and/or conflict resolution". Anton du Plessis (2008, 109) who looked at the case of South Africa describes defence diplomacy as "the use of military means for diplomatic purposes," while Gregory Winger (2014), in one of the latest contributions to the defence diplomacy literature, defined it as, "the peaceful use of the defence institutions of one country to co-opt the government institutions of another country in order to achieve a preferred outcome"; a definition that will be adopted by this paper.[3] The formulation of a definition is, by default, a difficult and complicated process in all academic fields. Although widely used in political and academic debates, defence diplomacy lacks a universally accepted definition, and there is no consensus, since a plethora of definitions is available (Mulloy 2007; Drab 2018).

Foreign Policy Maturity and Defence Diplomacy: A Set of Components

In the field of International Relations (IR), and particularly in diplomatic studies and Foreign Policy Analysis (FPA), "maturity" is not a widely researched concept; there are only sporadic references. These attempts broadly define foreign policy maturity as that which its objectives and aspirations are clearly defined and are commensurate to the needs and capabilities of a state (see Tziarras' introduction in this volume). The lack of sufficient analysis in the literature about the concept of maturity is also obvious in other aspects (subcategories) of the concept/practice, such as

---

[3] It should be noted that, although Wingers' definition is adopted in this paper, this does not mean that the researcher's approach to defence diplomacy is restricted to it.

defence diplomacy. What follows is a first attempt to discuss and determine some fundamental components of defence diplomacy that should be considered in evaluating its level of maturity. It should be clearly noted that this is not an exhaustive analysis but a brief and nascent attempt that can provide the basis for further research.

At the time of writing, no works have been found in the literature that collate the concepts of maturity with defence diplomacy or to examine the components which determine a mature defence diplomacy. In other words, there are no specific or general "criteria" based on which to define defence diplomacy maturity. The existing literature determines the level of maturity of this policy indirectly and unintentionally. Despite the lack of clear criteria, the maturity of defence diplomacy is determined indirectly by the quality and quantity of some key activities. Scholars determine what defence diplomacy is (or not), or the level of its development, by analysing the evolution of some "mainstream" activities of the practice.

The overwhelming majority of scholars base their analysis, either theoretical or empirical, on Cottey and Forster's (2004) seminal research that summarised the activities of defence diplomacy as follows:Bilateral and multilateral contacts between senior and military defence officials; appointment of defence attachés to foreign countries; bilateral defence cooperation agreements; training of foreign military and civilian defence personnel; provision of expertise and advice on the democratic control of armed forces; contacts and exchanges between military personnel and units, and ship visits; placement of military or civilian personnel in partner countries' defence ministries or armed forces; deployment of training teams; provision of military equipment and other material aid; bilateral or multilateral military exercises for training purposes. These activities (at least the majority of them) are like the archetype on which scholars rely in order to describe and analyse defence diplomacy.

As already noted, there are no maturity criteria in the literature and, as such, defence diplomacy maturity is evaluated indirectly and empirically which means that. In other words, the more developed the activities, the more mature the policy. Following the same reasoning, this paper sets as general maturity components of defence diplomacy some of these "mainstream" activities as found in the literature. To be sure, the choice of activities as maturity components is not random; they are the most frequently used ones and found in the majority of defence diplomacy studies.

Bilateral and Multilateral Defence Cooperation Agreements

Bilateral and multilateral defence cooperation agreements are a major part of defence diplomacy policy. The significance of these agreements lies in that they provide defence ministries with the necessary political and legal protocols for the structuring of cooperative actions (Ministerio De Defensa Espana 2012). These agreements ensure that the particular positions of each party may be stated and logged, in order to build trust and avoid potential misunderstandings (Muthanna 2011). Collaborative action, by providing points of synergy and joint working, smoothen the appreciation, which can include a wide variety of activities, like defence technology cooperation, use of each other's facilities for logistics and repairs, bilateral or multilateral military or rescue exercises, exchanges of military information, military exchanges, arms transfers, and foreign military financing in the form of grants and loans. To hold bilateral conventions and agreements with adjacent states is especially helpful, enabling initiatives in the field of defence to be instigated; countries can also share points of view, information, and plans.

Defence Attaches to Foreign Countries and Organisations[4]

A fundamental activity of defence diplomacy is the appointment of defence attaches (DAs)[5] to foreign countries and organisations, an activity that signifies a state's direction in defence diplomacy. A DA's duties include, among others, being an advocate for both their nation's security and their military capacity; representing their nation's military divisions and guaranteeing an armed network and security strategy that can function even when bilateral relations are strained or under threat; operating as advisors in terms of security and military matters to the staff of the embassy, including the ambassador; monitoring the prevailing environment in the host nation as regards security and relaying information to their home country etc. (DCAF 2007).

---

[4] Defence attachés are part of a permanent diplomatic mission and should not be confused with ad hoc military missions.

[5] DA is a term that covers personnel from all branches of the armed services, although some larger countries may appoint an attaché to represent an individual service branch, such as an air force or naval attaché.

Bilateral and Multilateral Foreign Visits

Foreign visits are central to defence diplomacy and have remained an effective tool in contributing to confidence building between states. Bi-level or Multi-level discussions help to facilitate mutual appreciation and consequently find common ground and points of shared interest (Muthanna 2011). Top-level meetings with senior defence ministry personnel, and reciprocal hosting from counterpart nations and organisations, assist in furthering and bolstering links, thereby, building meaningful dialogue, both politically and strategically (Ministerio De Defensa Espana 2012).

Joint Military and Search and Rescue Exercises

Joint military drills and search and rescue exercises are also significant defence diplomacy activities. Participation in such activities enables greater mutual understanding and provides an excellent occasion for promoting cooperation between countries. It is also a practical way of increasing interoperability among involved countries (Ministerio De Defensa Espana 2012).

Participation in Peace Keeping Operations

Peacekeeping operations are a critical part of a state's defence diplomacy and participant states in these missions can benefited variously. Participation in peacekeeping missions offers a lot of opportunities for the participant state to create a network among the other foreign defence establishments who participate in the mission. Also, peacekeeping missions can be an opportunity for the promotion of a country's image (Muthanna 2011), either in the local communities or to other states. The advantages of peacekeepers conducting military diplomacy are generally restricted to political and security gains, despite the fact that opportunities emerge to obtain benefits in other areas, particularly economic ones.

Training Foreign Military and Civilian Defence Personnel

The practice of training foreign military defence personnel can be traced back to the Cold War period, where the two superpowers, the Soviet Union and the United States (US), extensively offered training to their allies. To be sure, this practice is common nowadays as well. Apart from the obvious operational instruction, in all of these cases, training and political objectives could be delivered as well. Training programmes can be beneficial as they enable military officers to establish official or unofficial relations with foreign officers that would otherwise not exist. Training courses, however, can be beneficial only on a long-term basis.

Disaster Relief—Humanitarian Assistance—Development Aid to Foreign States

The participation of defence actors in actions that improve civilian lives has multiplied hugely in recent years and now forms a major element on the defence diplomacy agenda. Military resources are now used in different disaster relief operations, humanitarian assistance and developmental projects. Armies and military organisations have abilities and resources to enable humanitarian and developmental projects to be conducted on a big scale. This is especially so where there is need to increase training quickly and supply and coordinate provisions in the event of a sudden crisis needing a rapid response. The US military's relief efforts in Indonesia after the 2004 tsunami are an indicative example. The advantages of these activities were twofold: meeting international humanitarian conventions in providing necessary medical treatment for local people while succeeding in winning over 'hearts and minds'.

Provision of Facilities for Military and Defence Purposes

The provision of military facilities to foreign countries, such as allowing the docking of warships in ports and the provision of facilities for aircrafts, or even the provision of military bases, is among the most significant activities on the agenda of a states' defence diplomacy. The benefits from this activity can range from pure political-diplomatic and military to financial ones. The small state of Djibouti is a striking example of a country that provides military bases to foreign states, using its highly important geostrategic location with access to the Gulf of Aden and the Indian Ocean and a significant gateway to the Horn of Africa and the wider region of East Africa. With an area of 23,000 square km and a population of less than one million, Djibouti hosts the most foreign military bases in the world. The French maintain four military bases in Djibouti (which also house German and Spanish soldiers); the Americans two, while Italy, Japan, and, more recently, China have one (Styan 2016).

Other Factors

Beyond the above-mentioned activities, there are also some other criteria to be met for defence diplomacy to be considered mature. Namely, the ability of a given state to respond effectively to international needs and capitalise new opportunities that emerge in the international arena. This could be seen as an additional maturity component of defence diplomacy. Based on the limited literature on foreign policy maturity, it can be concluded that a mature foreign policy could be generally defined as that which has clearly defined and set goals/aspirations that match a state's needs and capabilities (see Tziarras in this volume). The same is applied to the case of defence diplomacy. Thus, another basic component of a mature defence diplomacy lies in the well defined goals and matching capabilities or means.

The role of elites, both political and the military, is another important factor in defence diplomacy. One the one hand, the political elite determines the general approach of a state's foreign policy and subsequently, the different tools, such as defence, work towards that direction. On the other hand, the role of the military is essential to the design and exercise of defence diplomacy. The examination of decisions-making in both political and military elites significant in evaluating of maturity. More specifically, the extent to which decision-making is rational needs to be examined. Namely, when governments take decisions that are not merely based on their ideological preferences but on the overall interests of the state.

Determining the maturity components of defence diplomacy should consider the particularities of each country case such as the size, defence, and financial capabilities to exercise defence diplomacy, etc. Thus, it is not here argued that a mature defence diplomacy policy should adhere to all the above components. However, a state's defence diplomacy could be considered (relatively) mature if it meets at least most of the components or some of them to a high degree. Additionally, it should be noted that the maturity level of defence diplomacy can be "measured" in comparison to the quality and quantity of past initiatives. For example, if country X had one defence attaché before 10 years and now maintains 15, this is a sign of maturity. However, numerical criteria vary and are relative to each case. Moreover, although the numerical rise in these components is a sign of maturity, the examination of this dimension alone cannot be conclusive; the conclusion needs to be a combination of other elements as well.

An important dimension that must be also raised is the relation between maturity and success. In many cases, maturity is incorrectly linked to success. Without a doubt, having successful policies in the long run indicates a degree of maturity. However, a mature policy is not necessarily successful and vice versa: a successful policy is not always mature.

In what follows, some basic components of a mature defence diplomacy policy are defined. To examine and assess the maturity level of a state's defence diplomacy, these components and their evolution vis-à-vis the case study under examination should be taken into account.

The Defence Diplomacy of the Republic of Cyprus and Its Drivers (2004–2020)

Defence diplomacy has not been a particularly popular idea in the RoC in the past. The conflict with Turkey was the main issue that the defence establishment of the country used to primarily focus on. Reluctance on the part of the RoC to use defence diplomacy was gradually relinquished as its benefits became clearer (both from the security and political standpoints). It can be argued that since 2004—and even more so since the early 2010s—the defence diplomacy of the RoC has gone through a process of gradual development. This section analyses the basic components of the RoC's defence diplomacy and its level of maturity during the 2004–2020 period. Moreover, to better examine how the RoC's defence diplomacy has matured across different areas of activity, this section briefly scrutinises the circumstances and dynamics under which the defence diplomacy of the RoC gradually emerged in a chronological order, starting with the milestone of the RoC's accession to the EU.

The RoC's Accession to the EU

One of the most significant factors that triggered the RoC's defence diplomacy was its accession to the EU in 2004. This development has undoubtedly offered major opportunities to the RoC's defence establishment to participate in EU defence organisations and agencies. It has also ushered the RoC's defence relations in a new era and became the cornerstone for the emergence of its defence diplomacy. To be accepted to the EU, the RoC had to fulfil a number of obligations and be harmonised with the EU *Acquis Communautaire*. The Ministry of Defence (MoD) had conventional obligations to follow because of its participation in the EU. The necessity to effectively respond to these led the RoC MoD and National Guard to create institutions and departments of international relations that did not previously exist (e.g. the Department of International Relations) and to appoint Cypriot officers to certain EU positions (e.g. military representatives in Brussels). It was the first time that the RoC's defence establishment got the chance to have a voice internationally. This exposure within the EU led to the gradual emergence of a culture of internationalism and extroversion in the defence establishment of the RoC.

The EU membership enabled the RoC to initiate defence relations with its counterparts in the Union, bilaterally and multilaterally. Indeed, prior to 2004, the RoC had much more limited defence relations with European countries in comparison to the post-accession period. Its participation in EU defence organisations and agencies was also created major opportunities for the RoC defence establishment in terms of gaining new know-how, educational and operational experiences, as well as synergies, partnerships, etc. During the same period, the EU defence sector was strengthened notably, with operations and missions to third countries. This gave members-states, especially small ones like the RoC, the opportunity to participate in such missions, as they could not otherwise do it alone. Overall, the EU accession played a key role in the evolution of the RoC's defence diplomacy. The new reality gave the opportunity to the RoC defence establishment to become more institutionalised, and later to better understand and conduct defence diplomacy activities.

New Geopolitical Developments in the Region

As the regional level has become more important in international relations, and as rapid geopolitical developments have had great effects, especially in the Middle East, the RoC was presented with new opportunities and the incentive to pursue a more central role in the Eastern Mediterranean. The most important developments that affected the RoC's defence diplomacy are listed below.

Lebanon War (2006). On 12 July 2006, the Lebanon War broke out between Hezbollah and the Israeli forces. Many foreign civilians were left stranded in Lebanon following the assaults on the country's international airport and the blockade of its ports. While the crisis was ongoing, the RoC government used its resources to accommodate the safe exit of 80,000 foreign citizens and Lebanese nationals (Samokhvalov 2013). The RoC became the centre of humanitarian assistance deliveries for Lebanese people (Ministry of Defence 2012). The 2006 Lebanon Crisis was not particularly revealing of Cyprus' geostrategic location in the Eastern Mediterranean. What it did reveal, however, was the fact that the RoC had the facilities needed to play the role of a humanitarian assistance centre.

After this event, several regional actors reassessed their views as concerns the role and importance of Cyprus in the Eastern Mediterranean. The international community has acknowledged the significance of the RoC as a pillar of stability in the troubled region of the Middle East. A defence attaché of a European country in Cyprus stated indicatively in an interview that "The Lebanon Crisis of 2006 was one of the major reasons that favoured the kick-off of our relations in the defence sector, since this situation revealed the capabilities and prospects of Cyprus as a potential logistics centre in the future" (interview no. 1). In what followed, many countries requested to use the RoC's defence and military infrastructures and resources for training purposes on rescue and evacuation operations. This resulted in the signing of status-of-forces agreements (SOFA)[6] with many countries, especially with those that participate in the peacekeeping force in Lebanon. The crisis in Lebanon was overall a very significant event, for it revealed the capabilities of the RoC to other countries and its potential as a stable partner in the region; in turn, the RoC established defence cooperation with other states as well.

---

[6] A status-of-forces agreement (SOFA) is an agreement between a host country and a foreign nation, stationing military forces in that country. SOFAs are often included, along with other types of military agreements, as part of a comprehensive security arrangement. A SOFA does not constitute a security arrangement; it establishes the rights and privileges of foreign personnel present in a host country in support of the larger security arrangement.

Hydrocarbons in Cyprus' Exclusive Economic Zone (2007)

Another significant factor behind the emergence of the RoC's defence diplomacy was the discovery of hydrocarbons in the country's Exclusive Economic Zone (EEZ).[7] This development gave rise to new needs and challenges in the RoC's defence that did not exist before. The new reality created a new circle of tensions with Turkey, which in many cases was directly or indirectly threatening both the RoC as well as interested hydrocarbon companies. In addition, the RoC had to ensure that the seismographic surveys conducted by these companies in its EEZ would continue uninterrupted. The potential construction of new infrastructure for the exploitation of hydrocarbons created the need for more security provision.

Against this background, the activation of the RoC's defence diplomacy through the signing of defence agreements with all interested parties was deemed necessary for the new challenges to be dealt with more effectively. As former Minister of Defence, Photis Photiou pointed out in December 2013, "The utilization of our defence diplomacy is crucial and has a special role to play in our more general strategic plans with regards to energy security" (*Philenews* 2013). In another interview with the researcher, Photiou also claimed that "through cooperation with other countries, we have tried to create an energy and maritime security umbrella that safeguards our sovereign rights in light of the new developments in our EEZ. We considered it vital to develop strong defence diplomacy, to contribute to this direction" (interview no. 3). These statements are indicative of how the RoC government was "forced" to activate its defence diplomacy because of the new security needs that occurred after the discovery of hydrocarbons. Moreover, the activity of major energy-related international companies (from the US, Israel France, Italy, Korea, UK, etc.) in Cyprus has provided the RoC with the opportunity to develop defence relations with the countries represented by these companies. In fact, defence diplomacy activities with interested countries were a consequence of working together in the energy sector. Defence diplomacy intended to secure the areas in which hydrocarbons were located and exploited, thereby addressing energy-related insecurities resulting from threats posed by Turkey.

---

[7] About the influence of the discovery of Hydrocarbons in the RoC foreign policy see, Kariotis (2011), Proedrou (2012), and Gürel et al. (2016).

Turkish Strained Relations with Regional States (2010–2017). The deteriorating relations between Ankara and neighbouring states undoubtedly had a positive impact on the RoC's foreign policy. The RoC capitalised the new state of affairs and initiated efforts to establish defence relations with neighbouring countries, mainly with Israel and Egypt.

Although Turkey was the first Muslim country to recognise the state of Israel, relations between the two countries deteriorated after a series of events starting from 2008, culminating in the 2010 Mavi Marmara incident (Migdalovitz 2010). The rupture in the Turkey-Israel relations prompted the closer relationship between the RoC and Israel. Israel, in line with its need to escape regional isolation, was forced to seek new regional partners. The RoC, as the only non-hostile state Israel shares maritime and air boundaries with, was an attractive option for cooperation. On the other hand, for the RoC it was a good opportunity to benefit in various ways from a strong state in the region, such as Israel. In January 2012, then RoC Minister of Defence, Demetris Eliades, became the first Cypriot defence minister to visit Israel (Kathimerini 2012). Since then, the defence relations of the two states were upgraded significantly. Beyond the regular high-level visits between the two defence ministers, Cyprus and Israel have conducted many joint military exercises, with the most known being *Onisilos-Gideon*. Moreover, the two ministries of defence signed several defence cooperation agreements.

After the mid-2013 uprising against the Egyptian government that resulted in the overthrow of the Turkish-backed Egyptian President, Mohammad Morsi of the Muslim Brotherhood, difficulties in the relations between Egypt and the Turkish government of Recep Tayyip Erdoğan emerged, partly because of the latter's pro-Muslim Brotherhood (*The Daily Star* 2013). The overthrow of Morsi was described by Erdoğan as "anti-democratic", and even "a massacre" (Al Jazzera 2013). Following this, joint military exercises between the two nations were suspended, and their ambassadors recalled (BBC News 2013).

Under these circumstances, foreign and defence relations between the RoC and Egypt improved gradually. Since 2015 their defence relations evolved rapidly, and this was demonstrated by the regular diplomatic visits and the signing of many bilateral agreements on defence-related issues. Based on the Memorandum of Understanding between the RoC and Egypt, the two states collaborate on many activities, such as joint exercises in the field of search and rescue (Ministry of Defence 2017). A significant development was the mutual exchange of defence attaches between 2016 and 2017. Beyond the above agreements and official visits, there were also exchanges of military personnel for educational purposes. It is from this perspective clear, that deteriorated relations between Turkey and other states of the Eastern Mediterranean have benefited the RoC which capitalised on the opportunity to develop or enhance defence and other relations with its neighbours.

The Turbulent Region of the Middle East (2010–11). The ongoing political and societal tensions in the Middle East have been producing great regional instability. The outbreak of the Arab uprisings in 2010–2011 gave rise to a new geopolitical landscape, security challenges, and uncertainty. Many states were affected and fell into politically turmoil. Tensions coming from the empowerment of political Islamist parties and sectarian factions threatened the region's security, even as Jihadist terrorism became a more imminent threat after the advancements of the so-called Islamic State (ISIS) in 2014 (Dokos 2016; Tziarras 2017). Under these circumstances, countries that had an interest in the region increased their military presence. Various reports in the press confirm that during that period many states, mainly superpowers, maintained military presence in the area of the Eastern Mediterranean for various reasons such us the Syria war, the international fight again ISIS and others (see indicatively, Naftermporiki 2015; The Times of Israel 2013; Kathimerini 2016).

As the former director of the RoC's defence diplomacy department (2008–2014) noted:

> The Middle East, especially at that time, was a volcano because of a series of events, such as the Arab Spring, the development of terrorism, etc. These events have highlighted the role of Cyprus as one of the few stable states in the region, which proved to be one of the drivers of co-operation with large states with interests in the region. (interview no. 2)

This view was confirmed by officials of other states as well. For example, a defence attaché of a European country in the RoC claimed that "developments in the Eastern Mediterranean region and the wider Middle East created turmoil and Cyprus was the only stable state in the area" (interview no. 1). The RoC exploited the unstable regional environment and branded itself as a stable pillar and reliable partner in the area. This approach led to a close cooperation in the defence sector with many countries that have an interest in the area, such as France, the UK, and the United States. The military presence of these states provided the RoC with the opportunity to build defence cooperation and synergies that led to concrete actions such as joint exercises, information exchange, etc.

Overall, the political stability of the island stands in stark contrast to the political instability of the region and given that third states with interest in the region were looking for a stable and reliable partner, the RoC managed to acquire more geopolitical importance and plays this role at least to a certain extent. It was in the context of the above regional and international dynamics that RoC governments started to "discover" defence diplomacy as a foreign policy tool.

RoC's Defence Diplomacy in the Process of Maturation (2004–2020)

Following the examination of the circumstances under which the RoC's defence diplomacy developed, this section looks at the evolution of its basic components and its level of maturity for the period between 2004 and 2020, taking into consideration the maturity components laid out previously. From 2004, and more so since the early 2010s, there is no doubt that there has been an unprecedented proliferation of defence diplomacy initiatives by the RoC. This can be seen in the evolution of various defence diplomacy aspects. Undoubtedly, the expansion and development of all the above components of defence diplomacy show at least a level of maturation in the state's defence diplomacy.

Defence Agreements

The RoC, mainly since 2007, has signed many defence cooperation agreements (see Appendix, Table 13.1), or other defence-related agreements like memoranda of understanding (MoUs) (see Appendix, Table 13.2), bilateral military programmes (see Appendix, Table 13.3), etc., which resulted in the significant expansion of the role that the MoD had in foreign relations. Prior to 2007, the MoD had signed very few defence-related agreements out of which only a few had noteworthy impact. For example, in 1999, an MoU between the RoC and South Africa was signed but was never implemented. In 2000 an MoU with the UK was also signed, but it concerned activities of only a limited scope at the British bases in Cyprus. In addition, a defence agreement was signed in 2002 with Armenia that remained idle for many years and was eventually activated only after 2010. During the 1990s and early 2000s, the only remarkable defence-related agreement of RoC was the one with Russia: it was the agreement for Military and Technical Cooperation of March 1996. This agreement fell within the framework of RoC efforts to develop a reliable air defence through the purchase of defence systems from Russia and particularly the antiaircraft missiles S-300.

From 2007 onwards, there has been a remarkable rise in the number of defence-related agreements between the RoC and other states. Between 2007 and 2013, defence-related agreements with numerous states such as Greece (2008, 2009, 2013), Serbia (2010), Montenegro (2011), Ukraine (2011), Czech Republic (2012), Italy (2013), Armenia (2013), Poland (2013), and Lebanon (2013) were signed. One of the most significant ones was the one with France (2007), namely, the Cooperation Agreement on Defence Affairs. Other significant agreements were the two defence related agreements of 2012 with Israel that permitted the Israeli Air Force to use the airspace and territorial waters around Cyprus in order to safeguard and protect crucial energy resources, also allowing the exchange of classified information (*The Jerusalem Post* 2016). In February of the same year, Benjamin Netanyahu, then Israeli Prime Minister, signed an agreement with then RoC President Demetris Christofias, allowing Israel to access the Cypriot airspace and sovereign waters to conduct search and rescue missions (*The Economist* 2012). In 2014, another two agreements were signed with Greece: a cooperation agreement on search and rescue operations, and an MoU on crisis management.

In 2015, a significant agreement occurred when an MoU in defence and military cooperation was signed with Egypt for the first time. Moreover, an MoU on maritime cooperation and an agreement in the military field were signed with the Russian Federation in February 2015. In 2017, MoUs were also signed with Jordan and Austria respectively. Within the framework of the above defence-related agreements, several bilateral cooperation programmes were signed and implemented with many states. Special mention should be made to the bilateral military programmes with the UK. During the 2010s, several trilateral cooperation programmes were also signed and implemented such as: Cyprus-Greece-Armenia, Cyprus-Greece-Israel, and Cyprus-Greece-Egypt (see Appendix, Table 13.5). Additionally, the RoC signed SOFAs (agreements that define the rights and obligations of each country's military personnel during joint activities) with all the states that participate in UNIFCIL (2006) as well as with the state of Israel (2016).[8]

Defence Attaches

The MoD of the RoC has gradually expanded the network of DAs over the last decade. In 2001 it appointed a Military Representative (initially with the status of observer until full accession) to the EU Military Committee (EUMC). The same officer was also appointed as a DA in Belgium.[9] In 2004, a military representative was sent to the Organization for Security and Cooperation in Europe (OSCE) in Vienna and was also given the duties of the DA in Austria. Therefore, the appointment of the first two DAs was complementary to their main duties as military representatives to the EUMC and the OSCE respectively.

The next DAs were appointed to Russia and France as the two states have been traditional providers of the RoC military arsenal, mainly with the provision of military materials, when many other western countries were refusing to provide materials to the RoC due to the arms embargo. In 2008 the RoC appointed a DA in Russia, who was also accredited in Armenia.[10] The DA in France was appointed from August 2009 until June of 2013, and it was not replaced due to financial constraints. The following appointment of a DA was in 2010 to Greece with accreditation in Bulgaria and Romania as well, two countries with which the RoC was cooperating within the framework of the HELBROC EU battle group (an acronym for Hellas, Bulgaria, Romania, and Cyprus, consisting of military units from these countries). The DA position in Greece was paused in

---

[8] See in Appendix: Table 13.4.

[9] The researcher has been informed by the Department of Defence Diplomacy, Ministry of Defence, Republic of Cyprus.

[10] In January 2017, the term of the DA expired, and the position was not replaced.

2014 due to budgetary cuts as was the case with France. In 2011, the defence attaché of Austria was also accredited in Slovenia, Slovakia, and Croatia.

During the period between 2014 and 2017, the DA network of the RoC expanded significantly both in European and neighbouring states revealing the new defence diplomacy orientation of the RoC. Initially, a DA was appointed to the UK in February 2017 with accreditation in Ireland. It was the first time that a Cypriot officer was tasked as a DA of the RoC in the UK. Moreover, the position of DA in France was filled again with accreditation in Italy. In November 2017, a DA was appointed to Egypt with accreditation in Jordan as well. During the same period, a DA was also appointed to Israel. Recently, the RoC also appointed a military attaché to the US in 2019. Thus, as it is obvious, the DA network of the RoC developed and expanded significantly as Nicosia maintains DAs in key European states and in most of its neighbouring states. The expanded network of Cypriot DAs demonstrates the Republic's growing understanding of the positive impact that this aspect of defence diplomacy can have.

High-Level Foreign Visits

High-level Foreign Visits by Defence Ministers or other High-Ranking Military and Civilian Officers help in boosting connections, thereby creating meaningful strategic and political dialogue. The RoC Ministers of Defence used to visit Greece almost exclusively during the 1980s and 1990s due to the close links between the two states. In recent years, however, the various Ministers of Defence of the RoC have carried out numerous foreign visits to other states as well as to different international organisations. Moreover, regular foreign visits are conducted by the General Chief of the National Guard, the permanent secretary of the MoD, and other high-ranking military officers, something that was not observed previously. The rise in the percentages of high-level foreign visits by defence ministers and other high-ranking military personnel is an important indicator of the new extrovert approach on the RoC's part.

Joint Exercises

Joint military drills and search and rescue exercises with other countries are a valuable instrument and make a significant contribution towards achieving defence diplomacy aims. The RoC used to conduct joint military drills almost exclusively with Greece, especially in the mid-1990s, under the Unified Military Defence Doctrine, or the Doctrine of the Joint Defence Area, that was declared in November 1993 and aimed at creating a Single Defence Space for the two countries; a policy that was essentially abandoned in early 2000s. After 2010, and especially after the signing of many defence-related agreements with several countries, the MoD along with its operational arm, the National Guard, started to conduct many joint exercises for both military and search and rescue purposes, both at the bilateral and multilateral level. Bilaterally, the National Guard has conducted many joint military exercises, mainly with the states of Greece, Israel, Egypt, Jordan, Lebanon but also with France, Austria, Armenia, USA and the UK.

One of the large-scale annual military exercises where the National Guard participates is that with Israel called ONESILOS–GEDEON, within the framework of the Annual Military Cooperation Program between the RoC and the State of Israel. The exercise scenario includes aircraft flights, air combat exercises, as well as attacks of specific targets at low and high altitudes and the deployment of air defence forces (Ministry of Defence 2020). Another important military exercise with Israel is called IASON in the field of tactical air operations, and the military exercise KINYRAS-SAUL which concerns the joint training of the Special Forces of the two countries, with simultaneous operation of the Control and Information Management System (Papaioakeim 2018, 101). A military exercise with high importance is that with France named TALOS, where the response of the air defence system of the RoC is evaluated and the personnel of the National Guard is trained in realistic conditions (Ministry of Defence 2021). Since 2015, the air force of the National Guard takes part in the multinational military exercise INIOHOS, that takes place every year in Greece with the participation of armed forces elements from Greece, the US, Canada, Cyprus, Israel, Slovenia, Spain, and the United Arab Emirates (UAE) (*Cyprus Mail* 2021). In addition, staff from the National Guard participate regularly in various military exercises abroad, via the participation of the RoC in the EU Battlegroups and the European Defence Agency.

In the search and rescue field, the MoD organises two annual, multinational exercises. A special role in the search and rescue exercises is carried out by the Joint Rescue Coordination Centre, which is the coordination agency. The first is ARGONAUT (since 2011), a multinational, joint civil-military operation that encompasses potential scenarios in terms of humanitarian aid, search and rescue, and methods of facing asymmetric threats through joint action with another state (Ministry of Defence 2012). NEMESIS is the second multinational cooperative initiative, which started in 2013. This exercise's main aim is to strengthen cooperation and coordination between the relevant agencies of the RoC and neighbouring friendly nations in the domain of emergencies on merchant ships or on oil/gas platforms, or other situations demanding a humanitarian response in the Eastern Mediterranean. A new initiative is the quadrilateral search and rescue exercise among Cyprus, Greece, France, and Italy, as part of the Quadripartite Initiative codenamed QUAD-EUNOMIA. The first exercise took place within Cyprus' EEZ in August 2020 and included a wide range of activities, including joint naval exercises and rescue search exercises (In-Cyprus 2020). In addition, several trilateral search and rescue exercises are conducted with France and Italy (Ministry of Defence 2021). The RoC also takes part (since 2014) in the annual aeronautical exercise NOBLE DINA with forces from Greece, France, the US, and Israel—the host country. The exercise includes various activities among them advanced manoeuvres and formations, escorts, tactical game, anti-submarine warfare, and aeronautical cooperation, as well as a search and rescue exercise (In-Cyprus 2021).

Furthermore, many search and rescue exercises are also conducted on a bilateral level, independently with France, Italy, the UK, Greece, Israel, and the United States. Indicative is the spectacular upward trend of the number of search and rescue exercises conducted yearly. From two (2) exercises conducted in 2011, the number jumped to thirty-one (31) in 2019 and dropped to twenty (20) in 2020 due to COVID-19 pandemic.[11] In general terms, the participation in and organisation of many joint military drills and search and rescue exercises bilaterally and multilaterally is another important indicator that RoCs' defence diplomacy is maturing.

---

[11] The researcher was informed by the Joint Rescue Coordination Centre, Ministry of Defence, Republic of Cyprus.

Participation in UN and EU Peacekeeping Missions

The RoC and particularly the MoD had never participated in any peacekeeping mission until 2006 when it started participating symbolically in the United Nations (UN) peacekeeping operation UNIFIL (United Nations Interim Force in Lebanon) with three military officers (National Guard). Beyond UN peacekeeping operations, the RoC has also participated in several peacekeeping missions under the auspices of the EU. RoC military officers participated both in the Operational and Tactical Headquarters of the missions. The last participation of Cypriot officers was in two operations. First, in the autonomous EU military operation EUNAVFOR ATALANTA that combats piracy off the coast of Somalia since 2008 with one officer at the Operational Headquarters (OHQ) in Northwood, England. Second, in the EUNAVFOR MED SOPHIA operation in the Southern Central Mediterranean, since 2015, in which the Republic participates with one officer at the Operational Headquarters (OHQ) in Rome.[12]

Provision of Facilities

Provision of facilities is the most significant parameter of the RoC's defence diplomacy for it is the most important comparative advantage the country has due to its geostrategic position. The RoC has provided military and other facilities to other states in many cases. In 2006, during the Lebanon Crisis, for example, the RoC made available to the peacekeeping force the ports of Larnaca and Limassol, the Andreas Papandreou military airbase in Paphos and its infrastructure for encampment and medical treatment (Ministry of Defence 2012). It also provided its facilities in 2013, since an agreement was ratified between the RoC and the UN Organization for the Prohibition of Chemical Weapons for the establishment of a supportive base on the territory of Cyprus and the provision of facilities to ensure the safe presence and conduct of the joint mission that monitored the destruction of Syrian chemical weapons stockpiles (SigmaLive 2013).

---

[12] On the participation of the RoC in EU missions, the author was informed by the Department of Defence Diplomacy and International Relations of the Ministry of Defence, Republic of Cyprus.

After the explosion of August 2020 in Beirut, the activities of UNIFIL have been transferred to Limassol. The decision was made after the huge disaster suffered in the port of Beirut. The request was submitted by the Permanent Representation of Cyprus in New York and was immediately accepted. Former Foreign Minister Nikos Christodoulides described the selection of Cyprus as a UNIFIL base by the UN as a vote of confidence (Alpha News 2020). On a bilateral level, the RoC has agreed with many states to provide facilities for humanitarian purposes. Dozens of landings and port calls are hosted by Cypriot ports and airports by foreign states every year. Indicatively, and as stated in a public statement by Foreign Minister, Christodoulides in 2017, "the Republic provided airport facilities in 672 cases and docking facilities in another 225 in our ports". Moreover, in 2018 "facilities were provided in 212 cases at airports and 207 in ports" (Press Information Office 2018).

Exploiting New Opportunities

The maturity of the RoC's defence diplomacy is also obvious in other areas beyond the qualitative and/or quantitative analysis of defence diplomacy activities. The country was able to respond to the various changes and exploit the new opportunities in the international and regional system. Two examples are indicative: the tensions between Turkey and neighbouring states had a positive effect, since the RoC capitalised the opportunity and, among other things, established defence relations with its neighbouring countries; also, the RoC exploited the unstable regional environment and promoted itself as a stable pillar and reliable partner in the area, cooperating in the defence sector with many countries with interests in the broader region. It must be noted that the ability to respond effectively in international affairs needs real depth of understanding of the fluctuations of international politics and current affairs. The ability thus far of the RoC to understand, react, and capitalise on new opportunities indicates maturity in its defence diplomacy and beyond.

Maturity of the Elites

All the above might not have had the same impact had the RoC's political and military leaders not developed a more rounded view of international politics and foreign policy that resulted in changes in the state's foreign policy approaches. One of the new approaches had to do with the Cyprus Problem which, indeed, was and still remains the issue that almost monopolises the RoC's foreign policy. However, more recently, engagement in other foreign policy domains is not excluded as it used to be the case in the past. Likewise, the military elites of the Republic realised the benefits of international extroversion and thus abandoned their isolationist and highly introvert policy. Introversion used to dominate the MoD due to the Turkish occupation on the island, but since the 2004 EU accession, as argued in this paper, a more extrovert policy has been pursued.

Another new approach of the RoC's foreign policy and, by extension, defence diplomacy, was the gradual disengagement from the excessive ideological anchorages of the past by some political elites that were in the power. Under the presidency of leftist Dimitris Christofias[13] (2008–2013), for example, defence relations were initiated with Israel without, however, relinquishing the sympathetic stance towards Palestine. In a similar way, Nicos Anastasiades,[14] President since 2013, was elected on a pro-western platform but has sought to strike a balance between the EU/US and Russia (Tziarras 2019). This RoC foreign policy approach in general and defence diplomacy in particular shows that these governments took decisions that were not merely based on their ideological preferences but also on the overall interests of the state; a fact that demonstrates signs of maturity.

From the above examination of the defence diplomacy components, it can be seen that the RoC's defence diplomacy has grown significantly, with some positive developments. The country expanded defence relations with several other European nations and kept close links with traditional allies inside and outside the EU, while establishing new relationships with most of its neighbours. These examples illustrate that the RoC's defence diplomacy has progressed to a more advanced and dynamic phase, displaying signs of maturity.

---

[13] Dimitris Christofias used to be the General Secretary of the communist AKEL (the Progressive Party of Working People).

[14] Nicos Anastasiades used to be the president of the conservative DISY (Democratic Rally). He was first elected in February 2013 and got re-elected in February 2018.

The Limits of Maturity

Undoubtedly, there are many and solid arguments that could be made regarding the maturation of the RoC's defence diplomacy. However, at the same time it can be claimed that despite the dynamism and signs of maturity in terms of its defence foreign relations, the RoC has still some way to before its foreign defence relations can be regarded as solid and fully mature. According to one definition, maturity is when someone/something reaches a very advanced or developed form or state (Wechsler 1950). As such there is a widespread consensus within the RoC defence establishment that the field of defence diplomacy has not yet reached the most advanced stage in its evolution process. The intense defence diplomacy efforts of the RoC were initiated very recently—essentially during the 2010s—and they, thus, need more time to mature. Additionally, although institutions were established for the exercise of defence diplomacy, there is much progress to be made for them to mature and grow in experience.

As argued in this paper, a significant indicator of the level of maturity is the quality and quantity of defence diplomacy initiatives. In the case of the RoC, several defence diplomacy activities have been undertaken. When compared to the situation of previous years, the RoCs defence diplomacy has made major steps forward. And yet, there are many other areas that have not been adequately developed (e.g. participation in peacekeeping missions abroad) or are underdeveloped. A significant criterion of a mature policy is the establishment of well defined aims and targets that match the needs and capabilities of a state. In the case of the RoC, there is an obvious focus on establishing relations with western European countries and of course with neighbouring states. Beyond the fact that this point to well defined aims in defence diplomacy, there are still certain things that are not clear, for there is a lack of a written defence grand strategy, e.g. a "white paper", that would specify the direction and aims of defence diplomacy. This fact often limits the effectiveness and efficiency of Cypriot defence diplomacy.

Considering all the above factors and components, one could argue that the RoC's defence diplomacy is currently in a process of transition: It is better organised, entering a dynamic phase, demonstrating at least some maturity. But it still has some distance to go before it can be considered solid and fully mature. From this perspective, the current defence diplomacy of RoC could be characterised as a *dynamic policy in the process of maturation*.

Conclusion

This paper set out to discuss some of the components that determine a mature defence diplomacy. As noted, this was a first attempt and further research needs to be done. However, the significance of this paper's attempt lies in that it sought to analyse a dimension that has hitherto been absent from the literature. Moreover, the paper has investigated the RoC's defence diplomacy between 2004 and 2020. Particularly, it analysed the various circumstances that played a role in the emergence of defence diplomacy, but mainly scrutinised the different components of the RoC's defence diplomacy and considered whether and to what extent it has matured since 2004. The main argument is that the RoC's defence diplomacy is still in transition. On the one hand, it has reached a more dynamic, targeted phase and shows many signs of maturity. But, on the other hand, and even though the RoC has shown much dynamism in its foreign defence relations, there is still much ground to be covered before the RoC's defence diplomacy fully matures. It is therefore *dynamic* but still *in the process of maturation*.

Acknowledgements The data was collected from: (a) the Department of Defence Diplomacy and International Relations, Ministry of Defence, RoC (b) Press Releases that were published to the Website of the Ministry of Defence, RoC and (c) official and/or unofficial interviews with military officers of the National Guard and political leaders (in the field of defence). The author would like to thank the Ministry of Defence of the RoC and particularly the Department of Defence Diplomacy and International Relations and the Cyprus Joint Rescue Coordination Center (JRCC) for their valuable help during his research. Special thanks go also to all the interviewees (named and anonymous) for their willingness and contribution.

Appendix

Table 13.1 Bilateral Defence/Military Agreements on Defence Related Issues

Year	Agreement
1996 (updated and modified in 1999, 2002, and 2015)	Agreement between the Government of the Republic of Cyprus and the Government of the **Russian Federation** for Military and Technical Cooperation
2002 (activated in 2006)	Agreement between the Republic of Cyprus and the **Republic of Armenia** for Military and Technical Co-operation
2007 (updated and modified in 2017)	Agreement between the Republic of Cyprus and the Government of the **French Republic** on issues concerning Defence Cooperation
2010	Agreement between the Republic of Cyprus and the **Government of Serbia** on issues concerning Defence Cooperation
2011	Agreement between the Republic of Cyprus and the **Government of Montenegro** on issues concerning Defence Cooperation
2011	Agreement between the Republic of Cyprus and the **Government of Ukraine** on issues concerning Defence Cooperation
2012	Agreement between the Republic of Cyprus and the **Government of Czech Republic** on issues concerning Defence Cooperation
2013	Agreement between the Republic of Cyprus and the **Government of Poland** on issues concerning Defence Cooperation
2013	Agreement between the Republic of Cyprus and the **Government of Italy** on issues concerning Defence Cooperation

Table 13.2 Bilateral Memoranda of Understanding (MoUs) on Defence Related Issues

Year	MoU
1999	South Africa
2000 (updated in 2014)	United Kingdom
2008	Greece
2009	Greece
2012	Israel
2013	Lebanon, Greece
2014	Greece
2015	Russia, Egypt
2017	Jordan, Austria
2021	United Arab Emirates

Table 13.3 Bilateral Annual / Biannual Military Cooperation Programmes

Since	Country
2012	Unite Kingdom
2013	Israel
2015	France
2015	Armenia
2015	Serbia
2016	Italy
2016	Egypt
2016	Lebanon
2017	Jordan
2017	Austria
Information not available	Germany
Information not available	Netherlands
Information not available	United Arab Emirates

Table 13.4 SOFA Agreements

Year	Agreement
2008	United States
2006	United Nations Interim Force in Lebanon (UNIFIL) (Other parties in the Agreement Germany, Denmark, France, Netherlands, Sweden, Norway)
2016	Israel

Table 13.5 Trilateral Military Cooperation Programs

Cyprus-Greece-Armenia
Cyprus-Greece-Israel
Cyprus-Greece-Egypt

The sources for the development of the above tables are listed below:

- Ministry of Defence, Republic of Cyprus, Bilateral Relations (https://mod.gov.cy/en/%CE%B4%CE%B9%CE%BC%CE%B5% CF%81%CE%B5%CE%AF%CF%82%CF%83%CF%87%CE%AD%CF% 83%CE%B5%CE%B9%CF%82.html).
- Law Commissioner Office, Bilateral Treaties (http://www.olc.gov. cy/olc/olc.nsf/All/5127B9EF26EA434EC225847300280E1F? Open Document).

References

Al Jazzera. 2013. "Envoys Recalled Amid Egypt-Turkey Spat," August 16, https://www.aljazeera.com/news/middleeast/2013/08/201381616342 1338342.html, accessed 15 June 2020.
Alpha News. 2020. "Στην Κύπρο μεταφέρονται τα πολεμικά πλοία της UNIFIL μετά από αίτημα του ΟΗΕ" [UNIFIL Warships Transferred to Cyprus After UN Request], August 10, www.alphanews.live/politics/ stin-kypro-metaferontai-ta-polemika-ploia-tis-unifil-meta-apo-aitima-toy-oie, accessed 18 April 2021.
BBC. 2013. "Egypt Expels Turkish Ambassador," November 23, http://www. bbc.com/news/world-middle-east-25066115, accessed 15 July 2020.
Buzan, Barry. 1997. "Rethinking Security After the Cold War." *Cooperation and Conflict* 32 (1): 5–28.
CNA. 2017. "First Trilateral Meeting Between Cyprus, Greece and Egypt Defence Ministers to Take Place Thursday in Larnaka," December 13, http://www.cna.org.cy/WebNews-en.aspx?a=b2c79c34eece4530a551ea2d bbafbb7e, accessed 5 May 2020.
CNA. 2017. "Cyprus and Jordan Sign Memorandum on Military Cooperation," May 23 http://www.cna.org.cy/webnews-en.aspx?a=390846c1fc8645f 3b137fffd6d0b73e6, accessed 15 April 2020.
Cottey, Andrew, and Anthony Forster. 2004. *Reshaping Defence Diplomacy: New Roles for Military Cooperation and Assistance.* Adelphi Paper 365. London: Oxford University Press.
Cyprus Mail. 2021. "Cyprus Takes Part in Multinational Military Exercise," April 16, https://cyprus-mail.com/2021/04/16/cyprus-takes-part-in-multinational-military-exercise/, accessed 18 April 2021.
DCAF. 2007. *Defence Attaches, Geneva Centre for the Democratic Control of Armed Forces.* DCAF Backgrounder Series.

Drab, Lech. 2018. "Defence Diplomacy—An Important Tool for the Implementation of Foreign Policy and Security of the State." *Security and Defence Quarterly* 20 (3): 57–71.

Forster, Larissa. 2015. "The Soft Power Currencies of US Navy Hospital Ship Missions." *International Studies Perspectives* 16 (4): 367–387.

Globes. 2012. "Israel, Cyprus Sign Defense Agreements–Reports," January 10, http://www.globes.co.il/en/article-1000714277, accessed 23 January 2020.

Gürel, Ayla, Harry Tzimitras, and Hubert Faustmann. 2016. *Global Energy and the Eastern Mediterranean*. Oslo, Nicosia, and New York: PRIO Cyprus Center.

Hillmann, Jörg, and Constantinos Hadjisavvas (eds.). 2012. *Military Capability Development in the Framework of the Common Security and Defence Policy*. Cyprus Presidency of the Council of the EU 2012/Ministry of Defence.

In-Cyprus. 2020. "Cyprus, Greece, France and Italy Hold Naval, Aerial Military Exercises," August 26, https://in-cyprus.philenews.com/cyprus-greece-france-and-italy-hold-naval-aerial-military-exercises/, accessed 1 September 2020.

In-Cyprus. 2021. "Annual Multinational Aeronautical Exercise 'NOBLE DINA-2021' Ends," March 12, https://in-cyprus.philenews.com/annual-multinational-aeronautical-exercise-noble-dina-2021-ends/, accessed 18 April 2021.

Joint Rescue Coordination Centre (JRCC). http://www.mod.gov.cy/mod/cjrcc.nsf/index_en/index_en?OpenDocument, accessed 10 May 2020.

Kariotis, Theodore. 2011. "Hydrocarbons and the Law of the Sea in the Eastern Mediterranean: Implications for Cyprus, Greece, and Turkey." *Mediterranean Quarterly* 22 (2): 45–56.

Kathimerini. 2012. "Βουλή: Επιτυχής η επίσκεψη του ΥΠΑΜ στο Ισραήλ" [Parliament: Successful Visit of MoD to Israel], January 26, http://www.kathimerini.com.cy/gr/politiki/75080/?ctype=ar, accessed 20 February 2020.

Kathimerini. 2016. "Το αεροπλανοφόρο 'Αντμιράλ Κουζνετσόφ' στέλνει στη Μεσόγειο η Ρωσία" [Aircraft Carrier Admiral Kuznetsov' Sent to Mediterranean by Russia], September 21, http://www.kathimerini.com.cy/gr/kosmos/249698/?ctype=ar, accessed 15 April 2020.

Lachowski, Zdzislaw. 2007. *Foreign Military Bases in Eurasia*. Stockholm International Peace Research Institute.

Meixner, Helen. 2005. "Gentle Warriors: Britain's Defence Diplomacy in Romania Since 1990." In *In and Out of Focus: Romania and Britain. Relations and Perspectives from 1930 to the Present*, edited by D. Deletant. Bucharest: Cavallioti.

Migdalovitz, Carol. 2010. "Israel's Blockade of Gaza, the Mavi Marmara Incident and Its Aftermath." *Congressional Research Service* (June): 1–17.

Ministerio De Defensa Espana. 2012. *Defence Diplomacy Plan*. Ministerio De Defensa Espana.

Ministry of Defence, Republic of Cyprus. 2009. *International Affairs Security and Defence*, 2nd ed.
Ministry of Defence, Republic of Cyprus. 2012. *International Affairs Security and Defence*, 4th ed.
Ministry of Defence, United Kingdom. 1998. *Strategic Defence Review: Modern Forces for the Modern World*. Whitehall. London.
Ministry of Defence. 2017. "ΔΙΕΘΝΗΣ ΑΣΚΗΣΗ ΕΡΕΥΝΑΣ-ΔΙΑΣΩΣΗΣ SAREX CYPEGYP-02/17" [International Search and Rescue Drill SAREX-CYPEGYP-2/17], http://www.mod.gov.cy/mod/mod.nsf/All/C1F 7F8ED0F953E02C2258204001FB48F?OpenDocument, accessed 10 May 2020.
Ministry of Defence. 2020. Exercise "ONESILOS-GEDEON 2020", November 19, https://mod.gov.cy/en/announcements/2020/11/19/%CE%BF%CE% BB%CE%BF%CE%BA%CE%BB%CE%AE%CF%81%CF%89%CF%83%CE%B7-% CE%AC%CF%83%CE%BA%CE%B7%CF%83%CE%B7%CF%82-%C2%AB%CE% BF%CE%BD%CE%B7%CF%83%CE%B9%CE%BB%CE%BF%CF%83-%E2%80% 93-%CE%B3%CE%B5%CE%B4%CE%B5%CF%89%CE%BD-2020%C2%BB/, accessed 13 June 2021.
Ministry of Defence. 2021. "Completion of Cyprus - France Air Defence Exercise 'TALOS 2021'," May 18, https://mod.gov.cy/en/announcem ents/2021/05/18/%CE%BF%CE%BB%CE%BF%CE%BA%CE%BB%CE%AE% CF%81%CF%89%CF%83%CE%B7-%CE%B1%CE%B5%CF%81%CE%BF%CF% 80%CE%BF%CF%81%CE%B9%CE%BA%CE%AE%CF%82-%CE%AC%CF% 83%CE%BA%CE%B7%CF%83%CE%B7-%CE%BA%CF%8D%CF%80%CF%81% CE%BF%CF%85-%E2%80%93-%CE%B3%CE%B1%CE%BB%CE%BB%CE% AF%CE%B1%CF%82-%C2%AB%CF%84%CE%B1%CE%BB%CF%89%CF%83- 2021%C2%BB/, accessed 13 June 2021.
Ministry of Defence. 2021. "International Aeronautical Exercise," April 4, https://mod.gov.cy/en/announcements/2021/05/18/%CE%BF%CE%BB% CE%BF%CE%BA%CE%BB%CE%AE%CF%81%CF%89%CF%83%CE%B7-%CE% B1%CE%B5%CF%81%CE%BF%CF%80%CE%BF%CF%81%CE%B9%CE%BA% CE%AE%CF%82-%CE%AC%CF%83%CE%BA%CE%B7%CF%83%CE%B7-% CE%BA%CF%8D%CF%80%CF%81%CE%BF%CF%85-%E2%80%93-%CE%B3% CE%B1%CE%BB%CE%BB%CE%AF%CE%B1%CF%82-%C2%AB%CF%84% CE%B1%CE%BB%CF%89%CF%83-2021%C2%BB/, accessed 13 June 2021.
Mulloy, Garren. 2007. "Japan's Defense Diplomacy and 'Cold Peace'in Asia." *Asia Journal of Global Studies* 1 (1): 2–14.
Muthanna, Brig K. A. 2011. "Military Diplomacy." *Perspectives* 5 (1): 1–15.
Naftermporiki. 2015. "Στην ανατολική Μεσόγειο θα αναπτυχθεί το γαλλικό αεροπλανοφόρο Charles de Gaulle" [French Aircraft Carrier Charles de Gaulle to Deploy to the Eastern Mediterranean], November 17, https://

www.naftemporiki.gr/story/1031527/stin-anatoliki-mesogeio-tha-anaptu xthei-to-galliko-aeroplanoforo-charles-de-gaulle, accessed 15 April 2020.
National Guard. 2017. *International Relations*, http://army.gov.cy/el/organi smos-inomenon-ethnon, accessed 10 May 2020.
Papaioakeim, Marinos. 2018. "The Rise of the Republic of Cyprus' Defence Diplomacy in its Neighbourhood." *Cyprus Review* 30 (1): 95–112.
Philenews. 2013. "ΥΠΑΜ: Στόχος η ομπρέλα ενεργειακής ασφάλειας" [MoD: An Umbrella of Energy Security Is the Aim], December 12, http://arc hive.philenews.com/el-gr/top-stories/885/175834/ypam-sto-philenews--stochos-i-omprela-energeiakis-asfaleias, accessed 15 April 2020.
Philenews. 2017. "Τεχνογνωσία και... 'Ζάσταβα' από Κύπρο προς Λίβανο" [Know-how and... 'Zastava' from Cyprus to Lebanon], October 30, www.phi lenews.com/eidiseis/politiki/article/447991/technogosia-kai-zastaba-apo-kypro-pros-libano, accessed 15 April 2020.
Plessis, Du Anton. 2008. "Defense Diplomacy: Conceptual and Practical Dimensions with Specific Reference to South Africa." *Strategic Review for Southern Africa* 30 (20): 87–19.
Press Information Office. 2018. "Γραπτή δήλωση του Κυβερνητικού Εκπροσώπου κ. Πρόδρομου Προδρόμου" [Written Statement of Government Spokesman, Mr. Prodromos Prodromou], December 5, https://www.pio. gov.cy/%CE%B1%CE%BD%CE%B1%CE%BA%CE%BF%CE%B9%CE%BD% CF%89%CE%B8%CE%AD%CE%BD%CF%84%CE%B1-%CE%AC%CF%81% CE%B8%CF%81%CE%BF.html?id=5139#flat, accessed 13 June 2021.
Proedrou, Filippos. 2012. "Re-conceptualising the Energy and Security Complex in the Eastern Mediterranean." *The Cyprus Review* 24 (2):15–28.
Reuters. 2015. "Russia, Cyprus Sign Military Deal on Use of Mediterranean Ports," February 26, https://www.reuters.com/article/us-russia-cyprus-mil itary/russia-cyprus-sign-military-deal-on-use-of-mediterranean-ports-idUSKB N0LU1EW20150226, accessed 15 April 2020
Samokhvalov, Vsevolod. 2013. "Cyprus." In *Strategic Cultures in Europe*, edited by Biehl Heiko, Giegerich Bastian, and Jonas Alexandra, 55–67. Potsdam: Springer VS.
SigmaLive. 2013. "Βάση της Αποστολής για τα χημικά της Συρίας η Κύπρος" [Cyprus Mission Base for Syria's Chemicals], October 24, http://www.sigmalive.com/news/local/72024/vasi-tis-apostolis-gia-ta-ximika-tis-syrias-i-kypros, accessed 15 April 2020.
Styan, David. 2016. "Djibouti: Small State Strategy at a Crossroads." *Third World Thematics: A TWQ Journal* 1 (1): 79–91.
Tan, See Seng, and Bhubhindar Singh. 2012. "Introduction." *Asian Security* 8 (3): 221–231.
The Daily Star. 2013. "Turkey PM blasts Egypt 'Coup' as Enemy of Democracy," July 5, http://www.dailystar.com.lb/News/Middle-East/2013/Jul-05/222

688-turkey-pm-blasts-egypt-coup-as-enemy-of-democracy.ashx, accessed 20 February 2020.

The Economist. 2012. "Israel and Cyprus – Getting Friendly," February 18, http://www.economist.com/blogs/newsbook/2012/02/israel-and-cyprus, accessed 15 April 2020.

The Jerusalem Post. 2016. "Israel's Alliance That Could Potentially Offset Enhanced Russian and Iranian Power," March 26, https://www.jpost.com/Jerusalem-Report/A-petite-entente-in-the-eastern-Mediterranean-446804, accessed 20 February 2020.

The Times of Israel. 2013. "Russia, France Deploy Warships to Eastern Mediterranean," August 29, https://www.timesofisrael.com/russia-france-deploy-warships-to-eastern-mediterranean/, accessed 15 April 2020.

Thorhallsson, Baldur. 2006. "The Size of States in the European Union: Theoretical and Conceptual Perspectives." *Journal of European Integration* 28 (1): 7–31.

Tziarras, Zenonas. 2016. "Israel-Cyprus-Greece: A 'Comfortable' Quasi-Alliance." *Mediterranean Politics* 21 (3): 407–427.

Tziarras, Zenonas. 2017. "Islamic Caliphate: A Quasi-State, a Global Security Threat." *Journal of Applied Security* Research 12 (1): 96–116.

Tziarras, Zenonas. 2019. "Cyprus's Foreign Policy in the Eastern Mediterranean and the Trilateral Partnerships: A Neoclassical Realist Approach." In *The New Geopolitics of the Eastern Mediterranean: Trilateral Partnerships and Regional Security*, edited by Zenonas Tziarras, 53–72. Nicosia: PRIO Cyprus Centre.

Vreÿ, Francois, and Nel Michelle. 2009. "Employing Armed Forces: The Rise of More Constructive and Ethical Secondary Roles." *Politeia* 28 (3): 22–40.

Wallin, Matthew. 2014. Military Public Diplomacy: How the Military Influences Foreign Audiences. *American Security Project*. White Paper.

Wechsler, David. 1950. "Intellectual Development and Psychological Maturity." *Child Development* 21 (1): 45–50.

Winger, Gregory. 2014. "The Velvet Gauntlet: A Theory of Defence Diplomacy." In *What Ideas Do?*, edited by Agata Lisiak and Natalie Smolenski. Vienna: IWM Junior Visiting Fellows Conference.

INTERVIEWS

Interview no. 1: Defence Attache (anonymous country) in the Republic of Cyprus. (December 21, 2018).

Interview no. 2: Georgios, Georgiou, Former Head of Defence Diplomacy and International Relations Department (2008–2014), Ministry of Defence, RoC (March 6, 2018).

Interview no. 3: Photis, Photiou, Former Ministrer of Defence, Republic of Cyprus (2013/14) (May 10, 2018).

CHAPTER 14

Foreign Policy Maturity and Grand Strategy: The Way Forward for the Republic of Cyprus

Zenonas Tziarras

INTRODUCTION

This chapter concludes the volume and has two main objectives: (a) to assess the "maturity" of the Republic of Cyprus' (RoC) foreign policy, and (b) to examine whether the RoC has—or is able to develop—grand strategic capacities. The first part of the chapter discusses the definition and components of grand strategy and identifies the overlaps and differences between grand strategy and mature foreign policy. This discussion sets the ground for the next section that—through a critical review of the limited literature—examines whether the RoC has a grand strategy or could develop a grand strategy while the resolution of the Cyprus Problem is pending. Further delving into this analysis, the following section assesses the overall foreign policy (im)maturity of the RoC. By

Z. Tziarras (✉)
PRIO Cyprus Centre, Nicosia, Cyprus
e-mail: zenonas@prio.org

© The Author(s), under exclusive license to Springer Nature Switzerland AG 2022
Z. Tziarras (ed.), *The Foreign Policy of the Republic of Cyprus*, Reform and Transition in the Mediterranean,
https://doi.org/10.1007/978-3-030-91177-5_14

extension, it explores whether the RoC can develop a grand strategy and, if so, under what conditions. The concluding section draws parallels between the RoC's foreign policymaking and its approach to the resolution of the Cyprus Problem—two issues that are intertwined.

The chapter argues that the Cyprus Problem has been inevitably and negatively affecting grand strategic formulation in the RoC even as it often complicates and hinders the country's day-to-day foreign policy and diplomatic practice. From this perspective, the popular understanding that the RoC can have long-term foreign policies or a grand strategy without the resolution of the Cyprus Problem is questioned. At the same time, it is argued that the RoC should not stop engaging in capacity building and a pro-active foreign policy while having the resolution of the Cyprus Problem as a strategic objective. Among other things, this will allow the country to reach its full potential in the region and the world. However, to achieve that, RoC governments will need to make difficult and critical decisions—necessary for the country's next steps—both regarding national strategy and national consensus.

ON GRAND STRATEGY AND FOREIGN POLICY MATURITY

Before assessing the maturity of the RoC's foreign policy and its grand strategic capacities, it is necessary to examine the concept of grand strategy and revisit the concept of foreign policy "maturity". The overlaps (and differences) between the two concepts will facilitate the analysis that follows.

Grand Strategy and Small States

Although the concept of grand strategy never really went out of fashion, it seems to be making a comeback in the twenty-first century. Grand strategy has been for years a contested concept and its definitions have been broadened enough "to include periods of peace as well as war" and thus peacetime objectives such as "political, economic, and diplomatic" (Dueck 2006, 9). This notion should not come as a surprise, we can also find it in more classical writings such as those of war theorist Carl von Clausewitz. In one of the most popular definitions of strategy Clausewitz holds that, it is "the use of engagement for the purpose of war" (Clausewitz 1989, 128, 177). However, he also writes "that war is not merely an act of policy but a true political instrument, a continuation of political intercourse, carried on with other means" (Clausewitz 1989, 87). If the purpose of war is by definition political (because war is politics) then engagement in warfare is not necessarily the only way for strategy to achieve the political end.[1] Strategy could exist outside the framework of warfare as well, not just within it. Against this background, a broader definition of strategy, not restricted to warfare, would be permissible: strategy is the use of available means for the achievement of specific ends.

Edward Luttwak supports that grand strategy is "the everyday form of strategy" that continues "even in the absence of warfare" (Luttwak 1987, 177). Bridging these two definitions, Paul Kennedy suggests that "the balancing of ends and means both in peacetime and in wartime" is grand strategy (Kennedy 1991, 4). In an older approach, Basil Liddell Hart provides a wartime definition of grand strategy that defines it as the "co-ordinat[ion] and direct[ion of] all the resources of a nation, or band of a nations, towards the attainment of the political object of the war" (Hart 1991, 322). Regardless of its wartime focus, this approach remains similar to the previous definitions in that it emphasizes the coordination of ends and means. Yet, beyond the core relationship between ends and means, the concept of grand strategy also involves "some willingness and ability to think about the future in terms of the goals of a political entity" (Murray 2011, 5). Or, as Lobell et al. (2012, 15) note, "It is a future-oriented enterprise involving considerations of external threats and opportunities, as well as the specific material, political, and ideological objectives of the state."

Taking all the above into account, a working definition for the purposes of this chapter could be the following: grand strategy is the coordination and direction of all available means of a nation, or band of nations, both in peacetime and wartime, with a long-term perspective and considering external threats and opportunities, towards the attainment of political, economic, ideological, warfare, or other objectives. To be sure, the literature identifies a number of factors that need to be considered for the better pursuit and application of grand strategy, such as the good management of resources, the skilful use of diplomacy to improve a "nation's

---

[1] A similar idea is put forward by Liddell Hart who argued that Clausewitz's definition of strategy "narrows the definition of 'strategy' to the pure utilization of battle, thus conveying the idea that battle is the only means to the strategical end," see Hart (1991, 319).

position-and prospects of victory-through gaining allies, winning the support of neutrals, and reducing the number of one's enemies," and the need for popular legitimacy vis-à-vis a state's endeavours (Kennedy 1991, 4–5). What is more, a grand strategy must be able to assess in real time the constantly changing and unexpected environment in which it operates. As Murray (2011, 5) puts it, "simply thinking about developing a concept of grand strategy demands not only a deep understanding of the past but also a comprehensive and realistic understanding of the present."

Another issue that begs resolution is the fact that the concept of grand strategy has by and large been applied to great powers throughout history such as Britain, the Roman Empire, the Byzantine Empire, China, the Soviet Union/Russia, Germany, and the United States (US) instead of smaller states. However, as Kennedy writes if in a short endnote, "No doubt it is theoretically possible for a small state to develop a grand strategy, but the latter is generally understood to imply the endeavors of a power with extensive (i.e., not just local) interests and obligations, to reconcile its means and its ends" (Kennedy 1991, 186n18). This might be because of how smaller states are more susceptible to external pressures—in relation to great powers—and possibly dependent on greater states in such a degree that a solid, long-term grand strategy becomes more difficult for them to develop and sustain. However, more recent research has expanded the study of grand strategy "beyond the well-trodden examples of a few great powers" and examined how "a variety of states (both 'great' and 'small') device and execute grand strategies" (Balzacq et al. 2019, 1). Such cases include the Nordic countries (Neumann and Heikka 2005), Israel (Shamir 2019), Saudi Arabia (Hetou 2019), and more recently Cyprus (Zachariades and Petrikkos 2020).

Certainly, much can be said about the "smallness" of a country. A small state could, for example, be defined as that which is too weak to project (material) power, impose its will in the international system as well as protect its national interests (Vaicekauskaitė 2017, 8). However, the strategic environment of states is also important in assessing their size relative to that of other states. As Vaicekauskaitė (2017, 8) rightly notes, "size does not prevent small states from being active or exercising their influence in international politics. Sweden, Finland, and Denmark, despite being small, are active participants of international military operations." Likewise, although the RoC may indeed have very limited power capabilities, it has managed to acquire a rather influential—and disproportionate to its size—role in the Eastern Mediterranean during the latter half of the 2010s by capitalizing on certain developments and contributing to the emergence of inter-state networks of cooperation (Tziarras 2019, 2016). There are, therefore, reasons, to explore the RoC's grand strategic capacities and prospects.

Foreign Policy (Maturity) vs Grand Strategy

Similarities as well as significant differences can be found between the concepts of foreign policy (maturity) and grand strategy. Simply put, foreign policy can refer to relations between states (Leira 2019, 187) or state behaviour in the international system (Jensen 1982, 9). The study or analysis of foreign policy (i.e. Foreign Policy Analysis, FPA) deals with how foreign policies are shaped and why certain foreign policy decisions are made or not (Hudson 2007, 3–7; Jensen 1982, 4–11). Foreign policy maturity as defined in the introductory chapter of this volume is when a state has clearly defined foreign policy objectives that match its needs, interests, and capabilities. In addition, a mature foreign policy has a well weighted strategy and is supported by the appropriate state institutions and policymaking mechanisms.

Immediately, the word "strategy" stands out as something common between foreign policy and grand strategy. Also evident is that in both cases, certain institutional and other capacities are needed. However, these do not mean that foreign policy and grand strategy are one and the same. After all, it would not be difficult to argue that all (state) policies (e.g. military, economic, cultural, educational) need a strategy, namely a purpose and a plan, as well as institutional capacities. From this perspective it seems that foreign policy, along with other policies, are encompassed by grand strategy. In the same vein, Paul Kennedy (1991, 5) suggests that "The crux of grand strategy lies therefore in *policy*, that is, in the capacity of the nation's leaders to bring together all of the elements, both military and nonmilitary, for the preservation and enhancement of the nation's long-term (that is, in wartime *and* peacetime) best interests." Therefore, grand strategy cannot be restricted to foreign policy. If we consider that grand strategy, according to our above-mentioned definition, coordinates all available means with a long-term perspective towards the attainment of a variety of objectives, then it must also incorporate crucial policy sectors such as defence and economy.

Given that foreign policy is distinct and separate from other policies, notwithstanding potential overlaps, discussions about foreign policy maturity and grand strategy, respectively, cannot be one and the same. However, the extent to which a foreign policy is mature is also indicative of whether the necessary conditions exist for a state to have a successful grand strategy—or have a grand strategy at all. That is because some of the elements of a grand strategy and a mature foreign policy overlap, especially as regards the need for appropriate institutions, defined objectives, and strategic plan. Through a review of different opinions in the literature, the next section examines whether the RoC has or can have a grand strategy.

Does or Can the RoC Have a Grand Strategy?

Can the RoC have a grand strategy? Theoretically, yes. Practically, the answer is more complicated. In the very limited literature and public discussion about the RoC's grand strategy, one can find two main schools of thought: (a) those who argue that the RoC *does* have a grand strategy, and (b) those who believe that the RoC *can develop* a grand strategy by utilizing certain means and power components. The second school is certainly more popular. Within the first school of thought, there is the opinion that the RoC has either always had a grand strategy or developed one in response to Turkish aggression. For example, Nikos Lygeros argues that the RoC's endeavour to delimit its Exclusive Economic Zone (EEZ) with neighbouring states and search for natural resources in the sea during the 2000s was the culmination of the RoC's grand strategy. In his words, "Cyprus' initiative is not a mindless move […] Nor is it a tactical move, as some experts believe. In reality, this initiative is merely the rational implementation of a grand strategy that was birthed with the need to exist of a state that has suffered an invasion and still withstands even now an occupation" (Lygeros 2012, 183–184). In 2019, Lygeros insisted on this view saying that through developments in the EEZ, the RoC's grand strategy in relation to the island's liberation from Turkish occupation is unfolding. And went on to argue that once a series of drillings for natural gas are realized in the RoC's EEZ along with the extraction of natural gas and the construction of a Liquefied Natural Gas (LNG) plant, the RoC will have the "energy background for a change of cycle at the strategic level" (Lygeros 2019).

This view holds that the exploitation of natural resources will enhance not only the RoC's internal balancing efforts (through the strengthening of its national power components), but also its external balancing efforts by attracting international interests and allowing Nicosia to form strong alliances and partnerships. The strategic objective of course is to counterbalance Turkey and, ultimately, liberate Cyprus from Turkey by shifting the power balances and applying pressure on the latter. While national security, energy security, state survival, and foreign policy can be parts of a grand strategy, the notion that the ultimate goal of a grand strategy is the resolution of the Cyprus Problem is very limiting. It does not see beyond the resolution of the conflict. What would Cyprus' purpose be after liberation? It does not explain how the new state of affairs will look like or how Turkey-Cyprus relations would develop. Nor does it explain the role (if any) that Turkish-Cypriots will have in these developments. Lastly, it does not adequately substantiate how this particular approach to internal and external balancing will yield the desired results.

A similar approach is adopted by Alexandros Zachariades and Petros Petrikkos who argue that "offshore natural resources can act as structural modifiers" since they enabled the RoC to form partnerships that provide support in its antagonism with Turkey (Zachariades and Petrikkos 2020, 124). Moreover, they hold the view that the RoC has had some sort of a grand strategy since its establishment: "Cypriot FP [foreign policy] grand strategy has changed a great deal since the nascence of the island-state in 1960. Nonetheless, the backbone of the state's grand strategy and its aims have remained unaltered; a solution to the Cyprus Problem, the removal of Turkish troops from the island and the non-recognition of the TRNC" (Zachariades and Petrikkos 2020, 123). The authors seem to conflate foreign policy with grand strategy without treating the two terms as separate or explaining the way in which they are associated. Nevertheless, they, too, support that the resolution of the Cyprus Problem and the riddance of Turkish occupation have been the primary objectives of the RoC's grand strategy, albeit pursued in a more "polythematic" rather than "monothematic" way.

At the same time, they hold that "Cyprus is in need of a grand strategy that acts as a theoretical tool that complements foreign, defence, and security strategy" (Zachariades and Petrikkos 2020, 94). Leaving aside the fact that foreign, defence, and security strategies are encompassed by grand strategy rather than complemented by it, the question remains: how is this grand strategy articulated by the RoC? Certainly, there is no such document, be it for grand strategy or National Security Strategy (NSS) for that matter. The authors acknowledge the lack of an institutionalized grand strategy but analyse the RoC's foreign policy in grand strategic terms.

The overarching issue here is similar to that encountered in Lygeros' argument, though Zachariades and Petrikkos acknowledge the limitations of the RoC and note that success in foreign policy is conditional on a number of factors.

The second school of thought revolves around the idea that the RoC can and should develop a grand strategy. Most authors in this category focus on how Cyprus could increase its material power capabilities and institutional capacities as well as on the linkage between means and ends. Although not specifically referring to grand strategy, former chief of the RoC armed forces, General Phoivos Klokkaris, suggests that the RoC should develop a security strategy to balance the Turkish threat. To that end, he suggests (Klokkaris 2016, 4) that the RoC should strengthen its internal (e.g. policymaking and security institutions, strategic documents, and defence capabilities) and external components (e.g. international alliances, role in international organizations, and cooperation with international hydrocarbon companies). Klokkaris' suggestions are correct in the context of a (grand or security) strategy, but the objective—though justified—is limited. In other words, it lacks a true long-term perspective that goes beyond Turkey and the Cyprus Problem. A similar approach can be found in Michalis Kontos' study on the RoC strategies of survival. Kontos suggests a number of internal and external capacity building strategies that would serve the development of a grand strategy of prosperity and survival for the next years. This otherwise comprehensive and multidimensional study is still confined to survival in the context of the unresolved Cyprus conflict or the efforts for dealing with it. Thus, there are limitations to the long-term aspect of the strategy as well.

A document by the Symmachia Politon (Citizens Alliance) political party offers a somewhat different take. It suggests that the resolution of the Cyprus Problem should not in itself be a strategic objective but a means to the strategic end of liberation from Turkish occupation. In turn, according to the document, this strategic end should serve three ultimate (or grand) strategic objectives: the survival of Cypriot Hellenism, the safeguarding of the interests of the RoC's citizens, and the creation of an EU member state (RoC) that will be effective and active (Symmachia Politon 2015, 5, 64–68). There are two fundamental problems with this approach. First, the resolution of the Cyprus Problem cannot be considered a means (regardless of the RoC's position on the matter) because its content is not yet certain and will likely be a product of negotiations—if and when it comes about. How can a strategy take a means as a given for the accomplishment of ends if the means is uncertain, fluid, and there is no indication as to when it will be available? Second, the ultimate objectives are very similar to the RoC's official negotiation objectives regarding the accomplishment of the strategic end, namely the liberation of the island (or, in diplomatic language, the resolution of the conflict). Moreover, as Symmachia Politon acknowledges, the ultimate objectives are to be pursued through the settlement of the Cyprus conflict. What is then the fundamental difference between the ultimate objectives and the end of settlement? And how could one strategize regarding the ultimately objectives if the achievement of the intermediate strategic end is in limbo?

Others are more specific, arguing that Cyprus' natural gas should be central to the formation of a grand strategy. For example, Member of Parliament with Democratic Rally (DISY), Nikos Tornaritis, argued that the prospects created with the discovery of hydrocarbons off Cyprus should be incorporated into "a multileveled framework within which Cyprus will plan and implement a grand strategy" (Tornaritis 2013). Similarly, Nikos Panayiotides suggested that the natural gas should be pivotal in any grand strategic planning, adding that it should be the "principal axis" of a Cypriot grand strategy (Panayiotides 2014). Both authors use the concept of grand strategy uncritically, taking as a granted that the RoC could have a grand strategy and that natural gas can be central to it, without considering the complications that the Cyprus conflict may create in the process. Spyros Litsas is more thorough in his approach proposing a "smart grand strategy" that will allow the RoC to "upgrade its role and presence in the region" based on the incorporation of smart power, flexible bureaucracy, the capacity of facing the sharp power of other factors, and the support of a realistic narrative with international appeal (Litsas 2019). As good as this concept is, it still bypasses the extreme systemic pressures that the RoC faces as a country under occupation and the disadvantageous position this puts it in vis-à-vis the development of a (smart) grand strategy conceived independently from the conflict's imperatives.

Constantinos Adamides captures these complexities well in his discussion of a prospective RoC NSS. On the one hand, he acknowledges that it is normal and necessary for "a state facing an overarching threat" (i.e. Turkey and the Turkish occupation) to "formulate its security strategies around a single source of threat." On the other hand, he explains that "this 'over-focus' on a single issue, as necessary as it may be, may lead to an insufficient NSS in terms of breadth … or in terms of the quality of the state security structure" (Adamides 2019, 92). This could be applied to the concept of grand strategy as well. Putting aside questions on smallness and capabilities, any grand strategic planning by the RoC will stumble on the intervening variable of the conflict's *status quo* (the overarching threat). It is of course necessary for the RoC to broaden its strategic purview beyond the Cyprus Problem, but the latter remains an objective obstacle that cannot be ignored for a multitude of reasons. Even in the scenario where grand strategy is temporal—or transitional—and has the settlement of the Cyprus conflict as its ultimate objective, the outcome is not guaranteed because it will likely be affected by an unfavourable balance of power and various other factors over which the RoC has little or no control. Drawing on this discussion, the next section provides a brief assessment of the RoC foreign policy (im)maturity and addresses its relationship to grand strategy, based both on theoretical insights and the findings of other papers in this volume. It ultimately suggests a number of conditions under which the RoC can or cannot develop a grand strategy.

THE RoC's FOREIGN POLICY MATURITY AND GRAND STRATEGIC CAPACITIES

We have so far touched upon the theoretical and practical challenges attached to the notion of an RoC grand strategy. Much of this discussion has revolved around the RoC's regional and international role, its national security, and its quest for survival against external threats—primarily Turkey. It is thus no surprise that grand strategy is often conflated with foreign policy or that related discussions—at least in the context of the RoC—are mostly focused on Nicosia's "Turkey problem" and relations with other countries. Although this is justifiable given that grand strategy determines a state's place and activity in the international system in times of peace and war, we have seen that grand strategy encompasses many other policy sectors, components, and capabilities as well. But because of the emphasis on foreign policy in the RoC context, assessing its maturity could help us understand whether the RoC can have a grand strategy from a capabilities and policy point of view.

Table 14.1 displays the chapters of this book that provided assessments on the RoC's foreign policy maturity in different sectors (e.g. energy security, defence diplomacy, international law, and international organizations). The big picture of the assessments is, perhaps unsurprisingly, neither that the RoC foreign policy is mature nor that it is entirely

Table 14.1 Assessing the RoC's foreign policy maturity

Authors	Policy sector/area	Assessment of maturity
Anna K. Prokopiou Petros Petrikkos	Foreign Policy Making Relations with the EU	Signs of maturity • Energy and Economic Cooperation; Security: *Mature* • Communications, Online Presence, EU Defence Structures, Health, Environment, and Cultural Heritage: *In a process of maturation* • Migration, Cybersecurity and Intelligence, Bureaucracy and e-databases, Civil Service: *not mature*
Alexandros Zachariades	Relations with the US	Lack of a mature policy towards the US
Costas Melakopides	Relations with Russia	Conditional maturity
Ioannis S. Ioannou	Institutional Capacities and Regional Relations	Immaturity
Nicholas Ioannides	International Law	A mature attitude in the shaping of international law
Constantinos Adamides & Josie Christodoulou	Gender Mainstreaming	In a process of maturation
Revecca Pedi & Kalliopi Chainoglou	Participation in IOs	A mature status seeking strategy in multilateral settings
Marinos Papaioakeim	Defence Diplomacy	In a dynamic phase of maturation

immature. Rather, most authors trace signs of maturity or a maturation process in different sectors, either with regard to dealing with the Cyprus Problem in various ways or in terms of developing a pro-active and far-reaching policy, beyond the Cyprus Problem. However, all of them acknowledge that foreign policymaking is tightly intertwined with the unresolved Cyprus Problem, with the latter constituting either a direct or indirect objective. In other words, very few are the times, if any, when the RoC foreign policy operates without examining how a given policy or foreign policy decision will assist the objective of conflict resolution (on beneficial terms). This is frequently highlighted by the government. For example, in late 2020, RoC Foreign Minister Nikos Christodoulides wrote that "the Cyprus problem continues to be the foremost priority, at the heart of our foreign policy, utilising all political and diplomatic tools at our disposal" (Christodoulides 2020, 2).

Having said that, the RoC Foreign Policy Executive (FPE) seems to fluctuate, and therefore so does the RoC foreign policy, between trying to find solutions, bargaining chips and leverages vis-à-vis the Cyprus Problem on the one hand, and developing a more mature foreign policy that would not be constrained by the Cyprus Problem on the other. But this creates a new problem: whenever the RoC starts to grow independent from the imperatives of the Cyprus Problem—or does not set its resolution as priority—domestic efforts for resolution become disconnected from foreign policy activism. As a result, the reality on the ground is that the strategic objective of solving the conflict is hindered, despite the positive image projected by the government, the media, and among the public about the country's new regional or international role. This is what happened when the RoC pursued an ambitious regional policy during the 2010s effectively contributing to an emerging network of international cooperation in the Eastern Mediterranean, including in the domain of energy. Although these efforts tried to develop a balancing effect against the Turkish threat, their success in that regard was minimal given that Turkey's coercive activity was not mitigated or deterred. In fact, it was exacerbated in the context of Turkey's revisionist geopolitical agenda and ushered the Eastern Mediterranean in a new round of international competition (Tziarras 2019, 2021). This had a direct effect on the Cyprus Problem dynamics, which became more complicated and difficult to manage, even as a significant shift was taking place regarding the solution model of the conflict, away from federation and towards confederation or two states (Reuters 2021).

This discussion reveals the weakness of the RoC in terms of its ability to clearly define its foreign policy strategic objectives and interests. That is, the Cyprus Problem is not consistently treated as a strategic priority despite proclamations to the contrary, while other foreign policy objectives are often not well defined—if defined at all—or not matched with the state's strategic needs and capabilities. Indeed, based on what was discussed in different chapters of this book, it could be argued that the RoC got more than it bargained for when it made its ambitious opening in the Eastern Mediterranean and beyond, given that it lacked the proper institutional capacity, strategic planning, and even a NSS. The same could be argued about the country's failure to either adopt a clear and consistent international orientation or strike a balance between the East and West.

In other words, the RoC may have demonstrated mature aspirations or made steps towards foreign policy maturity, but it did not fulfil to a satisfying degree the criteria of a mature foreign policy; namely, the clear definition of objectives and interests, a coherent strategic plan, functioning institutions, corresponding institutional capacities, and matching material capabilities or means (see, Tziarras 2022). To be sure this is not to suggest that the RoC's logic was wrong in principle, nor that the policy was not successful in contributing to regional cooperation on various levels. It was, after all, driven by necessity and facilitated by a permissive geopolitical environment. However, it has not yet produced the expected and needed results, particularly regarding Turkey and the Cyprus Problem.

Based on what has been discussed so far in this chapter, can the RoC develop a grand strategy? And if so, under what conditions? To address this question, we need to consider three elements previously analysed: (a) the role of the Cyprus Problem, (b) the articulation of strategy, and (c) the institutional and other material capabilities. It has been demonstrated that the RoC has still a long way to go in terms of the latter two. Nicosia needs to produce a document with short-term, medium-term, and long-term national-strategic objectives where possible, and a corresponding strategic plan that will consider threats, opportunities, and available means. As of 2021 such thing does not exist, at least not officially or publicly. At the same time, the RoC should invest funds and time in developing its material capabilities and institutional capacities. No strategic plan can be successful or sustainable if the state lacks the necessary capabilities and resources—or if the determined objectives are incompatible with the available means. This means that the RoC should revisit its strategic planning and capacity building on various levels such as natural resource and economic development, security, and defence capabilities, as well as institution building and development including the need for a National Security Council (NSC).

At this point, it is appropriate for this inquiry to finish the same way that it started—with the Cyprus Problem. As analysed previously, there are two ways of looking at grand strategy in relation to the Cyprus Problem: (a) as the ultimate objective of a grand strategy; or (b) as an obstacle (or a means) to the development of a grand strategy. It is here argued that to think of the Cyprus Problem as the ultimate objective of grand strategy is counterintuitive. Mainly because grand strategy encompasses a state's long-term role and position in the international system, along with various other objectives, in times of peace and war. Therefore, the objective of resolving the Cyprus Problem, though essential, is very limited/ing as an ultimate objective. Especially given that, otherwise, the RoC functions as any other state in the international arena, despite its inability to exercise sovereignty in the occupied territories of the north. Moreover, to bind grand strategy to the Cyprus Problem is to limit or complicate the strategy's long-term orientation. For how long should a grand strategy regarding the Cyprus Problem be planned—five, ten, fifty years? What happens if the resolution of the problem comes earlier or later than planned? What happens when the grand strategic objective or peripheral issues are affected by other dynamics, third parties (e.g. Turkey) or systemic factors? Certainly, a strategy must be able to adapt. Yet in this case, it seems that a RoC grand strategy focused on the Cyprus Problem would not only have to adapt; it would also be conditioned by exogenous factors that would render it unable to pursue its objectives.

The aspect of the Cyprus Problem as an obstacle or a means to grand strategy is even more important. The Cyprus Problem could be seen as a means to grand strategy because its resolution would clarify the status quo in Cyprus and the realities that grand strategic formulation would have to take into account. On the contrary, the Cyprus Problem can become an obstacle to grand strategic formulation if it remains unresolved. The reason is that, currently, there are two different entities on the island, an internationally recognized state, and a non-recognized de facto state. These two entities have different interests and visions regarding their present and future—what we could call "national" interests. Moreover, they are in conflict and competition. A truly long-term grand strategy should consider that with the settlement of the Cyprus Problem one of three things can occur: (a) a new federal state with a strong central government and weaker Greek-Cypriot and a Turkish-Cypriot constituent states, (b) a confederation (with more powers to the constituent states), and (c) a two-state solution. There are other scenarios as well, but these are the most plausible ones at this point in time.

In the case of a federal state, the "national" interest would be de facto re-defined, based on how the Greek-Cypriot and Turkish-Cypriot political and security cultures would be bridged and integrated (Sülün and

Tziarras 2017). Everything would change and therefore, whatever grand strategic calculations the RoC would have made would have to change. How do you pursue a national-strategic vision if the content of what is "national" changes abruptly? In the case of a two-state solution, the RoC will continue as it is, but it would now have to deal with a new internationally recognized state in the north. That would also affect grand strategic calculations based on the new—positive or negative—relations that would develop between the two states in Cyprus as well as between the RoC and Turkey among others. Confederation is a more complicated scenario which implies a weak central government and constituent states that are more independent. The extent to which the two constituent states would have common policies, especially in high-politics sectors such as foreign policy and defence, would depend on the agreed arrangement.

In any case, if we take seriously the long-term and multi-thematic character of grand strategy, the existence of the Cyprus Problem presents the RoC with great limitations in grand strategic formulation. To put it differently, the RoC, divided and occupied as it is, can develop a grand strategy only if it decides that it will continue its journey in history, navigating the international system, without the prospect of re-integrating the occupied territories. And even then, the question of what dynamics the status quo will keep producing remains open. As long as the Cyprus Problem exists, it will keep affecting the grand strategic and other political calculations of the RoC. Therefore, the RoC will need to decide what its next steps will be both in terms of foreign policy and grand strategy. A mature (foreign) policy would prioritize the Cyprus Problem and at the same time develop other sectors to advance the RoC's broader interests and also support the efforts for settlement. No suggestions are here made as to what the solution model for the Cyprus Problem should be. It is simply argued that for the RoC to play an upgraded role in the international scene, better secure its interests, and be able to have a grand strategy, the settlement of the conflict is a *sine qua non*. Figure 14.1 illustrates how the two main settlement scenarios work in relation to grand strategy (and foreign policy maturity).

Conclusions

Has the RoC foreign policy entered an age of maturity? Yes and no. Yes, because it has made significant steps forward both in vision and action. No, because it still has a long way to go before the efforts for a

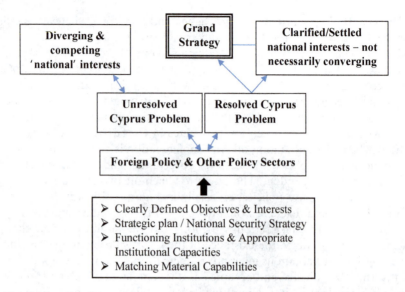

Fig. 14.1 Conditions for a cypriot grand strategy

mature foreign policy, as broadly defined in this book, become consistent, coherent, and do not bypass essential changes that need to be made, both at the institutional and strategic levels, so that the objectives make sense and are effectively pursued. Otherwise, the important progress that has been achieved since 2004 and especially during the 2010s, is in danger of becoming irrelevant with time given that mediocre or half measures are rarely effective, and more so for a state like the RoC which faces a constantly changing and challenging environment.

Leaving the big picture aside, it should be noted that foreign policy-making in the RoC can be seen as a mirror image of traditional weaknesses observed in the management of the Cyprus Problem. Since the late 1970s, when the RoC agreed to negotiate a solution to the conflict based on the Bizonal Bicommunal Federation (BBF) model, successive governments have done little to create a coherent national-strategic plan that would both define what the content of the sought solution was and how it would be pursued. Worse than that, the approach to the peace talks and the solution model itself changed multiple times as different governments succeeded each other through the decades. The political scene in the RoC remains deeply fragmented on the issue with no clear national-strategic framework to fall back to. The two sides of the conflict often try to find convergences through negotiation, but very few convergences can be found among RoC political parties regarding the model or outcome of the solution to begin with. This is a fundamental and long-standing issue.

It is no surprise, then, that similar issues can be identified in foreign policymaking, a domain that is de facto intertwined with the Cyprus Problem. With commitment and hard work, a NSC could begin to solve some of these issues, but such an institution is not a panacea if political will for national consensus does not exist. Moreover, and beyond the need for institutional capacity building, regarding both the Cyprus Problem and foreign policy RoC governments should start listening to the public, the civil society, groups and organizations that conduct relevant research, as well as the academic community. Not for the sake of listening, but with the purpose of learning, adjusting, and incorporating ideas. The RoC of the future and its foreign policy cannot be left vulnerable to the forces of luck and circumstance. There is too much at stake for superficial and half-hearted approaches. The road to maturity needs to be further travelled, and this can only happen with the vehicles of serious self-assessment, commitment to progress, peace-making, and consensus-building.

> *There was a little city with few men in it;*
> *and a great king came against it, besieged it,*
> *and built great snares around it.*
> *Now there was found in it a poor wise man,*
> *and he by his wisdom delivered the city.*
> *Yet no one remembered that same poor man.*
> *Then I said:*
>
> *"Wisdom is better than strength.*
> *Nevertheless the poor man's wisdom is despised,*
> *And his words are not heard.*
> *Words of the wise, spoken quietly, should be heard*
> *Rather than the shout of a ruler of fools.*
> *Wisdom is better than weapons of war;*
> *But one sinner destroys much good."*
>
> (Ecclesiastes 9:14-18, NKJV)

References

Adamides, Constantinos. 2019. "The Challenges of Formulating National Security Strategies (NSS) in the Presence of Overarching Existential Threats." *Cyprus Review* 30 (1): 71–94.

Balzacq, Thierry, Peter Dombrowski, and Simon Reich. 2019. "Introduction: Comparing Grand Strategies in the Modern World." In *Comparative Grand Strategy: A Framework and Cases*, edited by Thierry Balzacq, Peter Dombrowski, and Simon Reich, 1–24. Oxford: Oxford University Press.

Christodoulides, Nikos. 2020. "Cyprus Foreign Policy—The Way Forward." In *Depth* 17 (6): 2–5.

Clausewitz, Carl von. 1989. *On War*. Translated by Michael Howard and Peter Paret. Princeton: Princeton University Press.

Dueck, Colin. 2006. *Reluctant Crusaders: Power, Culture, and Change in American Grand Strategy*. Princeton and Oxford: Princeton University Press.

Hart, Basil H. Liddel. 1991. *Strategy*. London: Meridian.

Hetou, Ghaidda. 2019. "Saudi Arabia." In *Comparative Grand Strategy: A Framework and Cases*, edited by Thierry Balzacq, Peter Dombrowski, and Simon Reich, 239–261. Oxford: Oxford University Press.

Hudson, Valerie M. 2007. *Foreign Policy Analysis: Classic and Contemporary Theory*. Plymouth: Rowman & Littlefield.

Jensen, Lloyd. 1982. *Explaining Foreign Policy*. Englewood Cliffs: Prentice-Hall.

Kennedy, Paul. 1991. "Grand Strategy in War and Peace: Toward a Broader Definition." In *Grand Strategies in War and Peace*, edited by Paul Kennedy, 1–7. New Haven and London: Yale University Press.

Klokkaris, Phoivos. 2016. "The Security of Cyprus in the New Geopolitical Environment of the Eastern Mediterranean and the Middle East." *Eastern Mediterranean Policy Note* (5).

Leira, Halvard. 2019. "The Emergence of Foreign Policy." *International Studies Quarterly* 63: 187–198.

Litsas, Spyros. 2019. Μια έξυπνη υψηλή στρατηγική για την Κύπρο [A smart grand strategy for Cyprus]. *Phileleftheros*, 27 May. Accessed 30 May 2020. https://www.philenews.com/f-me-apopsi/paremvaseis-ston-f/article/710027/mia-exypni-ypsili-stratigki-ga-tin-kypro

Lobell, Steven E., Jeffrey W. Talliaferro, and Norrin M. Ripsman. 2012. "Introduction: Grand Strategy Between the World Wars." In *The Challenge of Grand Strategy: The Great Powers and the Broken Balance Between the World Wars*, edited by Jeffrey W. Talliaferro, Norrin M. Ripsman, and Steven E. Lobell, 1–36. New York: Cambridge University Press.

Luttwak, Edward N. 1987. *Strategy: The Logic of War and Peace*. London: Belknap Harvard.

Lygeros, Nikos. 2012. "Χαράζοντας την ΑΟΖ [Carving the EEZ]." In *Αποκλειστική Οικονομική Ζώνη: Από τη Στρατηγική Κίνηση στην*

Οικονομική Λύση [Exclusive Economic Zone: From the Strategic Move to the Economic Solution], edited by Vasilis P. Kikilias, 93–196. Athens: Kastanioti.
Lygeros, Nikos. 2019. Η Υψηλή Στρατηγική της Κυπριακής ΑΟΖ. *lygeros.org*, 22 November. Accessed 20 September 2020. https://lygeros.org/465 77-gr/.
Murray, Williamson. 2011. "Thoughts on Grand Strategy." In *The Shaping of Grand Strategy: Policy, Diplomacy, and War*, edited by Williamson Murray, Richard Hart Sinnreich and James Lacey, 1–33. New York: Cambridge University Press.
Neumann, Iver B., and Henrikki Heikka. 2005. "Grand Strategy, Strategic Culture, Practice: The Social Roots of Nordic Defence." *Cooperation and Conflict* 40 (1): 5–23.
Panayiotides, Nicos. 2014. Φυσικό αέριο, στρατηγική και Κυπριακό [Natural Gas, Strategy and the Cyprus Problem]. *Simerini*, 15 October. Accessed 30 May 2020. https://simerini.sigmalive.com/article/2014/10/15/phusiko-aerio-strategike-kai-kupriako/.
Reuters. 2021. "Greek Cypriots Say Turkish Two-State Offer Won't Work." 29 April. Accessed 10 July 2021. https://www.reuters.com/world/greek-cyp riots-say-turkish-two-state-offer-wont-work-2021-04-29/.
Shamir, Eitan. 2019. "Israel." In *Comparative Grand Strategy: A Framework and Cases*, edited by Thierry Balzacq, Peter Dombrowski, and Simon Reich, 217–238. Oxford: Oxford University Press.
Sülün, Emine Eminel, and Zenonas Tziarras. 2017. "Federal Cyprus in the Context of Regional Security." *Berghof Foundation & SeeD* Security Dialogue Project—Background Paper.
Symmachia Politon. 2015. Προταση Στρατηγικου Σχεδιασμού για Ανατροπή της Κατοχής Μέσα από τη Λύση του Κυπριακού [Strategic Planning Proposal for the Overthrow of the Occupation through the Resolution of the Cyprus Problem]. *Symmachia Politon*. http://forum.agora-dialogue. com/wp-content/uploads/2017/05/%CE%A3%CE%A4%CE%A1%CE%91% CE%A4%CE%97%CE%93%CE%99%CE%9A%CE%97-%CE%A3%CE%A5%CE% 9C%CE%9C%CE%91%CE%A7%CE%99%CE%91%CE%A3-%CE%9A%CE%A5% CE%A0%CE%A1%CE%99%CE%91%CE%9A%CE%9F%CE%A5.pdf.
Tornaritis, Nikos. 2013. Το Φυσικό Αέριο ως Υψηλή Στρατηγική. *Cyprus News*, 16 January. Accessed 30 May 2020. http://www.newsnowgr.com/art icle/334312/to-fysiko-aerio-os-ypsili-stratigiki.html.
Tziarras, Zenonas. 2016. "Israel-Cyprus-Greece: A 'Comfortable' Quasi-Alliance." *Mediterranean Politics* 21 (3): 407–427.
Tziarras, Zenonas. 2019. "Cyprus's Foreign Policy in the Eastern Mediterranean and the Trilateral Partnerships: A Neoclassical Realist Approach." In *The New*

Geopolitics of the Eastern Mediterranean: Trilateral Partnerships and Regional Security, edited by Zenonas Tziarras, 53–72. Nicosia: PRIO Cyprus Centre.
Tziarras, Zenonas. 2021. "International Competition and Cooperation in the New Eastern Mediterranean." *Oxford Research Encyclopedia of International Studies*, 1–19.
Tziarras, Zenonas. 2022. "Introduction: The Foreign Policy of the Republic of Cyprus. The Age of Maturity?" In *The Foreign Policy of the Republic of Cyprus: Local, Regional and International Dimensions*, edited by Zenonas Tziarras. London and New York: Palgrave Macmillan.
Vaicekauskaitė, Živilė Marija. 2017. "Security Strategies of Small States in a Changing World." *Journal of Baltic Security* 3 (2): 7–15.
Zachariades, Alexandros, and Petros Petrikkos. 2020. "Balancing for Profit: The Republic of Cyprus' Grand Strategy in the Eastern Mediterranean Sea." *The Cyprus Review* 32 (1): 89–136.

Index

A
Abkhazia, 162
Abraham Accords, 188
Acheson Plan, 25
Acquis communautaire, 85
Aegean, 116, 156, 158, 211, 212, 229, 234, 237, 258
Afghanistan, 6, 8
Africa, 26
Agriculture, 79
AKEL (Progressive Party of Working People), 10, 29, 32, 34, 46, 49, 83, 106, 107, 123, 124, 127, 128, 141, 159, 181, 229, 333
Akkuyu (nuclear power plant), 158
Alignment, 46
Alliance(s), 110, 111, 113, 121, 122, 128, 178, 184, 185, 191, 349, 350
Anastasiades, Nicos, 12, 46, 47, 55, 58, 59, 64, 66, 68, 82, 92, 93, 182, 333
Annan, Kofi, 88, 145
Annan Plan, 5, 47, 58, 60, 81, 88, 145, 153, 167, 180, 226, 229
Aphrodite field, 91, 92
Arab-Israeli conflict, 211, 224
Arab Spring, 183, 234, 235
Arab Uprisings, 112, 114, 183, 186, 187, 225, 233, 239, 324
Arab World, 66, 89
Archbishop Makarios III, 4, 20, 22, 50, 57, 107, 140, 180, 225
Armenia, 298, 326, 327, 329
Arms embargo, 327
Asia, 26, 27, 87
Assad, Bashar al, 187, 188, 191, 235
Association Agreement (1972), 33
Austria, 187, 326–329

B
Balancing
  external balancing, 348, 349
  hard balancing, 110, 111
  internal balancing, 348
  soft balancing, 106, 109–111, 115, 122, 127

Ball Plan, 24
Bandung Conference, 27
Bandwagoning, 110
Banking sector, 47, 64, 65
Beijing Declaration and Platform for Action, 269
Bipolar/bipolarity, 8
Bizonal Bicommunal Federation (BBF), 128, 358
Black Sea, 116
Blair, Tony, 162
Blue Homeland, 116, 157
Brexit, 67
Britain, 20, 21, 23–25, 31–33, 52, 254, 346
British Foreign Office, 32
British Indian Ocean Territory (BIOT), 252
British Overseas Territories (BOTs), 252
British Sovereign Base Areas (SBAs), 21, 140, 190, 246, 257, 262
Bush, George W., 162
Byzantine Empire, 346

C

Calypso field, 91
Capabilities, 6, 7, 289, 291, 302
power capabilities, 346, 350
Capitalism, 63
Caspian Sea, 211
Çavuşoğlu, Mevlüt, 236
Central Bank, 62
Central Intelligence Service, 49
Chagos Archipelago, 14, 252–257, 262
Charter of Fundamental Rights of the European Union, 84
China, 66, 67, 160, 169, 346
Christodoulides, Nikos, 47, 55, 56, 65, 66, 82, 83, 86, 89, 90, 92, 97, 117, 121, 225, 272, 332, 354
Christofias, Demetris, 10, 47, 62–65, 83, 106, 122–124, 127, 326, 333
Clark, Arthur Sir, 32
Clausewitz, Carl von, 344
Clerides, Glafkos, 27, 33, 36, 145
Climate change, 48, 65
Cold War, 8, 9, 50, 107, 123, 124, 137–139, 141–143, 180, 181, 225, 312, 316
Colonisation/colonialism/colony/ colonies/decolonisation, 27, 139, 249, 254–257, 262, 263
Common Foreign and Security Policy (CFSP), 82, 86, 89, 94, 260
Common Security and Defence Policy (CSDP), 93, 95
Commonwealth, 20, 28–30, 33, 37, 54, 246, 252
Communism/communist, 23, 29, 32, 34, 54, 58, 62, 63
Constitution/constitutional, 21–23, 30, 32, 37
Continental shelf (CS), 200, 232, 258–260
Convention on the Elimination of all forms of Discrimination Against Women (CEDAW), 269
Council for Geostrategic Studies, 190
Council of Europe (CoE), 14, 269, 288, 297–299
Council of Ministers, 63
Council on Foreign Affairs and Defence (KYSEA), 191
Covid-19, 48, 67, 185, 271, 281, 330
Crans Montana, 182, 224, 238
Crime, 79
Crimea, 169
Crisis management, 7
Cuba, 62

Cultural diplomacy, 51, 65, 68, 179, 193
Cultural heritage, 288, 292–294, 296, 298–303
Culture, 288, 289, 292, 294, 296, 297, 299–303
Customs Union, 34
Cyprus Intelligence Service (CIS), 190
Czechoslovakia, 142
Czech Republic, 36, 81, 187

D

Daesh, 183
Davutoğlu, Ahmet, 113, 114
Defence, 79, 89, 90, 93–95, 98, 278, 282, 311, 312, 314–317, 319–323, 325, 326, 329, 332–335, 347, 349, 350, 352, 355, 357
Defence Attaches (DAs), 315, 321, 324, 327, 328
Defence diplomacy, 7, 15, 311–320, 322, 324, 325, 328–335
Delek, 117, 118
Democratic Party (DIKO), 49, 83
Democratic Peace Theory, 87
Democratic Rally (DISY), 10, 83, 121, 152, 181, 182, 333, 351
Dendias, Nikos, 158
Denktaş, Rauf R., 225
Denmark, 346
Derviş Eroğlu, 153
Digital communication, 50
Digital diplomacy, 50, 68
Diplomacy, 9, 11, 12, 178, 180–182, 184–186, 189, 191, 193, 269, 270, 273, 277, 278, 283, 296, 299, 311–320, 322, 324, 325, 328–335, 345, 352
Direct Trade Regulation, 228, 238

Doctrine of the Joint Defence Area, 329

E

Eastern Mediterranean, 9–13, 15, 16, 47, 51, 66, 68, 79, 80, 82, 83, 87, 89–92, 98, 106, 107, 109, 111–113, 115–121, 123, 126–128, 138, 151, 152, 154, 156, 159–161, 168, 169, 177, 179, 181–184, 186, 189, 191, 192, 200, 204–210, 212–214, 216, 224, 230, 233, 234, 236–238, 257, 260–262, 320, 321, 324, 330, 346, 354
Eastern Mediterranean Gas Forum (EMGF), 48, 112, 207, 236
East Germany, 142
EastMed Pipeline, 127, 211, 212, 215
Economic crisis, 4, 8, 271
Economic diplomacy, 51, 68
Economy, 8, 12, 185, 300, 347
EDEK, 128
Egypt, 8, 9, 11, 48, 66, 89, 106, 111, 112, 114–119, 127, 154, 156, 159, 184–186, 189–191, 207–209, 211–213, 224, 230, 231, 233, 235–239, 258, 259, 281, 282, 323, 326, 328, 329
Energy, 79, 86, 87, 89, 91–93, 96, 98, 111, 113, 116, 117, 119–121, 123, 129, 204, 208–211, 213–215, 224, 230, 231, 233, 236, 282, 322, 326
energy diplomacy, 51
energy security, 7, 9–12, 15, 16, 67, 184, 189, 190, 192, 349, 352
ENI, 67, 91, 186, 189, 209, 212, 231, 232
Enosis (Union with Greece), 53, 245
EOKA, 28, 53, 139, 140
EOKA B, 4

Erdoğan, Recep Tayyip, 55, 113–116, 126, 138, 154, 156–160, 168, 169, 235, 237, 323
Erim, Nihat, 52
Eroğlu, Derviş, 49
Estonia, 36, 81
EU Council, 84
Eurobarometer, 229
Eurogroup, 64
European Central Bank (ECB), 47, 63
European Commission, 35, 82, 206, 226, 228, 269, 298
European Council (EC), 35, 36, 179, 207
European Defence Agency (EDA), 82, 329
European Economic Community (EEC), 33, 81
European External Action Services (EEAS), 269
Europeanisation, 50, 51, 56, 60, 62, 64, 68, 124
European Neighbourhood Policy, 207, 215
European Parliament (EP), 63, 226, 269
European Presidency, 63
European Security Strategy (ESS), 82
European Union (EU), 4, 19, 46, 62, 66, 78, 86, 90, 91, 105, 148, 179, 206, 207, 209, 214, 224, 237, 260, 268, 288, 311
Eurozone, 47, 51, 62, 64
Evros River, 158
Exclusive Economic Zone (EEZ), 8, 9, 13, 67, 91, 92, 113, 116–119, 121, 124, 138, 147, 150, 153, 154, 156–159, 165, 167, 181, 200, 230, 233, 236, 258–260, 322, 348
Extremism, 183, 185, 188
Exxon Mobil, 67, 91, 119, 209

F

Feminism/feminist, 269, 277, 278
Feminist foreign policy, 271, 272, 279
Financial Aid Regulation, 228
Financial crisis, 64, 96, 97
Finland, 346
Foreign Direct Investment (FDI), 87, 125
Foreign Policy Analysis (FPA), 5, 12, 313, 347
Foreign Policy, Defence and Security Council, 48
Foreign Policy Executive (FPE), 354
France, 9, 33, 48, 67, 94, 110, 112, 209, 237, 322, 325–330
Free market, 63

G

Gaddafi, Muammar, 186
Gas (natural gas), 113, 114, 117–119, 124, 126, 127, 189, 208–212, 230, 234, 236, 330, 348, 351
Gaza, 114, 235
Gazprom, 126, 127
Gender, 65, 268, 271–274, 278, 279, 281, 283
Gender equality, 267–273, 279, 280, 282, 283
Gender mainstreaming, 14, 268–270, 272, 279, 280, 283
Georgia, 6, 162
Germany, 67, 94, 110, 119, 151, 158, 346
Glafkos field, 91
Government of National Accord (GNA), 116, 212, 233
Grand strategy, 14, 15, 160, 343–352, 355–357
Greece, 3, 11, 20, 21, 26, 27, 30–32, 34, 46, 48, 52, 54, 106, 107, 111, 112, 116–120, 124, 138,

139, 142, 144, 148, 156, 157, 159, 160, 168, 179, 182, 184, 185, 187, 209, 211–213, 215, 224, 228, 230, 233–237, 245, 259, 298
Greek Cypriots (GC), 3–5, 13, 20, 47, 53, 57–61, 64, 85, 139, 146, 155, 167, 180, 182, 183, 213, 224–226, 228–232, 234, 236, 238, 300, 301
Greek Junta, 57, 142
Green Line, 199, 225, 227, 230
Green Line Regulation (GRL), 228
Grivas, George, 28
Güdeniz, Cem, 116
Gulf, 66, 67, 87, 156

H

Haftar, Khalifa, 116
Hariri, Saad al, 187
HELBROC, 327
Hezbollah, 321
Holy See, 299
House of Representatives, 29, 35
Human rights, 21, 267, 269, 271, 293, 294, 296
Human security, 57, 67
Hungary, 36, 81
Hydrocarbons, 8, 9, 11, 13, 47, 91, 92, 158, 190, 192, 200, 208, 209, 213, 224, 246, 257, 260, 262, 322

I

Iacovou, George, 47
Identity, 77, 86, 292
Incirlik, 126
India, 51, 66
Inonu, Ismet, 108
Institutional capacities, 347, 350, 355
Institutions, 7

Interactionist Role Theory (IRT), 200
Interest (national), 6, 54
International Court of Justice (ICJ), 246–249, 252–255, 260–262
Internationalization, 22, 23
International law, 11, 14, 53, 142, 144–147, 153, 157, 158, 167, 169, 245, 247–250, 253–257, 259–263, 292, 293
International Monetary Fund (IMF), 47
International Organizations (IOs), 14, 288–290, 297, 303
International Relations (IR), 5, 9, 14, 109, 113, 200, 202, 313, 320
Iran, 47, 62, 183, 188
Iraq, 8, 11, 110, 112
Ireland, 187
Isaak, Tasos, 57
Islamic State of Iraq and the Levant (ISIS), 93, 112, 183, 185, 187, 190, 324
Israel, 8–11, 48, 53, 66, 67, 106, 111, 112, 114, 115, 117–120, 124, 127, 154, 156, 159, 160, 184–186, 188–191, 207–209, 211–213, 224, 230, 233, 235, 236, 238, 239, 259, 281, 322, 323, 326, 328–330, 333, 346
Israel Defence Forces (IDF), 114
Italy, 9, 48, 67, 112, 158, 187, 209, 236, 296, 298, 299, 302, 318, 322, 326, 330

J

Japan, 110, 299
Johnson, Lyndon, 108
Jordan, 9, 48, 66, 111, 112, 156, 159, 185, 208, 236, 239, 282
Justice and Development Party (AKP), 113, 126, 235

K

Karamanlis, Konstantinos, 30–32
Kasoulides, Ioannis, 47, 54–56, 65, 154
Khrushchev, Nikita, 107, 141, 142, 161, 162, 164
Kissinger, Henry, 108, 142, 167
Kosovo, 14, 248–251, 255
Kosovo Declaration of Independence, 14, 246, 247
Kotzias, Nikos, 58, 181, 182, 194
Kozakou-Marcoullis, Erato, 47, 64, 140, 207, 274
Kyprianou, Markos, 47, 64
Kyprianou, Spyros, 32, 273

L

Lakkotrypis, George, 91, 154
Latvia, 81, 299
Lavrov, Sergey, 146, 150, 154, 164, 166, 168
Lebanon, 8, 9, 48, 67, 93, 111, 112, 156, 159, 183, 186, 187, 208, 211, 224, 230, 259, 282, 321, 326, 329
Liberal/liberalism, 79, 82, 87
Libya, 111, 116, 183, 185, 186, 212, 224, 233, 258
Libyan National Army (LNA), 116
Lillikas, Yiorgos, 47
Liquefied Natural Gas (LNG), 211, 348
Lisbon Treaty, 82, 95
Lithuania, 81

M

Maastricht Treaty, 35, 82
Malta, 81, 88
Mari, 47, 58, 62, 152, 181, 187
Masculinity, 277

Maturity/maturation/mature/immature, 37, 38, 78, 80, 95, 97, 98, 106–108, 127, 128, 177–179, 181, 182, 188, 192, 288, 289, 291, 301, 303, 312–314, 318, 319, 325, 330, 332–335
 foreign policy, 5–8, 15, 50, 70, 78, 80, 97, 98, 108, 169, 177, 178, 181, 313, 318, 343–359
Mauritius, 252–257, 262
Mavi Marmara, 114, 117, 124, 185, 236, 323
Mavroyiannis, Andreas, 49, 50
Mediterranean, 91, 96
Medvedev, Dmitry, 147, 150, 154
Menderes, Adnan, 31, 52
Merkel, Angela, 163, 237
Mexico, 299
Middle East, 9, 13, 15, 16, 26, 31, 51, 66, 82, 91, 95, 111, 112, 114, 115, 119, 121, 126, 179, 181, 183, 184, 189, 192, 193, 205, 207, 233, 234, 320, 321, 324
Migration/migrant/migrants, 51, 88, 89, 188
Military, 312–315, 317, 318, 321, 324–329, 331–333, 346, 347
Military drills/exercises, 316, 323, 328–330
Ministry of Defence (MoD), 51, 312, 321, 324, 329–331
Ministry of Finance, 51
Ministry of Foreign Affairs (MFA), 13, 49, 83, 93, 95, 98, 121, 178, 180, 190–194, 270, 271, 273, 279
Ministry of the Interior, 51
Mitsotakis, Kyriakos, 209, 237
Montenegro, 299
Montreux, 169

INDEX 369

Morsi, Mohamed, 114, 184, 185, 235, 323
Mubarak, Hosni, 112, 114, 184, 235
Muhammadans, 52
Multipolarity, 9
Muslim Brotherhood, 112, 114, 115, 184, 235, 323

N
National Council, 49, 191, 192
National Defence Authorization Act (NDAA), 115
National Guard, 125, 320, 328, 329, 331
Nationalism, 278
National liberation, 139, 167
National security, 349, 352
National Security Council (NSC), 48, 191, 237, 355
National Security Strategy (NSS), 49, 54, 193, 349
Natural resources, 66, 209, 224, 236, 238, 348, 349, 355
Netanyahu, Benjamin, 117, 124, 326
Nixon, Richard, 108
Noble Energy, 91, 117–119, 234
Non-Aligned Movement, 27, 28, 54, 81, 181, 225
Nord Stream 2, 119, 127
North Africa, 179, 183, 234
North Atlantic Treaty Organisation (NATO), 11, 19, 20, 23, 24, 27, 29–33, 37, 106, 107, 113, 119, 120, 122–124, 126, 138, 139, 141, 142, 144, 159, 161, 162, 169, 181–183, 248, 273
Northern Ireland, 254
Norway, 272, 281

O
Obama, Barack, 112, 114, 271

Omirou, Yannakis, 145
OPCW, 188
Organization for Security and Cooperation in Europe (OSCE), 280, 327
Ossetia, 162
Özersay, Kudret, 189, 232

P
Palestinian Authority/Palestine/Palestinians, 48, 111, 112, 185, 208, 236, 239, 282
Pandemic, 48, 51, 67, 185, 271
Papadopoulos, Tassos, 36, 47, 57, 58, 60–62, 64, 65, 83, 123, 147
Papaioannou, Ezekias, 29
Papandreou, George, 117
Partnership for Peace (PfP), 46, 122, 124, 128, 312
Patriotic Front, 29
Peacebuilding, 271
Peres, Shimon, 235
Permanent Structured Cooperation (PeSCo), 86
Persian Gulf, 205
Pilides, Natasa, 48
Pipeline, 211
Poland, 36, 81, 127
Political economy, 51
Pompeo, Mike, 209
Portugal, 298
Pragmatic idealism/pragmatic idealist, 138, 141–148, 150–152, 154, 164, 166
Public
  public diplomacy, 68
  public opinion, 50, 56–59
Putin, Vladimir, 115

Q

Qatar, 209
Qatar Petroleum, 209

R

Realism, 137, 138, 142, 143, 166, 167
Realpolitik, 141, 151
Referendum/referenda, 58, 59, 61, 81
Regional Security Complexes (RSC), 109, 111
Republika Srpska, 250
Rhodesia, 250
Rolandis, Nicos, 53
Roman Empire, 346
Romania, 187
Russia, 10–12, 63, 66, 67, 87, 105, 106, 110, 115, 119, 121, 123, 125–128, 137, 138, 144, 146–148, 150, 151, 154–156, 158–162, 166, 169, 181, 299, 326, 327, 333, 346

S

Sampson, Nikos, 108
San Marino, 298
Saudi Arabia, 51, 183, 187, 188, 235, 346
Schengen, 56
Search and Rescue drills/exercises, 316, 324, 328–330
Securitisation, 109, 111
Security, 6, 9, 12, 15, 46, 48, 51, 54–59, 65–68, 77–79, 82, 85–88, 90–93, 95, 96, 98, 201, 208–210, 212, 213, 224, 227, 233, 269, 271–273, 278, 313, 315, 319, 322, 324
    ontological security, 200–207, 210, 214, 215

Security culture, 356
Self-image, 201, 203, 204, 207, 209–216
Serbia, 144, 248, 249, 326
Shell, 118
Sisi, Abdel Fattah al, 115, 118, 185, 235
Slovakia, 81
Slovenia, 36, 81, 299
Small state(s), 288–292, 301–303, 311, 317
Soft power, 30, 85, 151, 169
Solomou, Solomos, 57
Soviet Union/Soviet, 78, 81, 138, 140–142, 161, 181, 316, 346
Spain, 158
Strategy, 7, 14, 15, 343–345, 347, 348, 350–352, 355–357
    strategic plan, 15
Survival, 349, 350, 352
    national, 20, 35, 37
Sweden, 271, 272, 346
Syria, 11, 47, 62, 111, 112, 115, 169, 181, 183–189, 191, 193, 224, 235, 258, 293, 324

T

TANAP, 210, 211
Terrorism, 96, 185, 189, 190, 192, 324
Third World, 27, 224, 225
TOTAL, 67, 209
Tourism, 148, 151, 152, 154, 169, 185
Trade, 178, 185, 189
Trans Adriatic Pipeline (TAP), 211
Treaty of Accession, 36
Treaty of Guarantees, 23
Treaty of Maastricht, 225
Trilateral
    alignment, 46

cooperation, 46, 48, 51, 68
diplomacy, 67, 68
meetings, 91
partnerships, 92, 106, 112, 117, 121, 127, 184, 185
Troika, 63
Tunisia, 235
Turkey, 3, 4, 8, 11, 13, 20–26, 28, 30, 31, 33, 34, 45, 49, 50, 52–57, 59, 65, 66, 68, 79, 85, 88, 92, 94, 106–109, 111, 113–120, 122, 123, 126, 127, 138, 140–145, 147, 150, 151, 153, 155–160, 167, 169, 179–185, 187–193, 200, 204–207, 209–216, 224, 225, 228–238, 246, 247, 258–262, 277, 278, 293, 319, 322–324, 332, 349–352, 354–357
Turkish Cypriot Chamber of Commerce, 226
Turkish Cypriots (TC), 3, 5, 13, 20, 53, 57, 59–61, 85, 139, 146, 178, 179, 182, 183, 213, 223, 224, 226–231, 233, 234, 236–238, 245, 300, 301, 349
Turkish Petroleum Corporation (TPAO), 190, 232, 237
Turkish Republic of Northern Cyprus (TRNC), 85, 108, 118, 147, 164, 189, 225, 226, 228–232, 238, 249
TurkStream pipeline, 115
Tylliria, 53
Tzionis, Tasos, 49, 56, 165

U
Ukraine, 119, 127, 162, 163, 169, 299
Underaggression, 6
Underbalancing, 6
Underexpansion, 6

UNDP, 300
Unemployment, 79
UN General Assembly, 25, 26, 28, 248, 253–255, 294
Unified Military Defence Doctrine, 329
Union for the Mediterranean, 269
Unipolar/unipolarity, 8
United Arab Emirates (UAE), 9, 51, 67, 235, 329
United Kingdom (UK), 66, 107, 139, 179, 246, 254, 297, 312
United Nations (UN), 3, 20, 53, 139, 224, 246, 288, 298, 331
United Nations Convention on the Law of the Sea (UNCLOS), 150, 157, 167, 234, 252, 253
United Nations General Assembly, 53
United Nations Interim Force in Lebanon (UNIFIL), 331, 332
United Nations Peacekeeping Forces in Cyprus (UNFICYP), 3, 24, 125, 140, 164, 165, 183, 230
United Nations Security Council (UNSC), 45, 53, 66, 185, 245, 246, 248, 271
United States (US), 5, 6, 23, 47, 81, 105, 138, 139, 148, 153, 163, 316, 346
Universal Declaration of Human Rights, 269
UN Security Council (UNSC), 21, 22, 24, 110, 125, 140, 145, 151, 156, 164, 296
UNSC 1325, 272
USSR, 23, 25, 29, 81, 87, 105, 107, 139, 142, 166, 312

V
Varosha, 48
Vassiliou, George, 34, 35, 123, 225

W

War on Terror, 8, 112

Warsaw Pact, 27, 181

Women's rights, 268, 270–272, 279–283

World War II (WWII), 138, 139

Y

Yeltsin, Boris, 145

Z

Zurich and London Agreements, 20, 21, 23, 25, 30–33, 37, 107, 205, 223

CPSIA information can be obtained
at www.ICGtesting.com
Printed in the USA
LVHW081120210322
713910LV00016B/79